D0794116

DISCARD

POETIC MADNESS
AND THE
ROMANTIC
IMAGINATION

FREDERICK BURWICK

POETIC MADNESS AND THE ROMANTIC IMAGINATION

The Pennsylvania State University Press
University Park, Pennsylvania

Library of Congress Cataloging-in-Publication Data

Burwick, Frederick.
    Poetic madness and the Romantic imagination / Frederick Burwick.

        p.   cm.
    Includes bibliographical references and index.
    ISBN 0-271-01488-1
    1. European poetry—18th century—History and criticism.
    2. European poetry—19th century—History and criticism.
    3. Romanticism—Europe. I. Title.
    PN1241.B87   1996
    809.1'9145—dc20   95-9868
                                                              CIP

Copyright © 1996 The Pennsylvania State University
All rights reserved
Printed in the United States of America
Published by The Pennsylvania State University Press,
University Park, PA 16802-1003

It is the policy of The Pennsylvania State University Press to use acid-free
paper for the first printing of all clothbound books. Publications on uncoated
stock satisfy the minimum requirements of American National Standard for
Information Sciences—Permanence of Paper for Printed Library Materials,
ANSI Z39.48-1992.

CONTENTS

ACKNOWLEDGMENTS

The sequestered mind, as I have learned from explanations of madness during the eighteenth and nineteenth centuries, is apt to lapse into solipsism—a sign of imminent aberration. I have been, therefore, especially grateful for the opportunities to test early versions of several chapters as conference papers, where they aroused useful discussion and wound up in print. Indeed, it was the lively response to the paper on the *furor poeticus*, presented at the Wordsworth Summer Conference in Grasmere (1989), that encouraged me to pursue the exploration into madness and romantic literature. That paper, published in the *Wordsworth Circle* 21 (Winter 1990), has now been reshaped and expanded as Chapter 1. An earlier version of Chapter 2 appeared in *Christianity and Literature* 39 (Summer 1990); of Chapter 5 in *Das Paradox. Historisch-systematischer Problemaufriß*, ed. Roland Hagenbüchle (Tübingen: Gunter Narr Verlag, 1992); of Chapter 4 in *Weimar Classicism*, ed. Gerhart Hoffmeister (London: Mellen Press, 1994). I thank the respective editors for permission to use these materials in their present revised form.

Among many helpful colleagues, I wish to thank Barbara Packer (UCLA), Marian Hobson (Cambridge), Kari Lokke (UC Davis), Walter Pape (Cologne), Karl Ludwig Pfeiffer (Siegen), Elinor Shaffer (East Anglia), and Barbara Stafford (Chicago), who share my interests in illusion and delusion, offered insight into theories of perception and cognition, and enriched my understanding of the representations of madness in literature and art. Roswitha Burwick (Scripps) guided me through the chapter on Arnim. I am especially grateful to Anthony Harding (Saskatchewan) and Thomas McFarland (Princeton), who read the manuscript in its entirety and advised me with revisions.

INTRODUCTION:
CREATIVITY AND MADNESS

"In vain does one knock at the gates of poetry with a sane mind."
—Plato, *Phaedrus*, 245a

"Poetry demands a man with a special gift . . . or a touch of madness."
—Aristotle, *Poetics*, 1455a

"No sane-minded poet could ever enter Helicon."
—Democritus, as quoted in Cicero, *De divinatione*, 1.80

"By some divine force the poet's mind is raised above the ordinary."
—Seneca the Younger, *Epistulae Morales*, 84.1–7

When Robert Schumann felt madness taking over his mind, he began to compose religious music, a mass and a requiem, and tried to communicate with the supernatural world, praising the "wonderful power" when a spirit he called forth in a séance rapped out "the rhythm of the first two bars of the C Minor Symphony." He spent his final years in an asylum, falling into a rage whenever his spirits accused him of plagiarism. The agony of the mind striving against the dark night of insanity has been told again and again in the biographies of poets, painters, and philosophers: Gogol passing out the pages of his unfinished novel to strangers, Van Gogh painting the starry whirlpools above the cypresses outside the insane asylum at Saint-Rémy, Nietzsche embracing a carthorse in an Italian piazza (Friedrich 69–70).

Psychoanalysis provides a variety of strategies to enable a suffering patient to explore the dark recesses of the mind. The suffering artist often devises his or her own strategy. If such a coping scheme suffices, the mind mends itself (see Youngquist on Blake, Colley on Tennyson). But often something more insidious is at work (see Packer on Cowper). Not until the beginning of the twentieth century were a test (the Wasserman, in 1906) and a cure (Ehrlich's, in 1910) found to put a stop to the spread of syphilis that had slowly and inexorably been eating away at the brains of 5 to 15 percent of the inhabitants of mental hospitals during the nineteenth century (Read 385). And only in the latter half of the century have doctors begun to identify the chemicals necessary to counter the biochemical imbalances that cause manic-depressive psychosis. The medicines for depression available to Virginia Woolf did little more than drug her into a stupor or put her to sleep (Caramagno).

"It would be difficult to find," wrote an anonymous reviewer of several early nineteenth-century works on the diagnosis and treatment of insanity, "in the whole range of medical science, a subject more interesting at first sight, or less satisfactory on further consideration, than the philosophical investigations of the causes and symptoms of insanity." The subject is interesting, of course, because virtually everyone experiences "at certain moments, some affections of the mind, which approach very near the character of true mania." The medical accounts, however, are disappointing because they reveal very little about either the causes or the cures of insanity. One problem, the reviewer notes, is the apparently "insuperable difficulty with regard to the correct definition of the term." At what point does an idiosyncracy become a serious aberration? Another problem is the classification. Physical disturbances, arising from disease or traumatic injury, are not properly discriminated from "morbid affections" that have their origin only in the mind. The latter category, which seems to defy the skills of medical science precisely because it is beyond physical treatment, is all the more challenging because its symptoms, in greater or lesser intensity, seem to be universal. Without a little madness, the author believes, life would be deprived of art: "The dreams of the poet, the fables of the mythologist, and the fictions of the romancer, may all be considered as subordinate varieties of the wanderings of an imagination, freed from the restraint of conformity with dull matter of fact" (*Quarterly Review* 2 [August 1809]: 155–80).

During the romantic period, the century-old notion of the *furor poeticus* was reinterpreted as a revolutionary and liberating madness that could free the imagination from the "restraint of conformity." Before the nineteenth century came to a close, Cesare Lombroso assembled an encyclopedic compilation, in the tradition of Burton's *Anatomy of Melancholy*, linking genius to a broad range of mental diseases and derangements, from alcoholism to epilepsy. The idea that a mental illness could liberate the imagination received significant scientific endorsement when Emil Kraepelin, professor of psychiatry at Heidelberg during the 1890s, identified and explained the manic syndrome. "Mania" he defined as an affection of the mind that may "set free powers that otherwise would be constrained by inhibitions." Mania in itself has nothing to do with the intellectual power of the mind; when it affects the mind of person of ability or talent, however, it can bring forth those gifts.

The notion that creative genius is impelled by madness has a venerable tradition. Yet, like many traditions, it has always had its opponents as well as its advocates (Delatte 28–79). Too, it has been subject to the constant permutations of cultural values. Madness, after all, is recognized by its very peculiarity, its deviation from social norms. Because the irrational is defined as a departure from the rational, its boundaries are renegotiated from age to age as norms change and tolerance for aberration waxes and wanes. During the Middle Ages, as Ernst Robert Curtius has noted, the topos of the mad poet was promoted by Statius, Nemesianus, and Fulgentius, for whom the idea of numinous inspiration (*ut insanus vates delirabam*) gave poetry special privilege as divinely sanctioned. Curtius also acknowledges that this lofty idea coexisted with the more vulgar appraisal of poetic enthusiasm (ἐνθουσιασμός) as drunken frenzy or demented raving (Curtius 474–75).

The contending currents of belief and skepticism flowed into the Renaissance. Even after Nicholas of Cusa (*On Learned Ignorance*, 1440) appropriated the Pauline doctrine of the fool in Christ (1 Cor. 4:10) and gave it a new intellectual spin of paradoxicality, Marsilio Ficino (*De furore divino*, 1457) could reaffirm naive mystical receptivity to divine ventriloquism. Although there still persisted a belief that divine wisdom might be bestowed upon the fool, or prophetic vision granted to the madman, the appeals to superstition and dogma were rapidly losing credibility. The debates engendered by the Reformation, and the rise of humanism, gave the bifurcated implications of inspired madman or fool a satirical currency in Erasmus's *Praise of Folly* (1511).

From the Middle Ages through the Renaissance, the *amabilis insanus* of the poet could, in various quarters, arouse admiration or scorn, piety or pity. Although madness was generally considered a failure of the mind to maintain order, the tactic of deliberate folly became part of the literary figure of the fool. The fool, as prankster, might even manipulate the follies that victimize others (Welsford 76–112). The Shakespearean fool, liberated from social constraints, observes the folly of others and exercises a mocking wit.

Shakespeare also dramatizes the fragility of reason, the unprotected borders between sanity and madness. Several of his major characters find themselves unable to sustain rational control. "Othello shall go mad," Iago confidently declares before he interviews Cassio (IV.i.100). "Let me not be mad, not mad," Lear cries out as he feels and fears the symptoms of debility, "Sweet heaven! / Keep me in temper: I would not be mad!" (I.v.46–47). The Doctor, witnessing Lady Macbeth walking in her sleep, declares that "unnatural deeds / Do breed unnatural troubles; infected minds / To their deaf pillows will discharge their secrets" (V.i.72–73). Polonius, as much a master of diagnosis as many modern practitioners of psychiatry, informs the Queen that her "noble son is mad: Mad I call it; for, to define true madness, / What is it but to be nothing else but mad?" (II.ii.93–94). Hamlet, confident that he is more than merely mad, offers an alternate diagnosis: "I am but mad north-north-west: when the wind is southerly I know a hawk from a handsaw" (II.ii.378–79).

Madness, according to Shakespeare in *Othello*, *King Lear*, and *Macbeth*, is largely a matter of reason being overwhelmed by the senses or feelings. But the case of Hamlet poses a rather different problem that fascinated the romantic critics. Hamlet's peculiarity, as Coleridge explained it, resulted from an intensity of imagination, an imagination that imposes upon the mind as vividly as the senses. Coleridge thus distinguishes between "the Madness of Imagination and that of Passion (*Lectures 1808–1819* [=*LL*] 2:419). Hamlet's madness is not a loss of reason, but a failure of judgment. Swayed by the power of his mental images, he gives more credence to his subjective experiences than to external circumstances. Hamlet's "view of the external world and all its incidents and objects were comparatively dim, and of no interest in themselves, and which began to interest only when they were reflected in the mirror of his mind. Hamlet beheld external objects in the same way that a man of vivid imagination who shuts his eyes, sees what has previously made an impression upon his organs of vision" (*LL* 1:386). Turning to Hamlet's feigned madness, Coleridge quotes (misquotes, but corrected here) Dryden's well-known couplet, "Great wits are sure to madness near allied, / And thin partitions do their bounds divide" (*Absalom and Achitophel* 163–64). Hamlet pretends to madness, says Coleridge, because he knows well "his own character, which with all strength of motive was so weak as to be unable to carry into effect his most obvious duty" (*LL* 1:388). For precisely this reason it is a dangerous disguise: "O that subtle trick to pretend to be acting only when we are very near to being what we act" (*LL* 1:541).

In describing Hamlet, Coleridge identified some of the peculiarities of which he often accused himself. A crucial problem, one that he also often pondered in his notebooks, was whether one could, in fact, watch one's own madness. Coleridge, who elsewhere insisted on distinguishing illusion from delusion (*LL* 1:133), wants to grant a rational self-awareness to certain modes of madness. Recent statistical studies on creativity and mental illness, as well as case studies of individual poets and artists, support Coleridge's claim that some modes of madness still permit the use of logic and reason. But even in his own day Coleridge would have found his opinions supported in a number of medical accounts, including those of Dr. John Abercrombie, personal physician and friend of Sir Walter Scott.

In his *Inquiries concerning the Intellectual Powers*, Dr. Abercrombie reports the case of a patient who is visited by a spectral apparition, yet on all occasions knows the ghostly visitor to be his own hallucination. Scott noted the similarities between Dr. Abercrombie's patient and a character in Le Sage's *Gil Blas*: Duke D'Olivarez was "haunted by an apparition, to the actual existence of which he gave no credit, but died, nevertheless, because he was overcome and heart-broken by its imaginary presence" (Scott, *Letters*, 28, 54–55). Dr. Abercrombie's patient seemed to have experienced in his hallucinations the very symptoms about which he had read in Le Sage. Dr. Abercrombie's own wife, after reading Hibbert's *Sketches of the Philosophy of Apparitions*, began to see various phantom figures posing in her sitting room and bedchamber. Sir David Brewster concurred with Dr. Abercrombie that these bizarre optical manifestations, stimulated by reading books, must be attributed to a "morbidly sensitive imagination" (Brewster 42–43, 49). Coleridge elaborated much the same diagnosis in his lectures on *Don Quixote* (*LL* 2:156–66, 414–20). While such symptoms may seem trivial and whimsical, Scott argues that the imagination has the power "to kill the body, even when its fantastic terrors cannot overcome the intellect" (*Letters* 26–32). The mind, conscious of its own hallucinations, may be relieved from the horror of thinking that nightmare images are real, but that awareness cannot dispel the torment of knowing it has no control over their presence.

Because the romantic period provides an overwhelming abundance of cases, it has been necessary to choose those few which best serve the major arguments of the book. Although a chapter is devoted to the visions of William Blake, it was necessary to omit discussion of mental aberrations experienced by other artists of the period. James Barry, for example, retreated into lonely isolation after being expelled from the Royal Academy in 1799; he spent the last seven years of his life as a "mad hermit" painting distortions of Reynolds's Grand Manner. Karl Blechen had no sooner achieved recognition as one of the most successful landscape artists of the Berlin Academy than he began to experience frequent delusions and could no longer trust his own perceptions;[1] in spite of the

1. Bettina von Arnim to Moritz August von Bethmann-Hollweg (1836): "Die Bilder, die er in seiner letzten Zeit gemalt und vorauf eine große Abspannung folgte, waren mit so ge-

aid offered by Bettina von Arnim during the four years preceding his death in 1840, Blechen gradually succumbed to the persistent and increasingly powerful hallucinations engendered by his own mind. Richard Dadd, convinced that his will was controlled by the god Osiris and that supernatural beings were communicating with him, began in the 1840s to paint the fairies and fantastic creatures of his visions; in 1844 he murdered his father, whom "secret admonitions" had revealed to be the Devil.

Were the scope of this book encyclopedic, it would have been interesting to devote attention to the mad artists and to examine in detail the fate of such figures as Charles Lloyd. In one of his contributions to *Poems by Coleridge, Lamb, and Lloyd* (1797), Lloyd described Coleridge as "rack'd by hopes that frenzy and expire, / In the long sabbath of subdued desire." These lines, which might have been applied with equal truth to Lloyd himself, embarrassed Coleridge as being "Too warm by a half." Coleridge was not embarrassed but angered by what he recognized as his own fictional portrait in Lloyd's novel, *Edmund Oliver* (1797). Lloyd's "infirmities," Coleridge assumed, had "been made the instruments of another man's darker passions." Only Robert Southey, Coleridge's brother-in-law, could have supplied the salacious details of Coleridge's past that Lloyd had given to the character of Edmund Oliver. Lloyd's "infirmities" had already in 1797 made it necessary for him to undergo treatment in Erasmus Darwin's sanitorium in Lichfield, and his wild hallucinations kept him in confinement for more than half of the remaining forty years of his life. Charles Lamb continued to befriend Lloyd during this troubled time, and the two collaborated on volume of poems, *Blank Verse by Charles Lloyd and Charles Lamb* (1798). Lloyd enjoyed a period of relative stability after his marriage in 1799, but by 1811 he was experiencing the intense auditory delusions, which Thomas De Quincey described in his reminiscences of Lloyd, which appeared in *Tait's Magazine* (March 1840)[2] shortly after Lloyd's death in France. Only death, De Quincey wrote, could open for Lloyd what "that fine mystic, Blake the artist, [called] a 'golden gate'— the gate of liberation from the captivity of half a life" (400). His creative work—poetry, plays, essays, and a second novel, *Isabel* (1820)—might

---

waltiger Phantasie, die, im Zügel gehalten und der Natur anschmiegend, das Unmögliche auf die Leinwand zauberte. In jedem kleinen Gegenstand spiegelt sich die Aufregung des Gemüts, in dem die Natur wühlt, um ihm begreiflich zu werden." The more he strove to capture the images of nature, the less he could trust his own perception: "War es optischer Betrug, daß er die Welt so schaute, war er's allein, dem die kühnen Massen, die er auf die Berge und Felsen pflanzte, so edel und groß erschienen? Und das Licht, das aus seinem Pinsel strömte, sollte das bloß Fiktion sein und keine Wahrheit?" Quoted in Fritz Böttger, *Bettina von Arnim*, 248–49.

2. "Society of the Lakes: Charles Lloyd," in *The Collected Writings of Thomas De Quincey* (=*DQ*), 2:381–402.

also have provided liberation, but the sustained effort exacerbated his nerves. Although "his mind was chiefly remarkable for a fine power of analysis," according to Thomas Noon Talfourd, Lloyd carried "this power of discriminating and distinguishing . . . almost to a pitch of painfulness."[3] When he was incapable of sustaining this power in writing poetry, when "ill health" and "much suffering" had "made it difficult for me to execute any thing at all," he turned to translation. But even in translation, as he confesses in his introduction to *The Tragedies of Vittorio Alfieri* (1815), he agonized over the "correctness and perspicuity" of his language (xxv).

Lloyd was one of those minor figures of the romantic period who achieved a certain centrality simply because he was well known to so many of the more prominent writers of the period. It was not just Coleridge, Lamb, and Southey during those early years who witnessed Lloyd's futile struggle with madness. William Wordsworth's brother Christopher had married Lloyd's sister Priscilla, and both families had settled in Ambleside, not far from the Wordsworths in Grasmere. During these years Priscilla, too, suffered periods of derangement. After De Quincey moved into Dove Cottage, he became Lloyd's friend and confidant. Several times, as De Quincey later recollected, Lloyd would seek sanctuary at Dove Cottage when he had escaped from the asylum. Lloyd's sad plight became for Coleridge, Wordsworth, Lamb, and De Quincey a reference against which to measure insanity: for Wordsworth when his sister-in-law Priscilla had her spells of depression, and perhaps even later when his sister Dorothy began to show the symptoms of mental debility; for Lamb when, at the very time Lloyd had moved into the Coleridge household in Kingsdown, his own sister Mary in a fit of insanity murdered their mother with a pair of scissors; for Coleridge and subsequently De Quincey as they slipped into the nightmare thrall of opium addiction. Much work, of course, has already been devoted to the romantic indulgence in alcohol, hashish, and opium (Hayter, Lefebure). Rather than focus on the extensive testimony of altered consciousness in the works of Coleridge, De Quincey, and Baudelaire, it might be rewarding to turn to their accounts of withdrawal and their records of how, after the chemically induced intoxication had passed and the body's biochemistry had been left in disorder, they continued to experience disruptions in perception and in physical and mental function.

But these are paths not taken. Instead, I have chosen to examine the strange entanglement of life and art, reality and imagination. Rather than impose the theories of Freud, or Jung, or Lacan, I have emphasized the prevailing social and medical attitudes toward madness and the so-called

---

3. *Final Memorials of Charles Lamb* (1848), 1:38.

poetic rapture. To demonstrate the dilemma of the mad rhapsodist during the later eighteenth and early nineteenth centuries, I have addressed three major topics: the appeal to poetic madness in critical theory, the thematization of the mad poet in literature, and the reception of mad poets.

In the first section, I examine the theoretical implications of the concept of the *furor poeticus*. In spite of its venerable tradition, the pose of the "mad rhapsodist" had always been suspect, for reasons that Socrates prompted Ion to acknowledge. Although Fénelon, in another enlightened age many centuries later, still insisted upon the miraculous inspiration of the prophets and the apostles,[4] the era of rationalism had rendered the religious as well as secular claims of the inspired mind virtually bankrupt. By defining "inspired" as possessed by or breathed upon by the Holy Spirit, the philosopher or critic substituted supernaturalism for the more difficult task of explaining the creative process.

Not in spite of, but rather because of the rationalist dismissal of enthusiasm and emotionalism in the arts, a number of critics during the latter half of the eighteenth century were prompted to refurbish and reinvest in the concept of inspiration. Although it was necessary to give the concept some intellectual credibility, it had to be located outside the domain commanded by the epistemologies of Locke, Condillac, and Leibniz. When Baumgarten staked out a new philosophical province for his *Aesthetica* (1750), he had to retrieve the aesthetic experience from the "lower faculties" of the senses and feelings (Baeumler 207–31). This could easily have been reduced to some "aesthetic" ritual of dipping one's net into the sloughs of base animal responses then attempting to wash off whatever slimy object one had caught under the clear waters of reason.

Artistic creativity and aesthetic experience ought to involve some activity of the "higher faculties" not comprehended by conscious analytical reason. "Original genius," as advocated by Young and Duff, by Herder and Goethe, was the mental faculty needed to reach beyond the constraints of reason and tradition to elevate the human consciousness to new heights. To exercise this faculty, however, is to oppose established norms, to adventure into obscure realms of mind not illuminated by the rational powers. One consequence of this endeavor is what Thomas McFarland has called the "originality paradox": the quest for the new keeps repeating the old. Another consequence is what Michel Foucault has called the "rationality paradox": every attempt to examine irrationality reveals only the

4. *Mémoire adressé à l'évêque de Châlons pendant les conférences d'Issy*, in *Oeuvres complètes*, 2:224, and *Traité du ministère des pasteurs*, chaps. 2 and 12, in *Oeuvres complètes*, 1:153 and 187.

rigorous categories of reason.[5] The dilemma arose, then, not in claiming inspiration beyond the reach of reason, but in trying to express it in the work of art.

It was not enough to affirm rhapsodic inspiration in a theory of the creative imagination. It was also necessary to account for the act of retrieving and representing. This two-part movement is evident in Coleridge's argument that the Primary Imagination, through which the creativity of the "infinite I AM" is repeated in the "finite mind," must be complemented by the Secondary Imagination, which "dissolves, diffuses, dissipates, in order to re-create" (*Biographia Literaria* [=*BL*] 1:304). Even without the devastating skepticism of Hume, Fénelon's affirmation of miraculous inspiration had become untenable. The "finite mind" could not be a mere passive recipient, and the expressive act required the exercise of will. Coleridge and De Quincey both found it necessary redefine the process as an active mental theogony. What, they asked, constitutes a miracle? How can one recognize divine intervention or divine inspiration? How does one distinguish a false prophet from a true?

Coleridge and De Quincey were not engaged in a mere metaphysical inquiry. From generation to generation many a fanatic has claimed divine inspiration. From them, however, emerge a few with the power to convince others of the truth of their visions. Such was the power of Richard Brothers, "the nephew of the Almighty," who had drawn many converts to his new religion before he was tried as a criminal lunatic in 1795 and confined in a private asylum in Islington. Such, too, was the power of Joanna Southcott, who commenced writing her prophecies in 1792, during the very years when Blake was engraving his illuminated works. Indeed, it was Blake's fellow engraver, William Sharp, who brought her to London to lead the cult that had once gathered around Brothers. To vast crowds of disciples and believers, she related her visions in incantatory verse and ecstatic, often incoherent prose. She wrote over sixty books, from *Strange Effects of Faith* (1801–2) and *A Dispute between the Woman and the Powers of Darkness* (1802) through the *Book of Wonders* (1813–14) and *Prophecies announcing the Birth of the Prince of Peace* (1814). In this last work, she announced that, like the Virgin Mary, she was about to give birth to the new Christ. Only a phantom, however, was delivered, for Southcott fell into a trance and died of a brain disease on 29 October 1814, a day that her followers, a religious sect of over 100,000 members, continued to worship as the advent of a new age.

With a mad king on the throne of England, mad prophets in the mar-

---

5. McFarland, *Originality and Imagination*, 1–30; Foucault, *Madness and Civilization*, 107.

ketplace, and mad poets in their midst, it cannot be surprising that many writers used their fiction to explore the conditions of madness. To discuss the mad poet as a character in romantic narrative, I commence the second section of this book with a study of Torquato Tasso, or rather with a study of the reception and representation of the Italian poet in Goethe's play and in the poetry and criticism of the Schlegels, Byron and Shelley, Peacock and Hazlitt. Part of my purpose in Chapter 4 is to consider the changing vantages from classical to romantic, but the dramatization of the madness of an actual poet also involves those entanglements, already mentioned, of life and art, reality and imagination. The mad poet as a literary topos invites a variety of self-reflective strategies. August Wilhelm Schlegel, who just a few years later was to express his enthusiasm for Tieck's *Puss-in-Boots* (1794) as a play about a play, is clearly excited about Goethe's offering a real poet as the object of poetic representation.[6]

The history of the drama has a long and well-established tradition of exhibiting the excesses of grief, remorse, or rage as passion transformed into madness. But madness as the trope of poetic creativity allows for a rather different strategy than one might witness in the raging Medea or the sleepwalking fits of Lady Macbeth. The poet steps forth on the stage to describe or even enact his visions. The theater itself becomes a madhouse, or troping that trope, as Charles Beys did in *Les Illustres Fous* (1634), the madhouse becomes theater. Persecuted lovers take refuge in a hospital for the insane in Valencia. There they meet with mad artists, poets, philosophers, and musicians. To entertain the curious nobility who visit the hospital, they put on a play in which they act out the circumstances that precipitated their madness. Within the romance plot of disguised and mistaken identities, the metadramatic play of the mad actors provides for an exploration of tension between the irrational origins and the rational forms of the dramatic art. When Molière attempted a similar self-reflexive, metadramatic debate on drama in *L'Impromptu de Versailles* (1663), he lacked the vantage of the mad artists who could personally document the irrationality of their dreams and desires.

Goethe's *Torquato Tasso* (1790) exploits that vantage with a vengeance. His Tasso is a poet who longs to fulfill the heroic roles of his own poetic imagination, a recluse who longs for the acclaim of the poet, but also the adventure of the soldier, the prestige of the statesman, the passionate joy of the lover. The artistic challenge to contain romantic exu-

---

6. A. W. Schlegel, review of Tieck's *Ritter Blaubart* and *Der gestiefelte Kater*, in *Jenaische Allgemeine Litteraturzeitung*, reprinted in *Kritische Schriften* (1828) 1:311–18; review of Goethe's *Schriften*, vols. 6–8, *Göttingische Anzeigen von gelerhten Sachen* 154 (1790), reprinted in *Sämtliche Werke*, ed. Eduard Böcking (Leipzig, 1846), 10:4–5.

berance within classical form is replicated in the personal tensions between reason and emotion. Goethe presents the mad Tasso not to exalt
the *visio beatifica* of original genius he had once celebrated in "Von
deutscher Baukunst" (1772) and the hymns of his Storm-and-Stress period, but rather to demonstrate the need to adhere to the formal structures of art and society.

Although tragedy had traditionally used outbreaks of derangement to
dramatize the emotional suffering of a character, the plays of the romantic period began to trace more carefully the causes and effects of madness. The more detailed literary attention to the "case history" of madness followed a new medical interest in nervous disorders and the rise of
psychology as a scientific discipline. Joanna Baillie, in her *Plays of the
Passions* (1798–1812), sought to dramatize the obsessive and compulsive
hold of one dominant passion on the life and mind of a character. Her
brother, Dr. Matthew Baillie, who had focused on the brain and abdomi-
nal organs in his *Morbid Anatomy* (1793), was encouraged by Joanna to
pursue his studies on the effects of disease on the spinal cord and nervous system. In 1797 he became physician extraordinary to George III,
who had already suffered spells of raving violence. Joanna Baillie attempted in her plays to dramatize the pathology of an idée fixe. This
meant, of course, that she had to somehow reveal internal motivation and
contrive to make her dialogue reveal the inner turmoil of her characters.
Scene and setting served to provoke the mimetic activity of her characters, who project their psychological experience onto the people and
things with whom they interact. The sense of external reality is gradually
transformed by the inner vision. Baillie dramatizes the process by which
a character becomes progressively deluded by his or her own mental
fixation: the supernatural fear that victimizes Osterloo in *The Dream*, the
paranoic fear that grips the title characters in *Orra* and *Ethwald*, the compulsive hatred that drives De Monfort to kill the honest Rezenvelt.[7] Elizabeth Inchbald, commenting on its first performance at Drury Lane (29
April 1800), found the playwright's hints of a progressive aberration too
subtle, so that "the most attentive auditor, whilst he plainly beholds defects, asks after causes; and not perceiving those diminutive seeds of hatred, here described, till, swollen, they extend to murder, he conceives
the hero of the tragedy to be more a pitiable maniac, than a man acting
under the dominion of a natural propensity."[8]

The new interest in mental pathology resulted in a different way of

---

7. Janice Patten, "Joanna Baillie: Passions of the Mind," in "Dark Imagination: Poetic
Painting in Romantic Drama," 61–96.

8. Elizabeth Inchbald, "Remarks" to *De Monfort*, in *The British Theatre* 24:2–6.

regarding aberrant behavior. Romantic literature, with its emphasis on subjective experience, quite naturally turned to expositions of madness that reflected contemporary developments in medicine and psychology. Among the many literary expositions of madness, not addressed in the ensuing chapters, one might think of the dialogue of the Visitor, the Physician, and the Patient in the madhouse scene of George Crabbe's *Sir Eustace Grey* (1807) or the tale of Peter Grimes, in Crabbe's *Borough* (1810), who in his hallucinatory guilt is persecuted by the phantoms of his father and the boys whom he has beaten and starved. In Wordsworth's poem "The Mad Mother" (1798), a woman rehearses to her nursing infant the woes and suffering that have driven her mad. Brother Medardus, in Hoffmann's *The Devil's Elixers* (1815), and Robert Wringhim, in Hogg's *Confessions of a Justified Sinner* (1824), both experience a confounded sense of identity and increasing derangement upon encountering a doppelgänger. My concern in Chapters 4, 5, and 6 is not simply with the literary representation of madness, even when it is said to be provoked by a "morbidly sensitive imagination," but more particularly with the portrayal of the mad poet. The major change that had taken place in the concept of the *furor poeticus* was that it could no longer be described simply as a moment of inspiration. From this time forward, it must bear the burden of psychiatric scrutiny. No longer miraculous, it was now definitely pathological.

In England, it may well be that the legacy of Chatterton, Cowper, and Smart influenced the fictional account of the poet (Porter 99, 146, 265–68). Clearly, a sad reciprocity between fiction and fact—as in the fashion of young men dressing in blue and yellow and the epidemic of suicides that followed the publication of *Werther* (1774)—extended to the poets and artists themselves, who often seemed incapable of escaping the mold into which they had been cast. The literary treatment of the mad poet seems to be inevitably tinged with autobiographical traits. There is a bit of Goethe, as he himself tells us, in his depiction of Tasso. E.T.A. Hoffmann put anecdotes from his own life into his *Kreisleriana*, the fictive episodes in the life of the mad composer, Johannes Kreisler. Nodier made his tale *Jean-François les bas-bleus* (1833) a repository for childhood recollections. And Georg Büchner formed a sympathetic bond with the mad poet of his *Lenz* (1836).

Jacob Michael Reinhold Lenz, who died in 1792, began to exhibit fits of insanity, perhaps schizophrenia, when he was in his twenties. His love poems to Friederike Brion were published as *Die Liebe auf dem Lande*, and his play, *Der Hofmeister* (1774), was performed in Hamburg in 1778. Because of his erratic temper and emotional outbursts, he soon lost his friends and supporters. He led a nomadic existence and was periodically confined for his wild behavior. Ludwig Tieck produced a three-volume edition of Lenz's works in 1828. Georg Büchner, whose plays *Woyzeck* and *Danton's Tod* demonstrate his preoccupation with the disturbances of the mind, transformed the troubled life of the poet into a haunting novella, *Lenz*. His immediate source was the diary of Johann Friedrich Oberlin, pastor of the little village of Waldbach in Steinthal, in whose home in 1778 Lenz had sought release from the hallucinations that were tormenting him.[9] From Oberlin's account of his attempts to care for Lenz, Büchner develops a strange third-person narrative in which the relation between narrator and character, caretaker and madman seem to merge into an autobiography with multiple subjects.

Not all of these tales found their way into my "Narratives of Madness." I discuss Nodier's *Jean-François les bas-bleus*, Hoffmann's *Der goldne Topf*, Shelley's *Julian and Maddalo*. And I devote a short chapter to Blake's account of the struggle between Los and Urizen. While Blake certainly represented with mythic intensity the grand labors of the artist in a world that seems to fear the rebellious energies of imagination, he was also unusually alert to social and political forces that work perniciously within the hierarchy of the classes. Perhaps only a poet of the lower classes could have observed, as Blake did, the epidemics of madness among the poor that resulted from marketing blighted grain. Blake himself, for all his visionary idiosyncrasy, may never have personally experienced the ergot poisoning he describes. But medical records confirm that Gerard de Nerval suffered the protracted effects of ergotism. In spite of extensive criticism on Blake and Nerval, much of which is devoted to their visionary experiences, no previous study has observed the relevance of ergotism.

The final section of the book, "Mad Poets," is in many respects a continuation of the "Narratives of Madness" section. Because the fictional representation of the mad poet invited an occasion for autobiographical indulgence, it is sometimes difficult to discriminate the "sane" narrator from the "insane" character. Strangely enough, as Evelyne Keitel points out, that duality of sanity and insanity is virtually a generic characteristic of psychopathography. The narration of psychosis, she observes, relies on intertextuality because the ability to sustain intersubjective communication breaks down (Keitel 28–29). The poets I discuss in this final section—Hölderlin, Nerval, and Clare—all adopted intertextual strategies in relating their visionary experiences: Hölderlin's hymn "Patmos" is a visionary endeavor to penetrate the visions of St. John; Nerval's "Le Christ aux Oliviers" enters into Christ's Sermon on the Mount by way of Jean

9. John Parker, "Some Reflections on Georg Büchner's *Lenz* and Its Principal Source, the Oberlin Record"; Francis Michael Sharp, "Büchner's *Lenz*. A Futile Madness."

Paul's "Rede des toten Christus"; and Clare, as a patient in the asylum of Dr. Matthew Allen, adopted a Byronic persona to write his own "Child Harold" and "Don Juan."

Although all three of these poets eventually collapsed under the debilities that held their minds in thrall, we must conclude that writing poetry provided them some therapeutic relief. One way of examining the thoughts and words of madness, as Coleridge suggested, is to presume that the mind retains its rational faculties. Both Dr. Abercrombie's patient and his wife were able to observe their vivid hallucinations fully aware that they were only hallucinations. The debate, however, still persists whether the relationship between creativity and madness is sequential or simultaneous. Wilhelm Dilthey, in his speech "Dichterische Einbildungskraft und Wahnsinn" (Poetic imagination and madness), argued the radical error of that traditional lore which equates genius with madness. Only the healthy imagination is capable of organizing images and impressions into a work of art. To claim that the creative imagination can function in and through madness mistakenly attributes to madness a degree of control it does not possess. As I point out in Chapter 5, Foucault may seem to agree with Dilthey when he exclaims that "*where there is a work of art, there is no madness.*" Although Foucault seems to support Dilthey's insistence that poetic imagination must be free from any tinge of madness, he actually embraces the opposite when he concludes that "madness is contemporary with the work of art."[10] Madness, no less than art, has its elaborate organization and meticulous structures. Art is twin-born with madness, Foucault affirms, yet the two grow apart because madness is self-centered, whereas art strives to communicate.

A more recent version of the debate over the relationship between creativity and madness is pursued in Albert Rothenberg's repudiation of the research of Nancy Andreasen. In the opening chapter of *Creativity and Madness*, Dr. Rothenberg reviews several versions of the "myth" that links creative inspiration to some irrational or suprarational experience—a dream, a vision, spontaneous revelation. Although perpetuated throughout history, the popular notions about the irrational origins of creativity "have *not* been empirically assessed or substantiated" (Rothenberg 3). Andreasen's studies of the creativity that accompanies mental illness, Rothenberg argues, are based on faulty assumptions and "a flawed research methodology":

10. Foucault, 288–89; also "Madness is precisely the *absence of the work of art*, the reiterated presence of that absence, its central void is experienced and measured in all its endless dimensions. . . . Madness is the absolute break with the work of art; it forms the constitutive moment of abolition, which dissolves in time the truth of the work of art" (287).

> Andreasen, who did her study with thirty writers who served during a period of fifteen years on the faculty of the University of Iowa Writer's workshop, reported that 80 percent of these writers experienced some form of affective illness. In arriving at this finding, Andreasen had personally carried out diagnostic interviews with the faculty members at the workshop as well as with a group of what she specified as "matched controls." The latter consisted of persons who were not in the creative arts but were comparable to the writers in age, sex, and education. She reported a statistically higher incidence of affective illness in the writers than in the matched control group. (150)

Rothenberg concedes that these results are impressive "on the surface," but he urges us not to accept her evidence. She has conducted her work as "sole interviewer," he says, and has failed to obtain proper documentation and corroboration. Because she had herself been duped by the "myth," Rothenberg argues, she ignored, "in assessing her own hypothesis, [that] some conscious or unconscious bias inevitably must have operated."

Rothenberg, it should be noted, refers to only one of Andreasen's many studies on creativity and mental illness published between 1974 and 1988. Much of this work was part of a team effort and was certainly verified by many experts. Andreasen has, in fact, conducted her research with several different groups: she not only studied the incidence of mental illness among creative writers and artists, she also examined creativity among the mentally ill. She went on to trace patterns of creativity and mental illness within families. The impasse, in answering the objections of Dilthey and Rothenberg, is whether artistic creativity is seen as occurring within the state of madness or as a "lucid interval" in which a person escapes the bondage of the affliction. Both Dilthey and Rothenberg dismiss the "myth" of simultaneous madness and creativity; both assert that creativity exhibits a healthy power of mental discrimination and organization. It seems to me that it is Rothenberg, not Andreasen, who makes the evidence suit the hypothesis. Admittedly, poets like Clare, Nerval, and Hölderlin gradually lost their creative ability to the ravages of debilitating mental illness; nevertheless, long after they suffered severe mental breakdown and had been confined to an asylum, the creative power still managed to assert itself. Indeed, Nerval produced his most stunning literary work during the dozen years that followed his first collapse and confinement.

Perhaps it is not creative irrationality but creative rationality that is the "myth." Only a portion of what takes place in the waking or dreaming activity of mind may be translated into the language of reason, yet the arts have always drawn from the otherwise untranslatable "aboriginal consciousness" (Shumaker 108–9) to find the images, symbols, rhythms which are recognized by humanity at large without ever being reduced to explicit logical meanings (Liebrucks 311–45). Bosch's "Garden of Earthly Delights" baffles the effort to interpret its symbols, but few have beheld the painting without recognizing something familiar to their own dreams. Art is twin-born with madness, Foucault asserted, and the two may be distinguished only by the capacity of the former to reassert itself within the rational world, while the latter remains trapped within the solipsism of irrationality. Yet that primal energy, bound within the individual consciousness, generates images we recognize because irrationality lurks within us all.

Art is able to communicate only because some portion of the population is willing to attend to it. The asylum was established, Foucault observes, to segregate and confine those whom the population did not want in their midst. Society is always anxious about the internal forces that threaten to destroy its cooperative order; yet it is also true that people will oppose an order that becomes too restrictive and oppressive. Art thus seems obligated to exercise two opposing attributes of its being, the impulses that Nietzsche identified as Apollonian and Dionysian.

In depicting the struggle between Urizen and Los, Blake not only acted out his own personal torment, Youngquist argues, the very act enabled him to secure his sanity. "Poetry itself cannot be mad," Youngquist asserts, and "Blake did not succumb to the madness so often imputed to him" (112). Many an artist has fought a similar battle. And many of those who ultimately lost the battle still managed to produce works of greatness.

Several theories have been forwarded to explain how mania influences creativity. One is that during the manic phase of the manic-depressive cycle, the mental processes are accelerated—ideas and associations simply come faster; another is that a more elaborate circuitry of connecting thoughts is brought into play, so that habitual patterns are replaced by surprising new combinations; still another is that mania alters perception so that images are apprehended more acutely or intensely. To the person who has lived through these manic-depressive cycles, the one phase may be as painful as the other. "I cultivate my hysteria," Baudelaire said, "with joy and terror." The "single-minded intensity" which possessed him during writing, Theodore Roethke observed, made him feel as if there were "some flaw in the motor" (Taylor 204–7).

The accounts of mania in Andreasen's studies, Frederick Goodwin and

Kay Jamison's *Manic-Depressive Illness*, and Shelley Taylor's *Positive Illusions* indicate that, at least in this form, madness is simultaneous with creativity. The mind is exhilarated and accelerated into a state of compulsive receptivity and productivity. But there are other forms of madness, which, in spite of the momentary flashes of genius that Lombroso emphasizes in his case studies, have dire and destructive consequences. Artistic genius may cross over the borders of madness, but it remains productive only if it can return again. But for many there is no return. We can understand Achim von Arnim's fond hope, in his "Walks with Hölderlin," that the poet had only gone forth on a mental journey of exploration, and that one day he would come back and tell us what it was like in the realm beyond the borders of rationality.

PART I
POETICS OF MADNESS

1

GENIUS, MADNESS, AND INSPIRATION

If the creative activity of inspiration and imagination transcends the material world, then the relevance of that activity to the rational order of things is suspect. Socrates, we know, convinces Ion that his moments of inspiration are fits of madness. The dilemma of the "mad rhapsodist," as we find it in Plato's *Ion*, *Phaedrus*, and *Timaeus*, involves an apparent impasse between the irrational source of inspiration and any possible rationality in its expression. To what extent is this dilemma recognized and resolved in those romantic theories of the imagination which assume that the mind has a capacity of reaching beyond the limits of logical or empirical knowledge? What rational control, for example, does Coleridge presume attendant to the "repetition in the finite mind of the eternal act of creation in the infinite I AM"? What happens, according to De Quincey, to an imagination "untouched by reality" or "untamed by the coarser realities of life"?

During the eighteenth century, aesthetic illusion was defined as emotion overpowering reason, so that representation was mistaken for reality. Among the variations on this prevailing theory, it was argued that illusion was a deliberate indulgence of the emotions, or a flickering alternation between dreamlike participation and aloof objectivity. We may credit Plato for promulgating the notion that poetry works through delusion. In the *Republic* the poet is banished because, in exciting the senses and the passions, his art exerts a dangerous influence. Indeed, the effect is the contagion and infection of the cause, for creative genius, too, is said to result from a pathological fit of the mind. Among the sources of madness, as delineated in the *Phaedrus*, is that which derives from the Muses and takes possession of "a tender, virgin soul and stimulates it to rapt passionate expression"; this "madness of the Muses" is needed because poetry cannot be produced by skill alone. In the *Ion*, the rhapsodist confesses that when he is inspired, he is carried out of himself; he becomes "possessed" and no longer in his senses; furthermore, he agrees that "the same effects" are produced in the spectators.[1]

Plato may have banished "mad" poets from his Republic, but Democritus demanded that sane poets be excluded from Helicon. To be a great poet, according to Democritus, one needed "a touch of divine madness." As Seneca phrased it, "There is no great genius without some touch of madness," and he attributed the same formula to Aristotle ("nullum magnum ingenium sine mixtura dementiae fuit"). Horace called poetic inspiration an "amiable insanity" ("amabilis insania").[2] And the pseudo-Longinus, whose *On the Sublime* was to have extensive influence on theories of literary expression during the Enlightenment, equated the power in language with the degree of felt emotion. These were the classical sources cited in the eighteenth century to define genius as an enraptured fit.

During the eighteenth century, the very predominance of rationalist and empirical thought prompted many poets and critics to claim a source or province for artistic endeavor apart from mundane experience and at odds with formal precepts. Creativity as well as the aesthetic response seemed to involve a spell, a rapture, a delirium, a momentary madness. Although they are by no means mutually exclusive, two definitions of genius are at work in the eighteenth century: one sees genius directly inspired by divine idea; another attributes to genius an acute sensitivity to the dynamism of nature. The former, as elaborated in the Neoplatonic tradition, describes the act of genius as a repetition of divine creativity. Thus in Ficino's *Theologia Platonica* (1482), the poet is referred to as a "god upon earth" ("est utique deus in terris"); in Scaliger's *Poetica* (1561), as "another god" ("alter deus");[3] and, moving from the Renaissance to the Enlightenment, in Shaftesbury's *Characteristics* (1711), as a "second maker, a just Prometheus under Jove." Shaftesbury, however, also turns to the latter conception of genius by insisting on the poet's natural insight in describing "men and matters." The poet's godlike power is revealed in

1. *Collected Dialogues of Plato* 221–22, 492, 827, 830.
2. Democritus, as quoted in Cicero, *De divinatione*, 1:80, and in Horace, *Epistles*, 2.3.295. Seneca, "De Tranquillitate," in *Moral Essays* 17:10, and *Problemata* 30.1. Horace, *Epistles*, 2.3.402.
3. Marsilio Ficino, *Theologia Platonica*, 16.6, in *Opera* 1:295, and Julius Caesar Scaliger, *Poetica* (1561), quoted in V. Rüfener, "Homo secundus deus."

naturally ordered representation: "Like that sovereign artist or universal plastic nature, he forms a whole, coherent and proportioned itself, with due subjection and subordinacy of constituent parts."[4]

The relationship between these two ways of defining genius resemble that interdependency Spinoza attributes to the *natura naturans* and the *natura naturata*.[5] The latter, admittedly, was more often repeated during the Enlightenment. "Great genius," as celebrated by Joseph Addison in *Spectator*, no. 160 (1711), is capable of creating "without any Assistance of Art or Learning."[6] The inspiration of genius is instinctive and natural. Edward Young, *On Original Composition* (1759), scorns the mediocrity produced by rules and reason in favor of the beauty and natural grace of genius. Whereas Young emphasizes the natural health of genius, William Duff, *Essay on Original Genius* (1767), suggests that, although it may naturally arise in a sanguine temperament, genius ill sustains disappointment and frustration and thus inclines to a gloomy and brooding preoccupation. In its most sublime and profound expression, genius is accompanied by melancholy. Whereas Addison and Young presume that inspiration would naturally assert itself in ordered expression, Duff harkens back to Aristotle's *Problemata Physica* (250, 253) and Ficino's *De vita triplici* (1:5) in observing the inclination of genius to morbid derangement. Alexander Gerard called for rational constraint to tame the wild excesses of natural genius: "It needs the assistance of taste, to guide and moderate its exertions" (*Essay on Taste* 76; *Essay on Genius* 391–416).

In Germany, where the cult of genius was carried to greater extremes than in England,[7] several critics came to recognize that their own endorsement of irrational enthusiasm left them trapped with a mode of artistic expression that could appeal only to the passions. Among the testimonies in behalf of epiphanic or ecstatic inspiration produced during this period were Hamann's *Socratic Memoires* (1759), Herder's "On Shakespeare" (1773), and Goethe's "On German Architecture" (1773).[8] Although

---

4. Anthony Ashley Cooper, 3d earl of Shaftesbury, *Characteristics of Men, Manners, Opinions, Times*, 1:207.

5. Spinoza, *Ethica*, pars prima, propositio xxix, scholium, in *Werke* 2:132–33.

6. Joseph Addison, *Spectator*, no. 160; see also no. 279, and "Pleasures of the Imagination," nos. 411–21 (1712).

7. Johann Caspar Lavater, *Physiognomische Fragmente*, 4:98, rhapsodizes the power of *Genie*: "The torch of the universe, the salt of the earth, the substantive in the grammar of humanity, the image of divinity, creator, destroyer, revealer of the secrets of God and men, guide of nature, prophets, priests and kings . . . super-Nature, super-Art, super-Learning, super-Talent, self-life . . . [whose] way is the way of lightning, or storm-wind or eagle" at the path of whose passage "we gaze with amazement," hearing its rush or seeing its majesty, but not knowing "the whither or whence of its going" or finding "the print of its feet."

8. Jochen Schmidt, *Die Geschichte des Genie-Gedankens*, 1:98–102, 133–35, 141–49, 193–

Herder and Goethe later retracted their notions of genius as irrational enthusiasm, Hamann did not swerve from his religious belief in inspired revelation.

Because he considered creativity not simply a divine gift but a manifestation of divine presence, Hamann dismissed the vain presumption of critics who supposed that art could be made, or even explained, according to rational criteria.[9] Hamann's literary model was the Bible: his poetics assumed a natural dialogue with God. From Bishop Robert Lowth's commentary on the Psalms in *De sacra poesi Hebraeorum* (1753), Hamann appropriated the analogical extension of biblical inspiration to all acts of poetic expression.

One major difference, however, sets Hamann apart from Lowth, and that is Hamann's account of the irony that inevitably occurs when reason disrupts inspired passion. Fallen reason intrudes upon the visionary moment. With the disruption of inspiration, revelation degenerates into self-conscious reflection; metaphoric presence lapses into metonymic absence. Fully aware of the difference, the poet resorts to ironic play with his scholarly learning. It is a Socratic but also a subversive irony, for Hamann opposes the pretenses of rationalism with the mystery of revelation. In Hamann's *Socratic Memoires*, the poet, who like Socrates "knows that he does not know," chooses therefore to make poetry out of "orgies and Eleusinian secrets."[10]

When he began proselytizing the cult of genius, Herder, too, imported his arguments from England. As in his English sources, his prime example of inspired genius was Shakespeare. In an essay "On the Means of Arousing Genius in Germany" (1767), Herder turned specifically to Young. "Why is it," he asked, "that Young's writing on Originality glows for us with a certain fire that we cannot discern simply through a detailed analysis?" And he answered, "Because the spirit of Young which prevails therein speaks from the heart directly to the heart, from one genius to another genius."[11]

95, discusses the problem of irrational inspiration in the works of Hamann, Herder, and Goethe. See also W. Schmidt-Dengler, *Genius.*

9. Johann Georg Hamann, *Sokratische Denkwürdigkeiten* (1759), in *Sämmtliche Werke* 2:75.

10. Hamann, *Aesthetica in nuce,* in *Sämmtliche Werke* 2:201–9, 214–15; Hamann, *Wolken* (1761), in *Sämmtliche Werke* 2:75, 89; Hamann, *Briefwechsel,* 2:118: "Eingebung und Gelehrsamkeit sind zwey stolze Pferde, zwey Hengste, die ich hier zum Gespann gemacht. Die Kunst kann nicht mehr übertrieben werden, als ich es hier gethan; wer Lust hat es von dieser Seite zu beurtheilen. Das Genie kann nicht unbändiger seyn, als ich es mir hier erlaubt."

11. Herder, "Über die Mittel zur Erweckung des Genies in Deutschland," in *Werke* 1:256: "Woher glühet uns bei der Youngischen Schrift über die Originale, ein gewisses Feuer an,

This intersubjectivity between individual and society, the one and the many, is a crux in Herder's criticism. To reconcile the apparent disparity between the isolated moment of inspiration and the universal ideal, Herder developed an organic and pantheistic account of poetic expression. Because Shakespeare creates an organized totality, we experience in his plays a universe not bounded by the mere limits of a finite text or a single performance. Emphasizing the organic unity, he says of *King Lear* that "everything in the play develops into a whole." Of *Othello*, he exclaims "what a world! what a whole! the living history of the rise, progress, eruption, and tragic end of the passion of this noble misfortunate!" Shakespeare had discovered "the divine touch of comprehending into One event a *whole* world of the most disparate scenes." The "divine touch" with which he combines the one and the many, Herder declares, makes Shakespeare the apotheosis of Spinoza's ideal: "The *whole* world is only body to this great mind: *all* scenes of nature limbs on this body, as *all* characters and modes of thought traits to this mind—and the *whole* may be named as that giant god of Spinoza '*Pan! Universum!*'"[12]

Goethe, who had studied under Herder in Strasbourg, appropriated Herder's humanized version of Spinoza in his description of the Strasbourg cathedral. But Goethe gives the idea of the artist's "godlike genius" a rebellious twist. With pointed irony, Goethe praises the architectural perfection of the cathedral as a revelation not of God's magnificence, but of "the magnificence of its lord and master," the architect Erwin of Steinbach. In praising the artist as another god, neither Scaliger nor Ficino had supposed a rivalry.[13] Although the idea is inherent in his

---

das wir bei blos gründlichen Untersuchungen nicht spüren? Weil der Youngische Geist drinn herrscht, der aus seinem Herzen gleichsam ins Herz; aus dem Genie in das Genie spricht."

12. Herder, "Über Shakespeare," in *Werke* 5:220–26: "Alles im Spiel! zu Einem *Ganzen* sich fortwickelnd" (221); "welche Welt! welch ein Ganzes! lebendige Geschichte der Entstehung, Fortgangs, Ausbruchs, traurigen Endes der Leidenschaft dieses Edlen Unglückseligen!" (221); "den Göttergriff eine *ganze* Welt der Disparatesten Auftritte zu Einer Begebenheit zu erfassen" (222); "die *ganze* Welt ist zu diesem großen Geiste allein Körper: *alle* Auftritte der Natur an diesem Körper Glieder, wie *alle* Charaktere und Denkarten zu diesem Geiste Züge— und das *Ganze* mag jener Riesengott des Spinosa '*Pan! Universum!*' heißen" (225–26).

13. See note 3. Prometheus as a model for the assertion of intellect and will is approved by Erasmus, *Opera omnia*, 10:1742B: "Prometheus est nobis imitandus, qui simulacro illi suo luteo vitam ex astris ausus est petere, sed tum demum ubi, quicquid humano artificio praestari potuit, adhibuisset." Cited in August Buck, "Über einige Deutungen des Prometheus-Mythos in der Literatur der Renaissance," 90. Bovillus, *Liber de sapiente*, chap. 19, also advises the wise man to imitate Prometheus: "hac enim in parte celebrem illum Prometheum imitatur") in order to strive for divine perfection and become a more godlike mortal ("terrenus quidam mortalisque deus." Cited in Ernst Cassirer, *Individuum und Kosmos in der Philosophie der Renaissance*, 320, 341. See also René Trousson, *Le thème de Prométhée dans la littérature euopéenne*.

example, Shaftesbury sought to conciliate the rival by calling him a "second maker, a just Prometheus under Jove." The young Goethe, as a moving force in the *Sturm und Drang*, declared Promethean justice on behalf of humanity, not "under Jove." The new archetype of the rebel genius, which Goethe proclaimed in his fragmentary play *Prometheus* (1773) and his hymn to "Prometheus" (1775), a bold celebration of the Titan's blasphemy ("I honor you? What for?"),[14] is also evident in the essay "On German Architecture" (1773).

Erwin becomes an apostle of the new religion of art. His genius, immanent in his work, is the altar at which we are to worship. We worship, Goethe explains, by fully appreciating beauty. By indulging our sensations of the beautiful, we participate in the mystical moment of artistic creativity.[15] Spinoza's sense of the dynamic *natura naturans* immanent in the *natura naturata* is transferred to the human artist and his creation.[16] Instead of Spinoza's rationalist insight into the order of divine creation, Goethe calls for a sensationalist ecstasy, a fully secularized mystical union with artistic genius.

Whether divine or natural, ordered or erratic, the very presumption of genius functioned to liberate the artistic endeavor. Genius, which conforms to the natural order of things, may effectively ignore traditional models, but it does not necessarily defy reason. Genius, which serves as an oracle of the supernatural, or even of the mystical power of human creativity, must presumably communicate in terms other than those dictated by rational experience. Because of its irrational origin, poetry conceived by the "mad rhapsodist" baffles the understanding. Although the frenzy of genius may delight, can it possibly teach? Reason and taste, conceded Herder and Goethe as well as Gerard, were required to translate the exuberant outpourings of genius and to give them intelligible shape, form, and meaning.

Although in his *Essay on Taste* (1759) he found it sufficient to observe the function of taste in guiding and moderating genius (76–77), in his later *Essay on Genius* (1774), Gerard considered it necessary to devote a whole chapter to "Taste Essential to Genius for the Arts" (391–416). Because genius itself lacks purpose and direction, Gerard argued the necessity of imposing interpretive and regulative control. Indeed, the essential solipsism as well as the disruptive influence of the experience prompted Herder to modify his earlier enthusiasm. In his essay, "Causes of the Decline of Taste" (1775), Herder borrows from Hume in observing that ge-

14. Goethe, "Prometheus" (1775), in *Werke* 1:44–46; see Oskar Walzel, *Das Prometheussymbol von Shaftesbury zu Goethe.*
15. Goethe, "Von deutscher Baukunst" (1773), in *Werke* 12:7–15.
16. Martin Bollacher, *Der junge Goethe und Spinoza*, 9–11.

nius is plural, "a multitude of intensive or extensive striving forces of the soul," whereas taste is singular and, thus, gives order, proportion, and unity to the manifold energy. "The more powers a genius has, the more rapidly the powers work, the more good taste is needed as a mentor."[17]

Herder argues the need to moderate the irrational force of genius even more urgently in his *On the Knowledge and Feeling of the Human Soul*: "One names the word imagination and customarily gives it to the poet as his due inheritance; [it is] very bad, however, if the imagination is without consciousness and understanding, [for then] the poet is only a raging dreamer."[18] Here, again, is the dilemma of the "mad rhapsodist": how is it possible to reconcile the irrationality of inspiration with the rationality of taste? Herder wants to unite these two opposites; the disparate experiences, he claims, are brought together by the understanding ("Verstand"), which he defines as "apperception with inner consciousness" (*Werke* 8:196). But in resorting to rationalist philosophy, Herder could not escape the radical opposition of knowledge and feeling. Either the emotions prevailed, or the reason. One might deliberate on an intense emotional experience after it had passed, but not while it was occurring. Herder's resolution, then, was to attribute a monitoring function to the understanding, by means of which the artist could, afterward, rationally reflect on his moment of inspiration.

Before the romantics began to set forth their own ideas on the nature of inspiration and imagination, critics of the Enlightenment had already added profoundly to the tradition of the "mad rhapsodist." The tradition bestowed three blessings on the poet: (1) freedom from the rational dictates that order the rest of society; (2) leadership as prophet or seer; (3) mystical union with the divine. It was the third and crucial blessing that eighteenth-century critics—Addison, Young, Rousseau, Herder, and Goethe—chose to reinterpret. Rather than mediating God's creative will as oracle or prophet, through mystical union or beatific vision, the poet was deemed to possess special affinity with nature, a capacity to read nature's hieroglyphs and translate natural phenomena into language and emotion. To explain this affinity between nature and feelings, critics like

17. Herder, *Ursachen des gesunknen Geschmacks*, in *Werke* 5:600–601: "so weiß jeder, daß Genie im Allgemeinen eine Menge in- und extensiv strebender Seelenkräfte sei; Geschmack ist Ordnung in dieser Menge, Proportion, und also schöne Qualität jener strebenden Größen." Also, "Je mehr Kräfte ein Genie hat, je rascher die Kräfte würken, desto mehr ist der Mentor des guten Geschmacks nöthig" (5:602). David Hume, *An Enquiry Concerning Human Understanding*, 24ff.

18. Herder, *Vom Erkennen und Empfinden der menschlichen Seele*, in *Werke* 8:195: "Man nennet das Wort Einbildungskraft und pflegt's dem Dichter als sein Erbtheil zu geben; sehr böse aber, wenn die Einbildung ohne Bewußtseyn und Verstand ist, der Dichter ist nur ein rasender Träumer."

Herder and Sulzer argued that poetic creativity replicated the organic processes at work in nature.[19] To Herder's credit, he recognized that the presumption of organic unity offered only a reconciliation post hoc, propter hoc to the apparent oppositions of reason and passion in human experience. Although organicism seemed as applicable to the processes of human nature as to those observable elsewhere in the natural world, it failed to resolve the old divisions of mind and body.

Not all romantics were willing to make concessions to "taste," or to accept affinity with nature as adequate substitute for religious experience. In order to render poetic inspiration rational, they stipulated an order of reason very different from that assumed by eighteenth-century epistemologies. Some vestiges of the old division remain. The battle between Los and Urizen is still that between reason and the creative imagination. But the battleground, at once individual and universal, psychological and historical, is far removed from that of the mental terrain which rational empiricism had mapped. Wordsworth's temporal separation of "the spontaneous overflow of powerful feelings" from the "emotion recollected in tranquility" may seem to repeat the division of inspiration and reflection required by rationalist aesthetics, but neither in spontaneity nor in recollection is reason divorced from emotion. Rather, Wordsworth uses his temporal advantage to demonstrate "how exquisitely the individual Mind / . . . to the external World / Is fitted" and, that rarer theme, "how exquisitely, too— / . . . The external World is fitted to the Mind." Wordsworth's division of spontaneity and recollection derives not from the exclusion of inspiration from rational deliberation, but rather from the "startling" and "hesitation" of the mind's vitality as well as nature's tutelary power to "kindle" and "restrain."[20]

This is not to say, however, that the "mad rhapsodist" suddenly recovered his sanity in romantic poetry. He springs forth from the pages of Purchas's *Pilgrimage* to voyage down the sacred river Alph in Coleridge's "Kubla Khan," and he wanders awestruck through the sublime architecture of De Quincey's dream-visions. For both, inspiration still depends on an act of the mind to reach beyond the sensible world. Whereas Herder and Gerard had defined "genius and taste" as contrasting, the true polarity for Coleridge and De Quincey was "genius and talent."

Although Kantian philosophy made available a new set of terms based on the distinction between the intuitive reason (*Vernunft*) and the discur-

19. Herder, "Versuch einer Geschichte der lyrischen Dichtkunst," in *Werke* 32:86–87. Johannes Georg Sulzer, *Allgemeine Theorie der Schöner Künste, Zweyter Theil*, 93–94. See Frederick Burwick, "Kant and Hegel," 153–93.

20. William Wordsworth, *Poetical Works*, 590, 148, and "Reply to Mathetes," in *Prose Works* 2:15.

sive understanding (*Verstand*), Kant himself held to the formula of the Enlightenment: genius produces, taste judges. Alexander Pope knew this much, and more. In the opening lines of *An Essay on Criticism* (1711), Pope questions whether a "greater want of skill / Appear in writing or in judging ill," and he goes on to acknowledge that "In true poets as true genius is but rare, / True taste as seldom is the critic's share." What Pope addresses, and Kant ignores, is that much called poetry is written with no genius at all. No less than Pope, Kant wants poets to write with genius and critics to judge with taste. But he does not want to separate creating from judging. He wants, rather, to redeem the products of genius from all taint of irrationality. Creative genius is the exercise of the imagination and intuitive reason; it interacts with, and is complemented by, the judgment.[21] In spite of having identified two different modes of intellectual production, Kant does not seem to recognize that even uninformed by intuition and imagination, the synthesizing activity of understanding and feeling might not content itself with judging and might also attempt to express itself in poetic form. What name should be given to this uninspired endeavor?

Choosing to damn with faint praise, Jean Paul in his *PreSchool of Aesthetics* (1804) named it "talent" and defined it as distinct from "genius." When earlier critics (Condillac, Lavater, Fuseli), had contrasted "genius" and "talent," they had subordinated the inspired invention of genius to the rational cultivation of talent.[22] In an earlier essay, "On the Natural Magic of the Imagination" (1795), Jean Paul had attempted to liberate the eighteenth-century concept of imagination as an associative, reproductive faculty by granting it a "sense of the infinite."[23] Samuel Johnson had paradoxically privileged judgment over genius under the rhetorical guise of doing the opposite when he praised genius as "that power which constitutes a poet; that quality without which judgment is cold and knowledge is inert; that energy which collects, combines, amplifies, and animates." We need not be surprised, granting his frequent caveats against sending "imagination out upon the wing," that Johnson should thus prefer to oc-

---

21. Immanuel Kant, *Kritik der Urteilskraft* (1790), in *Werke* 5:410: "Zur *Beurteilung* schöner Gegenstände wird *Geschmack*, zur schönen Kunst selber aber, d.i. zur *Hervorbringung* solcher Gegenstände, wird *Genie* erfordert." Also, "Zur schönen Kunst würden also Einbildungskraft, Verstand, Geist, und Geschmack erforderlich sein" (5:421), and "Die drei ersteren Vermögen bekommen durch das vierte allererst ihre Vereinigung" (Anmerkung) (5:421).

22. Jean Paul, *Vorschule der Ästhetik*, in *Werke* 5:50–51, 56. Earlier contrasts between "genius and talent" (J. C. Lavater, *Aphorisms on Man*, 10; Henry Fuseli, *Lectures on Painting*, 6) merely adapt the formula for "genius and taste"; that is, genius provides inspiration and invention, talent provides arrangement and order.

23. Jean Paul, "Über die natürliche Magie der Einbildungskraft," in *Werke* 4:195–205.

cupy the energies of genius with arrangement rather than invention. But we may find it peculiar that Jean Paul, no less than Johnson, was aware of, and wary of, "the dangerous prevalence of imagination" and the "power of fancy over reason."[24]

In his Shandyesque novels, Jean Paul warned against venturing too far into dreams or self-delusion.[25] At one pole, the imagination was apt to entangle itself in introspection; at the other, it might drift off in speculations on the Absolute. Thus, as in Coleridge's comic verse on Fichte's egocentric idealism ("Here on this market-cross aloud I cry: / I, I, I! I itself I"), Jean Paul argued against the solipsistic subjectivism of Fichte (*Werke* 3:1030). He also objected to Friedrich Schlegel (*Werke* 5:110) and, by implication, to Schelling as well, for having dissolved all identity, personal and divine, in the great wash of "poetic Nihilism."[26] Because it preserved the presence of God in the universe, it was Jacobi's treatment of Spinoza and Kant that most appealed to Jean Paul.[27] Having aligned his concept of genius with the intuitive reason of Kant, Jean Paul echoes the notion of its manifold plurality; but instead of subjecting it to the unifying imposition of taste, he grants it an instinct for totality, harmony, and divine order in opposition to the one-sided monotony of talent.[28] As long as the imagination sustains a sense of harmony, it will not fall into the irrational extremes of Fichtean introspection or Schlegelian nihilism.

De Quincey, too, distinguished genius from talent by invoking the total human being and an awareness of moral order:

> Genius is that mode of intellectual power which moves in alliance with *genial* nature—*i.e.* with the capacities of pleasures and pain, —whereas talent has no vestige of such an alliance, and is perfectly independent of all human sensibilities. Consequently, genius is a voice of breathing that represents the *total* nature of man, and therefore his enjoying and suffering nature, as well as his knowing and distinguishing nature; whilst, on the contrary, talent represents only a single function of that nature. Genius is the language which interprets the synthesis of the human spirit with the human

24. Samuel Johnson, "Pope," in *Lives of the Poets*, and "The Dangerous Prevalence of Imagination," in *Rasselas*, chap. 44.

25. Jean Paul, *Titan* (1802), *Flegeljahre* (1805), and *Der Komet* (1820). See Peter Michelsen, *Laurence Sterne und der deutsche Roman des 18. Jahrhunderts*; Uwe Schweikert, *Jean Pauls "Komet." Selbstparodie der Kunst*; and Kurt Wölfel, " 'Ein Echo, das sich selber in Unendliche nachhallt.' Eine Betrachtung von Jean Pauls Poetik und Poesie."

26. Coleridge, *Biographia Literaria* (=*BL*), 1:159.

27. Friedrich Heinrich Jacobi, *Über die Lehre des Spinoza*; Karl Brose, "Jean Pauls Verhältnis zu Fichte."

28. Jean Paul, *Vorschule der Ästhetik* (1804), in *Werke* 5:50–51, 56.

intellect, each acting through the other; whilst talent speaks only from the insulated intellect. And hence it is that, besides its relation to suffering and enjoyment, genius always implies a deeper relation to virtue and vice; whereas talent has no shadow of a relation to *moral* dualities any more than it has to vital sensibilities. A man of the highest talent is often obtuse and below the ordinary standard of men in his feelings; but no man of genius can unyoke himself from the society of moral perceptions that are brighter, and sensibilities that are more tremulous, than those of men in general.[29]

Talent, according to De Quincey, requires only the "insulated intellect," whereas genius involves "the synthesis of the human spirit with the human intellect." The terms of this distinction, it will be noticed, parallel his account of "the literature of knowledge" and "the literature of power."

"To many years' conversation with Mr. Wordsworth," De Quincey wrote, he owed the distinction between knowledge and power. In the Preface to the second edition of *Lyrical Ballads* (1800), Wordsworth had observed that the arbitrary "contradistinction of Poetry and Prose" was a source of confusion and should be replaced by "the more philosophical one of Poetry and Matter of Fact." To correct the older notion that taste moderates and directs genius, Wordsworth simply reversed the causal sequence. As he observes in the "Essay Supplementary" to the Preface of his *Poems* (1815), the poet's first task is "to call forth and communicate *power*"; power is the cause, knowledge and taste the effects; "to create taste is to call forth and bestow power."[30] In *Letters to a Young Man* (1823), where De Quincey first discussed the agency of knowledge and power in literature, he stressed a revision to Horace's "aut prodesse aut delectare": "The true antithesis to knowledge is not *pleasure*, but *power*." Twenty-five years later, in his essay on Pope (1848), De Quincey gave a more ample exposition of "the literature of knowledge" and "the literature

29. De Quincey, *DQ* 11:382–83; for later (1834, 1838, 1846, and 1853) variations of the distinction between genius and talent, also see 1:194, 3:34–35, and 1:195.

30. Wordsworth, "Essay Supplementary" to the Preface of his *Poems* (1815); cf. Preface to the second edition of *Lyrical Ballads*: "Much confusion has been introduced into criticism by . . . [the] contradistinction of Poetry and Prose, instead of the more philosophical one of Poetry and Matter of Fact, or Science." Elizabeth Schneider, *The Aesthetics of William Hazlitt*, 45n, has suggested a source in Hazlitt (from *The Morning Chronicle*, 1814): "Science depends on the discursive or *extensive*—art in the intuitive and *intensive* power of the mind. . . . In fact, we judge of science by the number of effects produced—of art by the energy which produces them. The one is knowledge—the other power." *Complete Works of William Hazlitt*, 18:8.

of power," and the informing ideas are evident throughout De Quincey's criticism.[31]

By substituting *movere*, which had been used to define the purpose of classical rhetoric, in the place of *delectare* in Horace's statement on the purpose of poetry, De Quincey effectively altered the opposition of reason and emotion, which had been the crux in eighteenth-century deliberations on inspiration and illusion. Even if Horace had not intended a radical separation between teaching and delighting, the division between reason and emotion in rationalist thought enforced the split. In consequence, rational taste had been given the governing role in shaping and ordering the irrational ecstasy of genius. Previous critics, in defining the ends of literature, had added Quintilian's "to move" to Horace's "to teach" and "to delight." But De Quincey was the first to absorb the full implications of the suasory ends of rhetoric into a definition of literature.

To make his new distinction effective, De Quincey had to alter completely the traditional categories. He not only replaced the *delectare*, he also refined the *prodesse*. In accord with the Kantian distinction between discursive understanding and intuitive reason, he acknowledged two modes of teaching. The didactic mode belongs to the "literature of knowledge." Poetry, however, is created exclusively as a "literature of power." "Didactic poetry," therefore, is obviously a *"contradictio in adjecto."*[32] Poetry teaches not didactically but by engaging the mind in the play of reason and passion. What it teaches are the abiding truths, which already have their germ in human consciousness. It teaches by stimulating and nurturing these dormant truths into vital activity. Its process is therefore organic.

Having appropriated the *movere* to the "literature of power," De Quincey also had to redefine traditional rhetoric. In shifting its province from "the urgent issues of politics and law," he established for rhetoric a new realm of appearances and possibilities:

> Whatsoever is certain, or matter of fixed science, can be not subject for the rhetorician: where it is possible for the understanding to be convinced, no field is open for rhetorical persuasion. (*DQ* 10:90–91)

> Rhetoric is the art of aggrandizing and bringing out into strong relief, by means of various and striking thoughts, some aspect of

31. De Quincey, "Letters to a Young Man" (1823), in *DQ* 10:46–47; "The Poetry of Pope" (1848), in *DQ* 11:53–59; and "Oliver Goldsmith" (1848), in *DQ* 4:308–9.

32. On didactic poetry, see De Quincey's postscript to the translation from Lessing's *Laokoon*, in *DQ* 11:213, 215, and 88.

truth which of itself is supported by no spontaneous feelings, and therefore rests upon artificial aids. (*DQ* 10:92)

Rhetoric . . . aims at an elaborate form of beauty which shrinks from the strife of business, and could neither arise nor make itself felt in a tumultuous assembly. . . . All great rhetoricians in selecting their subject have shunned the determinate cases of real life. (*DQ* 10:93–94)

Demosthenes, who would neither shrink "from the strife of business" nor stand impotent before "a tumultuous assembly," is excluded, along with all the "greater orators of Greece," from De Quincey's company of rhetoricians. His defining conditions are exclusively belletristic. His rhetoricians are all poets and philosophers devoted to speculation and to beauty. Their endeavor is further restricted, for De Quincey grants to rhetoric only the appeal to the intellect. The appeal to the passions belongs not to rhetoric, but to eloquence, which De Quincey defines in Wordsworthian terms as "the overflow of powerful feelings upon occasions fitted to excite them" (*DQ* 10:92). The highest form of literature, "the literature of power," is the interaction of rhetoric and eloquence brought into play by creative genius.

The discursive understanding, utilizing the forms of logic, expresses itself in a mechanical style: this is the "literature of knowledge" and its purpose is to teach. When the intuitive reason, exercising the suasory appeal of rhetoric, and the passions, overflowing in eloquence, come together in play, they engender an organic style: this is the "literature of power" and its purpose to move (*DQ* 11:54–55). But what is to be moved? And whither? De Quincey answers by contrasting *Paradise Lost* with "a cookery book":

What do you learn from *Paradise Lost*? Nothing at all. What do you learn from a cookery book? Something new, something that you did not know before, in every paragraph. But would you therefore put the wretched cookery book on a higher level of estimation than the divine poem? What you owe to Milton is not any knowledge, of which a million separate items are still but a million of advancing steps on the same earthly level; what you owe is *power*—that is, exercise and expansion to your own latent capacity of sympathy with the infinite, where every pulse and each influx is a step upwards, a step ascending as upon a Jacob's ladder from earth to mysterious altitudes above the earth. *All* the steps of knowledge, from first to last, carry you further on the same level plane, but could never raise you one foot above your ancient level of earth: whereas the very *first* step in power is a flight—is an ascending movement into another element where earth is forgotten. (*DQ* 11:58)

What is to be moved? Our "own latent capacity of sympathy with the infinite." And whither? "To mysterious altitudes above the earth, . . . into another element where earth is forgotten." Were this the language of the eighteenth century, we might rightly assume that these "mysterious altitudes" are the resort of irrational inspiration. For De Quincey, however, the "capacity of sympathy with the infinite" is fully rational. Indeed, the "intellectual capacity" of the intuitive reason is precisely what enables us to achieve our "highest state of capacity for the infinite."

By moving "the great *intuitive* [or nondiscursive] organ," literary works of power nurture the intellectual and moral capacity of mind. To be sure, De Quincey attributes the same power to dreams. But for De Quincey, dreaming, too, at least potentially, is a rational activity. In the introductory essay to the *Suspiria de Profundis* (1845), he asserts that, if suitably encouraged, the intuitive reason may contribute to dream-vision. "Habitually to dream magnificently one must have a constitutional determination to reverie." The activity of the waking mind is echoed by the mind in dreaming. "He whose talk is of oxen," De Quincey says, "will probably dream of oxen" (*DQ* 13:334). If the discursive understanding has not utterly dominated the waking mind, if the contemplative and reflective habits have been duly exercised, then, when the senses and understanding slumber, intuitive reason may take flight and reveal to the dreamer the grand vistas of the infinite.

The intellectual capacity to contemplate the infinite, however, is never confused by De Quincey with the capacity to comprehend. Just as the inquisitive nature of the intuitive reason takes the mind to the very brink of the irrational, De Quincey's dreamer, in a recurrent motif, is brought before the abyss of the unknown. Twice, for example, he translates Jean Paul's "Dream upon the Universe"—first in his *Analects from Richter*; then, in free adaptation, as the bravura conclusion to his *System of the Heavens* (1846).[33] Unlike Jean Paul, who exposes the dreamer to the terrors of the unknown only to restore faith with a beatific vision of the Virgin and Child, De Quincey leaves the dreamer engulfed by infinitude. There is revelation, but no resolution. De Quincey's challenge, and here

---

33. Jean Paul, "Traum über das All," in *Der Komet*, in *Werke* 6:682–86. De Quincey, "Analects of Richter," in *DQ* 11:290–93, and "System of the Heavens," in *DQ* 8:33–34. Frederick Burwick, "The Dream-Visions of Jean Paul and Thomas De Quincey."

he leaves his reader precisely where he leaves his fictive dreamer, is to grapple for meaning in the encounter with the incomprehensible.

The figure from beyond the bourn, who guides the dreamer into the vast unknown and communicates its mysteries, serves for De Quincey much the same function Diotima served for Plato in initiating Socrates into the Eleusinian mysteries. The possibility of transcending the limits of reason is entertained without risk, for it is only the imagination which takes the leap of faith. What is involved in assuming a report beyond the limits of reason and ordinary experience is explicitly developed in De Quincey's response to Hume's refutation of miracles—the topic I examine in Chapter 2. One of the great values of the dream, De Quincey argues, is that it enables the mind to delve into the very spiritual center of its being. Others writers, such as Gérard de Nerval, would find the dream experience fraught with dangers. For De Quincey, however, even the aching incomprehensibility aroused by the "Dream-vision of the Infinite" (*DQ* 8:33–34), or the recurrent dream of "sudden death" as recounted in the "Dream Fugue" (*DQ* 13:318–27) is ultimately restorative as revelation of divine benevolence.

De Quincey avoids rather than resolves the dilemma of the "mad rhapsodist." He defines the representation of irrationality as fictive; more important, he provides a literary rationale for the fiction. The rhetorical excursions of genius allow us to explore beyond the limits of discursive and demonstrative reason. After setting genius apart from talent in "Recollections of Charles Lamb" (1838), he praises himself: "I am the more proud of this distinction since I have seen the utter failure of Mr. Coleridge, judging from his attempt in his 'Table Talk'" (*DQ* 3:35). With which version of Coleridge's often repeated distinction De Quincey has chosen to find fault is uncertain. To be sure, in none of his several references to genius and talent in the *Table Talk* does Coleridge provide much more than a sketch. For example,

> Poetic taste, dexterity in composition, and ingenious imitation, often produce poems that are very promising in appearance. But genius, or the power of doing something new, is another thing. (*Table Talk*, 18 April 1830)

> Talent, lying in the understanding, is often inherited; genius, being the action of reason and imagination, rarely or never. (*Table Talk*, 21 May 1830)

Coleridge, too, relies on the distinction between the intuitive reason and the discursive understanding. De Quincey, of course, with his example of "the cookery book," has shown what is wrong with the criterion of "doing something new."

In his *Biographia Literaria*, Coleridge manages a more astute formulation and delineates the processes of intuitive reason and imagination in more meticulous detail than De Quincey. He is specifically concerned with extricating genius from all connotations of enthusism, fanaticism, and impassioned excess. Too little, rather than too much, "imaginative power" will "render the mind liable to superstition and fanaticism." When the mental capacity of mediating ideas and images is deficient, the mind becomes dependent on immediate sensations,

> but where the ideas are vivid, and there exists an endless power of combining and modifying them, the feelings and affections blend more easily and intimately with these ideal creations, than with the objects of the senses; the mind is affected by thoughts, rather than by things; and only then feels the requisite interest even for the most important events, and accidents, when by means of meditation they have passed into *thoughts*. The sanity of the mind is between superstition with fanaticism on the one hand; and enthusiasm with indifference and a diseased slowness to action on the other. For the conceptions of the mind may be so vivid and adequate, as to preclude that impulse to the realizing of them, which is strongest and most restless in those, who possess more than mere *talent* or the faculty of appropriating and applying the knowledge of others) yet still want something of the creative, and self-sufficing power of absolute *Genius*. For this reason therefore, they are men of *commanding* genius. While the former rest content between thought and reality, as it were in an intermundium of which their own living spirit supplies the *substance,* and their imagination the ever-varying *form;* the latter must impress their preconceptions on the world without, in order to present them back to their own view with the satisfying degree of clearness, distinctness, and individuality. (*BL* 1:31–32)

The distinction between genius and talent is defined in terms of the polarity between matter and idea, sensation and meditation. Although he liberates genius from irrationality, Coleridge leaves its sanity in a precarious balance. The sanity of genius is not separated from madness by "thin partitions," as Dryden phrased it; rather, as with Jean Paul, it is poised on a sliding scale between polar extremes. For Jean Paul, the extremes are self-centered subjectivity and nihilistic abstraction; for Coleridge, sensation-bound fanaticism and thought-indulgent enthusiasm. E.T.A. Hoffmann described as archetypal romantic genius the composer Johannes

Kreisler, who created perfect symphonies in his head and never bothered to write them down.[34] Coleridge's "absolute *Genius*" is of the same stamp: the creative process is so fully satisfied in the mind, that there is no accompanying need or urge for expression. Indeed, it is only the less consummate creativity of "*commanding* genius" that requires expression to complete the conception.

Coleridge's argument, however, is not that "absolute *Genius*" is solipsistic but that, untainted by the corruptive influences of material wealth and power, it is content to exhibit "a perfect poem"; whereas "*commanding* genius," necessarily committed to the material world, is swayed by public and political circumstance. The deficiency of genius and compensatory reliance on talent give rise to a dangerous breed of intellect, whom, in *The Statesman's Manual*, he describes as men of "Violence with Guile," the "mighty Hunters of Mankind, from Nimrod to Napoleon" (*Lay Sermons* [=*LS*] 65–66).

Fond as he is of polar oppositions, Coleridge does not everywhere sustain a convenient dialectic. In discussing the "compelling urgency" of Coleridge's commitment to "Polaritäts-Gedanken," Thomas McFarland makes the point that "Coleridge's incompleteness as a practicing polar schematist becomes a badge of honor" (*Forms of Ruin* 339–41). What McFarland refers to as the advantage of "diasparactive awareness," is a fitting response to the unpredictable and volatile nature of human events. The "tertium aliquid" is not a neutral ground, midway between opposing poles, but an entropic relationship.

Thus when Coleridge tells us that "absolute *Genius*" can "rest content between thought and reality," it is important to recognize the conditionality and responsive variability of this "intermundium." Its tranquility cannot be ensured by ignoring the contingencies of real life. The defining conditions of genius stipulate both "thought *and* reality." Rather than a Kantian, or even a Hegelian synthesis, Coleridge reserves the privilege of renegotiating relationships. He wants the logical convenience of a dialectic structure, but also the freedom of personal faith.

Even in arguing on behalf of intuitive reason, and against the irrational "hypothesis of inspiration," Coleridge hedges. The error in attributing inspiration to an external influence upon the mind, Coleridge argues, arose from inadequate understanding of the influx of intuition and the a priori capacities of mind. Similar assumptions underlie De Quincey's claim that the "literature of power" nurtures truths already latent in the mind. Universal ideas are not "immediate acts of divine agency" but have a priori existence within the mind. Failing to comprehend the "self-sufficing

---

34. E.T.A. Hoffmann, *Kater Murr* (1819–21) and *Kreisleriana* (1810–14), in *Sämtliche Werke* (1905). See also Klaus-Dieter Dobat, *Musik als romantische Illusion*, 155–67, 248–83.

power" that enables the mind to generate "vivid" ideas independent of "the immediate impression of the senses," philosophers have endeavored to explain all ideas in terms of external origin. "In fact [this is] the doctrine of Malebranche and of some other Cartesians [who] have taken refuge in the hypothesis of inspiration or immediate acts of divine agency— which may be *piety,* which may even be *truth;* but which most certainly is not *logic,* or philosophy logically deduced" (*Logic* 220). What is interesting in this passage is Coleridge's reluctance to refute the very contentions against which he is developing his analysis of intuitive reason: "The hypothesis of inspiration . . . may be *piety* . . . may even be *truth.*"

In his intellectual struggle to resolve the dilemma of the "mad rhapsodist" Coleridge wanted to have it both ways. He wanted to affirm the creative capacities of intuition and imagination without denying divine agency. Even in explaining inspiration through the dialectic of pure reason, he endorsed Christian belief in prophecy and revelation.[35] Just as he rejected the materialist model, which rendered the mind "always *passive*—a lazy *Looker-on* on an external world" (To Thomas Poole, 23 March 1801), he could not accept the idealist model, which presumed a divine ventriloquist with a prophetic dummy on his lap. Inspired poets and prophets cannot be "passive organs of dictation":

> There may be dictation without inspiration, and inspiration without dictation: they have been and continue to be grievously confounded. Balaam and his ass were the passive organs of dictation; but no one, I suppose, will venture to call either of those worthies inspired. It is my profound conviction that St. John and St. Paul were divinely inspired; but I totally disbelieve the dictation of any one word, sentence or argument throughout their writings. Observe, there was revelation. . . . Revelations of facts were undoubtedly made to John and Paul; —but is it not a mere matter of our very sense that John and Paul each dealt with those revelations, expounded them, insisted upon them, just exactly according to his own natural strength of intellect, habit of reasoning, moral, and even physical temperament? (*Table Talk,* 31 March 1832)

As Robert Barth has shown, the distinction between revelation and inspiration is crucial to Coleridge's thought.[36] Revelation is a thought or idea

---

35. J. Robert Barth, S.J., *Coleridge and Christian Doctrine,* 45–50. On the relationship between biblical inspiration and poetic voice in Coleridge, see Max F. Schultz, *The Poetic Voices of Coleridge,* 27–28, and Murray Roston, *Prophet and Poet,* 104, 157.

36. Barth, *Coleridge and Christian Doctrine,* 60; on the paradoxical nature of Coleridge's concept of inspiration, see Anthony Harding, *Coleridge and the Inspired Word,* 58–94.

mediated through external phenomena; inspiration must originate internally and involves the whole person and all the faculties. Coleridge was thus quite pleased to dismiss certain exhibitions of the "mad rhapsodist" as degenerate or pathological. In a paraphrase of George Chapman, he described "the Insania pseudo-poetica" as born of malice, vanity, or debility, and expressing itself in "nonsense conveyed in strange and unusual language." The *"Furor divinus,"* by contrast, is an "infusion of a celestial Health" and a "Surgeneration" of mind (*CN* 3216).

"If the mind be not *passive,*" as Coleridge went on to say in the same letter objecting to the degradation of mind as "lazy *Looker-on,*" "if it be indeed made in God's Image, & that, too, in the sublimest sense, the Image of the *Creator,* there is ground for suspicion that any system built on the passiveness of the mind must be false, as a system." Several systems fall under this indictment: that which defines the mind as *camera obscura,* passively receiving external sensory data; that which defines inspiration as oracle, passively echoing divine dictation; that which defines poetic *mimesis* as mirror, passively reflecting reality.

The humanistic and organic version of Spinoza's thought developed by Herder did not suit Coleridge precisely because it was too humanistic. In "On Poesy and Art," he draws a more apt version from Schelling: "If the artist copies the mere nature, the *natura naturata,* what idle rivalry! . . . Believe me, you must master the essence, the *natura naturans,* which presupposes a bond between nature in the higher sense and the soul of man" (Shawcross edition of *Biographia Literaria,* 2:257). When Schelling delivered his academy address *On the Relation of the Plastic Arts to Nature* (1807), he must have surprised some of his auditors by praising the foremost neoclassicist. Winckelmann had been right to reaffirm *mimesis* as the informing principle of art; he erred only, Schelling added, in insisting on objective nature as the matter to be imitated. What the artist must imitate is not nature but the mind's apprehension of nature. In the tradition of Plotinus, Schelling thus escapes Plato's charge that the artist in painting the carpenter's chair is thrice-removed from the ideal (*Republic* 10:596–98). Further, Schelling also claims that the artist accomplishes what the philosopher can only talk about. The philosopher can posit a reconciliation of subject with object, of conscious mind with unconscious matter. Such a reconciliation is performed and realized in the work of art. In this godlike creative act the artist imitates the *natura naturans.*[37]

In his lecture series of 1818, Coleridge repeats the account of a *mimesis* of mind superseding a *mimesis* of nature—replacing "Winckelmann" with

---

37. F.W.J. Schelling, *Über das Verhältnis der bildenden Künste zu der Natur,* in *Sämmtliche Werke* 7:289–329.

"Reynolds" (*LL* 2:220–21). The artist's task is to represent not nature, but the process of beholding nature. But how? What does it mean to imitate the processes of thought or perception? An unintentional irony in Schelling's work is that in praising the artist for accomplishing what the poet can only posit, he reveals himself very much a philosopher. His account of the creative reconciliation of subject and object remains abstract. Coleridge, of course, thinks in symbols and resorts frequently to examples. Even in Schelling's *Philosophy of Art* (1802), and I refer here to Crabb Robinson's transcription of the lectures,[38] the discussion of mythology and scripture is virtually barren of reference to specific texts or passages.

As Coleridge reveals in his *Confessions of an Inquiring Spirit*, he was not handicapped by Schelling's want of concrete demonstration, nor by Schelling's impersonal presentation of the artist. Indeed, much of what Schelling attributed only to the work of art is personalized by Coleridge in the consciousness of the poet and prophet.[39] By distinguishing illusion from delusion, Coleridge argued that only the latter referred to the deception of the mind, the former involved a conscious and deliberate indulgence of the imagination. His formulation of "the willing suspension of disbelief for the moment" put aside the eighteenth-century contention that aesthetic illusion was an instance of emotion overcoming the reason (*BL* 2:6; *LL* 1:135). Reason as well as emotion were fully operative through the activity of the imagination. He explains how it is possible to have an illusion and, at the same time, watch oneself having an illusion.

Similarly, Coleridge holds that it is possible for the creative imagination to respond to divine revelation and, at the same time, deliberate about its conditions. The poet may be inspired by what is beyond rational control or comprehension, yet communicate in a language accessible to human reason. Indeed, such terms are not at odds with Coleridge's definition of the primary and the secondary imagination (*BL* 1:304).[40] Challenging the imagination with its paradoxical duality—rational and irrational, natural and supernatural, finite and infinite—inspiration defies any representation through passive conventions (dictation, mimesis). Here, again, Schelling's notion of a *mimesis* of the mind proved attractive to Coleridge. The problem, of course, is that *mimesis* is a word fraught with historical tradition, a word that insists on the mirroring of nature and the reflection of reality, in spite of the effort to free it of the neoclassical context of a Winckelmann or a Reynolds.

38. Ernst Behler, "Schellings Ästhetik in der Überlieferung von Henry Crabb Robinson."

39. Coleridge, *Confessions of Inquiring Spirit*, in *Complete Works* 5:92–93, 589; also see Harding 58–73.

40. See McFarland, *Coleridge and the Pantheist Tradition*, 327–32, and "The Origin and Significance of Coleridge's Theory of the Secondary Imagination."

Thus Thomas McFarland's alternative is very useful. In contrast to the *mimetic* mode, "the imitation of what is there," he identifies the *meontic* mode, the imitation of "what is not there" (*Forms of Ruin* 384–85). As declarations of the meontic as opposed to the mimetic, he quotes Keats's distinction between himself and Byron: "He describes what he sees—I describe what I imagine" (To George and Georgiana Keats, 20 September 1819). McFarland also cites Blake's distinction between himself and Wordsworth: "Natural Objects always did & now do Weaken deaden & obliterate Imagination in Me Wordsworth must know that what he Writes Valuable is Not to be found in Nature" (*William Blake* 665); and Blake's distinction between himself and Reynolds: "Why are Copiers of Nature Incorrect while Copiers of Imagination are Correct this is manifest to all" (575).

The ontology, the ontic place, of "what is not there" may be grounded in the mind itself, in memory, desire, fear, or in the awareness of divine presence (McFarland, *Forms of Ruin*, 391–92). The mind gives as well as receives. The geometric patterns revealed when watching a swarm of ephemeridae by firelight provided Coleridge with an apt example of how the mind exerts its shaping presence in our perception (*Logic* 75).[41] Although the mind is inclined to such self-projections, inspiration is not a mere by-product of the illusion-making activity of mind or eye. Rather, inspiration is sparked by the discovery of an inherent truth in the illusion. "It is not the desire of attaching *Outness* and *externality* to our representations which is at the bottom of this Instinct; on the contrary this very attachment of Outness originates in this Instinct—But it is to possess *a ground* to know a fixed Cause generating a certain reason" (*CN* 3592).[42] Hamann saw irony as the only resort of human reason when the passions cease to soar with divine inspiration. Herder, by contrast, humanized the divine, and shifted the emphasis from genial inspiration to critical judgment. De Quincey affirmed the power of inspiration, but could claim its province, when reason balked at its boundaries, only through the mediation of dreams. Coleridge redeems the "mad rhapsodist" by allowing inspiration to coexist with insight.

In explaining inspiration as the participation of the individual artist in the absolute creativity of the "Infinite I AM" (*BL* 1:304), Coleridge deliberately countered those skeptics who demanded a rational and empirical basis for all knowledge. Like the older arguments of inspiration as a "divine frenzy," Coleridge's definition of the "primary Imagination" is at odds

41. J. R. de J. Jackson's note to this passage in *Logic* cites similar accounts: *CN* 549 ("Vortices of flies"), and *CL* 2:974 ("whirling round a live Coal").

42. On Coleridge's combination of religious and secular thought, see J. Robert Barth, S.J., *The Symbolic Imagination*, 115–22.

with rational, empirical demonstration. In Chapter 2, I examine more closely the romantic reaffirmation of religious supernaturalism as forwarded by Coleridge and De Quincey. To human comprehension, as the Voice out of the Whirlwind informed Job, God's creativity is beyond human reason. That one must accept the unseen and incomprehensible powers on faith is so essential to Christian belief that it is the first condition of the Nicene Creed: "*Credo in unum Deum, Patrem omnipotetem, factorem caeli et terrae, visibilium omnium et invisibilium.*" Thomas Burnet, the Anglican divine of seventeenth century, explained that he had no trouble accepting this doctrine of invisible powers: "*Facile credo, plures esse Naturas invisibiles quam visibiles in rerum universitate.*"[43] Nevertheless, as he also acknowledged, the uncertainty whence these powers came, and how they work upon the mind, often gave rise to anxiety and fear. Is religious experience a form of madness? Coleridge obviously shared the same concerns about the province and provenance of the supernatural when he borrowed this passage from Bishop Burnet as the motto to his "Rime of the Ancient Mariner." How Coleridge and De Quincey endeavored to defend the faith in miracles and to discriminate the divine from the demonic, true faith from mad frenzy, is the subject of the next chapter.

43. Thomas Burnet, *Archaeologiae philosophicae* (1692), 68; fifteen years before he added this passage as motto to "The Rime of the Ancient Mariner" in the *Sibylline Leaves* (1817), Coleridge had transcribed it in 1801–2 *Notebooks,* 1:1000H.

2

COLERIDGE AND DE QUINCEY: INSPIRATION AND REVELATION

In the great controversy over David Hume's account "Of Miracles" in *An Enquiry Concerning Human Understanding* (1748), Samuel Taylor Coleridge's response has received but little attention, and Thomas De Quincey's even less. What has been written of De Quincey's deliberations on miracles has been no more than incidental—mere mention in passing that essays concerned with revelation were among his writings in the 1840s. In his manuscript essay "On Miracles" (7 June 1847), De Quincey promises an extended treatment of the topic. In a marginal note, he cites that scene from *Timon of Athens* in which the Lords and Senators are seated at the banquet table expecting a sumptuous meal and praising their host as "the old man still" (III.vi.61). De Quincey apparently plans to combine his former idealism and present disillusion in a dual "mission." He and "the original man" shall be a team: "You shall see both of us," he tells the reader, ". . . sweeping the heart of some old nuisances." Curiously, Alexander Japp omits this and other passages from his edition of the *Posthumous Works*. It is also useful to reexamine the manuscripts in appraising Coleridge's deliberations on miracles. In previous studies of Coleridge, primary attention has been given to the work following *The Statesman's Manual* (1816), and justly so, for it was the later Coleridge who influenced theological developments throughout the remainder of the century. The crucial terms in his analysis of miracles, to be examined here, were formulated much earlier. When he turned his attention to the Gospel of John in his 1807 "Memorandum on Miracles," Coleridge put forth those arguments on the Johannine *logos* which were to have been elaborated as a major section of the *Opus Maximum*.[1]

Coleridge and De Quincey were fully aware of the vigorous rebuttal that had been put forth in the eighteenth century by David Hartley, George Campbell, James Beattie, and Joseph Priestley.[2] That debate, both pro and con, was conducted on Enlightened ground. Both Coleridge and De Quincey, of course, were outspoken opponents of the materialist and mechanist presumptions of Enlightenment philosophy. Reinterpreting the argument in romantic terms, they sought to clear the faith in supernatural mystery from all taint of weak-minded credulity. Hume approaches the miracle as if it had to be documented as a historical event. Coleridge answers Hume by arguing that a miracle works subjectively rather than objectively. Endorsing a doctrine of immanence similar to Coleridge's definition of *symbol*, De Quincey insists on the semiotic mediation of all humanly intelligible manifestations of the divine.

The primary source of knowledge, Hume states, is experience: "the evidence for the truth of our senses." While experience "must be acknowledged," it "is not altogether infallible." A range of experiences must be compared: the ratio of instances that confirm our expectations against those which oppose them provides our sense of probability. Because the range of our experience is limited, we rely on testimony to extend it. Testimony, of course, must be subjected to the same standard of proof and probability. We must judge its validity in relation to our own experience and observation. A miracle, as defined by Hume, "is a violation of the laws of nature." Any testimony regarding a miracle, therefore, presents a paradox: "As a uniform experience amounts to a proof, there is here a direct and full *proof*, from the nature of the fact, against the existence of any miracle; nor can such a proof be destroyed, or the miracle rendered credible, but by an opposite proof, which is superior." The very circumstances the witness must cite as evidence that a miracle has actually occurred are circumstances that render his testimony untenable. Hume concludes, then, "that no human testimony can have such force as

1. On Coleridge, see Barth, *Coleridge and Christian Doctrine*, 6–7, 37–42; Samuel Prickett, *Romanticism and Religion*, 44–45, 51–55, 61–64; Stephen Happel, *Coleridge's Religious Imagination*, 782–85; and Harding 39–40, 64, 76–77, 82–83. In spite of the anonymous reviewer's assertion that De Quincey's "reply to Hume upon miracles . . . well deserves the attention of students of divinity" (17–18), there has been no sustained study of De Quincey's religious thought and only incidental references to his essay "On Miracles as Subject of Testimony." See the biographies by Edward Sackville-West, 180, 245, and Horace Eaton, 447.

2. *Lectures 1795* 111–16; the editors cite the relevant passages from Coleridge's sources: Joseph Priestley, *An History of the Corruptions of Christianity*, 2:456; William Paley, *Evidences of Christianity* (1794), 31–37, and 38–194.

to prove a miracle, and make it a just foundation for any system of religion" (*Enquiry* 109–31; Flew 173–213).

When Coleridge delivered his Bristol lectures in 1795, he adhered closely to the refutation of Hume in David Hartley's *Observations on Man* (1749) and William Paley's *Evidences of Christianity* (1794). From Hartley, he borrowed the argument that the "laws of nature" have yet to be fully discerned by science:

> Nothing is more common or constant than the effect of Gravity in making all Bodies upon the surface of our Earth tend to its centre—yet the rare and extraordinary Influences of Magnetism and Electricity can suspend this Tendency. Now before Magnetism & Electricity were discovered and verified by a variety of concurrent facts, there would have been as much reason to disallow the evidence of their particular effects attested by Eyewitness, as there is now to disallow the particular Miracles recorded in the Scripture.[3]

Experience and probability, Hume's criteria, are only relative and may require radically different interpretation as new evidence emerges.[4] By reiterating Hartley's position, Coleridge was also challenging Hume's definition of a miracle as "a violation of the laws of nature." An act of the divine will may well demonstrate laws with which we are not yet acquainted. Even when he goes on to state that Christ's "system of morality . . . carries with it an irresistible force of conviction, and is of itself in the most philosophical sense of the word a Miracle," Coleridge repeats the arguments of Hartley and Priestley against Hume. Unlike his eighteenth-century predecessors, however, Coleridge is already thinking of the miracle not so much as the act or the expression, but more as the idea and the incumbent power. The evidence for the miracle of inspiration is its self-propagation. In a perfect "system of morality" resides a miraculous

3. Antony Flew, *Hume's Philosophy of Belief*, 196–97, acknowledges Hume's overconfidence in the knowledge and science of his own age and his failure to appreciate development and change. He cites, as an example, Herodotus's account of the Phoenician sailors who claimed to have circumnavigated Africa (ca. 600 B.C.). Herodotus discredits their story: "On their return they declared—I for my part do not believe them, but perhaps others may—that in sailing round Africa they had the sun upon their right hand" (bk. 4, chap. 42). The detail about the change in the relative position of the sun, which seemed unbelievable to Herodotus, is precisely the evidence which, in the light of subsequent knowledge, validates their account.

4. Coleridge, *Lectures 1795*, 160–61; David Hartley, *Observations on Man*, 146–48; Joseph Priestley, *Discourses*, vol. 5 and 11:337–38; see also Barth, *Coleridge and Christian Doctrine*, 6–7.

power. "Is it a Miracle," Coleridge asks, "that Jesus should be able to effect it? And no Miracle that Matthew or Luke or men of obscurer name should possess the Power?"

When Coleridge writes to George Fricker (4 October 1806), he confesses his own past Unitarian or Socinian beliefs and describes his reply "to a sceptical friend, who had been a Socinian, and of course rested all the evidences of Christianity on miracles." As he describes his "re-conversion" in the *Biographia Literaria*, he had been a "zealous Unitarian" only in respect to natural religion and had always deemed "the *idea* of the Trinity a fair scholastic inference from the being of God, as a creative intelligence" (*BL* 1:204–5). Natural religion, as argued by Grotius and Paley, he gradually recognizes as reductively mechanistic and too much at odds with his own "metaphysical notions."[5] Thus, in recounting to Fricker the advice to his Socinian friend, he argues that Grotius and Paley would never have been so influential, "if thinking men had been habitually led to look into their own souls, instead of always looking out, both of themselves, and of their nature." Even if the account of miracles had been bolstered by "delusion" and by "exaggeration," he asserts that Christian doctrine would not be altered by demonstrating their falsehood. In matters of doctrine, "the miracles are extra essential." In matters of faith, however, they are by no means "superfluous." Perception of a miracle is a demonstration of faith: "Even as Christ did, so would I teach; that is, build the miracle on the faith, not the faith on the miracle."[6]

Clearly, Coleridge has adopted a mode of reasoning very different from the one evident in the 1795 lectures. He has already formulated the idea that miracles operate through a bond of faith. As Robert Barth has described the major themes in Coleridge's discussion of miracles in *The Friend* (1818) and in subsequent unpublished letters and notebook entries, Coleridge totally controverted the mechanist reasoning in eighteenth-century apologetics. For the apologists, from Butler's *Analogy of Religion* (1736) through Paley's *Evidences of Christianity* (1794), miracles (1) were "departures from the ordinary course of nature," (2) "prove that God is master of His creation and testify that His revealed word is true," and (3) "were taken to be directed more to unbelievers than to believers." Coleridge, however, held that the contraries to these are true: "(1) the contravention of a law of nature is not the essence of a miracle; (2) the essential significance of a miracle is its sign value; and (3) faith *precedes*

5. Kathleen Coburn observes that Coleridge frequently levels combined attacks on Grotius and Paley (see *CN* 2:2640; 3:3135, 3911 f61) and on Priestley and Paley (*CN* 2:2509, 2640; 3:3817, 3897, 4312).

6. To George Fricker (4 October 1806), in *CL* 2:1189–90; cf. letters to Mary Cruikshank (21 September 1807) and J. J. Morgan (7 January 1818).

the perception of a miracle, that is to say, recognition of a miracle as such is a result of faith rather than its cause."[7]

In rejecting the mechanist and materialist grounds of eighteenth-century apologetics, Coleridge reinterpreted "law of nature," transformed the sign (of a miracle) into a symbol of faith, and grounded faith in the intuitive reason. To forge a new metaphysics capable of fortifying Christian faith, he turned, as we know, to Spinoza, Kant, and Schelling. This was problematic. Hume, after all, spoke of the "true atheism . . . for which *Spinoza* is so universally famous" (*Treatise* 240). Kant, too, had been accused of undermining traditional theology. And Schelling, who posited a "World-Soul" and an "Absolute Identity" yet refused to locate it in Godhead, consequently reverted to pantheism. Nevertheless, Coleridge drew from all three in interpreting the gospels and formulating his new account of the miraculous. As Thomas McFarland has shown, the philosophy of Spinoza and Schelling, no less than Unitarian and Socinian thought, left Coleridge trapped in the metaphysics of externality, the "it is."[8] The revisions in his thinking are first articulated—or, as I should say, are first documented—in August 1807, at the time of his meeting with De Quincey and his "warm conversation" with Thomas Poole.

The "eloquent dissertation" with which Coleridge entertained his youthful auditor (Coleridge was thirty-seven, De Quincey twenty-two) commenced, in response to De Quincey's gift of Hartley's *De Ideis* (1746), with a discussion of Hartley. Describing himself as "a reverential believer in the doctrine of the Trinity," one whose "mind almost demanded mysteries in so mysterious a system of relations as those which connect us to another world," De Quincey declares that he fully expected to encounter in Coleridge, whom he revered as a poet, a Unitarian, a Socinian, and therefore, to De Quincey's mind, a non-Christian. Nor was it any comfort to learn that Coleridge, by this time, had stepped within the circle of "the *alleszermalmender* Kant."[9] To De Quincey's surprise, Coleridge "penitentially" disowned his former Unitarianism and declared himself a believer in prayer, which he defines not as a passive rumination but as "the total concentration of the faculties." The act of praying, he informed De Quin-

7. Barth, *Coleridge and Christian Doctrine*, 38, asserting that "Coleridge treats of miracles (and we confine our discussion to scriptural miracles, as Coleridge does) in only one of the works published during his lifetime." Barth refers to the passages in *The Friend* (1818). Another published commentary on scriptural miracles appears in Coleridge's *The Statesman's Manual* (1816). See Coleridge, *Friend*, 431, 519, and *LS* 9–10.

8. See McFarland, *Pantheist Tradition*, 155–57, on Schelling's failure to reconcile the "I am" and "it is."

9. *DQ* 2:155. De Quincey appropriates the epithet "*alleszermalmender* Kant" from Coleridge; it was originally bestowed on Kant by Moses Mendelssohn in the preface to *Morgenstunden, oder Vorlesungen über das Dasein Gottes* (1790), Coleridge repeats it in the *BL* 2:89.

cey, is "the very highest energy of which the human heart was capable."[10] Coleridge's theme, then, was religious experience. "For about three hours he had continued to talk," De Quincey recollects, "and in the course of this performance he had delivered many most striking aphorisms, embalming more weight of truth, and separately more deserving to be themselves embalmed, than would easily be found in a month's course of select reading" (*DQ* 2:152–57).

During this visit with Coleridge in August 1807, De Quincey had been cordially received by Thomas Poole, a "polished and liberal Englishman." Poole, who possessed "a good library, superbly mounted in all departments bearing upon political philosophy," frequently hosted evening discussions with Coleridge.[11] One of Coleridge's fullest statements on miracles is an outline recapitulating ten propositions he had considered on one such evening. Poole wrote at the top of the manuscript: "The following was written by Coleridge after a warm conversation between him and me concerning miracles. <signed> Tho Poole Augst 1807." As the manuscript makes clear, their discussion of miracles had focused specifically on John's report of "one casting out devils" in Christ's name (Mark 9:38–39). The first six propositions, however, deal generally with supernatural powers and the possibility of a demonic as well as a divine origin of miracles. The discussion throughout concerns miracles as performed through the agency of a miracle worker.

Coleridge begins with the definition of a miracle as "that which appears . . . beyond the power of unassisted man," and goes on to state that "the only necessary & universal consequence of the belief in a miracle . . . is that the performer either is [himself,] or is assisted by powers[,] more than human." The question then arises whether the sources of power are divine or demonic. Although Coleridge elsewhere resists such incipient Manichaeism,[12] he here indulges the possibility of Satanic forces. The grounds for discrimination rest partly with God, partly with human beings. God, for His part, "would not permit either conspiracies of men of very superior knowledge, or evil spirits to produce those appearances,

10. Coleridge on prayer (*LS* 55); Kathleen Coburn, in her note to Coleridge's account of prayer "as a guard against Self-delusion" and "the sole instrument of regeneration" (July–August 1808), observes that prayer, "probably a frequent topic with him," was often the subject of discussions with Lady Beaumont. See *CN* 3:3355 and 3355n.

11. *DQ* 2:142–47. Coleridge was absent at the time of De Quincey's arrival; with no other company at dinner, Thomas Poole launched a discussion of Coleridge's "unacknowledged obligations." The conversation apparently concerned only a borrowed source in Coleridge's elucidation of a passage from Pythagoras. De Quincey departs from the narrative of his visit to interpose a lengthy digression on Coleridge's borrowings, most notably the "real and palpable plagiarism" from Schelling in the *BL*.

12. *BL* 1:205; see also the comparison of Schelling and Zoroaster in *CN* 3:4424.

which must to men in a given state of knowledge inevitably be received as miraculous." Human beings, for their part, have an intuitive capacity to recognize the traces of divinity. Manifestations of the divine are perceived, explains Coleridge, much in the same way the ear experiences harmony in sound: "supposing the parations of the Heart towards Doctrines thereby welcomed as soon as heard, almost even as an Ear acknowledges & welcomes harmony in sounds, demanding no extrinsic proof that it is harmony." One such doctrine, Coleridge maintains, is the divinity of Christ, "the assumption of human nature by the Eternal Mind." Once the harmony of such a doctrine is felt, "miraculous actions would be naturally anticipated, not as a cause of Faith, but as the *result* of it." Here is Coleridge's key proposition that miracles are perceived through faith: "The great Truths of Christianity are directly declared to be inward result of a certain moral state, incipient at least, and to be a revelation from God to minds in that state" (*CN* 3278n).

From these propositions, Coleridge turns to his argument (with reference to John 6:37, 44–45, 65) that Christ uses his miracles to mediate rather than to demonstrate: "Christ asserts that none come to him but immediately led by God—he no where attests miracles as proofs of Doctrine." That wonders might be wrought for evil purposes, as Coleridge had considered in his third and forth propositions, is directly addressed when the question is put to Christ, "Can a devil open the eyes of the blind?" (John 10:21). Christ himself warns against the "many who shall come in my name, saying I am *Christ*; and shall deceive many" (Mark 13:5–6, 21–22). To guard against the deception, one must simply distinguish the ends from the means. As Coleridge points out, Christ "states indeed more than once the benevolent application of these extraordinary powers as a proof, that the supernatural worker was not malignant or anti-moral." This, he reminds Poole, is the significance of the text they had discussed from Mark's gospel: Christ "in our passage (the message to John) enumerates these applications, as a strong presumptive argument that the supernatural power which worked them was identical with that which was to come." Because Christ had already warned of those who would come in his name to practice deception, John is troubled by one whom he has seen "casting out devils in thy name." Christ reassures him: "Forbid him not: for there is no man which shall do a miracle in my name, that can lightly speak evil of me" (Mark 9:38–39).

Coleridge sees in this passage, then, confirmation of the crucial element in his case for miracles. Christ often makes explicit that having faith makes the miracle possible, even if that faith is no larger than a mustard seed. By contrast, he says, Christ "no where assigns a miracle as an argument for Christian Faith, and so far from working miracles to produce

Faith he uniformly demands pre-existing Faith in him as a requisite of the miracle." Coleridge refers as well to Peter's affirmation of faith (Matt. 16:16; Luke 9:20): "It was not Christ's intention broadly to inforce on John, further than his own heart led him, an actual faith in his Incarnation & consequent Divinity, but when Peter (first of all) declared, —Christ blesses him with fervour." Faith must assert itself from within; it cannot be imposed from without. Peter's faith came through revelation, not from beholding "all the miracles." Through faith the incumbent power passes from Christ to the apostles and multiplies among "men of obscurer name." Christ concludes his parable of the fig tree with the caveat that "no man, no, not even the angels of heaven" could command a power capable of preventing "the coming of the Son of man" (Matt. 24:32–37). In Coleridge's interpretation, we are thus forbidden "to believe even an Angel of Heaven / whatever miracles and however astonishing he might perform, if in confirmation of new doctrines." Although the possibility of doctrines being founded on miracles is "absurd," Coleridge concludes that it would be a very dangerous absurdity: "the notion that miracles can prove doctrines" would indeed justify fears of evil deception, for it would expose "human nature to every species of delusion & sensuality" (*CN* 3278n).

Because of his emphasis on the mediating power of faith, it may seem strange that Coleridge chose to elaborate his case for the intersubjectivity of religious experience by turning to the only gospel which makes no mention of faith.[13] The word *faith* does not appear in the Gospel of John because faith is actively predicated in the Word. When the Word becomes flesh, faith is possible only as an act of believing, that is, as active engagement in the doing and suffering, the το ποιειν and το παθειν, of Christ. It was most probable that Coleridge began to see the profound metaphysical implications of the "Word" and the "I am" as set forth in John's gospel only after wrestling with Schelling's arguments on the reconciliation of subject and object.[14] His discovery of these implications is recorded in his notebook entries of June 1810. His later intention, announced in the *Biographia Literaria*, to write "a full Commentary on the Gospel of St. John" as

13. This is not just a peculiarity of the King James Authorized Version; *pistis*, the Greek noun for "faith," occurs 8 times in Matthew, 5 times in Mark, 11 times in Luke, not in John; the adjective *pistos*, "faithful," occurs 3 times in Matthew, 5 times in Luke. John relies exclusively on the verb *pisteuo*, "believe," which occurs 98 times in his text, as opposed to 35 times in the other three gospels.

14. *CN* 3:3764 (April–June 1810) and 3764n: Coleridge's poetic lines on "The body / Eternal Shadow of the finite Soul / The Soul's self-symbol" are related by Kathleen Coburn to Coleridge's marginal gloss to K. E. Schelling in *Jahrbücher der Medicin* (1805–1808), 2:200–201, sec. 25. Coburn, *CN* 3:3875, 4176, 42–65, also notes Coleridge's response to Schelling's efforts to reconcile body and soul and subject and object.

part of his demonstration of Christianity as "the one true Philosophy"[15] clearly has its inception in his recognition that, long before Schelling, John had succeeded in revealing how the "mysterious End" of Christianity consists "in tying together the two separate portions of a one truth in the schemes of Materialism & Immaterialism."

One of the peculiarities that he notes in the Gospel of John is the distinction between "miracle" and "sign." He finds "something very stupendous" in John 6:30. Following the feeding of the five thousand, the crowd seeks Christ on the opposite of side of the sea. Christ reproaches them: "Ye seek me, not because ye saw miracles, but because ye did eat of the loaves, and were filled" (John 6:26). Since this is the crowd "whom he had fed miraculously the day or two before," Coleridge observes, it is strange that they should now ask him for a sign: "What sign shewest thou then, that we may see, and believe thee? what dost thou work?" (John 6:30).

> Was it not natural for him to have referred to his stupendous miracles, done in their own presence, but a day or two before? Was it not natural for him to have shewn what so many of the Advocates of Christianity, have since done—that he had not only given signs & works as great as any of their prophets, even the greatest, are related to have done, but even greater, & more frequent? When he refuses *a sign*, he does not refuse it merely to the persons tempting him and as such unworthy of having a miracle wrought for their sakes (which is the common but insufficient solution) but to *this generation*? Shall we say that a *sign* meant something very different from *a miracle!* (*CN* 3846)

Although "sign" and "miracle" are used interchangeably in the synoptic gospels, Coleridge argues that John discriminates the terms in order to avoid the possibility of equating miracle worker with thaumaturgist.[16] This would explain, Coleridge argues, the "apparent discord between different sentiments of Jesus himself concerning these miracles, and the evident discord between his general Language, & that of the Truth of Gospel History."

In contrast to the synoptic gospels, John has reduced the number of

15. *BL* 1:136; to Daniel Stuart (12 September 1814) and to John May (27 September 1815), in *CL* 3:554, and 4:589–90, describing the projected "*Logosophia*: or on the *Logos*, divine and human, in six Treatises," part 4 of which was to provide "a full Commentary on the Gospel of St. John." See also McFarland, *Pantheist Tradition*, 191–95.

16. C. H. Dodd, *The Interpretation of the Fourth Gospel*, similarly emphasizes the sign as distinguished from the miracle; he describes the central narrative of Christ's teaching (John 2:1–12:50) as the Book of Signs.

miracles to seven. John's gospel stipulates an active believing, as Coleridge has already argued, for a miracle to be perceived. Only under these conditions can the message of the miracle, its inherent sign, be understood. Coleridge thus relates the *semeion* to the *Logos*. Where Matthew, Mark, and Luke tell of Christ born of the virgin Mary in a stable in Bethlehem, John defines Christ as born of the divine *Logos*: the Word that was with God, and was God, becomes the Word made flesh (John 1:1, 14). Thus John provides, as Coleridge recognized, a reconciliation of subject and object, idea and matter. Rather than standing in polar opposition to the "it is" of Spinoza and Schelling, as McFarland maintains,[17] the "I am" permeates and transforms the "it is." As the Word become flesh, Christ asserts his presence as "I am": "Before Abraham was, I am" (8:58). Again in contrast to the synoptic gospels, the Christ of John's text teaches not in parables but in metaphors of the self. Self-presentation is the tool of his teaching: "I am the bread of life" (6:35, 48, 50); "I am the light of the world" (8:12); "I am the one who bears witness to myself" (8:18); "I am from above" (8:23); "I am the door" (10:7, 9); "I am the good shepherd" (10:11, 14); "I am the resurrection and the life" (11:25); "I am the way, the truth and the life" (14:6); "I am the true vine" (15:1, 5).

Proposing that Christianity achieves its "mysterious End" by reconciling "the schemes of Materialism & Immaterialism," Coleridge claims that Christ in the Gospel of John gives primacy to the sign not the miracle. The failure to see the sign is a persistent problem. The crowd that saw the miracle and ate the loaves still crave for the sign that they failed to see. Can there be any sign more profound or more self-evident, Coleridge asks, than Christ himself as the sign, the divine "Logos" become flesh and blood? "To give a flesh-and-blood reality to those processes of the rational and moral Being, which considered as abstractly intellectual, thin away into eternal notions, that remaining always the same, partake not of the life and change of material forms, which belong equally to all, faintly interest any, and from their very permanence and independence possess the weakest affinity with Fear, or Hope, or Love?" (*CN* 3847). Christ is that Word which is at once signifier and thing signified. His great task as teacher is to communicate that Word, to make the "I am" apparent and accessible. Thus he teaches in terms of his own body. Christ's body, as the self-referential Word, is at once human and divine. In his effort to explain this notion of the word containing its own truth, Coleridge later, in *The Statesman's Manual* (1816), defines "symbols" as "tautegorical"

---

17. McFarland, *Pantheist Tradition*, continues to discuss the polarity of "it is" and "I am" throughout his chapter "The Trinitarian Resolution." See 191–255, esp. 195–97, 200–203, 210, and 216; also see his note on the Gospel of John, 373–74.

and "consubstantial with the truths, of which they are the conductors" (*LS* 29). Here, too, he discusses the "sign" as "symbol" mediating its own meaning. Christ's "body" does not simply refer to but *is* the life and the soul, moreover, because of the Word within the word, *is* eternal life and salvation. He is "the Teacher and the Doctrine, the Giver and the Gift":

> Whether Christ's Discourses do not in a constant vein of peculiar Thought imply, that the growth, diseases, and restoration of the Soul are not merely analogous to those of the Body, as ideas to their appointed Symbols (i.e. by a factitious analogy, the work of association) but strictly so, as *things* of one class to *things* of another, in the linked ascent of creation? —Whether the plain purpose of John VI. be not to establish that *specific* difference between Christ and all other Delegates from Heaven before & after him, that the faithful believe *them*, i.e. receive their *doctrines* as true and of divine Authority, but they not only are to believe Christ, but to believe *in* Christ—He is at once the Teacher and the Doctrine, the Giver and the Gift. (*CN* 3847)

In yet another contrast to the synoptic gospels, the Gospel of John omits the narrative of the Last Supper. Or rather, Coleridge argues, John replaces it with the eucharistic Discourse, "I am the bread of life" (John 6:35–58). The mediating Word absorbs whoever speaks it, knowing its meaning, into its meaning. The eucharistic mystery is not simply the presence of the body of Christ in the bread, but the presence of Christ in the body of whoever consumes it.

> These mysterious declarations in this Chapter so evidently connected with the miracle of the Loaves & Fishes narrated in the beginning of the Chapter, & seemingly, like the rest of Christ's miracles, bearing an intentional symbolical analogy to the declarations which follow as avowed comments on that miracle, and lastly, this Chapter considered as *a substitute* for the Texts in the three other Evangelists relating to the institution of the Lord's Supper accounts for & alone can count for, the beloved Disciple's Silence on this institution. (*CN* 3847)

For Coleridge, then, John transcends the historical sequence of the synoptic gospels. The entire narrative of the Last Supper, the Crucifixion, and the Resurrection is subsumed in the discourse of the "living bread." More important, that abyss between phenomenon and noumenon, which Kant had declared unbridgeable, is bridged.

Remember, that flesh & blood as phaenomena, must have a supporting Noumenon—that it does not follow, that the Noumenon
remaining, the Phaenomenon should likewise remain/ that this is
proved myriadfold in Chemistry & Physiology—and Scripturally
evinced by the changes in the phaenomena of Christ's Body after
the Resurrection, which yet we are bound to believe *persisted* as
his Body—. Remember, too, that Christ's Body, as represented to
the Eye, was a Phaenomenon—but that the Body = Noumenon,
with which the Logos was united, so becoming incarnate, was *Human Nature*—a mysterious thing, whose boundaries & laws of in-
dividualism we know not/ assuredly, as a Noumenon, it is not
bound to the conditions *of Space. (CN* 3847)

Although John affirms that in the Word made flesh the noumenon becomes directly accessible through the phenomenon, the intuitive reason
cannot reach beyond mere speculation into the mystery of God incarnate.
Spiritual truth is accessible, even among the immediate witnesses of
Christ, only to the willing believer. Scriptural evidence brings us this
close, and no closer, to philosophical resolution.

The scriptural evidence, however, is at odds with the Socinian interpretation. Coleridge calls attention to the passage in which Paul tells Timothy that the "great mystery" of "God . . . manifest in the flesh" is "without
controversy." God incarnate, writes Paul, was "seen of angels" (1 Tim.
3:6). If Christ was merely a man divinely inspired, "*psilos anthropos*,"
Coleridge asks, what could be the significance or purport of this passage?
"What could the Angels *see* that men could not?" "But if it were *o the-
anthropos*, God incarnate, then indeed Angels *might* SEE, i.e. have a direct
and *intuitive* knowledge of what men could only infer discursively & know
by faith" (*CN* 3858). Throughout the notebook entries for June 1810, Coleridge grapples with scriptural references to miracles and Christ's divinity.[18]
Although he acknowledges that a philosophical proof cannot be extrapo-
lated from the Bible, he is firmly convinced that Hume's attack on miracles as well as the whole company of refutations, from Hartley to Paley,
belabored the mere externalities. The true province of miracles is internal
and subjective.

In *The Statesman's Manual* (1816), Coleridge describes the internalizing
of the miracle as a necessary process of intellectual development. When
superstitious credulity prevailed, human beings externalized their hopes

18. *CN* 3:3846–47, 3886–89, 3892–93, 3897 (June 1810); also 3022 (February–May 1807);
3135 (September 1807); 3231 (1807–10); 3278 (February–March 1808); 4249 (May 1815); 4381
(January 1818); 4451–52 (October 1818); and Coleridge, *Letters, Conversations and Recollections* 1:87–89.

there was nothing! are self-contradictory. There is that within us which repels the proposition with as full and instantaneous light, as if it bore evidence against the fact in right of its own eternity. Not TO BE, then, is impossible: TO BE, incomprehensible. (*Friend* 1:514)

The intuition of the "it is" as "absolute existence" leads irresistibly to a contemplation of an informing and sustaining power, the "I am." No mode or method of reasoning directs the steps by which we come to this truth. It is a truth that "manifests itself," a revelation. Coleridge repeats, here, his argument that the means to spiritual truth resides *a priori* within the intuition. He grants, nevertheless, that the truth must unfold historically and culturally. Relative to our state of learning, we "move progressively towards that divine idea." As truth is divine revelation, so progress is divine intervention.

When John Henry Newman, some twenty-five years later, proposed the relevance of historical to religious development, he emphasized the way in which learning could reveal more and more of the original truths of biblical revelation (Prickett 55–56, 161–70). Coleridge sees the historical progression itself as revelation. The laws that govern "man's development and progression" derive from the a priori structures of the mind. Understanding and fancy, directly stimulated through the senses, are the first to be nurtured. When they interpret the intuition of divinity, they inevitably "break and scatter the one divine and invisible life of nature into countless idols of the sense." Thus it was "that men sent by God have come with signs and wonders" to break down the superstitious idolatry of the senses (*Friend* 1:518). Reiterating this argument from *The Statesman's Manual*, Coleridge declares that "in the case of miracles . . . wisdom forbids her children to antedate their knowledge, or to act and feel otherwise, or further than they know." The idea may be derived from Hartley, as Coleridge had earlier used it in the 1795 lectures, but he has added a remarkable philosophical refinement. Whereas natural phenomena at large reveal the laws of science, God's presence in nature reveals the laws of mind. As our understanding of both progresses, we will come to perceive miracles not in terms of exterior nature, but as revelations of the capacities of intuitive reason: "What we now consider as miracles in opposition to ordinary experience, we should then reverence with a yet higher devotion as harmonious parts of one great complex miracle, when the antithesis between experience and belief would itself be taken up into the unity of intuitive reason" (*Friend* 1:519). By appealing thus to historical development and a progressive maturation from faith to reason, Coleridge conveniently postpones the resolution of his argument. The history of philosophy remains conditional and inconclusive in recording the permutations of the essential spiritual truth, the "I am" in the "it is." Philosophy begins in wonder, Coleridge says, and ends in wonder. In the meantime, we fill the interspace with admiration and content ourselves with symbols that seem to conjure the mystery of Immanence.[19]

Unlike Coleridge, De Quincey in his analysis of miracles never constructed an epistemology of intuition and intersubjectivity. As he had acknowledged on the occasion of his first meeting with Coleridge, his "mind almost demanded mysteries in so mysterious a system of relations as those which connect us to another world." Because he accepted the mind's impulsive quest of the mysterious nexus between the natural and the supernatural world, De Quincey never struggled with the metaphysics of the relationship. Himself a dedicated dreamer with "a constitutional determination to reverie," he was more inclined to perceive the dream as an exterior world rather than as an interior construct of the mind. Thus, too, supernatural manifestations of the divine belong to "another world," which is not merely connected to, but coincident with, and sometimes visibly manifest in this one. Whereas Coleridge endeavored to bring all external traces of the miraculous into the internal space of "spiritual truth," De Quincey allowed for a subtle cooperation between the internal and external. He agreed with Coleridge, however, in attributing the essential power of miracles to the inherent "symbol" or "sign."

De Quincey seems to have borrowed Coleridge's definition of the symbol as *tautegorical,* that is, "expressing the same subject but with a difference" (*LS* 30; *AR* 199). For Coleridge, the symbol is akin to that "imperceptible infusion" of creative presence which distinguishes an "imitation" from a mere "copy" (*BL* 1:76; 2:43, 76, 212). For De Quincey, too, the simultaneous presence of identity and alterity is a crucial attribute of all art. In his marginalia to Jacob Böhme, Coleridge explains the Tri-unity of the Word that is God, the Word that is with God, and the Word become flesh (John 1:1, 14): "with God" combines the first—itself God, or *Idem*—and the last *Alter,* God become other (*Marginalia* (=M) 1:690; cf. 2:33). Commenting on the connection of faith with power as proclaimed by Christ in the "faith as a mustard seed" (Matt. 17:20; Luke 17:6), Coleridge responds that there is "no proper allegorism in Scripture/ *tauto en genei, allo* solum in gradu *alla agorei*" (*CN* 4186). De Quincey similarly describes symbolic action as *idem in alio* (*DQ* 1:51, 5:237, 10:369, 11:195–96). In its simplest formulation, "sameness in difference" is the principle that renders a marble statue aesthetically more dynamic than Madame

---

19. *Friend* 1:519; Coleridge, *Aids to Reflection* (=AR), 185: "In Wonder all Philosophy began: in Wonder it ends: and Admiration fills up the interspace."

Tussaud's most life-like wax figure. The wax mimics the flesh all too well: the difference is wanting (*DQ* 10:369). *Idem in alio* is what enables the whole to express more than the sum of its parts. A symbol reveals more than it means: "One part of the effect from the symbolic is dependent upon the great catholic principle of the *Idem in alio*. The symbol restores the theme, but under new combinations of form or colouring; gives back, but changes; restores, but idealizes" (*DQ* 1:51). The language of symbol thus has a power to transcend the limits of reason, to reach beyond experience, and to draw, like dreams, from a spiritual world. The "interlusory revealings of the symbolic" thus evoke, *idem in alio*, "the solemn remembrances that lie hidden below."

What is involved in interpreting a report beyond the limits of reason and ordinary experience is explicitly developed in De Quincey's response to Hume's refutation of miracles. It has been said that De Quincey simply adapted the arguments against Hume from Campbell's *Dissertation on Miracles* (1763). This opinion misses De Quincey's deliberately precarious reasoning in "Miracles as Subjects of Testimony" (1839) (*DQ* 8:157–75). The key word of the title is not "Miracles" but "Testimony"; not whether miracles occur, but the presumptions of their record. De Quincey's essay, then, is about rhetoric. The crux of Hume's refutation, he says, is the problem of language: "Besides the objection to miracles that they are not capable of attestation, Hume's objection is not that they are false, but that they are incommunicable." To summarize Hume's argument "On Miracles" De Quincey uses a mathematical formula[20] of plus and minus factors as an apt, and perhaps ironic, way to reflect Hume's concern with measuring the credibility of any report, pro or con, on a supposedly miraculous moment of divine intervention:

> Assume the resistance to credibility in any preternatural occurrence as equal to x, and the very ideal or possible value of human testimony as no more than x: in that case, under the most favorable circumstances conceivable, the argument for and against a miracle, $+x$ and $-x$, will be equal; the values will destroy each other; the result will be $= 0$. But, inasmuch as this expresses the value of human testimony in its highest or ideal form, —a form which is seldom realized in experience, —the true result will be different: there will always be a negative result, much or little according to the circumstances, but in any case enough to turn the balance *against* believing a miracle. (*DQ* 8:157)

20. David Masson apparently has this formula in mind when he objects that De Quincey's "counter-argument . . . is decidedly supersubtle, —too fine-spun and algebraic to be really effective" (preface, *DQ* 8:4).

As De Quincey rightly points out, Hume does not deny the possibility of miracles. He denies, rather, the credibility of any witness seeking to testify that a miracle had occurred. De Quincey's strategy is to shift the emphasis from historical to rhetorical, from verifying to persuading.

There are only three circumstances, De Quincey notes, in which a miracle might be witnessed (*DQ* 8:158):

1. It might happen in the presence of a single witness, —that witness not being ourselves. . . .
2. It might happen in the presence of many witnesses, —witnesses to a variable amount, but still (as before) ourselves not being amongst that multitude. . . .
3. It might happen in our own presence, and fall within the direct light of our own consciousness.

Hume's argument addresses only the problems of communication attending the first of these three cases. The third case is irrelevant to Hume's argument, because personal experience eliminates the need to determine the reliability of the witness or the validity of the communication. The second case seems to be pondered in Hume's fictitious example of the resurrection of Queen Elizabeth. Hume's supposed witnesses to this miracle are the Queen's physicians, who might well be suspected of collusion. De Quincey objects that Hume has thus excluded the strength of corroboration: "though three or four nominally, virtually they are but one man." If Hume seriously wanted to entertain a case of multiple witnesses, why not, De Quincey suggests, "call in the whole Privy Council—or the Lord Mayor and Common Council of London, the Sheriffs of Middlesex, and the Twelve Judges?" (*DQ* 8:160).

In constructing his refutation, De Quincey begins by noting that Hume has excluded corroborative testimony. He then observes that Hume has given no thought to various kinds of miracles. The basic discrimination, for De Quincey, involves internal and external miracles. By inner miracles he means those which occur "within the separate personal consciousness of each separate man." He lists three sorts of inner miracles: special providence, grace, and the efficacy of prayer. Whereas many "philosophic Christians doubt or deny" special providence, the divine agency of both grace and prayer are basic to Christianity (*DQ* 8:163–64). Hume's argument, since it addresses only the communication of miracles, does not bother with miracles of spiritual communion. The external miracles De Quincey divides into two sorts: "1. *Evidential* miracles, which simply *prove* Christianity; 2. *Constituent* miracles, which, in a partial sense, *are* Christianity, as in part composing its substance." Of the latter order, he insists upon "the miraculous birth of our Saviour, and his miraculous resurrection" (*DQ* 8:165).

The evidential miracles, De Quincey observes, were "occasional and polemic." Their whole function was "to meet a special hostility incident to the birth-struggles of a new religion." Hume's argument, therefore, is paradoxical and belated. Paradoxical, because, no matter how it might be judged by eighteenth-century criteria, the testimony as originally communicated was indeed highly effective; belated, because "a Christianised earth never can want polemic miracles again." Even "if Hume's argument were applicable in its whole strength to the evidential miracles, no result of any importance could follow." They have already worked their purpose in that early history, when people of faith struggled under "a dominant idolatry" (*DQ* 8:166).

Although De Quincey thus dismisses the relevance of the argument against evidential miracles, an adequate answer to Hume still requires a defense of the constituent miracles, the miracles so essential to the faith that they are codified in the Nicene creed. Hume held that the constituent miracles, however sacrosanct, were subject to the same criteria of analysis as any other claimed aberration of natural law. His fictitious resurrection of Queen Elizabeth is fully intended to duplicate the problems of witness and testimony accompanying the resurrection of Christ. Even in multiplying the factorial value of the testimony of the Apostles and reducing the testimony of the court physicians to a factor of one, De Quincey plays a game of numbers which leaves his rebuttal trapped by Hume's demand for material evidence. He seeks to avoid this trap by proposing two modes of valuation, a priori and a posteriori. Unlike Coleridge, De Quincey does not avail himself of the Kantian application of these terms.

The a posteriori valuation of testimony, De Quincey asserts, derives from the detection of motives that influence our judgment. An "abstract resistance to credibility," De Quincey grants, has abundant historical justification in pagan cultures, where supernatural events were proclaimed on the behalf of "ostentation" or "ambition." Magical phenomena, if not "blind accidents," were surely "blank expressions of power." The miracles of Christianity, by contrast, always have a moral purpose. As the temptations of Christ demonstrate, the miracles of his advent deliberately counter all claims to material power. Whereas the providence of Christ's miracles is exclusively moral, "to any other wielder of supernatural power, real or imaginary, it never had occurred, by way of pretence even, that he had a moral object" (*DQ* 8:169).

The a priori valuation also has abundant justification, not merely in the history of man, but in the natural history of life itself. As De Quincey put it, "Upon any hypothesis, we are driven to suppose—and compelled to suppose—a miraculous state as introductory to the earliest state of nature. The planet, indeed, might form itself by mechanical laws of motion, repulsion, attraction, and central forces. But man could not. Life could not" (*DQ* 8:171). God is "always already" present. This same sense of temporal priority informs Jesus' declaration: "Before Abraham was, I am" (John 8:58). An a priori mode of apprehending events is relevant to the gradual unfolding of both natural history and human history. Thus the great prophets could predict accurately events to come because they perceived the divine purpose. De Quincey cites the desolation of Babylon, fulfilling Isaiah's prophecy, as an a posteriori miracle demonstrating an a priori miracle.

De Quincey's final argument in "Miracles considered as Subjects of Testimony" is his crucial argument against Hume, and it is the one to which he returns in subsequent discussions of miracles. The very definition of God is predicated on "a *power* to work miracles." The notion of God "breaking" nature's law, which Hume has assumed as the necessary condition of miracles, is a paradox. Nature's laws are God's laws. The latter works through the former: the *natura naturans* is manifest in the *natura naturata* (to use the phrase Coleridge frequently quoted from Spinoza). Coleridge had followed Hartley in equating divine will and natural law (Hartley 2:142; *Lectures 1795* 111–16). De Quincey differs only in insisting upon the limits: advances in science can never allow more than a glimpse at the grandeur of infinite mystery. From a finite human vantage, science reveals only partially and obliquely those laws by which the divine will manifests itself. In terms of consequence, a posteriori, the constituent miracles function "to revolutionise the moral nature of man"; in terms of origin, a priori, the constituent miracles reveal an immediate and direct act of the divine will. They are manifest in the natural world, yet independent of natural causality. Because they proceed from the will rather than from nature, the birth and resurrection of Christ are best understood as an *epigenesis*, a reaffirmation on behalf of the moral order of humanity of that very act of *genesis* which brought nature and humankind into being (*DQ* 8:173–75).

Even before Newman aroused the controversy over "development," De Quincey had already formulated his own notion on the progress of human intellect as an organic revelation of inherent and persisting truths. His conviction that humanity cooperates in expanding revelation prompted him to reverse the strategy that had informed Hume's *Natural History of Religion* (1757). In tracing the development of belief, Hume acknowledged two sources of religion: "its foundation in reason" and "its origin in human nature" (*Natural History* 24). A third source, revelation, is historically excluded by the "universal" polytheism of early religion. Even the second, human reason, must be deemed a fairly late addition to a historical record dominated by irrationality and corruption. De Quincey, although capable of little tolerance toward pagan and non-Christian cultures, looked far more approvingly than Hume upon humanity's irrationality.

"Modern Superstition," which appeared in *Blackwood's* (April 1840) ten months after "Miracles considered as Subjects of Testimony" (July 1839), continued the deliberation on miracles. "It is said continually that the age of the miraculous and supernatural is past," De Quincey states in a typically polemical opening. "I deny that it is so in any sense which implies this age to differ from all other generations of man except one." In response to God's continuing revelation, human beings have gradually strengthened their capacity to perceive the divine presence. Our greatest asset in perceiving the divine has never been reason, but rather superstition. Careful to rid the word of its grosser implications of credulity and delusion, De Quincey specifies that he means *superstition* "in the sense of sympathy with the invisible." As such, superstition is no hindrance to the progress of humanity. It is, rather, "the great test of man's grandeur" which enables the reconciliation of the "earthly" and "celestial." Not only does it make available "the possibility of religion," De Quincey confidently declares that, so long as it is allowed to express itself, superstition will always and inevitably "pass into pure forms of religion as man advances" (*DQ* 8:404).

De Quincey traces two major modes of superstition, the Ovidian and the Ominous. "That function of miraculous power which, though widely diffused through Pagan and Christian ages alike, has the least root in the solemnities of the imagination, we may call the *Ovidian*." In this mode, "a movement of superstition under the domination of human affections" projects itself outward onto an object in nature that seems, then, to mirror its own passions and sympathies. The object is imaginatively transformed, thus "supporting that blended sympathy by a symbol incarnated with the fixed agencies of nature" (*DQ* 8:405). Although he names it after the *Metamorphoses*, he is quick to point out that the Ovidian mode persists in Christian lands, and he cites numerous examples of such lore as the imprint of St. Peter's thumb on the haddock, the blossoming of the thorn on Christmas morning, the shivering of the aspen in sympathy with the holy cross.

Nor is it easy to dismiss "all silent incarnations of miraculous power." Nature sometimes seems to mimic the human sympathies with peculiar precision, as, for example, when "we see lineaments of faces and forms in petrifactions, in variegated marbles, in spars or in rocky strata, which our fancy interprets as once having been real human existences, but which are now confounded with the very substance of a mineral product." Taking on the characteristics of immanence that Coleridge attributed to symbols, such natural phenomena seem to occupy "a midway station between the physical and hyperphysical." Because the illusion of intelligent agency appears incontrovertible, De Quincey declares, "the stream of the miraculous is here confluent with the stream of the natural" (*DQ* 8:410). His footnote to Novalis's "interesting speculations" on this confluence refers to the passage in *Heinrich von Ofterdingen* (1800) in which the Hermit of the Cave argues that no longer engendering new metals and gems, rocks and mountains, gigantic plants and animals, the creativity of nature has turned inward: "The more its procreative energy is exhausted, the more its plastic, ennobling, and companionable energies increase; its mood is more receptive and tender, its fantasy more various and symbolic. . . . [I]t becomes like man, and if it were once a rock wildly giving birth, it is now a still germinating plant, a mute human artist" (Novalis 1:262).

As if they were notes "in the ascending scale of superstitions," De Quincey plays next in "a more alarming key": the Ominous mode. Here the superstitious imagination is more alarming because more personal. In the Ovidian mode, we project our sympathies onto nature, seeing in nature reflections of human images in general. In the Ominous mode, the supernatural power reveals itself as intimate omen or augur to the individual. De Quincey begins with names and signs as self-fulfilling prophecies. *Nomen est omen* is a superstition that he documents with several instances, from the fate of Atrius Umber, an officer of the Roman legion (*DQ* 8:412–13), to Napoleon's presentiments that the loss of his boat, *L'Italie*, would be followed, as it was, by the loss of his Italian territory (*DQ* 8:416). What is said will come to pass: this superstition De Quincey documents in Christ's reply to Pilate's query after his Kingship, "Thou hast said it" (*DQ* 8:418). As we know from his *Confessions* and *Suspiria de Profundis*, De Quincey was fascinated with oneiromancy as practiced by Joseph in interpreting the dreams of Pharaoh (Gen. 41:1–37). Such auguries presume not only that supernatural ministrations attend and direct human events, but that individuals may interpret and participate in the supernatural processes. A peculiar and riddling example is the seeming success of rhabdomancy, the art of seeking out underground water or mineral deposits with a divining or dousing rod: "the experimental evidences of a real practical skill in these men, and the enlarged compass of speculation in these days, have led many enlightened people to a stoic *epoche,* or suspension of judgment, on the reality of this somewhat mysterious art" (*DQ* 8:434).[21]

21. Johann Ritter, noted for his discovery of ultraviolet, began in 1806 to investigate rhabdomancy in relation to subterranean electromagnetism. After witnessing Francesco Campetti perform with the divining rod, Ritter founded a journal, *Der Siderismus* (1808), to

De Quincey's point, as he summarizes it, is that "the spirit of the miraculous as it moulded and gathered itself in the superstitions of Paganism" is fully perpetuated "in the modern superstitions of Christianity." Indeed, that spirit has acquired a far more extensive domain. He has deliberately omitted from his purview the "peculiarly Christian" preoccupation with ghosts. "The Christian ghost," he says, "is too awful a presence, with too large a substratum of the real, the impassioned, the human, for my present purposes." It is enough to demonstrate "the high activity of the miraculous and the hyperphysical instincts" as a persistent attribute of human perception (*DQ* 8:443–44). Plutarch, in "On Superstition," blames superstition as an indulgence of cowardice and ignorance which "both supplied the cause for Atheism to come into being, and after it is come, furnished it with an excuse" (Plutarch 272–73). Sir John Cheke, in an essay appended to his translation of Plutarch (1540), narrowed the definition of atheism and in part redeemed the disparagement of superstition.[22] If atheism is the denial, not of God, but of God's active intervention, then superstition, as sensitivity to the invisible, may be a corrective rather than a provocation of atheism. De Quincey praises superstition as that vehicle of the imagination which enables the Christian to affirm his belief in God. Coleridge obviously shared the same conviction when he took as the motto to his "Rime of the Ancient Mariner," the words of Bishop Burnet: "Facile credo, plures esse Naturas invisibiles quam visibiles in rerum universitate."[23]

Following the completion of *The Logic of Political Economy* (1844) and the *Suspiria de Profundis* (1845), De Quincey returned to the problem of miracles and divine providence. His thinking on these topics had been rekindled by Newman's *Essay on the Development of Christian Doctrine* (1845). He wrote a series of papers expatiating upon Newman's concept of "development," which he planned to bring together in a book to be titled "Christianity in Relation to Human Development" (*PW* 1:xiv). In the manuscript "On Miracles" (7 June 1847), De Quincey reveals his excitement in preparing a major work on inspiration and development: "Ah reader you little dream of our mission. You shall see both of us—getting within the next 5 years getting at the heart and sweeping the heart of some old nuisances—it was unavoidable and granted as they turn down thumbs to the other, and as safe as they seem to themselves."[24] The letter

---

report sidereal and rhabdomantic experiments; see the studies by Klinckowstroem cited in the bibliography.

22. Sir John Cheke's translation and commentary, quoted in Michael J. Buckley, S.J., *At the Origins of Modern Atheism*, 9–10.

23. Burnet, *Archaeologiae philosophicae*, 62; see Chap. 1, n. 43.

24. Not in Alexander Japp's transcription. See *The Posthumous Works of Thomas De Quincey* (=*PW*), 1:173–76.

to his daughter Margaret, written three days later (10 June 1847), refers to his vile digestion, which made eating repugnant. Making a virtue of his plight, he repeats his promise to complete the new project in five years:

> To be a great philosopher, it is absolutely necessary to be famished. My intellect is far too electric in its speed, and its growth of flying armies of thoughts entirely new. I could spare enough to fit a nation. This secret lies—not, observe, in my hair; cutting off *that* does no harm; it lies in my want of dinner, as also of breakfast and supper. Being famished, I shall show this world of ours in the next five years something that it never saw before. (Page 1:343)

De Quincey, like Coleridge, constructed many more projects in his imagination than he ever brought to paper. But a good number of his essays, published and unpublished, clearly contribute to the planned work on inspiration and development. Among the first installments, he wrote "On Christianity as an Organ of Political Movement" (April/June 1846) to examine how religion has shaped political history.

Just two years earlier Karl Marx had declared that "religion . . . is the opium of the people" (Marx 175), and others had blamed the church for preaching passivity to the masses to render them docile. De Quincey tries to turn the indictment around, not by denying corruption within the church, but by insisting that the indictment itself is evidence of the moral benevolence of Christian doctrine: "Hence it has happened sometimes that minds of the highest order have entered into enmity with the Christian faith, have arraigned it as a curse to man, and have fought against it even upon Christian impulses (impulses of benignity that could not have had birth except in Christianity)" (*DQ* 8:207–8). The secret workings of Christianity, propagated as spiritual values, are always benevolent; the public workings, entangled in the material concerns of property and production, are often swayed by selfish interests. Even the latter, however, are held in check by the inspirational and doctrinal aspects of religion. Why, then, slavery? Why war among Christian nations? De Quincey confidently endorses the progress of social morality under Christian guidance. His own age had participated in the abolition of slavery, had contributed to the founding of charitable institutions, and had witnessed an expanding "*social* influence of woman" (*DQ* 8:233). He had no way of knowing, of course, that the twentieth century would be violently shaken by two global wars, but he did observe international tensions in his own day that required him to temper his optimism: "Shall I offend the reader by doubting, after all, whether war is not an evil still destined to survive through several centuries?" To bring about "the final step for its extinction," De

Quincey says, the world must cooperate in ratifying "a new and Christian code of international law" (*DQ* 8:236).

De Quincey's essay "Protestantism" (1847) is a reply to *A Vindication of Protestant Principles* (1847), a tract by John W. Donaldson, which, in turn, is a response to Newman's *Essay on the Development of Christian Doctrine* (1845). Although he agrees with Donaldson's position on inspiration, De Quincey takes him to task for his opposition to Newman's doctrine of development. Inspiration and development, De Quincey maintains, are fully compatible. Both the manner and matter of inspiration altered historically from the time of Moses and the Prophets to the time of Jesus and the Apostles. Not only the writing but also the interpretation of the text may be inspired and similarly subject to historical change. As Stephen Prickett has shown, Coleridge preceded Newman in arguing the progressive unfolding of biblical thought (Prickett 54–55). De Quincey, who had already adopted with Coleridge the basic hermeneutic idea that meanings could lie latent in a text until advances in knowledge made them accessible, readily endorses Newman's argument.

Donaldson's tract defined three basic attributes of Protestantism: "The sole sufficiency of Scripture, the right of private judgment in its interpretation, and the authority of individual conscience in matters of religion" (*DQ* 8:250). By insisting on individual rights, the Reformation gave intellectual dimension to the political concern with legal rights. These rights also required a new tolerance and a new intellectual responsibility. The problem, according to Donaldson, is that this intellectual right and responsibility leads to an inevitable confrontation between religion and science.

> That we stand on the brink of a great theological crisis, that the problem must soon be solved how far orthodox Christianity is possible for those who are not behind their age in scholarship and science: this is a solemn fact, which may be ignored by the partisans of short-sighted bigotry, but which is felt by all, and confessed by most of those who are capable of appreciating its reality and importance. The deep sibylline vaticinations of Coleridge's philosophical mind, the practical workings of Arnold's religious sentimentalism, and the open acknowledgment of many divines who are living examples of the spirit of the age, have all, in different ways, foretold the advent of a Church of the Future. (Donaldson ix)

Such is the crisis. In confronting it, Donaldson apparently wanted the church of the future to resist rather than to build on change. His "secret purpose," De Quincey observes, is to report "the latest novelties that have found a roosting-place in the English Church, amongst the most temperate of those churchmen who keep pace with modern philosophy." Tolerance toward these forces of change, Donaldson seemed to be urging, should not be led to sanction change. He attempts to show, De Quincey says, "how far it is possible that strict orthodoxy should bend, on the one side, to new impulses, derived from an advancing philosophy, and yet, on the other side, should reconcile itself, both verbally and in spirit, with ancient standards" (*DQ* 8:262). The church should remain, then, a repository of sameness amid difference.

One means of holding onto that sameness is through the appeal to the inspiration of the Bible. Here De Quincey agrees with Donaldson in opposing "bibliolatry" (the fundamentalist insistence on the literal truth of "the Bible as the Word of God"). He distinguishes between "inspiration as attaching to the separate words and phrases of the Scriptures" and "inspiration as attaching to the spiritual truths and doctrines delivered in these Scriptures" (*DQ* 8:265). How is inspiration to be ascertained, De Quincey asks, in a collection of texts that has been strangely pieced together during its long history of transmission and translation? It is precisely in the harmony and coherence, in spite of the disrupted and fragmentary composition, that De Quincey finds the evidence of sustained inspiration.

> On such a final creation resulting from such a distraction of parts it is indispensable to suppose an overruling inspiration, in order at all to account for the final result of a most elaborate harmony. Besides, —which would argue some inconceivable magic if we did not assume a providential inspiration watching over the coherencies, tendencies, and intertesselations (to use a learned word) of the whole, —it happens that, in many instances, typical things are recorded, things ceremonial that could have no meaning to the person recording, prospective words that were reported and transmitted in a spirit of confiding faith, but that could have little meaning to the reporting parties for many hundreds of years. (*DQ* 8:265)

Although he thus describes a guiding rather than a literal inspiration, De Quincey also anticipates the argument for development. Meanings are evolved as a part of the historical communication, gradual compilation, and ongoing reception of the Scripture. The key passage, always cited as the Scripture's own declaration of "*verbatim et literatim* inspiration" is in Paul's letter to Timothy: "All scripture [is] given by inspiration of God, and [is] profitable for doctrine, for reproof, for correction, for instruction in righteousness" (2 Tim. 3:16). De Quincey has already called attention to the paradox that "bibliolatry depends upon ignorance of Hebrew and Greek" (*DQ* 8:263). In keeping with his notion of the fragility and elusiveness of textual meanings, he provides a word-by-word exegesis of Paul's Greek. The crucial word, *theopneustos*, De Quincey translates literally as "God-breathed, or God-prompted." Whether it belongs to the subject or the predicate is ambiguous, for the Greek sentence has no copula. Thus God's breathing or prompting hovers indeterminately between *pasa graphe* (all writing) and *kai ophelimos pros didaskalian* (and/also serviceable toward doctrinal truth), between the text and the teaching. In his *Confessions of an Inquiring Spirit*, Coleridge had also scrutinized this passage to argue that the truth of the Bible resides not in the literal sense of its words but in "its declared ends and purposes" (67–68). No matter how Paul's words are construed, they cannot be made into a commandment of literalism. Elsewhere, as De Quincey reminds us, Paul preached that "the letter killeth, but the spirit giveth life" (2 Cor. 3:6). The *theopneustia* is better sought, therefore, not "in the corruptibilities of perishing syllables" but "in the sanctities of indefeasible, word-transcending ideas" (*DQ* 8:268).

The many translators, compilers, compositors, interpreters, who have been involved in handing down the Scriptures need not, each and every one, be deemed a prophet who infallibly grasps and conveys inspired truth. De Quincey recollects the scandal in seventeenth-century London when a drunken compositor left out the "not" in the seventh commandment (*DQ* 8:273). Because the missing word remains readily obvious from the context in Deuteronomy, only perversity could declare that the Bible recommended adultery. "The heavenly truths, by their own imperishableness, defeat the mortality of languages with which for a moment they are associated" (*DQ* 8:275). Not even the bibliolator *cum* philologist (*rara avis,* but Donaldson was one), having mastered Hebrew and Greek, would therefore approach the source of inspiration. Inspiration is communicated through the experience with the scriptural ideas. Through experience, too, the ideas may grow in individual consciousness and in the culture. Inspiration overrides the limits of language, enters into human actions, and thus contributes directly to development. This argument for development is opposed by Donaldson because he believes that it undermines the very origins of Christianity. Newman's doctrine, as he sees it, implies that "primitive" Christianity was in a state of error, or that Christ's own teachings were imperfect and have only come into perfection with the rise of modern learning.

De Quincey deftly corrects Donaldson's misapprehension by distinguishing "perfection" and "development": the former inheres in Christianity as "theory and system"; the latter is acquired by the Christian community through experience. Through "development" we perceive more and more of the original and abiding "perfection." De Quincey points out that Donaldson, when he is not condemning Newman, understands and endorses the idea of development: "at p. 33, when as yet he is not thinking of Mr. Newman, he says, 'If knowledge is progressive, the *development* of Christian doctrine must be progressive'" (*DQ* 8:294). De Quincey denies only the "must" in Donaldson's formulation. He goes on, however, to elaborate the modes of development, not in Newman's terms but in his own. He discusses the possibilities of philological, philosophical, and social development. Donaldson, he says, harbors, paradoxically, a surreptitious bibliolatry as well as a covert endorsement of development:

> It is past all denial that, to a certain extent, the Scriptures must benefit, like any other book, by an increasing accuracy and compass of learning in the *exegesis* applied to them. But, if all the world denied this, . . . [Donaldson] is the man that cannot; since he relies upon philological knowledge as the one resource of Christian philosophy in all circumstances of difficulty for any of its interests, positive or negative. . . . He denounces development when dealing with the Newmanites; he relies on it when vaunting the functions of Philology. (*DQ* 8:295)

Philosophical development, as "a mode of development continually going on, and reversing the steps of past human follies," may also be swayed by ideological fashions and made to waver in its quest for the good, true, and beautiful. De Quincey is optimistic, however, that philosophy is, in the long run, a reliable handmaid of religion: "All the texts and all the cases remain at this hour just as they were for our ancestors; and our reverence for these texts is just as absolute as theirs; but we, applying lights of experience which *they* had not, construe these texts by a different logic" (*DQ* 8:297). The best evidence of philosophical development is found in social development.

As in his essay "On Christianity as an Organ of Political Movement," he argues the benevolent influence on social progress. Scriptural inspiration nourishes spiritual and, indirectly, intellectual development. The two, nevertheless, remain separate. While it stimulates the intellectual pursuits, the Bible neither reveals, nor can be countermanded by, scientific knowledge.

> It is an obligation resting upon the Bible, if it is to be consistent with itself, that it should *refuse* to teach science; and, if the Bible

ever *had* taught any one art, science, or process of life, capital doubts would have clouded our confidence in the authority of the book. By what caprice, it would have been asked, is a divine mission abandoned suddenly for a human mission. . . . *The Bible must not teach anything that man can teach himself.* Does a doctrine require a revelation? —then nobody but God *can* teach it. Does it require none? —then, in whatever case God has qualified man to do a thing for himself; he has in that very qualification silently laid an injunction upon man to do it. (*DQ* 8:282–83)[25]

De Quincey means thus to escape the religion-science controversy that Donaldson had seen looming as the "great theological crisis" of the age. Galileo's excommunication for having proposed a scientific alternative to biblical cosmology is a prime example of the bibliolator's fanatical literalism. The Bible does not dictate scientific facts; it works, rather, through spiritual inspiration to excite intellectual inquiry into the riddles of the material world. By giving primacy to spiritual inspiration over intellectual inquiry, De Quincey inverts the Kantian postulate. After summarizing how Kant successfully collapsed the physico-theological proof, the cosmological proof, and the ontological proof "to demonstrate the indemonstrability of God," De Quincey observes that with the "same *apodeixis*, which he had thus inexorably torn from reason under one manifestation, Kant himself restored to the reason in another (the *praktische vernunft*)." Kant affirms God as a necessary "postulate of the human reason, as speaking through the conscience and will, not proved *ostensively*, but indirectly proved as being *wanted* indispensably, and presupposed in other necessities of our human nature" (*DQ* 8:261–62).[26] For Kant, reason is the given, from which follows a subjective need, and therefore a moral duty, to assume the existence of God. For De Quincey, a "sympathy with the invisible" is the given, from which follows the injunction to explore the unknown as far as reason will allow.

Inspiration means much more to De Quincey than scriptural revelation. He refers to "the pervading *spirit* of God's revealed command," to the efficacy of "the direct voice of God, ventriloquising through secret whispers of man's conscience." Development, as the reflex or reciprocal counterpart of inspiration, "is not so much a light which Scripture throws out upon human life as inversely a light which human life and its eternal evolutions throw back upon Scripture" (*DQ* 8:300–301). Inspiration in-

25. De Quincey later elaborated this argument in "On the True Relations of the Bible to merely Human Science" (1854; *DQ* 8:35–41), a postscript to "System of the Heavens" (1846).
26. See Kant's *Kritik der reinen Vernunft*, in *Werke* 2:523–63, and *Kritik der praktischen Vernunft*, in *Werke* 4:254–64.

trudes upon consciousness as an irrational or suprarational presence. It may itself resist rational scrutiny, but it arouses the rational faculties, stimulating an activity of mind, like Wordsworth's "correspondent breeze," "vexing its own creation." In their reciprocity, inspiration and development bring about revelation, and revelation promulgates continuing interaction: "It cannot be the policy or true meaning of revelation to work towards any great purpose in man's destiny otherwise than through the co-agency of man's faculties, improved in the whole extent of their capacities" (*DQ* 8:307).

When De Quincey returns to Hume's attack on miracles, he reconciles what he had earlier called the internal and external miracles. The fragmentary manuscript "On Miracles" (7 June 1847) employs that mode of argument he had developed in his celebration of a "literature of power."[27] The biblical record was not intended as a "literature of knowledge"; its revelations excite the intuitive reason rather than convince the understanding. Hume was more right than he realized: miracles, however they are reported, bear no immediate relation to the event they pretend to describe. The appeal to probability and experience, the criteria by which we judge the credibility of a report, are irrelevant to the report of a miracle. The factors that compel us to believe that a given event is a miracle, Hume declares, compel us also to reject the likelihood that it occurred. He offers, therefore, a general maxim: "That no testimony is sufficient to establish a miracle, unless the testimony be of such a kind that its falsehood would be more miraculous, than the fact, which it endeavours to establish" (*Enquiry* 115–16). He means, of course, to leave the testimony of miracles trapped in paradox. De Quincey, with his new insight into inspiration and development, dissolves the paradox. The "falsehood" of testimony, as a kind of negative miracle, is no miracle at all, nor ever could be. The true miracle resides not in the event, but in the testimony. The event is only a moment; the testimony endures.

De Quincey questions the purpose of "presenting Christ alive forever." By insisting on the physical presence of "Christ's going about and doing good" and "showing what commands one sense or other," mystery is bereft of its spiritual relevance. Quoting Christ's reply to the Pharisees and Saducees when they desired "a sign from heaven" (Matt. 16:1–4), De Quincey asks, "What else is it than the case of 'a wicked and adulterous generation asking for a Sign'—laying such a stress on miracles?" ("On

---

27. Critics usually document De Quincey's distinction between the "literature of knowledge" and the "literature of power" as it is developed in "Letters to a Young Man" (1823), in *DQ* 10:46–52, and "The Poetry of Pope" (1848), in *DQ* 11:53–59; he also expands upon the distinction in "Cause of the Novel's Decline," in *PW* 1:302–5.

Miracles"; *PW* 1:174).[28] The purpose of a miracle is not to display physical power but to reveal moral truth. Were the Bible introduced in court, how could one use as evidence "the mere *facts* of the Gospel"? "Who knows anything of the contrivances, as to circumstances, persons, interests in which the whole narrative originated, or when? All is dark and dusty." The facts prove nothing. The miracle is the testimony, a means of saying what cannot be said: "Nothing in such a case *can* be proved but what shines by its own light. . . . Nay, God Himself could not attest a miracle, *but* (listen to this)—*but* (hear this my friend)—*but* by the internal revelation or visiting of the Spirit—to evade which, to dispense with which, a miracle is ever resorted to" ("On Miracles"; *PW* 1:175).[29]

The seemingly miraculous physical circumstances, then, are an evasion, a subterfuge, a sleight of God's hand. Or, if you prefer, an event "misapprehended" by the reporter. The real miracle is "the internal revelation or visiting of the Spirit." Thus he speculates on what would have happened at that moment when the priests were taunting, "Let Him come down from the cross," if Christ had actually descended. "They would have been stunned and confounded for the moment, not at all converted in heart. Their hatred to Christ was not built on their unbelief, but their unbelief on their hatred; and hatred would not have been mitigated by another (however astounding) miracle" ("On Miracles"; *PW* 1:174). No more than the priests are we, or anyone, apt to experience a profound change merely at witnessing some surprising physical event. Something else must happen. Many of the physical events, De Quincey suspects, have been transformed by testimony too powerfully moved by the experience to attend to mere facts. What if Christ cured by *process* rather than by word or touch? The testimony may, then, report the awe and admiration, "Since the *unity* given to the act of healing is probably (more probably than otherwise) but the figurative unity of the tendency to mythos." What happened to the multitude who followed Christ into the desert? Did they risk that journey with no thought of food or water? In his earlier reply to Hume, he had used this account as an example of the corroborated validity of many witnesses. Now he is quite willing to dismiss the physical circumstances as mere "gossip." Perhaps there was no physical miracle at all, but, instead, the more profound and invisible miracle of unselfish sharing. "Such again as the miracle of the loaves—so liable to be utterly gossip, so incapable of being watched or examined amongst a

28. Japp's transcription, *PW* 1:174, omits the opening paragraph, approximately fifty-three words, and alters the word order of the sentence with the quotation from Matthew 16:4.

29. Japp's transcription, *PW* 1:175, omits at the marked ellipsis 175 words (including the passage on the author's "mission" quoted at note 24, and a passage on the impossibility of demonstration in religion and the necessity of compromise in moral compliance).

crowd of 7000 people. Besides, were these people mad? The very fact which is said to have drawn Christ's pity—viz. their situation in the desert, surely cannot have escaped their own attention in going thither. Think of 7000 people rushing to a sort of destruction; for less than that, the mere inconvenience were not worthy of divine attention" ("On Miracles"; *PW* 1:174).[30] Physical miracles command awe. "How clearly do the villains betray their own hypocrisy about the divinity of Christianity, and at the same time the meanness of their own natures, who think the Messiah or God's Messenger must 1st prove his own commission by an act of power" ("On Miracles"; *PW* 1:176).[31] A philosophy of materialism and an ideology of power are at odds with religion as "a new revelation of moral forces." But what sort of religion is founded upon a display of power? Let Christ move a mountain: "This would have *coerced* people into believing." But it would not be a willing and spontaneous act of faith; indeed, it would be no belief at all. Whence came the power? By what agency? "This obstinately recurrent question remains," De Quincey says, and "the pretended belief would have left them just where they were as to any real belief in Christ."

Like Coleridge, then, De Quincey has defined the working of miracles as subjective. But for De Quincey the medium through which miracles are propagated is language. True testimony "shines by its own light." If counterfeited or falsified it betrays its own imposture: "Suppose the Gospels written 30 years after the events, and by ignorant superstitious men who have adopted the fables that old women had surrounded Christ with. How does this supposition vitiate their report of Christ's Parables? But, on the other hand, they could no more have invented the Parables than a man alleging a diamond mine could invent a diamond as attestation. The Parables prove themselves" ("On Miracles"; *PW* 1:176). Thus he can proclaim in a subsequent note that miracles, even the constituent miracles, have their efficacy in the intuitive "power" inherent in their narration. Verification as documentary evidence ceases to be relevant. He again takes as his topic the priests' mocking taunt at the crucifixion: " 'Let Him come down from the cross.' "

In this note De Quincey explains why the profound influence of the spiritual Resurrection could not have been accomplished by other means. A physical display, such as Christ's descending from the cross, would have failed to work, whereas the miracle of the disciples' testimony did

30. The multitude is numbered five thousand (not seven thousand) in Matthew 14:21, Mark 6:44, Luke 9:14, and John 6:10.

31. Japp, *PW* 1:176, has altered the wording here to soften De Quincey's denunciation of hypocrisy: instead of "How clearly do the villains," Japp has substituted: "How dearly do these people."

work, and continues to work, most effectively. It would fail, De Quincey explains, because "inverting the order of every true emanation from God, instead of growing and expanding for ever like a $<$, it would have attained its *maximum* at the first. The effect for the half-hour would have been prodigious, and from that moment when it began to flag it would degrade rapidly, until, in three days, a far fiercer hatred against Christ would have been moulded" ("On Miracles"; *PW* 1:177–78). In elaborating his argument from "On Miracles," De Quincey lays the ground for the necessity of a spiritual rather than a physical miracle by establishing that the animosity of the priests sprang only from Christ's presumption of spiritual leadership, not from any doubts of the acts attributed to him. Thus the physical miracle of descending from the cross would not eradicate lurking suspicions "that He was an impostor in the sense that He pretended to a power of miracles which in fact He had not." This had never been the source of their hatred. "The sense in which Christ had been an impostor for them was in assuming a commission, a spiritual embassy with appropriate functions, promises, prospects, to which He had not title." Greeted by the multitudes upon his arrival in Jerusalem, Christ commenced teaching in the temple, confuting the Sadducees, reproving the Pharisees. It was not for "miraculous impostorship" that the priests denounced him, but for "spiritual impostorship." So successful they were in spreading their antagonism, that the multitudes, given the choice, called for the release of Barabbas not of Christ. Coming down from the cross, then, would have been a stunning demonstration of power. The rivalry would be restored. The hatred would increase. No spiritual victory would be won. The indictment of Christ's "spiritual impostorship" could only be answered by a spiritual miracle, and that miracle is realized in "the sublimity of His moral system" ("On Miracles"; *PW* 1:178).

For both Coleridge and De Quincey, miracles work subjectively. Whereas Coleridge attempts to trace their apprehension through the intuition and the willing action of faith, De Quincey attends to the inspiration and development operating through language. Both emphasize the mediation of meaning through symbols; both define the symbol as combining identity with alterity; and both attribute to the symbol a capacity to represent the unknowable through the known. They agree that the alterity in the self-referential identity of biblical symbolism has its origin in the *theopneustia*, as word-embodied, word-transcending inspiration, and they devise similar schemes for reading symbols. While the practical reason compulsively pursues what lies beyond its boundaries, Coleridge states, an a priori intuition responds harmonically to the still unfathomed meaning. De Quincey describes a rational affinity with the irrational. He advocates a Higher Superstition, a "sympathy with the invisible," informed by intellectual curiosity rather than driven by taboo-ridden credulity. A symbol, for him, provides a convenient "midway station between the physical and hyperphysical" (*DQ* 8:410).

Although Coleridge's deliberations on miracles can be traced throughout his career, it was his reading in 1810 that shaped his argument on intuition and the *Logos*. De Quincey's examination of miracles belongs to a period thirty to thirty-five years later. Coleridge discovers in the Gospel of John a resolution to the pantheist dilemma he had encountered in Spinoza, Kant, and Schelling. In recalling his first meeting with Coleridge, De Quincey lapses into a diatribe against the "essentially destructive" influence of Kant, who, "let him say what he would in books," privately professes "the horrid Ghoulish creed" of atheism (*DQ* 2:155–56). Coleridge, of course, had also read Kant's *Tisch-Rede*, but responded very differently: "I can never without indignation read these most groundless attacks on Kant's System: which I distinguish from Kant's own personal opinions respecting Prayer & Miracles. But his System is most friendly to the Christian Faith—were it only, that it proves the utter worthlessness of all the Ground against its doctrines" (*M* 185–86).[32] De Quincey also grants as much to Kant (*DQ* 8:260–61), but he does not elaborate, as did Coleridge, the intuitive reason as the effective ground for refuting the Humean claim that the "philosophical testimony on which the truth of the miracle rests is historical, that is, experiential" (Coleridge, *Logic*, 191).[33] To counter Hume, Coleridge turns to the Gospel of John and interprets Christ's miracles in terms of the intersubjectivity of philosophical idealism. Following Newman, De Quincey emphasizes the reciprocity of inspiration

32. Coleridge's notes (ca. 1825–26) to Wilhelm De Wette, *Theodore oder des Zweiflers Weihe*, 2 vols. (Berlin, 1822): "There is nothing (says Kant) in right Reason *against* it—tho' Reason has no means of demonstrating its truth/ for this plain reason, that Religion is not *Science* but Faith!" (*Die Religion innerhalb der Grenzen der blossen Vernunft*, vol. 4, sec. 2, and Allgemeine Anmerkung, 264–65, 298–99, 302–8; prayer is "a superstitious delusion"; *Religion* III Allgemeine Anmerkung, 116–124, "it is pointless to question miracles or even interpret them; sensible people admit that miracles are possible, but act as if there were none." (*Marginalia* [=*M*2:185–60]. Cf *M* 2:184, 202, 204); also the marginal gloss to Edward Stillingfleet's assertion that "a *power of miracles* is the clearest *evidence* of a Divine *Testimony*." Stillingfleet *Origines Sacre* (London, 1675), in Brinkley 375–76.

33. On Hume's objection "to the truth of miracles," Coleridge, *Logic*, 191, wrote, "Here one constituent only of the judgment is the legitimate or possible object of experience. The other half, the miraculous substitute of the antecedent, is not the possible object of human experience and therefore not a legitimate object of human history. Nay, even though the supersensual A were admitted to exist, there would nevertheless result no right of asserting a causal connection between it and the phenomenon B: for *this* would be an act of the judgment; but the necessity in the *causal* connection is, according to Mr Hume, no act of the judgment, far rather, it is no act at all, but a mere *affection* of the animal sensibility, a passive *feeling*."

and development, with the argument that the progress of learning reveals more and more of the hidden mysteries of Christ's miracles. Although Coleridge, too, endorses a doctrine of historical development, he addresses that development primarily in terms of individual mind (*AR* 183).[34] De Quincey, however, observes a benevolent expansion of Christian ethics enlightening and transforming the culture as a whole. Confronting the failure of reason to reconcile the "it is" and "I am," Coleridge ultimately finds no better alternative than reliance on faith. Accepting supernatural mystery and the persuasive rhetoric of the irrational, De Quincey sought no better alternative.

34. *AR* 183: "Reason . . . either predetermines experience, or avails itself of a past experience to supersede its necessity in all future times; and affirms truths which no sense could perceive, nor experiment verify, nor experience confirm." On reason versus understanding, see *AR* 167–85, 344–45, and *Friend* 1:154–61.

3

THE AESTHETICS OF THE "OTHER HALF"

> . . . the feverish slumbers of the mind:
> The bubble floats before, the spectre stalks behind.
> —De Quincey, "Ode to Tranquillity," in *PW* 1:361

In November 1808, one year after his first meeting with Coleridge and Wordsworth, De Quincey became a resident at Allan Bank, where he remained for nearly four months while Coleridge was preparing *The Friend* for publication. Before returning, in November 1809, to occupy Dove Cottage, De Quincey helped see Wordsworth's *Convention of Cintra* through the press and endeavored to promote subscriptions for *The Friend* in London. Coleridge sought to enlist De Quincey's aid in another ambitious project, an examination of psychology and the senses. De Quincey was contemplating a study of the mind to be titled *De Emendatione Humani Intellectus*.[1] Coleridge, in a note on a theory of volition to be derived from sensory awareness, records his intention "To urge M^r De Quincey to execute my old plan of collecting from all the Transactions of Academies (Royal, Edinburgh, Berlin, Petersburgh, Paris, Madrid &c &c) Magazines, & Medical Books, Moritz &c &c all the facts relative to the Senses, and to psychology" (*CN* 3587). Although Kathleen Coburn offers no explanation of the "old plan" to which Coleridge here refers, she had previously observed that several notebook entries during the stay in Nether Stowey, in 1807 (*CN* 3071, 3072, 3074), are clearly related to Coleridge's marginalia in

---

1. Recounting his studies for this work in *Confessions of an English Opium-Eater*, De Quincey acknowledges the presumption in borrowing his title from Spinoza. See *DQ* 3:431.

Thomas Poole's set of the *Philosophical Transactions*. Coleridge failed to secure De Quincey's assistance in searching the medical and scientific journals. Although this "old plan," like many others, was never realized, it was neither abandoned nor forgotten.

The planned study of psychology and the senses is still echoed nine and ten years later when Coleridge lectured on the madness of Don Quixote (20 February 1818; 25 March 1819). As Reginald Foakes observes, Coleridge's account of the madness of Don Quixote follows the same scheme he had presented in his essay "The Soul and Its Organs of Sense" in section 174 of *Omniana, or Horae Otiosiores* (Coleridge and Southey 2:14–16). Coburn, too, refers to this brief essay in her commentary on Coleridge's notebook entries on the various kinds of madness (*CN* 3431, 3605). None of Coleridge's commentators has mentioned, however, that the categories of mental aberration set forth in "The Soul and Its Organs of Sense" are borrowed from Kant. It is not, however, Coleridge's source for these categories that interests me here, but how he relates the thresholds of madness to his discussion of "Outness," "Halfness," and the referentiality of symbols.

The two arguments Coleridge presents in "The Soul and Its Organs of Sense" may well seem unrelated. In the first, he claims that discourse which relies on a materialist vocabulary cannot persist long without contradicting itself. In the second, he argues that madness is properly understood as an imbalance of one of the major faculties. What holds these two arguments together is their shared premise "that the mind makes the sense, far more than the senses make the mind." In setting forth that premise, he reiterates his "old plan" to document a study of the senses and powers of mind with reports drawn from the *Philosophical Transactions* and other scientific proceedings: "If I have life and health, and leisure, I propose to compile (from the works, memoires, transactions, &c. of the different philosophical societies in Europe, from magazines, and the rich store of medical and psychological publications furnished by the English, French, and German press), all the essays and cases, that relate to the human faculties under unusual circumstances (for pathology is the crucible of physiology)" (*Omniana* §174). The first half of the essay is devoted to a refutation of the misguided attempts to explain biblical miracles with materialist arguments. With the same appeal to development that we examined in Chapter 2, Coleridge objects to the reductionist ends of natural religion and the failure to recognize that "the language of the scriptures is as strictly philosophical as that of the Newtonian system." The mistake is in trying to address the account of divine influence as if it were the historical record of material events. Scripture relies on the language of *appearance*. "And what other language," Coleridge asks, "would have been consistent with divine wisdom?" Neither the philosophy nor the science of biblical times made available a language which would not have been subsequently condemned as falsehood. And had a language been available which reached beyond the immediate historical context and "anticipated the terminology of the true system," it would have necessarily remained "without any revelation of the system itself, and so have become unintelligible to all men." Or grant that God might intervene upon centuries of scientific and philosophical striving and struggling to reveal "the true system," what then would become of the intellectual integrity of humanity? "Left nothing for the exercise, development, or reward of the human understanding," such an act of intervention would have usurped the benefits of intellectual inquiry "instead of teaching that moral knowledge, and enforcing those social and civic virtues, out of which the arts and sciences will spring up in due time, and of their own accord."

The language of the materialist must inevitably lapse into self-contradiction, for it has no means of acknowledging or addressing consciousness, whether individual, universal, or the "the common consciousness of man, as man." The language of mind, unfortunately, is also fallible. This is why Coleridge, with or without De Quincey's help, wants to organize a new psychology to be arranged according to "the different senses and powers":

> As the eye, the ear, the touch, &c; the imitative power, voluntary and automatic; the imagination, or shaping and modifying power; the fancy, or the aggregative and associative power; the understanding, or the regulative, substantiating, and realizing power; the speculative reason . . . *vis theoretica et scientifica*, or the power by which we produce, or aim to produce, unity, necessity, and universality in all our knowledge by the means of principles *a priori;* the will, or practical reason; the faculty of choice (*Germanicé, Willkühr*), and (distinct both from the moral will, and the choice) the sensation of volition, which I have found reason to include under the head of single and double touch.

Not only the divisions of the proposed psychology are Kantian, so, too, is the ensuing pathology. Kant had first outlined the species of madness in five installments in the *Königsbergsche Gelehrte und Politische Zeitung*. He later revised the pathology to conform to his critical philosophy.[2]

2. Kant, "Versuch über die Krankheiten des Kopfes," in the *Königsbergsche Gelehrte und Politische Zeitung*, in *Werke* 1:887–901; *Kritik der Urteilskraft* (1790, 1793), secs. 29, 42, 54, in *Werke* 5:363–71, 395–400, and 434–41; and *Anthropologie in pragmatischer Hinsicht* (1798), in *Werke* 6:462–66, 512–37.

Coleridge borrows from Kant's *Critique of Judgment* (1790) and the *Anthropology from a Pragmatic Vantage* (1798).

Kant recognized that because the mind gives structure and meaning to external phenomena, the disturbed mind distorts external phenomena. In his *Anthropology*, he describes how the five senses contribute to the inner sense, but also how the inner sense is subject to delusions and debilities. Admittedly, the *Anthropology* is a pastiche, more anecdotal than analytical, but as a pastiche it attempts to reassemble from his earlier writings a composite picture of human being, not as it has been formed by nature (the concern of a physical anthropology), but as it has shaped itself (it is this pragmatic approach that also enables Coleridge to declare that "pathology is the crucible of physiology"). Kant recapitulates, from the *Critique of Pure Reason*, his examination of the a priori categories and the ordering of the senses. From the *Critique of Judgment*, he repeats his concern with the modality of judgment and tensions of sensory response. And he reaches back to his early newspaper account to describe the debilities and diseases of the soul in respect to the mental powers.

In describing the disorders of the senses, the reason, the imagination, and the judgment (*Anthropologie*, secs. 42–50), Kant distinguishes between affect and passion (*Urteilskraft*, sec 29) both of which influence desires (*Anthropologie*, secs. 71–83). An affect, as "a surprise of sensation," is involuntary and blind; it defies rational deliberation and is generally incapable of relieving the feeling that prompted it. An affect of pleasure or pain cannot be suspended while the reason deliberates whether it should be indulged or avoided (*Anthropologie*, sec. 73). Driven by passion, the reason may be perverted; compelled by affect, the reason is incapable of willful choice. Two sorts of madness may thus influence the imagination, a madness of affect which produces the Enthusiast, or a madness of passion which is the malady of the Phantast (sec. 42). Similarly, when the senses are disrupted by an affect the result is Hypochondria, by a passion, Mania (sec. 47). Kant objects to the legal question "whether the plaintiff at the time of his act was in possession of his natural understanding and judgment" (sec. 48). Although he recognizes a madness of the understanding or judgment, he also argues that madness of the imagination or senses may leave the understanding and judgment unimpaired. For Kant the suspension or debility of the will is the crucial factor.

Those who project their own lust or anger onto external events and circumstances may well have full volitional control over their actions; their sickness is in exercising choices from subjective rules that are at odds with the objective rules of experience. A person overcome with an affect (such as those aversions or fears now known as "phobias") may be fully conscious that his response is irrational but still lack volitional control to resist its hold. Perception may be seduced by jealousy or rage: the victim sees what he chooses to see; perception may be influenced by affect: the victim is aware of the delusion but cannot dispel it. To his definition of the "Phantast," who habitually and deliberately substitutes imagination for experience, Kant adds the "Enthusiast," who is involuntarily subject to affects of rapture or delirium (*Urteilskraft*, sec. 29; *Anthropologie*, sec. 42). In the midst of imaginative play with aesthetic illusion (*Urteilskraft*, sec. 54), the artist may succumb to the spell he is trying to create. Pygmalion fell in love with the statue he was sculpting. The so-called *furor poeticus* ("dichterische Begeisterung") thus sweeps genius across the threshold of madness. Nor is the spell of the imagination easily broken: "A sustained attention to one and the same object leaves behind, as it were, its echo" (*Anthropologie*, sec. 44). An exciting tale holds the listener as powerfully as the Ancient Mariner's "glittering eye." When the spell is lifted, the listener is "distracted," not quite capable of controlling his attention to experience, still fascinated with the echoes of the enchantment that haunt the mind like an irrepressible melody. The danger of reading too many novels, Kant says, is that it makes distraction a habitual state of mind. Coleridge's advocacy of *poetic faith* as a "willing suspension of disbelief," Kant would have considered perilous. Continually surrendering to illusion, the reader's voluntary control gradually dissipates. The illusion of art is a waking dream that lulls the reason and will while the reader blindly follows the free play of imagination. The mind remains preoccupied by the illusion, neglecting its immediate surroundings (sec. 44).

Although Coleridge is intrigued by the subjective "pragmatism" in studying how one shapes his or her own mind, it should be noticed that in "The Soul and Its Organs of Sense," he avoids directly implicating a diseased will as source of madness. To be sure, he at one time calls for a "Gymnastic Medicine" for treating mental derangement by "forcing the Will & *motive faculties* into action." The will may be incapacitated by other disturbances of the mind. In order to identify and exercise the one malfunctioning faculty, "the genus Madness should be extended & more classes & species made" (*CN* 3431). This was the advantage he found in appropriating the Kantian division of the mental faculties:

> Thence I propose to make a new arrangement of madness, whether as defect, or as excess of any of these senses or faculties; and thus by appropriate cases to shew the difference between, I. a man, having lost his reason, but not his senses or understanding—that is, he sees things as other men see them; he adapts means to ends, as other men would adapt them, and not seldom, with more sagacity; but his final end is altogether irrational. II. His having lost

his wits, i.e. his understanding or judicial power; but not his reason, or the uses of his senses. Such was Don Quixote; and, therefore we love and reverence him, while we despise Hudibras. III. His being out of *his senses,* as is the case of the hypochondrist, to whom his limbs appear to be of glass. Granting that, all his conduct is both rational (or moral) and prudent; IV. or the case may be a combination of all three, though I doubt the existence of such a case; or any two of them; V, or lastly, it may be merely such an excess of sensation, as overpowers and suspends all; which is frenzy or raving madness.

Madness, according to this Kantian plan, is not a passive dementia, but an overcompensation in one of the mind's usual modes of relating the subjective and objective. The mind is accustomed to compensating for the limitations of its various faculties. Compensation and complementation are spontaneous. If one sense or faculty is baffled or impaired, another will be called to action. As an example of this compensatory activity, Coleridge cites the case of John Gough, the blind botanist of Kendal: "As to plants and flowers, the rapidity of his touch appears fully equal to that of sight; and the accuracy greater. Good heavens! it needs only to look at him . . . ! Why, his face sees all over! It is all one eye! I almost envied him: for the purity and excellence of his own nature." When the story of John Gough is told in Wordsworth's *Excursion* (*Poetical Works* 7:498–527), the Wanderer interprets his skill as proof "that faculties, which seem / Extinguished, do not, *therefore,* cease to be. / And to the mind among her powers of sense / This transfer is permitted." Coleridge, on the other hand, takes the very words from his "Soul and Its Organs of Sense" and gives them a macabre twist in "Limbo," when he describes the blind old man:

> his eyeless face all eye; —
> As 'twere an organ full of silent sight,
> His whole face seemeth to rejoice in light!
> Lip touching lip, all moveless, bust and limb—
> He seems to gaze on that which seems to gaze on him!
> (Ll. 26–30)

In contrast to a John Gough who seeks, acts, discovers, the blind man here is trapped in delusion and immobility. He only "seems" to participate in an exchange with nature. The sad fact is that both versions of this story substantiate the argument "that the mind makes the sense, far more than the senses make the mind." The "sense" that the mind makes, alas, may well be nonsense.

Essential to Coleridge's criticism is his assumption of aesthetic complementation. The synecdochal nature of art creates the illusion of a part fully representative of the whole.[3] Because of the constitutive nature of perception, the mind not only assembles the data of the senses but also fills in the missing details. This corrective activity becomes so habitual that it takes an optical experiment to remind us that there is a blind spot in the middle of our field of vision. Although perception itself is fragmentary, not until it is baffled by an optical illusion does the eye expose its own inadequacy and limitation. Precisely because complementation is habitual and spontaneous, Coleridge finds it necessary to isolate its peculiarities. He emphasizes, for example, the phenomenon of "double touch" to remind us that in rubbing our fingers across a surface we feel not only its texture, its roughness or smoothness, we feel also the sensation within our fingers. We feel the object, but we also feel our own feeling.[4] The tendency, he grants, is for consciousness to refer to the external cause. Attentive to the objects around us, we ignore the subjective processes. It takes an act of the will to turn awareness inward. Indeed, volition itself seems to have its origin in self-conscious reflexivity.[5]

Even as it excites the sense organs, the external stimulus also enables us to contemplate the processes of internal response. Key terms in Coleridge's exploration of the liminality of sensory awareness are "Halfness" and "Outness." One version of that "halfness" is evident in Wordsworth's celebration of this "mighty world of eye and ear, / Both what we half create and what perceive." Hesitation at the very threshold between mind and nature is a moment that frequently recurs in romantic poetry. In sorting out which half belongs to mind, which to something beyond it, Coleridge borrowed Berkeley's concept of "Outness" to help discriminate the confusions of "Halfness." "Outness," for Berkeley, referred to a capacity of spatial orientation not immediately derived from sense-data alone.[6] Coleridge works with both these concepts in defining *symbol*.

3. According to Plato, *Theaetetus*, 204–5, the whole is greater than the sum of the parts; according to Aristotle, *Politics*, 1.2.1253a, the whole is prior to the parts. Also see McFarland, "Fragmented Modalities and the Criteria of Romanticism," in *Forms of Ruin* 3–55, and Marjorie Levinson, *The Romantic Fragment Poem*.

4. *CN* 3:4046n; Coburn cross-references additional accounts of "double Touch": *CN* 1:1039, 1188, 1827; *CN* 2:2399, 2402, 2405.

5. Karl Christian Wolfart, *Mesmerismus*, vol. 2, flyleaf, and 2:188; cited in Coleridge, *Philosophical Lectures*, 432–34. Coleridge speculated that by concentrating mental effort and exercising "earnestness of Volition," mesmerism involved processes akin to sensory response "& will confirm my long long ago theory of Volition as a mode of *double Touch*."

6. George Berkeley, *An Essay Towards a New Theory of Vision*, *A Treatise Concerning the Principles of Human Knowledge*, part 1, sec. 43, in *Works* 1:55–56, 93, and 1:176–77; see also Kathleen Coburn's note to *CN* 3325.

Because the mind applies its leverage to external events only in terms of "Halfness," art, too, must work its effects by halves. Coleridge defines the symbol as something that is at once itself "& its *Other half.*"

> All minds must think by some *symbols*—the strongest minds possess the most vivid Symbols in the Imagination—yet this ingenerates a *want, pothon, disiderium,* for vividness of Symbol: which something that is *without,* that has the property of *Outness* (a word which Berkeley preferred to "Externality") can alone gratify/ even that indeed not fully—for the utmost is only an approximation to that absolute *Union,* which the soul sensible of its imperfection in itself, of its *Halfness,* yearns after, whenever it exists free from meaner passions . . . every generous mind not already filled by some one of these passions feels its *Halfness*—it cannot *think* without a symbol—neither can it *live* without something that is to be at once its Symbol & its *Other half.* (*CN* 3325, May 1808)

Convinced that the only adequate response to art depends upon an awareness of what is not inherent in, but simply evoked by and external to, the work, he develops critical strategies to verify the *outness* of an art object and to justify the "half-faith" in its illusions.

In desynonymizing illusion and delusion, Coleridge declared that the latter depends on the failure of the understanding to discriminate the representation from reality, whereas the former allows the mind to appreciate the thing represented with full awareness of its mode of representation. Don Quixote's madness results from his delusion in entering into the fictions of knight errantry as if they were reality. Illusion, by contrast, requires a conscious act of will. In order to define "poetic faith" as the "willing suspension of disbelief for the moment," it is necessary for Coleridge to consider the will, the act of volition, in terms of the primacy of mind over matter. As Kant had explained it, all striving of mind toward matter is born of desire, and the will arises from the self-conscious reflexes of desire. When Coleridge addresses "the higher Volition" as "das obere Begehrungs-vermögen" (the same notebook entry in which he proposes that De Quincey might "execute my old plan"), he is responding not to Kant but to Fichte.[7] The *Begehrungsvermögen,* for Kant, is the capacity of mind, through its own representations, to become the cause of the reality of these representations. We propagate certain images as a way of indulging our desire for the object the images represent. Desire may also arouse that choice and determination of reason which Kant called the will

7. *CN* 3587, July–September 1809; *M* 2:639–40.

or "das obere Begehrungsvermögen."[8] Fichte elaborated the Kantian concept of the will as rational desire by making it the ground of divine revelation.

Is it possible, Fichte asked, that the willful representations of desire might be acts of delusion rather than illusion? He proposes to investigate "whether the consciousness of self-activity occurring in willing may not perhaps deceive us."[9] The implications, as Coleridge saw, were irreverent and demeaning. Creativity would be debased as a deliberate self-indulgence: "Surely, to the highest Wollen, viz. the *Creative* act, it would be contradictory as well as irreverend to attribute ein Begehrungsvermögen? This is no trifling error; but a vice in the first concoction, according to which there would be no *will* at all, but a mere impulse, differing from the total mechanism of the mind only as the Current of a River from the River" (*M* 2:640). Even in granting it the self-consciousness of reason, the will thus derived from desire seems caught in the mechanism of stimulus and response. What is necessary, Coleridge claims, is to transform the self-centered constraints, so that "Self becomes evanescent, or transfigured" and the will, "aided by Grace," becomes "perfectly free" (*M* 2:642). Coleridge agrees with Fichte's distinction between natural and revealed religion, and even with his claim that both, indeed all forms of religion, have their basis in sensuous needs, as in the "*want, pothon, disiderium,* for vividness of Symbol." How the need for vividness is fulfilled, however, requires further discrimination. Illusions may be engendered by desire, but how are they felt or perceived? The illusions of natural and revealed religion are not perceived in the same way: "Surely that the one is conscious, that it is an illusion, and the other thinks the illusion (not <as> the vehicle or inward metaphor of the Truth, but) the true Reality itself, —surely this makes a distinction." Coleridge's language here is similar to his discussion of illusion and delusion, but rather than discriminating conscious awareness from deception, he sets that illusion which the mind knows it has created itself apart from that illusion it knows has been revealed to it. The one is an "inward metaphor of the Truth"; the other reveals "the true Reality itself."

The problem remains, of course, that what we thus deem to be a revelation of "the true Reality" may be self-deception. Fichte himself can only give subjective reinforcement to the illusion of objective reality: "A determination of the faculty of desire [*Begehrungsvermögen*] drives us to choose a positive judgment." Recognizing the solipsistic trap of Fichte's

---

8. "Vorrede," in *Kritik der praktischen Vernunft,* in *Werke* 4:114; *Kritik der Urteilskraft,* sec. 10, in *Werke,* 5:299.

9. Johann Gottlieb Fichte, *Versuch einer Kritik aller Offenbarung;* Coleridge, *M* 2:639–46.

claim that we can therefore confidently "yield to this determination," Coleridge again insists on the awareness of illusion as illusion. A capacity to experience revelation objectively and subjectively at the same time is what keeps the experience from lapsing into hallucination and delusion. This does not mean that revelation may appear only as a pale shadow, a weakly glimmering will o' the wisp: "Surely there is no impossibility (however improbable it may be) that the Holy Spirit may give the Soul an intellectual Intuition, equal to—'I see.'" When the gift of intuition is received with faith, "a willing suspension of disbelief," the revelation may appear vivid and powerful. Even with all the *outness* of "I see," we still know that the illusory presence is possible only because it is "conjoined with a *positive* waking Faith" (*M* 2:644).

The power of the symbol resides in its ability to reveal in its vivid "Outness" the truth of the "Other Half" that lies beyond. The difficulty is that to the uninitiated the pretensions to such power look very much like madness—"Beware! Beware! / His flashing eyes, his floating hair!" Given as he was to hallucinations, Coleridge had decided to record them in his notebooks "as a weapon against superstition." He came to this decision while on Malta, upon seeing the phantom image of Robert Dennison seated in an empty chair (*CN* 2583, 12 May 1805). A few years later, while he was struggling to prepare his first series of Shakespeare lectures in his little room above the *Courier* office, he saw the wallpaper momentarily open into a passageway (*CN* 3280, 23 March 1808). On both of these occasions, Coleridge claimed that he could restore his rational control and avoid the irrational confusion of the hallucination with reality. But he was not always able to avoid the confusion. What really happened at the Queen's Head "that dreadful Saturday morning" (*CN* 2975, 27 December 1806)? "But a half a minute with ME—and all that time evidently *restless & going*—An hour and more with . . . <Wordsworth> *in bed*—O agony!" (*CN* 3328). Whatever had prompted his vision of forbidden intimacy between Wordsworth and Sarah Hutchinson, Coleridge was utterly incapable of sorting out illusion and delusion. With its "strange power to represent the events & circumstances even to the Anguish or the triumph of the *quasi*-credent Soul," the imagination may override the judgment. He thus refers to the "Strange Self-power in the Imagination, when painful sensations have made it their Interpreter," and confesses his inability to control its images: "Did I *believe* it? Did I not even *know,* that it *was* not so, *could* not be so? . . . Yes! Yes! I *knew* the horrid phantasm to be a mere phantasm: and yet what anguish, what gnawings of despair, what throbbings and lancinations of positive Jealousy!" (*CN* 3547; cf. 3148, 3236).

In his notes on Coleridge's lecture on Cervantes (20 February 1818),

Henry Crabb Robinson complained that "his digressions on the nature of insanity were carried too far" (*LL* 2:157). The complaint may have been justified if Coleridge had introduced his "old plan" only as a digression, as a psychological scheme obliquely relevant to the diagnosis of Quixote's madness as an excess of imagination and a deficiency of judgment. In fact, as he stressed in his outline for his lecture the following year (25 March 1819), Coleridge intended to demonstrate the connection between "madness and its different sorts—(considered without pretension to medical science); and the nature and eminence of Symbolical Writing." As Coleridge sees it, Cervantes thematized in the adventures of the knight of La Mancha the dilemma of all encounter with symbols.

Symbol-making tends to become pathological to the degree that we forget the symbols in a desire to confirm the "Other Half" which symbols merely mediate. Humor, Coleridge declares, "consists in a certain reference to the General, and the Universal, by which the finite great is brought into identity with the Little, or the Little with the <Finite> Great, so as to make both *nothing* by comparison with the Infinite." Humor works through juxtaposition and evokes a sense of the "ridiculously disproportionate." A symbol, however, even as it mediates through its own finitude the presence of something far more vast, attempts to reconcile the difference, to reveal itself as an essential part of the larger whole. The most immediate example to explain the presence of the infinite within the finite, Coleridge says, is the mind itself: "The Mind, the *idea* of the World, &c is *sine finibus*—subjectively infinite" (*LL* 2:417). The concept of mind, therefore, "leads us at once to the Symbolical, which cannot perhaps be better defined, in distinction from the Allegorical, than that it is always itself a *part* of that of the whole of which it is representative."

Because allegory and symbol are distinguished by the mental processes through which they are engendered, Coleridge sets them apart in much the same terms as fancy and imagination (*BL* 1:304–5). Although the similitudes of allegory are always "spoken consciously," "it is very possible that *the general truth* represented may be working unconsciously in the Poet's mind during the construction of the symbol—yet proves itself by being produced out of his own mind." The symbol is not wrought with full rational control. The conscious mind merely lends, as it were, a word to mediate that which works unconsciously. The proof of that unity of the unconscious in the conscious, the infinite in the finite, is the symbol itself. Thus we behold the creation of "Don Quixote out of the perfectly sane mind of Cervantes." The rational representation of the irrational, Coleridge argues, is not created "historically" or by "outward observation," but by revealing what lies hidden in the unconscious. "The advantage of symbolical writing over allegory," he says, is "that it presumes no disjunction of Faculty," but only "simple predomination" (*LL* 2:418). But madness, too, asserts itself through predomination rather than disjunction.

It is in this context of explaining the symbolic function of Cervantes's narrative that Coleridge again presents the scheme of his "old plan": "Madness—1. Hypochondriasis, or out of his *senses*—2. Derangement of the Understanding, or out of his Wits—3. & Loss of reason—4. Frenzy— or derangement of *the Sensations*" (*LL* 2:418).[10] Don Quixote is not only himself a symbol, he enacts the symbol-making process in his hallucinatory transformation of the material world: "In these day-dreams the greater part of the History passes & is carried on *in Words* & look forward to *Words* as what will be said of them." By allowing us to see now from the vantage of Sancho, now through the eyes of Quixote, Cervantes shows how the real world is transformed into the imaginary world of chivalric romance. That "real world," of course, is itself only the illusion of Cervantes's art. Within that illusion he conjures the delusion of Quixote's mind. At the beginning of his tale, Cervantes depicts the gradual foment of delusion in Quixote's "colloquies with the village priest and the barber surgeon." The purpose, Coleridge says, is to show how "the fervour of critical controversy feeds the passion and gives reality to its object." Madness, as an exacerbation of one of the mental faculties, causes that faculty to respond in excess. Instead of the usual progression of observation and inquiry, the mind becomes preoccupied then obsessed with one idée fixe. "What more natural," Coleridge asks, "than that the mental striving should become an eddy? —madness may perhaps be defined as the circling stream which should be progressive and adaptive" (*LL* 2:161).

As example of the illusion of delusion, Coleridge reads from the account of Quixote first sallying forth, inventing as he goes the history of his own past deeds and transforming the landscape into the visible record of that imaginary history: "how happily already is the abstraction from the senses, from observation, and the consequent confusion of the Judgement, marked in this description—. The Knight is describing objects *im-*

10. Cf. *LL* 2:164–65 (*New Times*, 23 February 1818): "Here the lecturer entered into some curious remarks on madness, which he distinguished into four species: —1st, Frenzy, wherein the whole physical and mental organisation is disturbed—2d. Hypochondriasis, wherein a man is *out of his senses*, feeling as if he were made of glass, or as if his nose was too big to enter a door, etc.—3d, Fatuity, where a man *loses his reason*, and can no more argue on cases and consequences than an infant—And, 4thly, such madness as that of *Don Quixote*, where the senses are perfect, and the reason faculty is accurate enough; but the man is totally mistaken in his judgment. Grant him but one assumption and every thing he does is not only reasonable, but admirable. Admit that *Don Quixote* really lived in an age of Knight Errantry, that the Inn was a Castle, and the Windmill a Giant: and Alexander or Julius Caesar could not have behaved with more true courage, or more noble magnimity."

mediate to his senses & sensations without borrowing a single trait from either." Even the practical-minded Sancho learns how to engage these imaginative transformations. When Sancho tells the story of the three hundred goats, then leaves Quixote the task of completing the story by counting the imaginary herd as they are ferried one by one across the river, he deliberately makes a game of the transformations which Quixote has compulsively played all along. "O how admirable a symbol," Coleridge exclaims, "of the dependence of all *copula* on the higher powers of the mind" (*LL* 2:419).

Cervantes has thus made his hero a symbol of the transforming power of the mind and has also given him, in the symbol-making of his mad adventures, the quixotic quest to realize the "Other Half." The halfness of Quixote's character is portrayed in two different ways: On the one hand, he is at once himself and the self-image of his madness, "the imaginary Being, he is *acting*." On the other, he is but half a character, not complete without his counterpart Sancho: "Put him and his master together, and they form a perfect intellect; but they are separated and without cement; and hence each having a need of the other for its own completeness, each has at time a mastery over the other" (*LL* 2:162). Cervantes prepares for a dialogue between "the language of *appearances*" and "the language of materialism": "Don Quixote's leanness and featureliness are happy exponents of the excess of the formative or imaginative in him, contrasted with Sancho's plump rotundity, and recipiency of external impression" (*LL* 2:160). Nor was it enough for Cervantes to cast common sense and imagination in the roles of *eiron* and *alazon*, he also saw to it that they constantly exchanged roles: "These two characters possess the world, alternately and interchangeably the cheater and the cheated." Coleridge observes the ironic subtleties as Cervantes manipulates the reader through the paradoxes of a madness induced by reading too many books, and he cites, as "contrast between the Madness of Imagination and that of Passion," the passage in which Cardenio tells Quixote that "that great villain master Elizabat lay with Queen Madasima" (2:419). Inside the book, we have reference to another book; and the book-mad character Quixote leaps to defend the character in the other book as if she were real. At the same time, however, he is also defending his interpretation of the other book. Certainly the character in the book he has read behaved in no such way. The aesthetic experience is confounded with the critical, the passionate with the imaginative.

This confusion, however, is not just the symptom of Quixote's madness. It is in the nature of a symbol to provoke confusion between the intuition and the practical reason. In its very liminality, a symbol serves the intellectual quest for certainty as well as the fascination with the unknown. Art, as art, always involves illusion. Themes of madness, aesthetic illusions of delusion, enable the artist to explore the constitutive faculties of the mind gone awry. In developing a theory of poetic creativity that called for the mind to transcend the finite and to participate in the "Infinite I AM," Coleridge imposed upon himself, and all others who have tried to make use of his theory, the task of rendering that flight of the primary imagination intelligible to the rational world. Coleridge himself placed the burden on the secondary imagination. To fulfill the task of reconciling opposites, the symbol had the special function of revealing the infinite within the finite. Complaining that a truth made too concrete is made too small, Coleridge argued that the known must be pushed as far as possible into the unknown. Thus the symbol wavers ambiguously on the brink of irrationality.

In the notebook draft of the essay "On Certainty" (*CN* 3592, August–September 1809; cf. *Friend* 1:104–5, 2:71), Coleridge explains why illusion, not delusion, is crucial to art. The contest between Parrhasius and Zeuxis, as recounted by Pliny, was judged according to the criterion of delusion: that work of art was deemed best which tricked the viewer into mistaking it for reality (Pliny 9.310–11). Coleridge asserts, however, that "even in the Imitative Arts, that are supposed to have their being in fiction, a well-disciplined mind is offended by actual Delusion." Illusion allows us to see what is represented with full awareness that it is a representation. Because the mind is intrigued rather than cheated, the experience may be sustained: "The meanest Taste finds its pleasure in a painted marble Apple or Peach exhausted after it has been once or twice seen and handled—while the Fruit-piece of some eminent Dutch Painter which had never appeared to him other than a picture will give him increased pleasure in proportion as he can be induced to look at and think of it." Aesthetic illusion excites the curiosity and sends the mind in search of explanation. The mind, Coleridge assumes, instinctively pursues a "sufficient ground." The very energy the mind expends in grappling with perceptions provides a "sense of Power" and also "supplies the conviction, that there is a certain ground." Whereas the delight in the Dutch still-life may derive from the illusion of "Outness," Coleridge valorizes not the illusion but the mental quest that makes the illusion possible. "It is not the desire of attaching *Outness,* an *externality* to our representations which is at the bottom of this Instinct <the Instinctive Pursuit of a sufficient ground>; on the contrary this very attachment of Outness originates in this Instinct—But it is to possess *a ground* to know a fixed Cause generating a certain reason." Although the mind always seeks certainty, certainty is itself illusory. The knowledge of truth toward which we strive always eludes our mortal comprehension. "For now we see through a glass, darkly; but then face to face; now I know in part; but then I shall know even as also I am known" (1 Cor. 13:12). Certainty, then, is a religious as well as philosophical ideal: "The very end and Final bliss of the glorified Spirit is represented as a plain aspect, an intuitive Beholding of Truth in its eternal and immutable Source." The instinctive quest for certainty can only "betray itself" in the delusion that it has found what it can only seek.

The real, no less than the ideal, is removed from the immediate grasp of the mind. Coleridge could not, like Marlowe's Dr. Faustus, "Bid *on kai me on* farewell" (I.i.12). Nor did he deem it possible to separate being from not-being. Any representation of the ontic is inevitably engulfed in the meontic.[11] Being, he observed, could claim no primacy as a ground of certainty. If not like Faustus, then very much like Kant, Coleridge placed objective being at a noumenal distance beyond the ken of phenomenal experience: "Our Senses in no way acquaint us with Things, as they are in and of themselves: that the properties, which we attribute to Things without us, yea, that this very *Outness*, are not strictly properties of the things themselves, but either constituents or modifications of our own minds" (*CN* 3605; August–September 1809). Empirical perception, "blended with the sense of real Presence," Coleridge distinguishes from "a renewal of this by the memory or in the imagination, with or without an act of will" (*CN* 3605). Although Coleridge seems here to reiterate the Kantian distinction between empirical and subjective *Vorstellungen*,[12] he claims for the latter what Kant attributed only to the former: a mental presence equivalent to "I see." Even in the empirical moment of "I see," perception is half created by mind. In conjuring perceptual "renewal," art may solicit an illusion of the "other half" and thus give to absent images the power of presence.

To perform such conjuration, art must rely on symbol. But symbol is by no means the exclusive property of artists or poets. In the well-known distinction between symbol and allegory in *The Statesman's Manual* (1816), Coleridge deliberately prescinds the symbol from its familiar rhetorical and literary context. A symbol, as he defines it, is no mere trope: "By a symbol I mean, not a metaphor or allegory or any other figure of speech or form of fancy, but an actual and essential part of that, the whole of which it represents" (*LS* 79). As we have seen, he used this very formulation in his lecture on Don Quixote when he described the symbol as "always itself a *part* of that of the whole of which it is representative"

11. On ὄντα and μή ὄντα, see Plato, *Sophist*, 263d, and Plotinus, *Ennead*, 6:8–9. See Heidegger, on the ontic, *Sein und Zeit*, secs. 3–4; McFarland on the meontic, in *Forms of Ruin* 384–418.

12. Kant, *Kritik der reinen Vernunft*, in *Werke* 2:97–98, 325.

(25 March 1819; *LL* 2:417). In notebook entries as early as 1810, Coleridge attributed to the symbol a capacity to mediate conscious awareness of the elusive "other half." By 1811, he was prepared to posit, not just mediation, but actual participation in the noumenon.

By extending the concept of "language" to include "whatever accompanies any perception, act, or sensation," Coleridge was able to talk about "How the human Soul *is* affected" by these "*logoi*" which communicate "directly to the spirit with whom they are conjoined, and mediately to any other whom it communes with." In speculating on how a language of the soul might operate through "symbolical effluxes" of perceptions and sensations, he ponders the possibility that accompanying this symbolic intercourse there might be "actual effluences" hidden to human sensation and perception. Just as the physics of attraction and repulsion act upon matter, are essential to its "conceivability," yet remain "incompatible with *materiality*," so too might invisible forces operate on the human psyche. As did Schelling in his *Naturphilosophie* (*Sämtliche Werke*, vol. 2), Coleridge speculates whether the energy evident in the polarities of attraction and repulsion might not "have some analogy or ratio to all other spiritual Being" (*CN* 3810; May 1810).

The problem with a secret intercourse of "actual effluences" beyond a language of "symbolical effluxes" is not just that it necessarily remains meaningless to the conscious mind, but that the mind can receive such "effluences" only passively. Because he insists on an active and willing engagement, Coleridge must rely upon the language of consciously perceived symbols. He succeeds in overcoming the limited notion of symbolic mediation by confronting the paradox of wholeness—a paradox clearly descended from temporal and spatial paradoxes of Zeno of Elea:

> Now it is absolutely impossible to think of a material Universe, or even of a world of spirits, as an aggregate of separate Finites, under the idea of *a Whole*—we might say, These are all that there are—but never these are all that there *can* be—and why not more? If in basic attempts to answer this latter question, the imagination goes on adding, and if to hide from itself its perpetual failure, & to evade the perpetual recurrence of the same question, why not more yet?—it takes the salto mortale, and vaults at once into the transcendental Idea, of Infinity—yet still how can this Infinity of Finites be *a Whole*? To be *a Whole* it must in some sense or other *be one*. Totality is Multitude participating of Unity. *A World* therefore in order to be a World (*cosmos, Universum*) supposes a god—an infinite *one*—*one* not by participation, or union, but one essentially—and infinite not by an infinity of finite parts,

but absolutely infinite.—Now to *conceive* this is impossible—but to assume it is necessary. (*CN* 4047; January 1811)

A "finite whole" thus becomes a contradiction in terms. An oak tree is not a whole distinct from the organic processes that contribute to its being.[13] It stands not separate and apart from the soil, rain, and sunshine which nourish it, nor from the seasons which regulate its growth, nor from the acorn whence it germinated, nor from the parent oak of that acorn. The circumstances by which its being is constituted are so integrated into the infinite web of causality that the "wholeness" of the oak baffles comprehension. Yet the visible oak tree participates in that wholeness and effectively communicates its being to the beholder. To recognize the oak, however, it is necessary to abstract general characteristics and criteria. We formulate a universal idea, in which any given oak may participate. Coleridge offers the example of "a mathematical Circle" as "the *Idea*, to which we *regulate* all material or imaginable circular Objects." We cannot construct a "perfect circle," yet even if we could, it is unlikely that our meager senses, "thro' which alone we receive all knowledge of reality, could distinguish it from a thousand figures, each less circular than the other" (*CN* 4047).[14]

Both the noumenal and the phenomenal are thus caught in the paradox of the whole: the external object exists only in and through an infinite web of causal factors; the subjective idea may be manipulated in endless permutations.[15] As he phrased it in his lecture on Don Quixote, "the Mind,

13. The concept "organic whole" refers to form as process, growth, and change, not to form as fixed and finite. For the relationship between organicism and vitalism in Coleridge's thought, see J. H. Haeger, "Samuel Taylor Coleridge and the Romantic Background to Bergson," in *Crisis in Modernism*. In *Theory of Life*, according to Haeger, "Coleridge sought to show that what biological science might interpret as an evolution of life forms resulting from progressively higher and more complex combinations and structures of organic matter was in reality the manifestation of *a priori* force."

14. As evidence of the constitutive nature of cognition, Coleridge collected numerous examples of the mind's capacity to project geometric shapes onto external reality. Such an example is the one, first recorded by Reimarus, of the triangular patterns to be observed in the whirling flight of ephemerae: "Emphemerae . . . by the exceeding velocity of motion actually present to our eyes a symbol of what Plotinus meant when, speaking of the geometricians and then of Nature as acting geometrically, he says θεωρουσα θεωρηματα ποιει, her contemplative act is creative and is one with the product of the contemplation" (*Logic* 74). Coleridge refers to Plotinus, *Ennead*, 3.8.4; quoted again in *Logic* 245, and *BL* 1:173.

15. *CN* 4058 (March–April 1811): "In explaining all into one it is not sufficient to have detected some one character common to all—it is necessary to manifest, *that* they all & *how* they all, spring out of this one. Else we substantialize generalization, not much wiser than those who worshipped the Goddess, Multitudo. We must therefore minutely examine, each in all its manifestations, as far as we can . . . for ever be this my Motto/ 'When I

the *idea* of the World, &c is *sine finibus*—subjectively infinite" (*LL* 2:417). But what is the mind to do with ideas that dilate unto infinity? Is not infinity just as apt to "tease us out of thought, / As doth eternity"? Clearly it was necessary for Coleridge to seek some compromise between a materialist vocabulary (denounced in "The Soul and Its Organs of Sense" as doomed to self-contradiction) and the inanity of infinite referentiality. Rather than surrender to the anarchy of inane diffuseness, he enfranchised a "despotism in symbols" (*CL* 4:836). Symbols enabled him to anchor ideas in finite experience.

A symbol hovers liminally between the finite and the infinite. Like the images of imagination, it is at once "*in* us" and "*out* of us." The image (or ειδολον) of sensory perception lacks this liminality. Because the visual image excites a sense of presence, we attend only to its *outness*. The imagination, at least for the sane mind, is always conscious of its own activity: its images are both *in* and *out*. Coleridge speculates on the capacity of imagination to project its images: "Definites, be they Sounds or Images, . . . must be thought of either as being or as capable of being, *out* of us. Nay, is not this faulty?—for an Imagination quod Imagination cannot be thought of as capable of being out of us? Answer. No. For while we imagine, we never do think thus. We always think of it as an *it*, & intimately mix the Thing & the Symbol" (*CN* 4058, March–April 1811). Following Kant's distinction between empirical and subjective *Vorstellungen*, Coleridge separates "Definites combined with the sense of their real presence" from "Definites combined with a sense of their Absence." Unlike Kant, as we have noted, he allows for an easy interchange from the sense of presence to absence: "To have an Ειδολον & to notice it, two very different Things/ when we notice it, we compare, & judge, & thus inoculating it with our own activity we make an *Idea* of it." The ειδολον has the multistability of an optical illusion, such as the Necker cube, that seems to change shape as we behold it. So, too, may any image of perception change as we shift attention from the empirical awareness of its *outness* to the bodily sensations and mental structures that constitute our perception.

Coleridge's sense of multistability is evident, as well, in his first deliberations on the imagination as opposed to the fancy. Because it responds passively to images as objects, the fancy remains detached, its images lifeless. The imagination, by contrast, actively enters into and animates

---

worship, let me unify; but qui bene distinguit, bene *docet*.' To be wise I must know all things as *One*; to be knowing I must perceive the absolutely indivisible as infinitely distinguishable. And this holds from the Universe to a Grape-cluster/ even as the human Intellect in the infinite divisibility of matter attributes the same infinity of component parts to a Grain of Sand as to a System of Worlds/ & Infinites of Infinites/ we *understand* them not."

its images. The former have only inanimate "outness"; the latter share a sensory intimacy with the beholder as being *"in* us" as well as *"out* of us."

> The image-forming or rather re-forming power, the imagination in its passive sense, which I would rather call Fancy . . . may not inaptly be compared to the Gorgon Head, which *looked* death into every thing—and this not by accident, but by the nature of the faculty itself, the province of which is to give consciousness to the Subject by presenting to it its conceptions *objectively* but the Soul differences itself from any other Soul for the purposes of symbolical knowledge by *form* or body only—but all form as body, i.e. as shape, & not as forma efformans, is dead—Life may be *inferred,* even as intelligence is from black marks on white paper—but the black marks themselves *are truly "the* dead letter." Here then is the error—not in the faculty itself, without which there would be no *fixation,* consequently, no distinct perception or conception, but in the gross idolatry of those who abuse it, & make that the goal & end which should be only a means of arriving at it. Is it any excuse to him who treats a living being as inanimate Body, that we cannot arrive at the knowledge of the living Being but thro' the Body which is its Symbol & outward & visible Sign? (*CN* 4066, April 1811)

To regard the bodies around us as more than a welter of outward things, we must somehow respond to the inward and informing life. It is this "fusing power" of intersubjectivity, Coleridge says, which gives to "poetic Imagination" its "worth & dignity." Through symbol-making a human being may nourish humanitarian benevolence. The fancy merely "fixes" the image in its "outness." The imagination in "fixing unfixes & while it melts & bedims the Image, still leaves in the Soul its living meaning" (*CN* 4066).

In a subsequent notebook entry, perhaps of the following day, Coleridge continues his thoughts on the vacillation of "fixed" and "unfixed" images. While "feelings seem, to *organize* themselves into Images," an image acquires "<perfect> Individuality" only in objective detachment. The very sensibility which accompanies the "fusing power" thus "bedims the image": "the more *Feeling* & less *Image,* the more substance yet the less Individuality." There is, of course, a possible synthesis, "a certain middle state where there is a *particular,* and yet not quite a definite, sharply-outlined *Individual"* (*CN* 4068, April 1811). He had previously observed that the mystics, in order to open their minds to religious raptures, had nurtured a "state midway between mere Reason, and mere sensuality" (*CN* 3937, June–July 1810; cf. *CN* 3973, September 1810). Al-though sensual indulgence tends to unlimn the image, it nevertheless makes it more immediate. We sacrifice clarity of outline, "a necessary condition of *distance*," in order to gain intimacy and presence. This is the advantage of the amorphous: even though you cannot touch a millionth part of the ocean, you seem to feel the whole in the moment of immer-sion; or "when you take a bit of Jelly mass you know, you touch only that bit, and yet you somehow or other seem to touch the *whole*" (CN 4068). Similarly, because it invites sensual as well as rational response, the sym-bol opens into the whole, even though it is of that whole only a part.[16]

The capacity to convert sense-data into self-reflexive ideas, or to pro-ject an idea outward as if it were a part of an exterior reality provides the multistable flexibility of mind that Coleridge calls upon in that "willing suspension of disbelief for the moment which constitutes poetic faith." We are thus able "to transfer from our inward nature . . . a semblance of truth," which enables us to animate the inanimate or engage absent things as if they were present (*BL* 2:7). Quixote's madness, as Coleridge explained it, arose from a lack of conscious control over the mind's multi-stability. Hamlet's madness, too, he attributed to a loss of that essential flexibility in alternating between the inward and outward sense. Accord-ing to Coleridge's "old plan," Quixote, deprived of understanding or judg-ment, treated internal ideas as if they belonged to external reality. Ham-let, too, suffers a debility of judgment, but he gives priority to the internal over the external. In interpreting Hamlet's response to his mother, "'Seems', Madam! nay it is; I know not 'seems'" (I.ii.76–86), Coleridge di-agnoses the pathology: "The aversion to externals, the betrayed Habit of brooding over the world within him, and the prodigality of beautiful words, which are as it were the half embodyings of Thought, that make them more than Thought, give them an outness, a reality sui generis and yet retain their correspondence and shadowy approach to the Images and Movement within" (*LL* 1:540). Hamlet dismisses outward actions as mere semblance and disguise "that a man might play." He chooses to rely, in-stead, on the *outness* of his inward thoughts: "I have that within which passeth show." No less than Quixote, Hamlet has lost the ability to bal-ance the inward and outward modes of perception.

The ability of mind to project its images or to give animate vitality to

16. *CN* 4253 (May 1815): "Symbols = 'the whole, yet of the whole a part'—P. Fletcher's Purple Island." Coburn, in her note to this entry, quotes the pertinent passage from Phineas Fletcher ("which like an index briefly should impart / The sum of all; the whole, yet of the whole a part." *The Purple Island*, canto 1, stanza 43) and observes that the reference to *Symbols* is Coleridge's, not Fletcher's.

images in the subjective theater of consciousness, is in itself sound and healthy.[17] Pathological is the loss of conscious and volitional control of this mental activity in our waking experience. Coleridge, as we have seen, was personally chary of those momentary lapses in which "the *quasi-credent* Soul" is deluded by the "strange self-power in the Imagination" (*CN* 3537). Such moments, he insisted, are not necessarily pathological. We all experience a sort of madness in dreams, as well as in that state between waking and sleeping.

As Coleridge writes in *The Friend*, it is no wonder that the midnight hour is "*the true witching time.*" Susceptible to "those rapid alternations of the sleeping with the half-waking state," the mind becomes "the fruitful matrix of Ghosts." The encounter between Hamlet and the Ghost of his father is set at midnight, "the season / Wherein the spirit held his wont to walk" (I.iv.5–6). Hamlet is thus introduced at the very threshold between the rational and the irrational. He succumbs to the lure of the "other half." Even Luther, Coleridge observes, was subject to such spells:

> I see nothing improbable, that in some one of those momentary slumbers, into which the suspension of all Thought in the perplexity of intense thinking so often passes; Luther should have had a full view of the Room in which he was sitting, of his writing Table and all the Implements of Study, as they really existed, and at the same time a brain-image of the Devil, vivid enough to have acquired apparent *Outness,* and a distance regulated by the proportion of its distinctness to that of the objects really impressed on the outward senses. (*Friend* 1:140)

Tossing an ink-pot at the devil, then, was no symbolic gesture in the moment of action. It might well become symbol, however, in subsequent reflection, once the hallucination is overcome and the multistability of mind is restored.

There may be more truth than jest in Coleridge's retort that he had seen too many ghosts to believe in them. He was nevertheless steadfast in insisting that the supernatural deserved, rather than belief, "a willing suspension of disbelief." Thus in the *Biographia Literaria* he confidently celebrates the triumph of reason over the irrational intrusions of the supernatural: "Of all intellectual power, that of superiority to the fear of the invisible world is most dazzling. Its influence is abundantly proved by one circumstance, that it can bribe us into a voluntary submission of our better knowledge, into suspension of all our judgment derived from con-

17. Wordsworth similarly recommends a salubrious interchange of inward and outward intellectual activity in "Reply to Mathetes," in *Prose Works* 2:14.

stant experience, and enable us to peruse with the liveliest interest the wildest tales of ghosts, wizards, genii, and secret talismans" (*BL* 2:217–18). Coleridge, however, did not mean to imply that intruders from the "other half" could no longer invade the mind. He merely states that the intellect has the power to distance itself from "the invisible world" with such confidence that it can reenter it, through "a willing suspension of disbelief," with equanimity. Supernatural forces might nevertheless prey on the unwary. Such forces, however, do not belong to the rational or the visible world. As meontic images of the "other half," they are ipso facto irrational. Without contradicting his confidence in intellectual "superiority to the fear of the invisible world," Coleridge also entertained the possibility that "a departed Spirit" might "act on an embodied Spirit" and "produce in the Brain a corresponding Appearance, which in proportion to the vividness of the impression will have apparent *outness.*" While such an intrusion may well occur, Coleridge is quick to add, "the Beholder of the Ghost (on *this* theory) admits, that he was *not in his Senses* at the time" (*LS* 81).

Although it would serve as well as a gloss to Hamlet's insistence, "Nay it is; I know not 'seems,'" it was in response to Schelling's argument on sense perception that Coleridge penned the marginal note on "it is" versus "it seems": "The *Sense* can only say, It seems; that 'it *is*', is a decision of the Reason, judging, by the instrument of the Understanding, or the phaenomena according to their participation of its own constituent attributes. . . . Experience is—the Reduction of the notices of the Senses to the a priori Forms of the Understanding" (marginalia to Schelling in *LS* 18). As R. J. White has pointed out, this same distinction between "it is" and "it seems" is repeated in a note added in 1827 to *The Statesman's Manual.* Coleridge asserts that an "act of faith" is the necessary "copula" to all possible knowledge:

> I mean that but for the confidence which we place in the assertions of reason and conscience, we could have no certainty of the reality and actual outness of the material world. It might be answered that in what we call 'sleep' every one has a dream of his own; and that in what we call 'awake', whole communities dream nearly alike. It is!—is a sense of reason: the senses can only say—It seems! (*LS* 18)

This, of course, is an obvious conclusion for a constitutive theory of cognition. Just as Coleridge stipulates a "poetic faith" as requisite to the aesthetic experience of the "other half," he claims that an "act of faith" is equally necessary to the experience of reality. The conditional "certainty" that distinguishes waking from dreaming, reality from fantasy, is provided by the reason. To enter into the dreamworld where the River Alph spills forth from Xanadu, down the romantic chasm and on to the sunless sea, we willingly engage an illusion of delusion, a rational construct of irrationality. We consciously control that multistability of mind that enables us "intimately <to> mix the Thing & the Symbol" (*CN* 4058).

As a poet of fragments and disrupted visions, Coleridge built a large province of his poetry amid unsaid words, and he offered various apologies for incompleteness. The person from Porlock disrupted the poet in the midst of writing down his dream of "Kubla Khan." While he privately claimed that personal suffering from the satirical attack in Charles Lloyd's *Edmund Oliver* (1798) "prevented my finishing the Christabel" (*CN* 4006), he publicly stated, "I have only my own indolence to blame." The introductory stanzas to "The Blossoming of the Solitary Date-Tree" were lost, he said, when the first page of the manuscript was torn away. His poems are not only presented as the remains of something lost, they are about that lostness. The poet of "Kubla Khan" seeks to revive the lost "symphony and song" of the Abyssinian maid and thereby to rebuild the vanished "pleasure dome." The solitary date-tree is disquieted by the very incompleteness of its own rich imagination and aches with a longing for the missing "other half."

Much of his critical theory is concerned with retrieving what merely lurks, allusively and elusively, in the remnants of language. He defines the symbol as the tool for seeking out and interpreting the hidden other half of utterance. Although it transcends the rational and may well partake of the irrational, the symbol is nevertheless a tool of reason. Indeed, it is the only tool that allows us to gain intellectual leverage on the world beyond the range of our phenomenal experience. The danger is in failing to maintain the conscious and willing control over the symbol-making process, in allowing ourselves to become, like Quixote or Hamlet, victims to "the invisible powers of our nature, whose immediate presence is disclosed to our inner sense" (*Friend* 1:172).[18] Properly used, it reveals the living character of an otherwise unknowable and inaccessible world. It allows the universal to appear in the particular, the whole in the part—"*Forma formans per formam formatam translucens*" (*BL* 2:215).[19]

18. *Friend* 1:172: "What the eye beholds the hand strives to reach; what it reaches, it conquers and makes the instrument of further conquest. We can be subdued by that alone which is analogous in kind to that by which we subdue: therefore by the invisible powers of our nature, whose immediate presence is disclosed to our inner sense, and only as the symbols and language of which all shapes and modifications of matter become formidable to us."

19. *LS* 30: "A Symbol (ὁ ἔστιν ἀεὶ ταυτηγόρικον) is characterized by a translucence of the

An aesthetics of the "other half" is essential, for art, both in its creation and its reception, is a yearning for completion. The great frustrations and the great joys in life derive from life's paradoxical progress by halves. We learn to make a virtue of necessity. That the "Half" may thus "become better than whole," prompts Coleridge on one occasion to compile a tentative list with the pledge "To note down the instances as they suggest themselves," wherein we may readily acknowledge the advantages of halfness: a "Marriage bed," for example, or "the Parson's Sermon" (*CN* 3680, January–February 1810).

For better or worse, the poet remains only half in control of the making and shaping of the' literary text. The "other half," beyond the reach of rational deliberation, may well taint the whole with the ferment of irrationality, a "dilemma of the mad rhapsodist," which has been made, self-reflexively, the very subject-matter of literature.

Special in the Individual or of the General in Especial or of the Universal in the General. Above all by the translucence of the Eternal through and in the Temporal. It always partakes of the Reality which it renders intelligible; and while it enunciates the whole, abides itself as a living part in that Unity, of which it is the representative."

PART II
Narratives of Madness

4

IRRATIONALITY IN GOETHE'S
TORQUATO TASSO

As a classical trope, the *furor poeticus* allowed the poet to claim sources of inspiration beyond the province of mere human reason. A contrary tradition, upheld by Horace, insisted on "clear understanding" as the primary requisite for good writing, and the elder Seneca scorned the notion of poetry "ready-made" in a fit of frenzy.[1] Through the Reformation and Counter-Reformation, the claims of divine inspiration were variously praised as personal revelation or denounced as blasphemy, Satanism, or lunacy. Whatever its provenance, the visionary gift brought no blessing to those recipients persecuted by the Inquisition. The debate concerning the nature of inspiration thus persisted through the Renaissance[2] and took still another ideological turn in Enlightenment aesthetics, when "poetic madness" justified a resistance to the dictates of rational authority.

Early in his career, Goethe participated in the "cult of genius" and asserted its claims for inspiration from beyond the boundaries of reason. Throughout this period, such works as "Von deutscher Baukunst" and "Prometheus" proclaim the advantages of an irrepressible enthusiasm in artistic creativity. In the Weimar period, Goethe began to emphasize, in-

1. Horace, *Epistles*, 2.3.295–301, ridicules would-be poets who think by their eccentricity they will gain the entry into Hélcion which Democritus denied to the "sane-minded poet." The doctrine of "divine frenzy" is also denounced by the elder Seneca, *Prologue*, 1ff., and *Suasoriae*, 3.7, but defended by the younger Seneca, *Epistolae Morales*, 84.1–7.

2. In Scaliger's *Poetica* (1561), the poet is referred to as "another god" ("alter deus"); in Ficino's *Theologia Platonica* (1576), as a "god upon earth" ("est utique deus in terris"). Marsilio Ficino, *Theologia Platonica*, 16.6, in *Opera* (Basiliae, 1576), 1:295, and Julius Caesar Scaliger, *Poetica* (1561); both quoted in V. Rüfener, "Homo secundus deus."

stead, the values of classical order. The opposition of two aesthetic ideals, originality and passion versus tradition and reason, inform plot and character in several works completed after his return to Weimar from his Italian journey. In *Torquato Tasso*, Goethe thematizes and problematizes the pretenses of the *furor poeticus* in relation to the structure of classical drama and the strictures of classical poetics.

Goethe found these dramatic tensions between the rational and irrational, the classic and romantic, readily available in his source materials. Tasso himself, in composing *La Gerusalemme liberata*, had struggled with the opposing demands of epic and romance, history and fantasy. He labored too with his religious themes, anxious of critical judgment but also fearful of the Inquisition. His confinement for madness is often taken as evidence of a turmoil of reason and passion that he could not control, and many critics have claimed that Tasso also failed to reconcile these extremes in his epic poem. It is no wonder, then, that *La Gerusalemme liberata* has aroused controversy since it first appeared.

Most critics concede that Goethe's dramatic portrait of Torquato Tasso as the "mad" poet in the court of Alfonso II in Ferrara bears little biographical similarity to Goethe's own experience in the court of Carl August in Weimar. Goethe himself, however, declared that he had combined attributes of his own life with that of Tasso.[3] Many circumstances in the play suggest that Goethe intended his account of Tasso's passion and paranoia in a courtly world of rivalry and intrigue to critique the contemporary plight of the poet. Unlike his Tasso, who laments that the Duke excludes him from any serious consideration of the affairs of state, Goethe achieved prominence in the Weimar court precisely because he was an astute counselor as well as gifted poet. Tasso's anxieties, however, about measuring himself against the great poets of the past and about the reception of his own endeavors in the midst of political turmoil are anxieties that Goethe may well have shared.

The pathology that weakens Tasso's character Goethe attributes to a poetic imagination not balanced by an adequate practical understanding. As he explained the play to Caroline Herder, *Tasso* dramatizes "die Dis-

---

3. *Gespräche mit Goethe* (6 May 1827): "Ich hatte das *Leben* Tassos, ich hatte mein eigenes Leben, und indem ich zwei so wunderliche Figuren mit ihren Eigenheiten zusammen warf, entstand in mir das Bild des Tasso, dem ich, als prosaischen Kontrast, den Antonio entgegenstellte, wozu es mir auch nicht an Vorbildern fehlte. Die weiteren Hof-, Lebens- und Liebesverhältnisse waren übrigens in Weimar wie in Ferrara, und ich kann mit Recht von meiner Darstellung sagen: sie ist Bein von meinem Bein und Fleisch von meinem Fleisch." That he sought to merge his own experience with that of Tasso was not a belated afterthought; he made the same assertion at the time of composition: "Meine Absicht ist, meinen Geist mit dem Charakter und den Schicksalen dieses Dichters zu füllen." *Italienische Reise* (28 March 1788); quoted in Hans Gerhard Gräf, *Goethe über seine Dichtungen*, 4:302.

proportion des Talents mit dem Leben."[4] Tasso has nourished his fantasy in solitude, as the other characters often remind us, and is ill at ease in society. Faust diagnosed his own psychological dilemma as the antagonism between worldly and spiritual inclinations: "Two souls, alas! reside within my breast, / And each withdraws from, and repels, the other" [Zwei Seelen wohnen, ach, in meiner Brust! / Die eine will sich von der andern trennen, 1112–13]. The split of the human being into two opposing halves is externalized in the characters of Antonio and Tasso. Each possesses attributes the other lacks. The shrewd statesman and the sensitive poet, as Leonore observes, are "in opposition because nature / Failed to make one man out of both of them" [darum Feinde . . . , weil die Natur / Nicht einen Mann aus ihnen beiden formte, III.ii].

The action in *Torquato Tasso* is minimal: the poet presents his finished draft of *La Gerusalemme liberata* to the Duke in act 1; in act 4 he wants it back; in act 2 he quarrels with Antonio, the Duke's secretary of state, and rashly draws his sword; in act 5 he is no sooner released from house arrest than he again trespasses propriety by passionately embracing Princess Leonore d'Este, the Duke's sister. With the exception of the symbolic bestowal of the wreaths in act 1, these are the only moments of overt action, but they effectively mark the dramatic tensions affecting Tasso's poetic creativity and his role at court. Even though he is pampered, he must satisfy the Duke's expectations by providing a worthy "ornament" of his art. He may mingle freely with court nobility, but he must recognize his subservient place in the courtly hierarchy. In *La Gerusalemme liberata*, the poet could project himself into the hero and the lover. In reality (as represented in the two major incidents of Goethe's play), he fails miserably in either role.

Tasso is admired by Princess Leonore d'Este and Countess Leonore Sanvitale (referred to as Princess and Leonore in Goethe's play). The Princess confesses that she loves him and feels herself attracted to him in spite of herself:

> To love a thing I had to treasure it:
> I had to love it for its power to make
> My life a life such as I'd never known.
> At first I said: avoid him, keep away!
> I did draw back, yet with each step drew closer,
> So sweetly lured, and so severely punished.[5]

4. Caroline Herder to Herder, between 16 and 20 March 1789: "Ich habe die Fortsetzung von 'Tasso' wieder abgeschrieben. Goethe kam dazu. . . . Von diesem Stück sagte er mir im Vertrauen den eigentlichen Sinn. Es ist die Disproportion des Talents mit dem Leben." Quoted in Gräf, *Goethe über seine Dichtungen*, 4:309.

5. The German text is quoted from the Hamburg edition of Goethe's *Werke*; the English

She makes clear, however, that it is a Platonic love of "Entbehren" (II.i; III.ii). Necessary to that deliberately imposed renunciation, she must disassociate the poet from his poetry. If she must acknowledge an irresistible attraction, it must not be for the man but for the art that he produces. Even in her confession to Leonore, she describes her love for "a thing," not for a vital and passionate person. Leonore, however, is not one to adopt self-denial or "Entbehren" as a way of life. "Do you love him then?" she asks herself, "If not, what is it that make you so unwilling / To do without him?" Her motive, she admits only in monologue, is to lure him to her court in Florence, where she imagines that, just as Petrarch immortalized Laura, Tasso will immortalize her in song (III.iii). The quarrel with Antonio, who chides him as a dreamer, is a breaking point for Tasso's already exacerbated sensibility. In return for the comfort and support the Duke has lavishly provided, he must return a suitable poem in tribute and honor to his patron. Tasso wants his gift to be perfect, yet he no sooner gives it than he begins to worry about its imperfections. His self-recriminations make him all the more sensitive to the criticism of others. Already inclined, as the other characters reveal by recalling his previous behavior, to suspect dark plots at work against him, he begins to imagine that his friends have turned to enemies and are set on his utter ruin.

The historical Tasso charged himself with heresy and fled from his confinement under Alfonso II. After years of wandering, he returned in 1579 to the court of Ferrara, where he was again imprisoned for his frenzied accusations during the celebrations that Alfonso had prepared for his bride, Margherita Gonzaga. During the seven years of his incarceration for apparent insanity in the hospital of Sant' Anna, he continued to revise *La Gerusalemme liberata*, but he also wrote several philosophical dialogues, which established his reputation as literary theorist and critic. To these years of his confinement belong *Cavaletta, or On Tuscan Poetry* (1585), *Gianluca, or On Masks* (1585), and *Discourse on the Art of the Dialogue* (1585), as well as *Malpiglio, or On the Court* (1585), in which he insinuates how malevolent intrigues may be hidden by the very dazzle and splendor of courtly life. After regaining his freedom in 1586, Tasso was

---

text is from Michael Hamburger's translation for the Suhrkamp edition. Goethe, *Torquato Tasso*, III.ii.1887–92:

> Ihn mußt ich ehren, darum liebt ich ihn;
> Ich mußt' ihn lieben, weil mit ihm mein Leben
> Zum Leben ward, wie ich es nie gekannt.
> Erst sagt' ich mir: entferne dich von ihm!
> Ich wich und wich, und kam nur immer näher,
> So lieblich angelockt, so hart bestraft!

granted sanctuary at the court of Duke Vincenzo Gonzaga in Mantua, where he completed *Il re Torrismondo* before returning to his restless wandering. Following the publication of his *Discourses on the Poetic Art* (1590), he went on to elaborate his critical tenets in *Discourses on the Heroic Poem* (1594). The reactionary religious temperament of the Inquisition did not make it easy to satisfy ecclesiastic authority during the Counter-Reformation. Eager that his account of the Crusades would gain church approval, Tasso brought forth a revised version of his epic, *La Gerusalemme conquistata* (1593). His religious epic, *Sette Giornate del Mondo Creato* (1594), was intended to win the favor of Pope Clement VIII.

Goethe shifts the emphasis away from the religious preoccupation, although he does have Tasso declare his need to go to Rome to consult his friends in correcting his poem. More important to Goethe is the poet's inability to convince his courtly audience of the high accomplishment of his art. In adapting his historical sources, Goethe subtracts some ten years from Tasso's age, not so much to lend the impetuosity of youth to the poet's forbidden love for the Duke's sister, but rather to excuse his inexperience with the wiles of the court. Dismissing Tasso's brash expectations of instant friendship, the reserved statesman rebukes the poet as a spoiled child accustomed to having his way:

> With full sails you drive on! And it would seem
> You're used to winning battles.
>
> . . . .
>
> So, the too hasty boy should take by storm
> The confidence and friendship of a man?[6]

Goethe needs this harsh voice of repudiation, for the theater audience might otherwise lose all sympathy with the petulant and sulking "hero" of this play. Antonio betrays enough envious pique and haughtiness for the audience to take Tasso's side against him, in spite of the partial truth in Antonio's scorn for Tasso's behavior.

When Goethe began his composition of *Tasso* in 1780, he relied on the biography by Giovanni Battista Manso, which attributed Tasso's madness to his unrequited love. The Ur-Tasso was, no doubt, a character much like Werther. Before completing the play in 1789, Goethe had read the

6. Goethe, *Torquato Tasso*, II.iii.1287–88, 1362–63:
> Du gehst mit vollen Segeln! Scheint es doch,
> Du bist gewohnt, zu siegen.
>
> . . . .
>
> Der übereilte Knabe will des Manns
> Vertraun und Freundschaft mit Gewalt ertrotzen?

new and more historically accurate biography by the Abbate Pierantonio Serassi, which presented evidence of the conflict with Antonio Montecatino.[7] In weaving together these two accounts of Tasso's mental duress, Goethe neglected neither Tasso's poetry, nor Tasso's poetic principles.

In his *Discorsi del Poema Eroica* Tasso conscientiously documents his poetic principles with references to Plato and Aristotle, Cicero and Horace, and with passages cited from Homer and Virgil. Nevertheless, he is far from endorsing a revival of Greek or Roman classicism. In defining *mimesis* as an imitation of "human and divine action," for example, he modifies Aristotle to include the supernatural and the marvelous. *Mimesis* for Aristotle required a replication in art not simply of the external consequences, the *praxis,* but, more important, of the subjective springs of action in deliberating and choosing, the *dianoia.* Tasso, however, wants the poet to attend more extensively to subjective processes. Poetry cannot imitate the divine except through the human sense of the marvelous. Adapting from Aristotle and Horace, Tasso declares that "the epic poem is an imitation of a noble action, great and perfect, narrated in the loftiest verse, with the purpose of moving the mind to wonder and thus being useful."[8]

During the *quattrocento,* as C. P. Brand reminds us, the Italian epic appropriated and elaborated the magic and enchantment of the chivalrous romances. Religious and patriotic fervor were replaced by whimsy and sensual indulgence. Pulci's *Morgante* (1486), Boiardo's *Orlando Innamorato* (1494), and Ariosto's *Orlando Furioso* (1516–32) fully exploited the romantic motifs of passionate love and fantastic adventure, yet they did so with an aloof irony that remains fully conscious of its own wild fictions. Educated amid the humanist zeal to reclaim the classical models, Tasso's generation turned to Homer and Virgil and criticized Pulci and Ariosto for their disorder and lack of seriousness.[9] Schooled in Aristotle's *Poetics* and Horace's *Ars Poetica*, Tasso intended to give his epic poem the structure and solemnity that his predecessors had neglected. The problem was, of course, that he was himself far too fond of chivalric romance to subordinate adventure and enchantment in his narrative.

In order to preserve the integrity of the Crusades and the Christian

7. Giovanni Battista Manso, *La Vita di Torquato Tasso* (Venice, 1621); Abate Pierantonio Serassi, *La Vita di Torquato Tasso* (Rome, 1785; Bergamo, 1790). In his *Italienische Reise* (28 March 1788) Goethe records: "Ich lese jetzt das Leben des Tasso, das *Abbate Serassi* und zwar recht gut geschrieben hat." Gräf, *Goethe über seine Dichtungen*, 4:302. See also H. G. Haile, *Artist in Chrysalis*, 187–89.

8. *Discourses on the Heroic Poem*, 10, 17.

9. Brand, *Torquato Tasso*, 57–59.

ideals of his heroes, Tasso could not assume the kind of ironic detachment that enabled Ariosto to tell of Orlando's mad passion without implicating narrator and reader in the emotional turmoil of the romance. Although by no means infected by Orlando's demon, as Giambattista Marino suggested in his sonnet,[10] Tasso does indeed conjure with madness, and his narrative strategy is to make that madness participatory. The reader, no less than the characters, is caught up in the confusion and misperceptions in the poet's frequent scenes of deception and disguise, as when Erminia dons the garb of Clorinda (canto 6), or a mutilated corpse is dressed in the armor of Rinaldo (canto 8). Ismén's conjuring in the haunted forest (canto 13) and the vision in the Hermit's cave of Armida enticing Rinaldo with her sexual allures (canto 14) are difficult to reduce to a strictly allegorical interpretation.[11] Although they may well represent the temptation and evil that distract the wavering Christian from his religious duty, the erotic and the marvelous have a narrative vitality of their own. Tasso may seem to lack Ariosto's fecund imagination, but unlike Ariosto, his magic seems real. His characters feel their experiences with a palpable intensity. His enchantments may not have the splendor of Ariosto's, but his spells are more binding, precisely because they reflect fantasies and deceptions familiar to the reader from the real world.

This is not to deny the confounding of historical reality with the charms of romance in the *Liberata*, but rather to suggest that the heroic epic serves as vehicle for Tasso's desire to master and manipulate the flirtations and intrigues of the court. The Christian vicissitudes of the Crusades and the promised redemption of Christ are made more, not less, relevant by introducing a seductive temptress and a magic castle. In cre-

---

10. Joseph Tusiani, in the introduction to his translation of *Jerusalem Delivered*, 17, quotes from Giambattista Marino, "Torquato Tasso":

> Raising at last my trumpet for a more
> melodious sound, as Ariosto has done,
> I sang of arms and battles, knights and war.
> O cruel destiny! To imitate
> the Furioso's genius and his song,
> I shared the madness of Orlando's fate.

11. Although Tasso's *Allegoria della Gerusalemme liberata*, written in 1575 and appended to the poem as published by Feba Bonnà in 1581, does provide an allegorical reading of his own poem, it is by no means an adequate and satisfactory interpretation. Rather, it reveals the poet's concern in defending the orthodoxy of his religious and political ideas. As is evident in his *Discourses on the Heroic Poem*, Tasso preferred not to isolate allegory as an independent mode of poetry. He endorses, instead, Dante's discrimination of fourfold meaning: literal, moral, allegorical, and anagogic. The first is directed to the understanding, the second teaches, the latter two modes of poetic discourse are directed to the intellect, stimulating speculation on worldly and on spiritual matters (153).

ating Clorinda, Armida, and Ermina, Tasso may well have appropriated directly from his perception of feminine roles in court. Although there is no evidence to support the contention that the poet expressed his own forbidden attraction to the Duke's sister in the highly charged eroticism of Rinaldo's embrace of Armida (canto 16), biographers did indeed record that Tasso had dared to embrace the Princess. Although Goethe develops a multifaceted account of the poet's madness, the romantic poets tended to see Tasso's imprisonment as punishment for his rebellion against aristocratic authority.

The Romantic Reception

The reception of Tasso through the ensuing centuries perpetuated the legend of the poet who strove to perfect the classical epic but succumbed to the disorder of his own irrepressible fits of inspiration, whose reason was overwhelmed by passion and paranoia. The romantic critics, who contributed to that legend in the decades immediately following Goethe's *Torquato Tasso*, explored the ambiguities of the poet's seeming paranoia: was Tasso the victim of his own unbridled imagination?

Not according to Byron's account in his "Lament of Tasso." Confined in his cell at Saint Anna's Hospital, the defiant Tasso inveighs against the duplicity and cruelty of his oppressors.

> Long years! —It tries the thrilling frame to bear
> And eagle-spirit of a child of Song—
> Long years of outrage, calumny, and wrong;
> Imputed madness, prison'd solitude,
> And the mind's canker in its savage mood,
> When the impatient thirst of light and air
> Parches the heart; and the abhorred grate,
> Marring the sunbeams with its hideous shade,
> Works through the throbbing eyeball to the brain,
> With a hot sense of heaviness and pain.
>
> (1–10)

Although his confinement to a madman's cell might in itself have left the "taint" of "long infection," his refusal to recant, he says, enables him to hold on to his sanity. Even if they have failed to control his mind and dictate his thoughts, Tasso, by his own declaration, has been transformed. He feels the changes working within his brain:

> Yet do I feel at times my mind decline,
> But with a sense of its decay . . .
>
> (189–90)

> I once was quick in feeling—that is o'er;
> My scars are callous, or I should have dash'd
> My brain against these bars . . .
>
> (208–10)

As part of his strategy to hold on to his sanity, according to Byron's fiction, Tasso passed the hours in his cell composing his *Liberata*.

> For I have battled with mine agony;
> And made me wings wherewith to overfly
> The narrow circus of my dungeon wall,
> And freed the Holy Sepulchre from thrall;
> And revell'd among men and things divine,
> And pour'd my spirit over Palestine,
> In honour of the sacred war for Him.
>
> (21–27)

But once this "pleasant task is done," his thoughts are left to brood on his own fate while the cries of madmen ring from the adjoining cells (65–75).

He was once, he claims, a poet of love, who saw love permeating all things and who found its ideal in the person of Leonore d'Este.

> I knew my state, my station, and I knew
> A Princess was no love-mate for a bard;
> I told it not, I breathed it not, it was
> Sufficient to itself, its own reward;
> And if my eyes reveal'd it, they, alas!
> Were punished by the silentness of thine,
> And yet I did not venture to repine.
> Thou wert to me a crystal-girded shrine,
> Worshipped at holy distance
>
> (122–30)

He does not explicitly blame her for having betrayed him, but even his declarations of love seem perversely accusatory: "They call'd me mad—and why? / Oh, Leonora! wilt not *thou* reply?" (48–49). Byron's Tasso, as Regina Hewitt has observed, may well be an assertive romantic rebel against tyranny;[12] nevertheless, he remains entangled in that masculine ideology which distances women from practical involvement in the concerns of state.

Idealizing is a strategy of marginalizing. In her "crystal-girded shrine," the Princess is effectively removed from the political action of court. Paradoxically, as "Sister of my Sovereign," she remains identified with the tyrannical authority that has conspired against him: "Thy brother hates— but I cannot detest; / Thou pitiest not—but I cannot forsake" (109–10). She is at once removed from, yet implicated in, the punishment that has befallen him. She was "ashamed / That such as I could love"; she "blush'd to hear / To less than monarchs that thou couldst be dear" (228–29).

The "Lament" closes with a prophecy in which Tasso foretells the doom that awaits the Duke and his sister. When the Duke's realm and "hearthless halls" have crumbled, the poet's cell will be visited as "a future temple" (219–27). And long after "all that Birth and Beauty throws / Of magic round thee is extinct," he says of the Princess, she will be remembered only for the love she inspired in the poet:

> No power in death can tear our names apart,
> As none in life could rend thee from my heart.
> Yes, Leonora! it shall be our fate
> To be entwined for ever—but too late!
>
> (244–47)

Byron's Tasso has made the fiction of aristocratic superiority parallel the fiction of the ideal female. With his focus on the former, neither Byron nor his Tasso seems to comprehend that the concluding lines, as Kari Lokke has described them, "sound more like a threat or a curse than an expression of love."[13]

Just as Byron made Tasso into a Byronic hero, Shelley planned a tragedy of a persecuted Shelleyan poet. The tribulations of Tasso would not be an unlikely subject for the poet who described the agony of Prometheus, the untimely death of Adonais, and even portrayed his own sad plight as one who falls on the thorns of life and bleeds. Indeed, for many of Shelley's critics, the "atrocious assassination" which he claimed to have escaped at Tanenyenrallt in February 1813, would be proper evidence that he had enough firsthand experience with paranoic delusions to write with some insight into the torments of Tasso.[14]

Shelley, as he informed Thomas Love Peacock (20 April 1818), intended

12. Regina Hewitt, "Torquato Tasso—A Byronic Hero?"
13. Kari Lokke, "Weimar Classicism and Romantic Madness," 202.
14. Richard Holmes, *Shelley, The Pursuit*, 187, describes the incident and summarizes the various critical explanations as hoax and as hallucination.

to devote the summer of 1818 and the year following "to the composition of a tragedy on the subject of Tasso's madness." Upon first reading Manso's *La Vita di Tarquato Tasso*, Shelley was convinced that the subject would be, "if properly treated, admirably dramatic & poetical." Only ten days later, however, his enthusiasm began to falter: "I have been studying the history of Tasso's life, with some idea of making a drama of his adventures and misfortunes. [How] such a subject would suit English poetry [I cannot tell]" (30 April 1818). In fact, all that remains of this endeavor are the two fragments, "Scene from 'Tasso'" and "Song for 'Tasso'."[15] Perhaps realizing that a tragic drama on Tasso might prove too unwieldy, Shelley did not pursue the attempt. Rather than abandon the figure of the mad poet, Kari Lokke has argued, Shelley chose to incorporate him into "Julian and Maddalo," completed later that same year.

While he was still preoccupied with writing on madness, Shelley delved into classical accounts of the *furor poeticus*. "What a wonderful passage there is in *Phaedrus*," he wrote to Peacock,

> in praise of poetic madness, and in definition of what poetry is, and how a man becomes a poet. Every man who lives in this age and desires to write poetry, ought, as a preservative against the false and narrow systems of criticism which every poetical empiric vents, to impress himself with this sentence, if he would be numbered among those to whom may be applied this proud, though sublime, expression of Tasso: *Non c'è in mondo chi merita nome di creatore, che Dio ed il Poeta*. (*Le Hers*, 16 August 1818)

The conjunction, here, of Tasso's "sublime" equation of God and the poet as the sole true "creators" and Socrates' claim that the "madness" of the poet is "heaven-sent" reveals much about Shelley's interpretation of Tasso's plight. The "gates of poetry" can be entered, according to Socrates, only when divine madness "seizes a tender, virgin soul and stimulates it to rapt passionate expression, especially in lyric poetry, glorifying the countless mighty deeds of ancient times for the instruction of posterity."[16] Although Socrates insists that such madness is not evil but a blessing, he did not anticipate the perils that might beset "a tender, virgin soul" amid the real evil lurking beneath the surface gallantry of the Italian court. Such perils were to provide the dramatic substance of Shelley's play: the virtue and genius of the poet as victimized by the greed and guile of the tyrant.

Motives of jealousy and rivalry are deftly sketched in the twenty-seven

15. Donald Reiman, ed., *Shelley and His Circle, 1773–1822*, 6:590–92, 851–65.
16. Plato, *Phaedrus*, secs. 244a-245a, in *Collected Dialogues*, 491–92.

lines, in which Shelley introduces four characters: Maddalo, a courtier; Malpiglio, a poet; Pigna, a minister; and Albano, an usher. Maddalo is impatient that Duke Alfonso has delayed in granting him audience; Malpiglio is vexed that Lady Leonora has scorned the sonnet he has dedicated "to her fame"; Pigna is puzzled that the Duke has been distracted from affairs of state and lingers with the Duchess. The explanation, according to Albano, is that Duke Alfonso and the Princess are "buried in some strange talk" together with young Tasso. This report immediately provokes rivalry and anger that Tasso should thus be privileged. Maddalo deliberately goads Malpiglio: "Thou seest on whom from thine own worshipped heaven / Thou drawest down smiles—they did not rain on thee." Malpiglio replies with a curse on Tasso: "Would they were parching lightnings for his sake / On whom they fell!"

The second fragment, "Song for 'Tasso'," is a lyric lament in three seven-line stanzas (rhyme scheme, *aabbcccc*) spoken by the poet confined to his cell. His words, however, are not like the ravings of the madman in "Julian and Maddalo." Shelley's Tasso is fully capable of discriminating the images in his mind from reality. He despairs that love may have no immortal soul and is doomed to perish with the body. He once had thoughts that transcended mortality,

> Keen thoughts and bright of linkèd lore,
> Of all that men had thought before,
> And all that Nature shows, and more.

Although the images that now assault his mind are no longer free and revelatory, it is not because his mind is deranged, but because his freedom has been taken away. "Still I love and still I think," he affirms, but he also acknowledges that his once "bright" thoughts are now tarnished by the ugliness of his present condition:

> And if I think, my thoughts come fast,
> I mix the present with the past,
> And each seems uglier than the last.

In his confinement, images of love and freedom appear only to tease momentarily and then disappear. The image of Leonora in "a silver spirit's form" flees from his cell and fades with a sigh beyond "the grated casement's ledge." As if he were still grasping after that faded image of freedom, the sigh seems to echo the sound that "sedge / Breathes o'er the breezy streamlet's edge." But the echo, too, fades, and nothing follows.

A further clue to how Shelley might have developed the characters of

Tasso and Duke Alfonso is in the account of his visit to Ferrara. "I always seek in what I see," he writes in a letter to Peacock (7 November 1818), "the manifestation of something beyond the present and tangible objects." Thus merely seeing the manuscripts and entering Tasso's cell conjure for Shelley a dramatic scenario:

> Some of those Mss of Tasso were sonnets to his persecutor which contain a great deal of what is called flattery. If Alfonso's ghost were asked how he felt these praises now I wonder what he would say. But to me there is much more to pity than to condemn in these entreaties and praises of Tasso. It is as a Christian prays to {and} praises his God whom he knows to [be] the most remorseless capricious & inflexible of tyrants, but whom he knows also to be omnipotent. Tasso's situation was widely different from that of any persecuted being of the present day, for from the depth of dungeons public opinion might now at last be awakened to an echo that would startle the oppressor. But then there was no hope. There is something irresistibly pathetic to me in the sight of Tasso's own hand writing moulding expressions of adulation & entreaty to a deaf & stupid tyrant in an age when the most heroic virtue would have exposed its possessor to hopeless persecution, and—such is the alliance between virtue & genius—which unoffending genius could not escape. —We went afterwards to see his prison in the hospital of Santa Anna and I enclose you a piece of wood of the very door[17] which for seven years & three months divided this glorious being from the air & the light which had nourished him in those impulses which he has communicated to thousands. The dungeon is low & dark, . . . a horrible abode for the coarsest & the meanest thing that ever wore the shape of man, much more for one of delicate sensibilities and elevated fancies.

Much like Jupiter, Cenci, and other Shelleyan tyrants, Duke Alfonso lacks all redeeming qualities. The poet, of course, is all "virtue & genius." What prevents Shelley's conception from lapsing into an oversimplified conflict between good and evil is his sense of the conspiracy of religion and power that duped even the poet. Upon the intervention of the Cardinal,

17. Although "Tasso's cell" may have been simply contrived for the tourists, Shelley is obviously acting the tourist in cutting a splinter from the door to send to Peacock. When Byron and John Cam Hobhouse visited Ferrara, Hobhouse also helped himself to a souvenir; two years later the librarian who exhibited the Tasso mss. had not forgotten "'the English Milord' . . . who had taken & since stampatoed the copies of the Epic-maker's washing list" (3 June 1819). *Byron's Letters and Journals,* 6:145–46.

the Duke grants leniency by allowing the prisoner a fire to expel the "un-
wholesome damps" of the cell. The Church, however, does not denounce
the injustice or demand the prisoner's release. Shelley closes his letter
with an anecdote of a penitent "in a ghost like drapery" suffering "for
some crime known only to himself & his confessor." The tyrannical abuse
persists, concludes Shelley, in "the power of Catholic superstition over
the human mind."

In *Melincourt* (1817), Peacock uses Tasso's *La Gerusalemme liberata*
much in the way that in *Ulysses* (1922), James Joyce was later to use
Homer's *Odyssey*. Marilyn Butler has described an intertextuality evident
in both the symmetry of the narrative structure and the chivalric idealism
of the principle characters, who, she asserts, "are not characters in a
novel, but figures from a romance." Because *Melincourt* is not a heroic
romance, Forester, Sir Oran, and Anthelia are radically displaced and
must negotiate their actions amid the naturalistic conventions of nineteenth-century fiction and Peacock's own satirical ploys.[18] Anthelia Melincourt, whom Mrs. Pinmoney calls "a romantic heretic from the orthodox
supremacy of fashion" (Peacock, *Works*, 2:22), has envisioned her ideal
suitor as an "enthusiast" who possesses the "spirit of the age of chivalry"
(2:23, 86, 98). Tasso, as might be expected, is her favorite poet. Mr. Forester may not fulfill her ideal, but he certainly wins Miss Melincourt's
approval when he tells her that the stained-glass windows of her library
"would recall to an enthusiast mind the attendant spirit of Tasso" and
that the sounds from the "waving cedars beyond" remind him of the "melody which flowed from the enchanted wood at the entrance of Rinaldo,
and which Tasso has painted with a degree of harmony not less magical
than the music he describes." No other poet, he exclaims, offers description "so congenial to the tenderness and delicacy of the female mind."
(2:164). Miss Melincourt responds that he has "a better opinion of the
understandings of women" than most men. Other men, she has observed,
fear "that the friend of Tasso might aspire to the acquaintance of Virgil, or
even to an introduction to Homer and Sophocles" (2:168).

Although Peacock does advocate a liberal education for women with
his argument that familiarity with the Greek and Roman classics should
not be the sole province of men, the case that I want to emphasize here is
not that Peacock has endorsed a feminist cause, but that he has a romantic notion of classical literature. Far from agreeing with the writer for the
Eclectic Review who claimed that Tasso's "moral purity and religious fervour were pledges that his descriptions would not be intended to conceal

18. Marilyn Butler, *Peacock Displayed*, 67–68, 82; see also Butler's diagram of the sym-
metrical structure of *Melincourt* (on page 85), and her observation (on page 324 n. 52) that
Sir Oran's campaign occupies the same central place in the narrative as the assault on
Jerusalem in Tasso's epic.

any erotic passions,"[19] Peacock's silence on the poem's explicit sexuality, especially in canto 16, may well be conspiratorial. In part, he invites our amusement at Forester's "ardour and animation" in conjuring scenes from Homer, Aeschylus, Sophocles, Euripides, and his "figurative idea of wandering among them with a young and beautiful female aspirant." Forester's "imaginary wanderings through the classic scenes of antiquity" succeed in prompting Miss Melincourt to share "in her congenial mind the brightest colours of intellectual beauty" (2:168–69). She, in turn, has him follow her lead when he discovers her "splendid edition of Tasso, printed by Bodoni at Parma," ornamented with her own "magic" drawings in which "the wild and wonderful scenes of Tasso seemed to live under his eyes."

Peacock, however, does not mean us to reject this "visionary" mode of reading the classics. In two fragmentary tales, Peacock attempted to construct a satire out of the confrontation of classical and modern attitudes. In "Calidore," a mythic being out of classical antiquity arrives as a stranger on British soil; in "Satyrane," a ship of English missionaries arrives on an island populated by nymphs and satyrs. In both tales, Peacock apparently intended to show the power of classical myth to challenge the repressive sexual mores of Christianity (*Works* 8:297–341). Years later, in *Gryll Grange* (1860), Peacock has the Reverend Doctor Opiman expound upon the differences between "classical ghosts" and the ghosts of Gothic fiction. "The ghosts of Patroclus in Homer, of Darius in Aeschylus, of Polydorus in Euripides are fine poetical ghosts," he grants, "but none of them would make a ghost story." Although the aesthetics of fear and the demonic supernatural were elaborated by a later age of Christian dogma, Greek and Latin literature was not bereft of such dark tales. Peacock delights in expounding the romantic narratives of classical antiquity. He has Reverend Opiman remind us of Goethe's retelling, in the *Braut von Korinth*, of the woman who rises from the tomb to embrace her lover in Phlegon's Περὶ Θαυμασίων. Opiman goes on to retrieve two more macabre tales from the *Cena Trimalchionis* of Petronius Arbiter (Peacock, *Works*, 5:348–55). For Peacock, classical literature is not defined in terms of formal purity, but rather as a repository of the imagination. He refused to accept the claims of traditionalism and innovation as mutually exclusive. Tasso is thus appropriately cited as the poet who combined the classical and the romantic.[20]

---

19. *Eclectic Review* (November 1825), 461; quoted in Brand 272.

20. Thomas Peacock, "The Four Ages of Poetry" (1820), in *Works* 8:14–15, finds the modern equivalent of the iron age in the chivalric romance: "These legends, combined with the exaggerated love that pervades the songs of the troubadours, the reputation of magic that attached to learned men, the infant wonders of natural philosophy, the crazy fanaticism of the crusades, the power and privileges of the great feudal chiefs, and the holy mysteries of

Although Friedrich Schlegel emphasizes the feeling and lyric passion of the poet, his account of Tasso does not repeat the various anecdotes of the poet's madness. More typical of the reception in the period was Simonde de Sismondi's *De la Litterature de Midi de l'Europe* (Paris, 1813). In his critique of this four-volume history for the *Edinburgh Review* (June 1815), William Hazlitt observes that Sismondi is much more gifted as a political than as a literary historian. The best commentary, he asserts, occurs when Sismondi traces "the rise or fall of letters with the political independence or debasement of the states in which they flourished or decayed" (16:24). Sismondi's literary principles, as he himself acknowledged, are derived from such sources as "Boutterwek on modern literature . . . Tiraboschi and M. Guiguené on the Italian literature . . . and William Schlegel for the dramatic literature" (16:25).[21] Despite his recognition of Sismondi's strength in showing how literature responds to political circumstances, Hazlitt rejects Sismondi's appraisal of Tasso as a poet superior to Ariosto. He grants that Sismondi's "classification of their different styles, and the enumeration of their particular excellencies or defects" are correct, "but," he adds, "we should be inclined to give preference the contrary way" (16:49). Although "Tasso has more of what is usually called poetry," Hazlitt objects that it is the poet's very attention to classical form and style, to "tropes and ornaments" and to "splendid and elaborate diction" that burden the lively impulses with "artifices of composition" (16:50).

Hazlitt, usually an astute observer of the impact of political ideology on literary manner, apparently does not recognize the political implications of the poet's struggle to reconcile the fervor of romantic adventure with the new humanist emphasis on classical models. Because he fails to see that Tasso has Armida exercise such wiles as might be practiced by an Italian courtesan, Hazlitt judges that she is basely "tricked out with all the ostentatious trappings of a prostitute." Hazlitt betrays a lack of sensitivity to the subtleties and nuances of Tasso's style, to the "real passion" that Tasso has concealed in the elegance of courtly and classical mannerism. Beholding only the surface, "the lofty philosophical elegance" and "the grandeur of the general ideas," Hazlitt misses the undercurrents of "indi-

---

monks and nuns," contributed to a poetry of "love and battle." In the poetry of the succeeding golden age, the materials of the iron age were liberated by "an infinite license, which gave to the poet the free range of the whole field of imagination and memory."

21. Friedrich Bouterwek, *Geschichte der neuern Poesie und Beredsamkeit* (1801–19); Giolamo Triboschi, *Storia della Letteratura Italiana* (1772–82); Pierre Louis Guiguené, *Rapport sur les travaux de la classè d'histoire et de litterature Ancienne* (1807); A. W. Schlegel, "Vorlesungen über dramatische Kunst und Literatur (1809–11)," in *Kritische Schriften und Briefe*, vols. 5–6.

vidual feeling" and "immediate passion" (16:50–51). Nor, when he quotes a lengthy passage (over 600 words) recounting the events of Tasso's confinement and madness (16:51–52), does Hazlitt comment on the political machinations that Sismondi makes evident.

Tasso's fatal error, according to Sismondi, was trespassing against the aristocracy by venturing to woo women of rank. Both Leonora Sanvitale and Leonora d'Este attracted his attentions, as did Lucrezia Bendido, a maid of honor in service to the Princess. When Tasso dared to embrace the Princess in an impulsive "transport of love," the Duke declared that he had "gone mad" and had him locked away. This confinement, declares Sismondi, "enfeebled" his body and "disordered" his mind. Tasso's symptoms of derangement were provoked by his cruel imprisonment: "he believed himself by turns poisoned, or tormented by witchcraft; he fancied that he saw dreadful apparitions, and passed whole nights in painful watchfulness."[22] Tasso's desperate appeal for assistance from powerful heads of church and state did not go unheeded: "The princes of Italy in vain interposed for his release, which the Duke refused to grant, chiefly to mortify his rival, the Medici." Tasso was thus used as a pawn in the Duke's rivalry with other principalities. His release was granted only as a favor to Vincenzo Gonzago, duke of Mantua, "on the occasion of the marriage of the sister of this nobleman with the unrelenting Alphonso."[23] From *Il re Torresmondo*, dedicated by Tasso to his liberator, Sismondi quotes the final chorus: "Like the swift Alpine torrent, like the sudden lightning in the calm night, like the passing wind, the melting vapour, or the winged arrow, so vanishes our fame; and all our glory is but a fading flower. What can we hope, or what expect more? After triumphs and palms, all that remains for the soul, is strife and lamentation, and regret; neither love nor friendship can avail us aught, but only tears and grief." The "profound pathos" of this passage, writes Sismondi, may also express Tasso's own misfortunes and sense of "glory . . . vanishing from him" (16:52).

In referring to Tasso as a "keusches und zartes Gemüt" (like the "tender, virgin soul" seized by divine madness, *Phaedrus* sec. 245a) and as a "Romantischer Dichter *malgré lui*,"[24] August Wilhelm Schlegel clearly endorses the notion that for all his attention to classical principles Tasso

22. Hazlitt translated from the French edition of Sismondi's *Littérature du midi de l'Europe* (Paris, 1813). The English translation by Thomas Roscoe was published in 1823. Howe surmises that since Hazlitt was unable to read Italian, he probably enlisted the help of Leigh Hunt to translate the passages quoted by Sismondi (Hazlitt, *Complete Works*, 16:421–22).

23. As Brand, 23, observes, "extravagant legends have grown up concerning Tasso's madness and his imprisonment." Sismondi reverses the chronology: Tasso was imprisoned, not released, on the occasion of the Duke's wedding to Margherita Gonzaga in February 1579.

24. A. W. Schlegel, *Geschichte der romantischen Literatur*, in *Kritische Schriften* 4:222.

remained a romantic poet of feeling. And in Goethe's play, he observes the peculiar self-reflexivity in making an actual poet the object of poetic representation.[25] Adam Müller, too, is intrigued by the significance of *Tasso* as "ein Gedicht *über* den Dichter." Emphasizing the dialectic of art and nature in Goethe's work, Müller claims that it was precisely his ability to contain the inner strife of character within the formal symmetry of the drama that enabled Goethe to represent the agony of Tasso upon the stage. While Leonore competes with the Princess for the favor of the poet, Antonio enters as a rival who resents the attentions with which the poet is favored. Not the external rivalry, but the internal conflict between illusion and reality in the poet's own mind is central to Goethe's drama. As Müller puts it, "What had seemed to be already attained, swam ever higher and more unattainable among the stars, as a fortunate interpretation; just as, through the seriousness of life, the play becomes infinite, and, through the technical, painstaking management of the historical matter, of language and rhythm, and aesthetic laws, the freedom of poetry is perpetuated."[26] Focusing on the dilemma of the poet, *Tasso* not only thematizes the opposing demands of life and art, it also adopts the antagonism between classical form and romantic feeling as structural principle.

The same tension between the classic and romantic is noted by Friedrich Schlegel, who, like Hazlitt, did not approve of Tasso's classicism. Tasso could have developed more freely as a poet, Schlegel asserts, had he not held to the Virgilian model, which restricted his poetic spirit and occasionally led him astray (6:220). Schlegel approves the Christian content and the combination of history and romance. The historical facts of the Crusades are enhanced by the marvelous episodes of chivalric adventures, which allow the poet to engage the emotions. Rather than undermine the historical "truth," the romantic episodes actually enable the poet to represent the superstitious fear, patriotic enthusiasm, and religious zeal that accompanied the Crusaders to the Holy Land.

It was his adherence to "the Virgilian form" and his occasional awkwardness in manipulating his "epic machinery" that kept him, according

25. A. W. Schlegel, review of Goethe's *Schriften*, vols. 6–8, *Göttingische Anzeigen von gelerhten Sachen* 154 (1790); in *Sämtliche Werke*, ed. Eduard Böcking (Leipzig, 1846), 10:4–5: "Der Gedanke den Charakter eines wirklichen Dichters zum Gegenstand einer dichterischen Darstellung zu machen, hat etwas so Natürliches und auffallend Anlockendes, daß man sich wundern muß, ihn nicht häufiger benutzt zu finden."

26. Adam Müller, *Vorlesungen über die deutsche Wissenschaft und Literatur*, lecture 11: "Was schon gewonnen schien, schwebt immer höher und unerreichbarer zwischen den Gestirnen: als glückliche Deutung, wie eben durch den Ernst des Lebens, das Spiel erst zu einem unendlichen wird und wie durch die technische, mühsame Behandlung des Stoffs, der Sprach und des Rhythmus oder durch das Gesetz, sich die Freiheit der Poesie erst verewigt." See also Müller, *Die Lehre vom Gegensatze*, bk. 1, pp. 97–101.

to Schlegel, from fully realizing the richness of his subject. He was more gifted in tapping the immediate subjective response than in creating vast narrative panorama. His narrative might falter, but his evocations of the emotions experienced and aroused by his characters—Armida's enticements, Clorinda's beauty, Armida's love—were always powerful and thoroughly convincing.[27] The emotional depth he thus lends to his characters make them seem alive and real. He had peopled his mind with such vivid figures, Schlegel affirms, that Goethe was certainly right in having Tasso deny that they were mere shadows wrought by madness (II.i.1102–3). Schlegel apparently does not see that these lines have a very different meaning in context. Tasso lays claims to a primary image which he then transforms into the characters of his poetry:

> No vague and merely mental image hovers
> Before me when I write, now brightly close,
> Now dim again, withdrawing from my soul.
> With my own eyes I've seen the prototype
> Of every virtue, every loveliness;
> What in that image I have made, will last:
> Tancred's heroic love for his Clorinda,
> Ermina's tacit, unacknowledged faith,
> Sophronia's greatness and Olinda's plight;
> These are not phantoms conjured from delusion,
> I know they will endure, because they are.[28]

---

27. Friedrich Schlegel, *Geschichte der alten und neuen Literatur*, in *Kritische Friedrich Schlegel Ausgabe* 6:267: "Er gehört im ganzen mehr zu den Dichtern, die nur sich selbst und ihr schönstes Gefühl darstellen, als eine Welt in ihrem Geist klar aufzufassen, und ihr eignes Selbst in dieser zu versetzen und zu vergessen im Stande sind. Die schönsten Stellen in seinem Gedichte, sind solche, die auch einzeln oder als Episoden, in jedem anderen Werk schön sein würden, und die nicht wesentlich zum Gegenstande gehören. Die Reize der Armida, Clorindens Schönheit und Erminias Liebe, diese und ähnliche Stellen sind es, die uns an Tasso fesseln."

28. Goethe, *Torquato Tasso*, II.i.1093–1103:
> Es schwebt kein geistig unbestimmtes Bild
> Vor meiner Stirne, das der Seele bald
> Sich überglänzend nahte, bald entzöge,
> Mit meinen Augen hab' ich es gesehn,
> Das Urbild jeder Tugend, jeder Schöne;
> Was ich nach ihm gebildet, das wird bleiben:
> Tancredens Heldenliebe zu Clorinden,
> Erminiens stille, nicht bemerkte Treue,
> Sophroniens Großheit und Olindens Not,
> Es sind nicht Schatten, die der Wahn erzeugte;
> Ich weiß es, sie sind ewig, denn sie sind.

In addressing these words to the Princess, Tasso seems identify in her beauty and virtue the origin of his "Urbild" and the source for "Was auch in meinem Liede wiederklingt." Although the praise turns to denunciation after he is imprisoned for his impetuous embrace, he still acknowledges the Princess as inspiring image, an Armida disguised as Clorinda (canto 7):

> How long your holy image hid from me
> The mere seductress at her little games.
> The mask has dropped: I see Armida now
> Stripped of all her charms—yes, that is who you are.
> Prophetically my poem sang of you![29]

Insisting that Tasso is a poet of feeling ("Gefühlsdichter"), Schlegel claims the heightened emotions make Tasso a genius of the lyric, yet inhibit his efforts to create an epic. Goethe also represents Tasso's subjective and introspective nature, but he emphasizes the poet's response to external events and circumstances. In Goethe's play, Tasso's acute sensitivity not only informs but distorts and even usurps his perception. Goethe calls attention to passages in Tasso's poetry where the confounding of objective reality and subjective response is often thematized, and he makes it clear, as well, that Tasso felt himself victimized by the deceitful mannerisms of courtly behavior. Schlegel grants the glowing passion, enthusiasm, and musicality of Tasso's poetry, but attributes his dilemma to frustration in his efforts to sustain epic narrative. Worse, in Schlegel's judgment, Tasso's religious anxieties and increasing moral reserve led him to revise compulsively, ultimately eradicating his most beautiful evocations of love and passion (6:268–69).

With his assumption that Goethe, too, saw in Tasso a poet of essentially lyrical disposition, Schlegel, in the *Gespräch über Poesie* (1800), describes *Torquato Tasso* as the ordeal of a poet so committed to "Reflexion und Harmonie" that he struggles desperately to render even disharmony harmoniously (2:342). The conflict is one of "Antithese und Musik" in which the sensibilities of the pampered poet are strained beyond his fragile tolerance: "The misbehavior of a pampered virtuoso must and should become apparent: but they revealed themselves almost endearing in the beautiful, floral adornment of poetry. The whole hovered in an atmosphere of artificial alliances and misalliances among the eminent classes, and the consequence is

---

29. Ibid., V.v.3339–43:

> Wie lang verdeckte mir dein heilig Bild
> Die Bühlerin, die kleine Künste treibt.
> Die Maske fällt: Armiden seh' ich nun
> Entblößt, von allen Reizen—ja, du bist's!
> Von dir hat ahndungsvoll mein Lied gesungen!

only enigmatic when calculated from a position where reason and will are the only determinants, and the feeling is virtually silenced" (2:343).[30] The "misalliance," Schlegel says, lies in the very character of Goethe's Tasso. When this raw nerve is exposed, the poet no longer holds his passions in harmony but succumbs to the cacophony of rage.

With his emphasis on Tasso as a lyric rather than an epic poet, Schlegel declared that passages from the *Liberata* were often sung. Not Schlegel but his English translator had added the whimsical detail that "individual parts and episodes of his poem are frequently sung in the gondolas of the Arno and the Po."[31] As if he had expected to hear these lyrics wafting along the canals of Venice, Byron expressed his disappointment at the opening of *Childe Harold*, canto 4, that "Tasso's echoes are no more, / And silent rows the songless Gondolier" (19–20). Shelley wrote to Peacock (8 October 1818) that "the silent streets are paved with water, & you hear nothing but the dashing of oars & the occasional curses of the gondoliers. (I heard nothing of Tasso.)" Expressing his scorn for the presumptuous style with which "this German talks of gondolas on the Arno— a precious fellow to dare to speak of Italy," Byron compared Schlegel to Hazlitt, "who *talks pimples*—a red and white corruption rising up (in little imitation of mountains upon maps), but containing nothing, and discharging nothing, except their own humours" (29 January 1821, *Letters & Journals* 8:38–39). Like Shelley and Peacock, Byron saw in Tasso a poet who was victimized not so much by the vigor of his own passionate imagination as by the effort of Alfonso d'Este to dictate and direct its power. His madness resulted not from his inability to control himself, but rather from his unwillingness to submit to the controls being forced upon him.

Goethe's Tasso and the Historical Tasso

In his enthusiastic account of the Golden Age (II.i), Tasso tells the Princess that it exists in the ideal of freedom. The free creatures of nature

---

30. Friedrich Schlegel, *Gespräch über Poesie*, in *Kritische Friedrich Schlegel Ausgabe*, 2:343: "Es mußten und sollten Unarten eines verzärtelten Virtuosen zum Vorschein kommen: aber sie zeigten sich im schönsten Blumenschmuck der Poesie beinah liebens-würdig. Das Ganze schwebt in der Atmosphäre künstlicher Verhältnisse und Mißverhältnisse vornehmer Stände, und das Rätselhafte der Auflösung ist nur auf den Standpunkt berechnet, wo Verstand und Willkür allein herrschen, und das Gefühl beinah schweigt."

31. Byron was reading the translation of Schlegel's *History of Literature* (Edinburgh, 1818) in January 1821; see *Byron's Letters and Journals*, VIII, 38–40. Where Schlegel simply affirmed the adaptation into song ("Die einzelnen Stellen und Episoden des Gedichts sind oft gesungen worden," in *Kritische Friedrich Schlegel Ausgabe* 6:268), the translator gave them specifically to the gondoliers.

conveyed their message to mankind: "Erlaubt ist, was gefällt" [Permitted is what pleases]. Goethe has taken the line from Tasso's pastoral play, *Aminta* (1573), where it has moral legitimacy only because pleasure is prescinded from responsibility. Tasso must have known that it was a dubious doctrine, for it echoes Semiramis's rationale for her incest in Dante's *Inferno* (canto 5, line 56: "libito fé licito").[32] The Princess's response, "Erlaubt ist, was sich ziemt" [Permitted is what is proper], repeats the *bon mot* of another poet of the Ferrara court, Giovanni Battista Guarini, whose pastoral drama, *Il Pastor fido* (1580), countered the hedonistic liberty of Tasso's *Aminta*. Guarini's words are heard again when Antonio expresses to Leonora his contempt for Tasso's flirtations:

> He boasts of two great flames! He ties and loosens
> Now this knot, now the other, and he wins
> *Such* hearts with *such* an art. Is that to be
> Believed?[33]

Goethe has simply translated from a sonnet in which Guarini mocks his rival poet.[34] Although he uses Guarini's critique of Tasso, there is no room in his plot for Guarini himself: Goethe has already introduced a rival poet in the haunting presence of Ariosto. Goethe focuses attention on the mind of the poet through the attractions of Leonore and the Princess, as well as through the rivalry with Ariosto and Antonio. Because the poet's response, marked not by reserve but by an excitable sensitivity, is in itself dramatic and "stagy" ("bretterhaft"), Goethe simply engages Tasso's intensity to present the imagination as a power capable of arousing the passions and confounding practical reason. In devoting himself to his poetry, Tasso misapprehends the actual contingencies of court. Goethe, exactly as he stated, has located the conflict in "die Disproportion des Talents mit dem Leben."

32. Dante had the phrase, in turn, from Paulus Orosius, *Historiarum adversum paganos libri septem*, who thus records Semiramis's justification of incest: "praecepit enim, ut inter parentes ac filios nulla delata reverentia naturae de coniugiis adpetendis ut cuique *libitum esset liberum fieret*." *Inferno*, 50 (text), 77–78 (commentary).

33. Goethe, *Torquato Tasso*, III.iv.2094–97:
> Er rühmt sich zweier Flammen! knüpft und löst
> Die Knoten hin und wieder und gewinnt
> Mit solchen Künsten solche Herzen! Ist's
> Zu glauben?

34. Wolfdietrich Rasch, *Goethes "Torquato Tasso."* Noting that Goethe could have found Guarini's sonnet in Serrasi's biography of Tasso, Rasch quotes the lines Goethe gave to Antonio: "Di due fiamme si vanta, e stringe e spezza / Più volte un nodo, e con quest'arte piega / (Chi 'l crederebbe!) a suo favore i Dei."

Tasso was twenty-nine when he wrote *Aminta*, and thirty-one when he finished *La Gerusalemme liberata*. In Goethe's play, however, Tasso is repeatedly referred to as a youth, and his uncontrolled emotionality is attributed, in part, to his immaturity. The concluding scene of reconciliation between Tasso and Antonio opens the possibility that Tasso may yet learn to control his mental and emotional excesses. Antonio's praise of Ariosto (I.iv) suggests that the statesman is not totally deficient in poetic sensibility. Not until the concluding scene, in which Antonio patiently consoles the raving poet, does that sensibility become fully manifest. The clash occurs when Antonio coldly disdains to offer Tasso his hand in friendship. When he stretches forth his hand at the play's close, Tasso desperately clutches it, clinging to Antonio as his sole remaining hope. In the bravura piece at the end of act 1, Antonio gives tribute to the power of *Orlando Furioso*, in which "Madness on a lute well-tuned will seem / To strum at random to and fro, / And yet in loveliest rhythm keeps its bounds." Antonio also insinuates that Tasso lacks the ability to keep his madness in measure. Tasso deserves his laurel wreath not for his poetic genius, says Antonio, but rather for his boldness: "Whoever ventures to that great man's side / For his mere boldness deserves a garland."[35] The passage accomplishes several dramatic purposes: it acknowledges the high honor accorded courtly poets; it injures Tasso by reminding him of the great predecessor whom he presumes to rival; it initiates the hostility between Tasso and Antonio.

Antonio's reference to the "Kranz" further elaborates one of the major symbols of the play. In the opening scene, the Princess and Leonore are weaving wreaths for the garden hermae of the two poets, Virgil and Ariosto. The Princess places her wreath of laurel on the head of Virgil, Leonora's wreath of flowers decorates the brow of Ariosto. When Tasso arrives with his copy of *La Gerusalemme liberata* for the Duke, the Princess takes the laurel wreath from Virgil and presents it to him. The symbolic portent of this coronation almost overwhelms Tasso:

> O take it off my head again, remove it!
> It singes me, I feel it burn my temples.
> And like a sun's ray that too hotly were
> To strike my forehead, it consumes my power

---

35. Goethe, *Torquato Tasso*, I.iv.731–35:

> auf wohlgestimmter Laute wild
> Der Wahnsinn hin und her zu wühlen scheint
> Und doch im schönsten Takt sich mäßig hält.
> Wer neben diesen Mann sich wagen darf,
> Verdient für seine Kühnheit schon den Kranz.

To think, numbs and confuses. Feverish heat
Stirs up my blood. Forgive me. It's too much.[36]

Where else in literature has the poet expressed the burden of the past
with such agony, the anxiety of influence with such excruciating pain?
Ariosto, Tasso's immediate predecessor in the court of Ferrara, has been
awarded the wreath of flowers because, Leonora declares, his "jests never
fade" and he allows us to dream of a Golden Age. Ariosto (1474–1533)
entered the service of Cardinal Ippolito d'Este in 1503, and after 1518
resided in the court of Duke Alfonso I. *Orlando Furioso* was written during the period 1516–21, with an additional six cantos added in 1532. The
sensuality and the fantasy of his epic brought acclaim to Ferrara and
stirred the envy even of the powerful neighbor to the north, Venice, home
to Titian, Veronese, and Tintoretto. Tasso (1544–95) began his service to
Cardinal Luigi d'Este in 1565, and under the protection of the princesses,
Leonora and Lucrezia, subsequently became a member of the court of
Alfonso II. He is thus successor, as court poet, to the greatest Italian poet
of the age. He claims his debt, however, to an even greater poet. Not
Ariosto's *Orlando Furioso* but Virgil's *Aeneid* will be his model and the
standard against which his own *La Gerusalemme liberata* shall be mea-
sured.

Although he follows Virgil, Tasso enhances his historical and heroic
materials with scenes of Christian zeal and erotic passion. His fantastic
narrative and strophic form reveal a closer kinship to *Orlando Furioso*
than Tasso willingly acknowledged. Because his epic is to be a tribute to
the court of Ferrara, he claims as his subject the First Crusade. The Crusades contributed much to shaping the aristocracy of the age. The House
of Este received its dominion of Ferrara in 1208, following the sack of
Constantinople in the Fourth Crusade. After the devastating Muslim
(re)conquest of Acre, the church revised its position on the Crusades.
The historical Tasso, not as naive about the politics of church and state
as Goethe's poet, thus felt compelled to revise his poem to comply with
the new orthodoxy. The *Liberata* may have brought glory to the court of
Ferrara, but the House of Este was not long to prevail.

When Antonio returns from his meeting with Pope Gregory XIII, in

36. Ibid., I.iii.488–93:
> O nehmt ihn weg von meinem Haupte wieder,
> Nehmt ihn hinweg! Er sengt mir meine Locken!
> Und wie ein Strahl der Sonne, der zu heiß
> Das Haupt mir träfe, brennt er mir die Kraft
> Des Denkens aus der Stirne. Fieberhitze
> Bewegt mein Blut. Verzeiht! Es ist zuviel!

Goethe's play, he informs the Duke of a successful diplomatic mission. The Duke declares that "Rom will alles nehmen, geben nichts." Antonio reports that the Pope has extended the grant to Ferrara:

> He sees the small things small, the large ones large.
> In order to rule a world, he willingly
> And graciously gives in to all his neighbours.
> The little strip of land he grants to you
> He values greatly, as he does your friendship.[37]

For his diplomacy, Alfonso declares, Antonio deserves a wreath of oak leaves. A cue that prompts Antonio's attention to the floral and laurel wreaths. Referring to the laurel worn by Tasso, he remarks that "in rewarding . . . / Alfonso is immoderate" [im Belohnen / Alfons unmäßig ist]. The deserved praise, he emphasizes, belongs to the floral-wreathed Ariosto.

Whatever success Antonio, as fictional statesman, may have achieved in Rome, in reality the court of Ferrara was doomed. With the death of Gregory XIII, there was great turmoil in the Vatican. Four popes (Sixtus V, Urban VII, Gregory XIV, Innocent IX) followed within the next six years. When Clement VIII assumed the papal seat in 1592, he began to reclaim lands for the Papal State. In 1598, Ferrara was once again under papal authority. The historical materials would have made it easy for Goethe to have written a play richly woven with allusions to religious heresy, to rivalry among the ruling houses, to tensions between aristocracy and papal authority. In fact, there is a minimum of such reference, and that minimum functions to give credibility to the role of Antonio rather than to introduce factional intrigues at work against Tasso. His madness, in Goethe's play, is aggravated by his own incapacity to reconcile life and poetry. Because the Duke has indeed, just as Tasso laments, excluded him from the practical affairs of state, Tasso must struggle all the harder in his isolation to make his poem speak to a courtly audience from which he remains effectively estranged.

The very suppression of physical action, which is confined to the poet's anxieties about his poem and the eruption of his pent-up emotions, force all the dramatic tensions into dialogue. Even the dialogue exhibits the

---

37. Ibid., I.iv.616–20:
> Er sieht das Kleine klein, das Große groß.
> Damit er einer Welt gebiete, gibt
> Er seinen Nachbarn gern und freundlich nach.
> Das Streifchen Land, das er dir überläßt,
> Weiß er, wie deine Freundschaft, wohl zu schätzen.

strain of self-consciously measured language. Turbulent energies are made to wear the stately dress of courtly speech. Meaning is robed in a style that is mannered, elegant, yet often duplicitous. Not even in Tasso's emotional outbursts does language tumble wild and naked across the stage. Rather, it dons the garb of high tragedy, the language of Tasso's own *Il re Torrismondo*. No sooner, however, does Tasso adopt a poetic pose, than he begins to believe it. He is carried away by his own words. In dramatizing Tasso's gestures as heroic fighter and lover, Goethe adapts from his biographical sources: Tasso had drawn his blade against a servant whom he suspected of spying on him, and he had publicly embraced the Princess. Both of these moments, in Goethe's play, occur in consequence of Tasso's being impelled by his own verbal excesses.

In drawing his sword against Antonio, Tasso is not resorting to a weapon after having been vanquished in the verbal fencing. He draws the sword, rather, to parry Antonio's trope. The turn in their play of wit comes when Antonio suggests that Tasso has taken his laurels too seriously: "Mistake a gracious bounty for reward, / Fortuitous frippery for true ornament." At this point Tasso ceases to be awed by Antonio's appeal to restraint and mature wisdom. He is now convinced that the proffered friendship has been rejected because of Antonio's petty jealousy: "Your meaning's clear to me now. That's enough. / Deep into you I look, and for a lifetime / Now know you through and through."[38] When Antonio tells Tasso that he is "Held und Sieger" only when no other play is involved but "Lippenspiel and Saitenspiel" [play with lips and with the strings of an instrument], Tasso recognizes an implicit challenge and returns the trope by declaring himself ready for the "Wagespiel der Waffen" [daring play with weapons]. Antonio seems not to have anticipated that his mockery would agitate his excitable opponent to such a rage. It is not his sword that trespasses the propriety of the place, Tasso insists, but Antonio's words.

Tasso, to be sure, claims that he is in full control of his language even when he dissembles. When he justifies to himself the explanation he has given to the Duke in requesting the return of his epic poem and the permission to leave the court, he confesses in soliloquy that the whole dialogue was a deception:

38. Ibid., II.iii.1313–17:
> ANTONIO. Er halte gnädiges Geschenk für Lohn,
> Zufälligen Putz für wohlverdienten Schmuck.
> TASSO. Du brauchst nicht deutlicher zu sein. Es ist genug!
> Ich blicke tief dir in das Herz und kenne
> Fürs ganze Leben dich.

You found it hard, for never yet you had
The wish or power so to disguise yourself.
You clearly heard: he did not speak *his* mind,
Nor in *his* words. It seemed to me that only
Antonio's voice resounded from *his* lips.
Yes, take good care! You'll hear that voice henceforth
From every side. So you stand fast, stand fast!
Only one moment more is needed now.
A man who learns dissembling late in life
Profits by that because he seems sincere.
It will work out, just let them teach you how![39]

But his pretense at controlling the voice of his dissembling self collapses with the entrance of the Princess in the scene that immediately follows. While his imagination may give rise to his manneristic posturing in language, his language also seems to stimulate his imagination to defy ethical boundaries.

At first feigning concern solely for his poem, Tasso betrays increasing excitement, as the dialogue progresses, at his own words. If he is aided by his friends in Rome, he says, "With care and patience there perhaps I'll give / My poem the last touches it still needs." He will then proceed incognito to Naples, in spite of the ban against him, to visit his sister. The Princess expresses her concern for his safety and tells him that in parting he takes away the pleasures they might have shared: "[You] deprive us / Of what with us alone you could enjoy." This indication of her sadness in his parting prompts an abrupt change in his tone and manner: "It's not your wish, then, quite to banish me? / Sweet utterance, a dear and lovely comfort!"[40] He pleads with her to give him sanctuary in one of the country

39. Ibid., V.iii.3091–3101:

> Es wird dir schwer, es ist das erstemal,
> Daß du dich so verstellen magst und kannst.
> Du hörtest wohl: das war nicht sein Gemüt,
> Das waren seine Worte nicht; mir schien,
> Als klänge nur Antonios Stimme wieder.
> O gib nur acht! Du wirst sie nun so fort
> Von allen Seiten hören. Fest, nur fest!
> Um einen Augenblick ists noch zu tun.
> Wer spät im Leben sich verstellen lernt,
> Der hat den Schein der Ehrlichkeit voraus.
> Es wird schon gehen, nur übe dich mit ihnen!

40. Ibid., V.iv.3113–14, 3175–78:

> TASSO. So leg ich da mit Sorgfalt und Geduld
> Vielleicht die letzte Hand an mein Gedicht.
>
> . . . .

estates. No sooner has he envisaged this setting than he animates it with an image of himself as a menial tending her gardens. If he is to surrender to what he has already conceived as bondage, it is no self-degradation to serve as gardener rather than as poet. His desperate fantasies, however, alarm the Princess:

> My vision casts about for some kind god
> To succor us, I search for some good potion
> Or rare remedial herb that to your senses
> Might give some peace and rest, and so to us.
> The truest word that human lips can speak,
> The best of medicines is powerless now.
> I have to let you be, though never my heart
> Can leave you.[41]

What must he do, Tasso asks, to gain her forgiveness, and her brother's? She replies that he must forgive himself: "No thing that you are not we ask of you, / If only you will be yourself, and like it." She laments that he cannot be helped unless he is able to respond to the friendship that is offered him, "As long as you refuse the helping hand / Your friend extends in urgency, in vain."[42]

With these last words the Princess inadvertently touches the wound left by Antonio's haughty refusal to offer his hand. Tasso is deeply moved: "It's you entirely, as you were when first, / A holy angel, you appeared to

---

PRINZESSIN.   [du] nimmst uns weg,
Was du mit uns allein genießen konntest.
TASSO. So willst du mich nicht ganz und gar verstoßen?
O süßes Wort, so schöner, treurer Trost!

41. Ibid., V.iv.3214–21:

Mein Auge blickt umher, ob nicht ein Gott
Uns Hilfe reichen möchte, möchte mir
Ein heilsam Kraut entdecken, einen Trank,
Der deinem Sinne Frieden brächte, Frieden uns.
Das treuste Wort, das von der Lippe fließt,
Das schönste Heilungsmittel, wirkt nicht mehr.
Ich muß dich lassen, und verlassen kann
Mein Herz dich nicht.

42. Ibid., V.iv.3229–30, 3236–37:

Wir wollen nichts von dir, was du nicht bist,
Wenn du erst dir mit dir selbst gefällst.

. . . .

du nicht selbst des Freundes Hand ergreifst,
Die, sehnlich ausgereckt, dich nicht erreicht.

me." From a melancholy brooding his mood swings suddenly into an ecstatic outburst:

> What a feeling!
> Is it confusion that attracts me to you?
> Is it a madness? Is it that heightened sense
> Which grasps the highest and purest truth?
> Yes, it's that feeling which alone can make me
> Supremely happy on this earth of ours,
> And which alone could leave me so downcast
> When I resisted it and strove to drive it
> Out of my heart. For to subdue that passion
> I did my utmost, fought and fought against
> My deepest being, shamelessly destroyed
> My own true self, to which so wholly you [belong]—[43]

The source of his ecstasy, he seems to acknowledge, may be his own
madness. Here he admits that the mind may confound reality with its self-
engendered images. Goethe has Tasso discriminate three modes of delusion: error, which results from the mind seeking to substantiate a subjective feeling by confirming it in the objective world; delirium, in which a
person acts upon delusion; heightened sense, in which the mind sees
through the veil of manner and custom to discover the essential truth.
Tasso, of course, grasps this third possibility. His feeling of love is the
truth that can no longer be repressed. For the Princess, however, a certain repression is necessary in governing the otherwise unruly feeling. In
their earlier intimate exchange, the province of love, so declared the
Princess, was to be governed by restraint. "Entbehren" (self-denial, absti-

---

43. Ibid., V.iv.3238–39, 3245–56:

> Du bist es selbst, wie du zum erstenmal,
> Ein heiliger Engel, mir entgegenkamst!
>
> . · . · . · . · . · . · . ·
>   Welch ein Gefühl!
> Ist es Verirrung, was mich nach dir zieht?
> Ists Raserei? Ists ein erhöhter Sinn,
> Der erst die höchste, reinste Wahrheit faßt?
> Ja, es ist das Gefühl, das mich allein
> Auf dieser Erde glücklich machen kann.
> Das mich allein so elend werden ließ,
> Wenn ich ihm widerstand und aus dem Herzen
> Es bannen wollte. Diese Leidenschaft
> Gedacht ich zu bekämpfen, stritt und stritt
> Mit meinem tiefsten Sein, zerstörte frech
> Mein eignes Selbst, dem du so ganz gehörst—

nence), as she recognizes, has lost the battle to "Leidenschaft" (passion). Perhaps Tasso is right in claiming that it is a battle that has also destroyed his identity ("Mein eignes Selbst"). She now sees it threatening her as well. "Tasso, if I'm to listen to you further, / Dampen this ardour, for it frightens me." But Tasso is beyond such restraint. He is "Free as a god," he declares, "For ever you have made me wholly yours. / So take, too, the gift of all I am."[44] In his rapture he takes her in his arms and presses her close to him. Her cry, "Hinweg!" at his impulsive embrace echoes Tasso's earlier plea to her, "Nehmt ihn hinweg!" when she placed the laurels upon his head.

Having constrained physical action, Goethe intensifies symbolic and metaphoric action. The crowning of Virgil and Ariosto in the opening scene is a symbolic ritual in which Goethe introduces into the external action the literary tradition in which Tasso struggles to gain a place. Throughout the following scenes, the very word "Kranz" reinvokes the celebration of the two poets of the past and Tasso's agony as the new poet laureate. Instead of reconciling himself with the poetic past, he declares himself a spectator. If he is to wear the laurels, he announces, he shall wear them in the same solitude where he is accustomed to indulging his dreams:

> Alone there I shall wander, where no eye
> Reminds me of good fortune undeserved.
> And should some clear well show me there by chance
> In its pure mirror the image of a man
> Who, strangely garlanded, in light reflected
> From heaven, among the trees, among the rocks,
> Pondering, rests, then it will seem I see
> Elysium limned upon that magic surface.
> Quietly I shall think a while, and ask:
> Who could that dead man be? That young man there
> Out of an age long past? So proudly wreathed?
> Who'll tell me the man's name? Or what he did?

44. Ibid., V.iv.3257–58, 3265, 3274–75:

> PRINZESSIN. Wenn ich dich, Tasso, länger hören soll,
> So mäßige die Glut, die mich erschreckt.
>
> . . . .
>
> TASSO. Ich fühle mich von aller Not entladen,
> Frei wie ein Gott . . .
>
> . . . .
>
> Du hast mich ganz auf ewig dir gewonnen,
> So nimm denn auch mein ganzes Wesen hin!

> I wait for a long time, thinking: Oh, if only
> Another now would come, and then another
> To join him here in friendly conversation!
> If I could see the heroes and the poets
> Of ancient times conjoined around this well!
> If I could see them gathered here for ever,
> Inseparably bonded, as in life.[45]

As the dream of poetic fantasy unfolds, it ceases to matter whether other poets have dreamt the same dream. Although he has Tasso refer to poetic imagination with the commonplace metaphor of a mirror, Goethe clearly distinguishes its poetological significance from the mimetic principle of holding up the mirror to reality. More important for Tasso's dilemma, he also sets it at odds with that variation of *mimesis* which holds that poets must imitate the great literary models of the past. Goethe's Tasso affirms a version of the doctrine of imitation that was to become prominent in the romantic period: the poet imitates not the external object, but his own internal process of apprehending the object.

Tasso's mirror is thus a "Zauberfläche" that reflects the images of his own mind. At once the aloof observer and a participant in the magic scene, he watches his projected self moving in a world perhaps not of his own making but held together by the magnetic power of his own imagination, which draws images into its force field and holds them there.

45. Ibid., I.iii.530–48:

> Dort will ich einsam wandeln, dort erinnert
> Kein Auge mich ans unverdiente Glück.
> Und zeigt mir ungefähr ein klarer Brunnen
> In seinem reinen Spiegel einen Mann,
> Der, wunderbar bekränzt, im Widerschein
> Des Himmels zwischen Bäumen, zwischen Felsen
> Nachdenkend ruht, so scheint es mir, ich sehe
> Elysium auf dieser Zauberfläche
> Gebildet. Still bedenk' ich mich und frage:
> Wer mag der Abgeschiedene sein? der Jüngling
> Aus der vergangenen Zeit? so schön bekränzt?
> Wer sagt mir seinen Namen? sein Verdienst?
> Ich warte lang und denke: Käme doch
> Ein andrer und noch einer, sich zu ihm
> In freundlichem Gespräche zu gesellen!
> O säh ich die Heroen, die Poeten
> Der alten Zeit um diesen Quell versammelt!
> O säh ich hier sie immer unzertrennlich,
> Wie sie im Leben fest verbunden waren!

> As by its power the magnet holds together
> Iron and iron, in firm conjunction,
> So one urge binds the hero to the poet.
> Homer forgot himself, his whole life was
> Devoted to his thoughts about two men,
> And Alexander in Elysium
> Hurries to seek out Homer and Achilles.
> O that my living eyes might look upon
> The greatest spirits, all assembled now![46]

In the movement of this passage, Goethe marks the intensity of Tasso's imagination. What begins in speculating on a possible encounter with his own reflected image in a secluded spring, becomes complicated by imagining that it is reflected from the past, and then progressively animated by calling first upon the poets of antiquity and then upon the heroes from their works. The reflecting surface of the water is utterly forgotten. In his enthusiasm Tasso is ready to spring into the midst of the imaginary company of Alexander, Homer, and Achilles. Leonore calls out to him to awaken, to return from what is "gegenwärtig" only in his mind in order to acknowledge those who are "gegenwärtig" in the immediate reality.

The Princess, however, praises him for speaking so "menschlich" when he speaks to the phantom images of his mind. Tasso's poetic power lies in the strength of his imaginative vision. He creates a poetic presence in which the poet and the hero are united. His imagination is the magnet that holds this fictive world together. He is no sooner called forth from his vision than he finds himself catered to, humored, yet inevitably excluded from any practical deliberations in court. The magnet works its power only in seclusion and has power only over the images of fantasy. Antonio, in the very next scene, returns triumphant from Rome. His jealous repudiation of the poet is evident from his very first words to Tasso.

As the Princess asserts in the opening scene, it is still possible to dream one's way into the Golden Age of poetry (I.i.23). She must acknowl-

---

46. Ibid., I.iii.549–57:
> So bindet der Magnet durch seine Kraft
> Das Eisen mit dem Eisen fest zusammen,
> Wie gleiches Streben Held und Dichter bindet.
> Homer vergaß sich selbst, sein ganzes Leben
> War der Betrachtung zweier Männer heilig,
> Und Alexander im Elysium
> Eilt, den Achill und den Homer zu suchen.
> O daß ich gegenwärtig wäre, sie,
> Die größten Seelen, nur vereint zu sehen.

edge, however, that it is only a dream, and not untroubled by the disruptive presence of reality. The Princess, Leonora says, possesses a constancy of mind that elevates her above the vain appeals of flattery. Although the Princess responds by reminding her that these very words are spoken in the language of flattery, Leonora is too much the lady of the court to seek an alternative to the well practiced banter of praise. The Princess and her sister, she goes on, have used their intellectual powers to bring fame to the House of Este and have made themselves the most highly honored women of the age. The Princess recognizes the truth of Leonora's claim that the arts serve to display power and to satisfy "the princely appetite for fame" [die fürstliche Begier des Ruhms], but she also argues that they provide a means for exalting the human life itself. When Leonora says she wants "to linger on the island / Of poetry, and walk in its laurel groves," the Princess tells her that even in a land of poetry she would still seek the poet:

> Pleasant enough, we think, it would be, then,
> At the right time to meet him, all on fire
> To find in us the treasure that in vain
> The wide world over he has been looking for.[47]

Let the poet cross over alone to explore the realm of poetry, the Princess argues, for upon his return he might enable us to share in the strange vision. Leonora agrees:

> In his own magic circle that strange man
> Moves, has his being, and attracts us others
> To move with him and share his marvellous realm:
> He seems to approach us, yet stays far from us;
> He seems to look at us, yet in our place
> May well see only ghosts, phantasmal shapes.[48]

47. Ibid., I.i.151–54:

> Da wär' es denn ganz artig, wenn er uns
> Zur guten Stunde träfe, schnell entzückt
> Uns für den Schatz erkennte, den er lang
> Vergebens in der weiten Welt gesucht.

48. Ibid., I.i.167–72:

> In diesem eignen Zauberkreise wandelt
> Der wunderbare Mann und zieht uns an,
> Mit ihm zu wandeln, teil an ihm zu nehmen:
> Er scheint sich uns zu nahen und bleibt uns fern;
> Er scheint uns anzusehen, und Geister mögen
> An unsrer Stelle seltsam ihm erscheinen.

Having debated the relationship between the dream of a golden age and the realization of worldly power, the Princess and Leonora in this opening scene effectively anticipate the opposing forces with which Tasso must contend. In order to serve the Muse, the Renaissance artist must also manage to serve God and Mammon as well. As the Italian principalities vie with one another through the display of pomp and splendor, poet and painter, sculptor and architect gain social importance but must nevertheless surrender their independence and perhaps even their artistic integrity. The conflict between the ideals of art and the designs of the court repeats itself in the personal struggle of the artist. He must somehow fulfill his creative vision and, at the same time, obey the religious and worldly authorities over him. As Leonora phrases it, "What history offers, what this life can give him / At once and willingly his heart takes up." Or, in the words of the Princess, he "hovers on the plane of honeyed dreams / And yet . . . real things too / Attract him strongly and can hold him fast." Can Tasso discriminate the "honeyed dreams" and the reality, the "phantasmal shapes" and the aristocracy he must serve?

The overt action is starkly limited, as I have already noted, to the presentation of the epic poem and the request for its return, to the thwarted duel with Antonio and the impulsive embrace of the Princess. With all of Tasso's energies and efforts stifled, frustrated, and repressed, his only action is the action of words. Yet even his words, he is told, must conform to courtly principles. When he is called to self-denial, Tasso seeks gratification. When he is told that he must come to his senses, he lapses further into self-deception. Denied actual physical expression, the action is dramatically subverted into intense psychological confrontations in the dialogue ("entbehren" versus "befriedigen," "besinnen" versus "betrügen").

When "moderation" ("Mäßigkeit") is held up as a moral and aesthetic commandment, the intimidated poet is all the more impelled to excess. Antonio praises Ariosto as a poet whose "loveliest rhythm keeps its bounds" [im schönsten Takt sich mäßig hält, I.iv.733] even when he may seem to wallow in frenzied madness. When Tasso accuses him of coldness, Antonio replies, "The moderate man quite often is called cold" [Der Mäßige wird öfters kalt genannt, II.iii.1222]. The command to moderation pushes Tasso further into that immoderation perceived as ranting and raving ("toben und rasen"). Observing his mounting excitement, the Princess warns him that he must moderate his ardor ("mäßige die Glut," V.iv.3258). He responds, in his last gesture of physical action, by clasping her in his arms.

The Golden Age of poetry, as conceived by the Princess, is an ideal that will restore moderation and self-denial to those whose feelings grow pampered and spoilt. Tasso, however, imagines a Golden Age "When on a free earth human beings roamed / Like happy herds, to pasture on delight" [Da auf der freien Erde Menschen sich / Wie frohe Herden im Genuß verbreiten, II.i.980–81]. Where the Princess seeks to reassert moral order ("Erlaubt ist, was sich ziemt"), Tasso longs to escape moral restraints ("Erlaubt ist, was gefällt"). Confined to house arrest after his quarrel with Antonio, Tasso reflects upon the apparent futility of his dream of gratified desires:

> Have you awakened from protracted dream
> And has the dear delusion suddenly left you?
> The very day of your consummate joy
> Did a sleep cage you, to hold and awe your soul
> With heavy fetters now? There's no denying,
> You dream, awake.[49]

The soliloquy might have been an occasion for him to recognize the folly of his self-delusion. He seems to acknowledge that his "protracted dream" was but "dear delusion." But he is not ready to abandon the dream. Indeed, he resolutely declares and is all the more determined that he will continue the dream now wide awake and free of the fetters of sleep.

Tasso's dream of pleasure inevitably gives rise to nightmares of persecution. His very belief that a "consummate joy" is at hand requires him to believe, as well, in deliberate plots to foil its realization. When Antonio offers his diagnosis of Tasso's madness to Duke Alfonso, he lays the blame upon "immoderation." Antonio explains, in terms very different from Tasso's, the causes and consequences of dreaming while awake:

> There is no doubting it: an immoderate life,
> Just as it gives us wild and heavy dreams,
> Will make us waking dreamers in the end.
> What's false mistrust, suspicion, but a dream?
> In every place he thinks himself surrounded
> By enemies. No one perceives his talents
> Who doesn't envy him, and, envying,
> Hates him and persecutes him cruelly.

49. Ibid., IV.i.2189–94:
> Bist du aus einem Traum erwacht, und hat
> Der schöne Trug auf einmal dich verlassen?
> Hat dich an einem Tag der höchsten Lust
> Ein Schlaf gebändigt, hält und ängstet nun
> Mit schweren Fesseln deine Seele? Ja,
> Du wachst und träumst.

> How often has he vexed you with complaints:
> All those forced locks and intercepted letters,
> Poison and dagger! Phantoms that beset him!
> You've had each case investigated, looked
> Into it yourself, and found—less than a glint.
> No ruler's aegis makes him feel secure,
> No friend's affection comforts or assures him.
> Can you give peace or joy to such a man?
> Can you expect that man to give *you* pleasure?[50]

Antonio's account of Tasso's madness culminates in a crushing indictment not only of the madman but of the poet as well. Because of his delusions of persecution, Tasso has engulfed himself in torment. Not only has he become personally incapable of feeling "peace or joy," he can no longer as a poet give pleasure through his poetry. Duke Alfonso, although he looks on Tasso as an investment, still believes that it is worth spending more to succor the potential bounty of his literary power. With patience and tolerance, he replies, Tasso may still be encouraged to make full use of his great talents.

In the course of the play the concept of madness shifts. Rather than referring to his raptures of inspiration, Tasso's wild actions are perceived as fits of delirium. Although it is feared, even in the first act, that he spends too much time alone, absorbed in his own thoughts, his madness is still excused as dithyrambic ("wild begeistert"). Tasso himself is content with this definition of his peculiarity. He assures the Princess, for example, that her presence has cured him "Of all obsession, every devious urge":

50. Ibid., V.i.2914–30:

> Es ist gewiß, ein ungemäßigt Leben,
> Wie es uns schwere, wilde Träume gibt,
> Macht uns zuletzt am hellen Tag träumen.
> Was ist sein Argwohn anders als ein Traum?
> Wohin er tritt, glaubt er von Feinden sich
> Umgeben. Sein Talent kann niemand sehn,
> Der ihn nicht neidet, niemand ihn beneiden,
> Der ihn nicht haßt und bitter ihn verfolgt.
> So hat er oft mit Klagen dich belästigt:
> Erbrochne Schlösser, aufgefangne Briefe
> Und Gift und Dolch! Was alles vor ihm schwebt!
> Du hast es untersuchen lassen, untersucht.
> Und hast du was gefunden? Kaum den Schein.
> Der Schutz von keinem Fürsten macht ihn sicher,
> Der Busen keines Freundes kann ihn laben;
> Und willst du einem solchen Ruh und Glück,
> Willst du von ihm wohl Freude dir versprechen?

As one enchanted by deluded frenzy
Is promptly, willingly cured when gods are near,
So I was cured of every fantasy,
Of all obsession, every devious urge,
Cured by a single glance that met your glance.[51]

Tasso, of course, was not cured by that "single glance" of the Princess. Instead, her very presence further arouses the urges and obsessions that dictate more and more of his actions. The rational order of classicism gives way to the emotional excess of romanticism. After he has dared to take her into his arms, Duke Alfonso orders his attendants to escort Tasso to his confinement: "He's out of his mind. Hold on to him!" [Er kommt von Sinnen, halt ihn fest! V.iv.3277].

The opposition of the classic and romantic is better understood as a dialectic than as an absolute. Far from being mutually exclusive, the classic and romantic derive energy from each other and are typically defined in terms of relationship. Goethe's diagnosis—that the classic is the healthy and the romantic is the sick[52]—is reappraised as an inevitable cyclical recurrence in Herbert Grierson's definition of the classic and the romantic as "the systole and diastole of the human heart in history."[53] The romantic sickness is not fatal, but vital—a periodic hibernation during which poetry gives up its vigilant observation of external being and retreats into reverie and introspection. As Goethe acknowledges, the classic and romantic result from the poet's own objective or subjective inclination. In *Über naive und sentimentalische Dichtung*, Schiller demonstrated to Goethe that his classical presumptions were not as classical as he might want to believe. Comparatists the world over often cite *Faust* in discussions of European romanticism. Reluctant to accept Goethe's admission, "daß ich selber wider Willen romantisch sei,"[54] many Germanists continue to oppose the notion of a romantic Goethe as a gross misunderstanding of the poet's manner and meaning.

Perhaps it would be better to appraise the relation of classic and ro-

---

51. Ibid., II.i.874–78:
>   Wie den Bezauberten von Rausch und Wahn
>   Der Gottheit Nähe leicht und willig heilt,
>   So war auch ich von aller Phantasie,
>   Von jeder Sucht, von jedem falschen Triebe
>   Mit einem Blick in deinen Blick geheilt.

52. "Das Klassiche nenne ich das Gesunde und das Romantische das Kranke" (2 April 1829), in Johann Peter Eckermann, *Gespräche mit Goethe*, 313.

53. Herbert J.C. Grierson, "Classical and Romantic," 256, 287.

54. Eckermann, *Gespräche mit Goethe*, on Schiller's "Über naive und sentimentalische Dichtung," and classic and romantic as objective and subjective (21 March 1830), 390–91.

mantic motifs in terms of "container" and "thing contained." The transparency or opacity of one or the other would effect how that relationship might be perceived. Although we might invoke the term *vehicle* with I. A. Richards's sense of an implicated *tenor*,[55] the presence of the romantic in the classic, and *vice versa*, involves more than the metaphorical texture of a work. Even metaphorical reference, as Samuel Levin has argued, may be cognitively immediate or interactive, rather than synecdochic or structural.[56] In a perceptive and well-documented essay, "The Raven and the Bust of Pallas: Classical Artifacts and the Gothic Tale," Patricia Merivale explains why the prophetic bird perches upon the bust of Pallas Athena over the chamber door of the tormented scholar, and why so many other tales of sinister derangement implicate classical symbols of rational order. The classical artifact is a reminder of rationality, yet it may also represent a failure and perversion of classical ideals. Although Byron's Manfred is ready to scorn the classical τὸ καλόν, he must nevertheless admit its allure: "It will not last, / But it is well to have known it, though but once" (III.i.14–15). While Manfred may resign himself to a fleeting perception of the unattainable ideal, many another character in romantic fiction (among her examples, Merivale examines Josef von Eichendorff's *Das Marmorbild* and Prosper Mérimée's *La Vénus d'Ille*) is victimized by a quest to embrace the classical ideal. The very symbol of rational order thus becomes an instrument of irrational desires.

Just as romantic narrative may invoke the classical, so too a classical work may enclose within its rational order the ferment of romantic irrationality. Not every instance of madness in classical literature should be viewed as an outbreak of romantic temperament. Euripides, after all, provided a classical model for the tragic struggle with one's own irrational self in *Medea*. Fully aware of the evil of her act, Medea confesses simply that her passion (θυμός) is stronger than her will or reason (1078–80). As E. R. Dodds demonstrates in *The Greeks and the Irrational*, irrationality is not only celebrated in bacchanalia and maenadism, it persists in Greek literature from the temper (μένος) and delusion (ἄτη) of the Homeric hero through the subversions of rationalism in the drama of the classical age.

There is a difference, however, between the madness that recognizes the constraints of classical norms and the madness that envisions an alternate world. Yet even Don Quixote, who is smitten by romance and tries to reenact its fictions, is made to suffer his satirical mishaps in a

55. I. A. Richards, *Philosophy of Rhetoric* (1936), chaps. 5–6.
56. Samuel R. Levin, *Metaphoric Worlds,* describes literary conditions which render the covert implications inadequate and require the reader to accept the epistemological consequences of metaphor as a direct reference to a cognitive world.

world where pragmatic reason prevails. But once the poet presents a mad poet as spokesman, interpreter, perhaps even as *alter ego,* how can the reader or spectator sustain confidence in rational order? When Goethe introduces Tasso into the classical theater of Weimar, he complicates dramatic representation by insisting upon the validity of the poetic imagination even as he exposes its excesses. By showing how Tasso both controls and is controlled by the fictions he creates, how he observes, or thinks he observes, other fictions operative in the Duke's court, Goethe allows his Tasso to give free rein to the imaginative ardor of the romantic poet.

This does not mean that Goethe was willing to have it both ways. Byron and Shelley, as we have seen, championed the romantic rebel against external authority. Peacock believed that the classical and rational elements found a harmonic reciprocity in Tasso's great epic. Schlegel called him a poet of feeling, whose pretenses to classical form were ineffective. Goethe's dramatic representation exhibits in the character of Tasso the power of inspiration and passion on the individual imagination. But it also confirms the rational order upheld by the Princess, the Duke, and his Minister. Even in the midst of his raving in the final scene, Goethe's Tasso retains enough insight into his dilemma to know why his classical principles must guide his romantic impulses. The paradox of creative irrationality is resolved, if only within the confines of Goethe's play, by having the tormented poet acknowledge that rational order must ultimately prevail.

5

PARADOXES OF RATIONALITY AND REPRESENTATION

The patterns of paradox most pervasive in romantic literature are, in fact, the legacy of Enlightenment thought. With the emergence of aesthetics as a philosophical discipline in the eighteenth century came the attendant difficulty in establishing its claims to intellectual integrity. The problem, of course, was that the response to art had been relegated to the so-called "lower faculties." It was deemed an emotional rather than a rational experience. The illusion that art engenders was supposed to result from the emotions overpowering the reason.[1] While many of the paradoxes of rationality and representation may be attributed to an oversimplification of aesthetic experience, even a more complex account of perceptual process and psychological response, as developed during the romantic period, failed to dispel or resolve those dyads of representation apparently necessary to artistic expression.

Because illusion was considered the natural and proper effect of art, some advocated that artists should strive to create "perfect" illusion. In Germany, for example, both Johann Friedrich Schink and Christian Felix Weiße argued on behalf of bourgeois drama that it could provide such an accurate representation of domestic life that the spectators could become perfectly convinced during the performance that they were looking at real events and real persons.[2] For other critics, such as Jean François Marmon-

---

1. Alfred Baeumler, *Das Irrationalitätsproblem*, 18–64; Armand Nivelle, *Kunst- und Dichtungstheorien zwischen Aufklärung und Klassik*, 20; Marion Hobson, *The Object of Art*, 6–8, 47–50, 150–51, 174.
   2. Johann Friedrich Schink, *Dramaturgische Fragmente*, 458; Christian Felix Weiße, pref-

tel and Louis Sébasten Mercier, the purpose of the drama is to provide pleasure; thus we willingly indulge illusion in order to experience most fully the pleasure that dramatic fiction affords. But Mercier also stipulated that the illusion should not be continuous and complete.[3] Those who describe the emotional response as involuntary make no distinction between illusion and delusion. They dismiss the possibility of any conscious awareness of the fictionality of the performance to attend the illusion; indeed, they condemn any intruding awareness as a disruption that destroys the illusion. Those who argue the voluntary nature of illusion, however, savor both modes of response: aesthetic immediacy and aesthetic distance. But are the two modes of response possible simultaneously, or only consecutively? Modifying the concept of a complete and overwhelming illusion, Erasmus Darwin and Johannes Georg Sulzer were among the critics who appealed to the analogy of that twilight state in which we shift between dreaming and waking. Conceding that illusion was never long sustained, they claimed that drama could seduce the mind into a kind of reverie in which believing and disbelieving alternated.[4]

Although Diderot, in *Les Bijoux indiscrets* (1748), ridiculed the notion of perfect illusion, his description of the paintings of Vernet in his *Salon de 1767*, develops one of the most elaborate accounts of the illusionist experience in eighteenth-century art criticism. While he advocated the illusionism of bourgeois drama, his dialogue between author and character in *Entretien sur "Le Fils naturel"* also observed its pretensions and limitations.[5] Throughout his works, Diderot reveals a love of paradox.[6] Whether we read *Le Neveu de Rameau* (1762), or *Le Rêve de d'Alembert* (1769), or *Jacques le fataliste* (1775), we find Diderot so dexterous in juggling dia-

ace to *Das Fanatismus, oder Jean Calas*, 2–3. See also the anonymous "Rezension: Trauerspiele von C. F. Weiße" and Albert R. Schmitt, "Christian Felix Weißes *Jean Calas*—Dokumentarisches Theater im 18. Jahrhundert."

3. Jean François Marmontel, *Poétique Française*, 2:112, and "Illusion"; Louis Sébasten Mercier, "De Défauts à éviter dans le Drame," 140–47, also on 142: "Si l'illusion étoit entière, parfaite & d'une duré continue, elle cesseroit d'être agréable."

4. Erasmus Darwin, *The Botanic Garden*, 2:87; Johannes Georg Sulzer, "Täuschung," in *Allgemeine Theorie der schönen Künste* 4:514–16. For a later version of this argument, see Stendhal, *Racine et Shakespeare*, 60: "La fréquence de ces petits moments d'illusion, et de l'état d'emotion où, dans leurs intervailles, ils laissent l'âme du spectateur."

5. Denis Diderot, *Entretiens sur "le Fils naturel"* (1757), *Discours sur la poésie dramatique* (1758), in *Oeuvres Complètes* (= *OC*), 7:85–168, 299–394; *Salons*, vol. 3; and *Paradoxe sur le Comédien* (1773), in *Oeuvres esthétiques* (= *OE*).

6. Although Diderot's reliance on paradox has been denied by Yvon Belavel, *L'Esthétique sans Paradoxe de Diderot*, most critics persist in recognizing paradox as Diderot's master trope; see the review of Belavel by Herbert Dieckmann in *Romanic Review*; André Villiers, "A propos du *Paradoxe* de Diderot," 379–81; and Marian Hobson, "Le 'Paradoxe sur le comédien' est un paradoxe."

logical contraries that his exposition of alternatives seldom closes on a fixed and definite resolution.[7] The efforts at determining "truth" are indeterminate, conclusions remain inconclusive, paradoxes replace resolutions. Diderot exercised a variety of verbal and logical strategies for producing different sorts of paradox. Many "truths," as De Quincey was later to observe, deserve paradoxical exposition for they are not "truths" at all, but matters that may be viewed from opposite sides; paradox may thus reveal the error of popular opinion and challenge the orthodox by exclaiming: "Here, reader, are some extraordinary truths, looking so very like falsehoods that you would never take them for anything else if you were not invited to give them special examination."[8]

Indeed, some paradoxes defy resolution. For example, if my friend says of me, "This man always lies," and I confirm my friend's assertion, we have a paradox, for if he speaks the truth, then my confirmation must be true, but if it is true, then his statement is not, and neither is my confirmation of it. His statement and mine, like images between two mirrors, reverse each other in an endless series of counterreflections. The possibility of resolution is baffled.[9] Diderot, when he investigates the nature and experience of illusion, redresses several contradictions to orthodoxy, but he also exploits some inherent and some only seeming contradictions. Our task in reading his excursions on illusion requires that we sort our way between resolvable and irresolvable, real and apparent paradoxes.

Because dramatic illusion was generally defined during the eighteenth century as the heightening of emotional response to the point that the reason is overwhelmed, the spectator was presumed to be affected by the dramatic imitation as if it were reality. Illusion in these circumstances was often attributed directly to the success of the actor. The actor, so it seemed, ceases to be himself and becomes the character he plays. In examining how this apparent transfer is wrought, critics argued the same

7. Furst, *Fictions of Romantic Irony*, 159–87; see also Hans Robert Jauß, "Der dialogische und der dialektische *Neveu de Rameau* oder: Wie Diderot Sokrates und Hegel Diderot rezipierte," "Diderots Paradox über das Schauspiel (Entretiens sur le Fils Naturel)," and "Nachahmungsprinzip und Wirklichkeitsbegriff in der Theorie des Romans von Diderot bis Stendhal"; and Geoffrey Bremner, *Order and Change. The Pattern of Diderot's Thought*.

8. De Quincey, "Rhetoric" (1828) and "Secret Societies" (1847), in *DQ* 10:90–91 and 7:205–6; *paradox* distinguished from *fallacy* on 1:199 and 9:137. A similar definition of paradox is forwarded by Dieckmann in his review of Belavel: "Very few of Diderot's critics seem to be willing to read the *Paradoxe* and take it for what it is, or what, at least at the outset, it meant to be: a well-known classical genre, in which the author treats a statement which is contrary to general or received opinion and in appearance absurd, but in reality partly well founded" (42:63–65).

9. Robert L. Martin, *The Paradox of the Liar*; Intisar Ul-Haque, *A Critical Study of Logical Paradoxes*; William Poundstone, *Labyrinths of Reason*.

distinction between reason and emotion in acting that they had assigned to audience response. But here the argument took a different turn. The idea of artistic control conflicted with the notion of "feeling" the part.

Diderot takes up this problem in *Le Paradox sur le Comédien*. Actors actually in the throes of emotion lose all command of their skills in mime, gesture, and elocution. Thus to create the illusion of powerful emotion, actors are obliged to play their roles with studied deliberation. This enables them to concentrate on performing the very extremes of passion. Diderot refers to the acting of David Garrick and Claire-Joseph Clairon as examples of this paradoxical doctrine of the illusion of overwhelming emotion achieved through total rational constraint.[10] Should an actor actually surrender to the sway of feelings, the performance would be awkward and uneven. The paradox thus has a positive and negative aspect: if the spectator ceases to behold the actor and sees only the character caught up in emotional agitation, then it is certain that the actor has repressed emotion to achieve that effect; contrarily, if the spectator is aware of the actor and an inconsistent representation, then it may well be that the actor has allowed him- or herself to be affected by the emotional conditions of the role. The emotional response is excited in the audience only when it is mediated, not felt, by the actor.[11]

Having asserted at the opening of his *Laokoon* that the nature of both poetry and painting is illusion, presenting absent things as present, Lessing found it necessary to discuss the problem of signs. Following Plato's *Cratylus*, he accepted the distinction between natural and arbitrary signs together with the assumption that in the former the thing signified somehow is reflected with little alteration. Too, this distinction grants to the visual arts a medium of natural signs, but to verbal description only arbitrary signs. Thus *ekphrasis*, the verbal imitation of the visual, is not simply paradoxical but futile. Lessing's point, however, is that the illusion is broken in the ekphrastic moment of poetry not simply because its signs are arbitrary, but because its medium is consecutive. A static scene cannot be described with a flow of words. Conversely, process and change can be and are most properly described by language.[12]

In current semiotics, it is acknowledged that visual signs are no less

10. David Garrick, *Private Correspondence*; in his letter to Jean-Baptiste-Antoine Suard (7 March 1776), Garrick promises a commentary on Diderot's *Paradoxe sur le Comédien*. Also see Claire-Joseph Clairon, *Mémoires d'Hippolyte Clairon*, and H. C. Lancaster, *French Tragedy in the Time of Louis XV and Voltaire, 1715–1774*.

11. Denis Diderot, *The Paradox of Acting*, xii. See also Blanquet's edition of Diderot, *Paradoxe sur le Comédien*, 79–137.

12. Gotthold Ephraim Lessing, *Laokoon: oder über die Grenzen der Malerei und Poesie* (1766), in *Werke* 6:9, 52, 112–13, 116. For a critique of Lessing's attempt to undermine the credibility of *ut pictura poesis*, see Murray Krieger, *Ekphrasis*, 44–55.

arbitrary than verbal signs; even body language, gesture, and pantomime are the product of cultural conventions.[13] Nevertheless, literary critics still wrestle with the paradox of reference at the heart of aesthetic illusion. In Plato's dialogue between Cratylus and Socrates, those signs are said to be natural which echo or reflect what they signify, whereas the arbitrary signs convey their reference as instruments of convenience. The former are called primitive and mimetic, the latter derived and conventional. Primitive or primary nouns imitate what they represent; secondary nouns "have a meaning to those who have agreed about them" (*Cratylus* 383–89, 424, 433–34). The dialogue retains its importance, not for its linguistic validity, but for its close consideration of how words are perceived. Certainly, some words conjure virtual images, whereas others merely name without any sense of intimacy with their referent.

The rhetorical terms *metaphor* and *metonymy* provide another way of talking about the relative presence of the signified elicited through the signifier. Metaphor conjures the illusion that what is absent is present. Metonymy, however, calls attention to its own referentiality, discriminating itself from what it signifies.[14] There would be no paradox of reference if there were, in fact, discrete classes of words: one fixed vocabulary of metaphor, another of metonymy. What renders reference paradoxical is that the metaphor turns into metonymy, not just as the result of its altered reference in different contexts, but even as it functions within a given line of poetry. As Coleridge and De Quincey both recognized in formulating the *idem in alio*,[15] identity may coexist with difference. Although the *idem in alio* is a basic trope in all discourse, either of its polar constituents may be modulated with varying degrees of intensity.

Among the English romantic poets, Shelley was by far the most attentive to the flux of metonymic and metaphoric reference. The first two verse paragraphs of *Mont Blanc* reveal the strategy of reversing the subject-object dialectic crucial to his poetic argument. The poem begins with a metaphorical account of idea and thought as a river rushing down a mountain:

> The everlasting universe of things
> Flows through the mind, and rolls its rapid waves,
> Now dark—now glittering—now reflecting gloom—

---

13. Louis Marin, "Eléments pour une sémiologie picturale," in *Études Semiologiques* 17–43.

14. Murray Krieger, *Poetic Presence and Illusion*, xi–xii, 183–85. The Greek *metaphora* (*metapherein*, to carry over) implies a transference, whereas *metonymy* (*meta* + *onyma*) simply a change of names.

15. Coleridge, *M* 1:690, 2:33; and *CN* 3:4186. *DQ* 1:51, 5:237, 10:369, and 11:195–196.

Now lending splendour, where from secret springs
The source of human thought its tribute brings
Of waters, —with a sound but half its own,
Such as a feeble brook will oft assume
In the wild woods, among the mountains lone,
Where waterfalls around it leap for ever,
Where woods and winds contend, and a vast river
Over its rocks ceaselessly bursts and raves.

The second verse paragraph turns the reference around: if the mind is like the mountain, the mountain must be like the mind. With the first metaphorical set already in place, Shelley delays the equation in this second verse paragraph. He first establishes the conditions for his intended reversal. As the mind is informed by the universal flow of ideas, so too an external power permeates nature. That power seems immanent in the river Arve.

Thus thou, Ravine of Arve—dark, deep Ravine—
Thou many-coloured, many-voiced vale,
Over whose pines, and crags, and caverns sail
Fast cloud-shadows and sunbeams: awful scene,
Where Power in likeness of Arve comes down
From the ice-gulfs that gird his secret throne,
Bursting through these dark mountains like the flame
Of lightning through the tempest; —thou dost lie,
Thy giant brood of pines around thee clinging,
Children of elder time, in whose devotion
The chainless winds still come and ever came
To drink their odours, and their mighty swinging
To hear—an old and solemn harmony;
Thine earthly rainbows stretched across the sweep
Of the aethereal waterfall, whose veil
Robes some unsculptured image; the strange sleep
Wraps all in its own eternity; —
The caverns echoing to the Arve's commotion,
A loud, lone sound no other sound can tame.

Forever frozen, the glacier seems to replicate the Platonic ideal—fixed, permanent, and unchanging. Like that ideal, it spills forth into the world of flux, change, and mutability. Metaphors of religion and authority are blended in, as the mountain mimics the structures of human community and history. In proclaiming the active and creative processes at work in nature, Shelley implicates several minor metaphorical reversals that subtly anticipate the major reversal when he closes the equation. Transposing the epithets "earthly" and "aethereal," he makes the otherwise ethereal rainbow an earthly captive within the ravine, while the waterfall caught within the ravine is, in its unimpeded energy, liberated and ethereal. Its veil conceals the image it carves, a creative work to be contrasted with the sculpture of the human artist. It is with the emphasis on the restless spirit that seems to reside in the echoing ravine that Shelley closes the equation:

> Thou art pervaded with ceaseless motion,
> Thou art the path of that unresting sound—
> Dizzy Ravine! and when I gaze on thee
> I seem as in a trance sublime and strange
> To muse on my own separate fantasy,
> My own, my human mind, which passively
> Now renders and receives fast influencings,
> Holding an unremitting interchange
> With the clear universe of things around.

The mountain, then, is like the mind. At this point, however, the metaphor has become metonymy. Shelley makes us consciously aware of the trope as trope by introducing the narrative "I" in the act of reflecting on its "own separate fantasy." The mountain is *not* identical with the mind, but merely an image that seems to mimic the mind as it "renders and receives fast influencings." Of course, "the clear universe of things around" is very different from "the everlasting universe of things" with which the poem opened. Not until the concluding lines is the disparity reconciled in "The secret strength of things / Which governs thought." The task that remains is to discriminate the ideal from its material and mutable manifestations, "Seeking among the shadows that pass by, / Ghosts of all things that are" (45–46).

What renders that task problematic if not impossible, as Shelley states at the beginning of the third verse paragraph, is that the mind cannot always distinguish revelation from delusion.

> I look on high;
> Has some unknown omnipotence unfurled
> The veil of life and death? or do I lie
> In dream, and does the mightier world of sleep
> Spread far around and inaccessibly
> It circles?

$$(52–57)$$

The mountain, we are told at the end of the paragraph, has a voice "to repeal / Large codes of fraud and woe." Not everyone is capable of understanding that voice. The fourth paragraph interprets the language by which the mountain might "Teach the adverting mind" a lesson in the cataclysms of natural history. In the final paragraph, the mountain is bereft of mind; however, the power and strength still reside amid the silent winds and voiceless lightning. Its meaning, to the extent that its voice may be still be heard, depends completely on the human mind:

> And what were thou, and earth, and stars, and sea,
> If to the human mind's imaginings
> Silence and solitude were vacancy?
>
> (142–44)

An added problem of metaphorical referentiality in *Mont Blanc* is that Shelley has used the mimetic structure—the mind is like the mountain; the mountain is like the mind—as a means of representing those attributes of power that remain hidden in "silence and solitude." It may seem, then, that metaphor, the trope of identity and presence, has been called to serve the office of metonymy, the trope of difference and absence. What has happened, however, is that Shelley has shifted from the mimetic to the meontic mode. Instead of imitating what is there, he seeks to imitate what is not there. Although the meontic artist must also work with "the sensible forms of psychological perception," as Thomas McFarland has explained, "he uses those forms to bridge the *chorismus* between his own imperfect existence and the realm of true being" (*Forms of Ruin* 401).

Recurrent in romantic poetry are absences and negations. Shelley celebrates the inconstant visitations "of some unseen Power" which "Floats though unseen among us / . . . Like memory of music fled." "Heard melodies are sweet," Keats declares, "but those unheard / Are sweeter." If he could only remember the unheard melody of his vision, Coleridge assures us, he could build in air the images of his lost dream. Although akin to the classical tropes of omission and disruption, the romantic appeal to the unseen or unheard involves a very different strategy. The tropes of *occupatio* and *aposiopesis* have long been used to enlist the auditor in the narrator's task. The romantic poets seem to require something more, not merely to supplement the language, but to complement the creative act. The listener is called upon to participate in the very conjuring of the aesthetic experience.

When we hear one of Shakespeare's characters tell us that something cannot be told, the trope does not leave us doubting how to fill in the blank space. We are not called upon to ponder imponderables. The meaning is readily available to the audience even if there are those on the stage who are baffled by the unsaid or unsayable. Only Lear is foolish enough not to appreciate Cordelia's simple assurance that "my Love's / More richer than my tongue" and that she can say nothing to rival the language of her sisters. "Nothing will come of nothing," Lear warns her, "speak again." She replies, "I cannot heave / My heart into my mouth" (I.i.79–92). The unsaid words of Desdemona are no less immediately implicit when she is left without speech or even tears to reply to the harsh accusations of Othello: "I cannot weep; nor answer have I none, / But what should go by water" (IV.ii.103–4). The romantic poets may seem to rely on a similar rhetoric, but the conditions are not the same. Byron gives additional torque to the classical *occupatio*, when he resigns himself to silence in *Childe Harold*:

> Could I embody and unbusom now
> That which is most within me, —could I wreak
> My thoughts upon expression, and thus throw
> Soul, heart, mind, passions, feelings, strong or weak,
> All that I would have sought, and all I seek,
> Bear, know, feel, and yet breathe—into *one* word,
> And that one word were Lightning, I would speak;
> But as it is, I live and die unheard,
> With a most voiceless thought sheathing it as a
>   sword.
>
>   (III.xcvii)

Byron wants his language to engender another Byron, "unbusomed" from his own being and "embodied" in his text. The "embodied" word must be given all the vital attributes and energies of the speaker. Prepared to sacrifice himself to the blast in uttering forth the lightning word of power and passion, he surrenders to the opposite extreme, to "die unheard" with a "voiceless thought." Yet his is neither the one fate nor the other, and the reader is left with the paradox of contradictory alternatives.

If the concern with representing what is not there were conducted with a certain skeptical distance, content to leave absences absent, the writer might well rely on metonymy. Hughes Mearns's well-known "Antigonish" (no doubt prompted by one of his Lincoln School pupils mistaking "Antigone" for "Anti-gone") may have haunting implications, but the play with negation makes fun of the very illusion, or delusion, it pretends to describe.

> As I was going up the stair
> I met a man who wasn't there.

He wasn't there again today.
I wish, I *wish* he'd go away.[16]

Mearns has given us the simple paradox of negation, as in Lichtenberg's "handleless axe without a blade."[17] But what if the author seriously endeavors to conjure the nonexistent? The mimetic endeavors to make absent things present; the meontic reaches beyond the material world of things to draw nonbeing into being. In order to make its absence present, he must rely on symbol. Metaphors are functionally mimetic, but in imitating what is there, they may also allow what is not there to shine through. It is this capacity of mediating what cannot be mimetically represented which, according to Coleridge, defines the symbol (*LS* 30, 79).

The paradox of reference occurs when metaphor is abruptly turned to metonymy, or the mimetic to the meontic. Such a text leaves us with irreconcilable meanings. The aubade to Asia in Shelley's *Prometheus Unbound* attempts to describe her perfection, but the language remains bound by the material limits of metaphor. Metaphor turns to metonymy, and the metonymy negates itself.[18] Asia remains unseen even in the very moment she is beheld:

> Fair are others; none beholds thee,
> But thy voice sounds low and tender
> Like the fairest, for it folds thee
> From the sight, that liquid splendour,
> And all feel, yet see thee never,
> As I feel now, lost for ever!
>
> (II.v.60–65)

The metonymy of this aubade is complex, for the effect does not simply substitute the cause, it cancels the cause. The beauty before us is meontic: "Fair are others," but the fair features of Asia radiate in evanescence; her voice is "Like the fairest," but its very sound disembodies her presence. Cause and effect are caught in paradox: "none beholds thee, / But thy voice sounds low and tender"; when thus "thy voice sounds," "it folds thee / From the sight." To see is to hear; to hear is to see no more. The effect dissolves "that liquid splendour" of the efficient cause; seeing evokes the voice that renders invisible. The conditional "none beholds

16. Hughes Mearns, "Antigonish" (27 March 1922), in Franklin Pierce, *Innocent Merriment. An Anthology of Light Verse*, 239.

17. Georg Christoph Lichtenberg, *Schriften und Briefe*, 3:452: "Ein Messer ohne Klinge, an welchen der Stiel fehlt."

18. Frederick Burwick, "The Language of Causality in *Prometheus Unbound*."

thee" becomes absolute: no one *can* behold thee. This beauty may be felt, not seen: "all feel, yet see thee never." Such feeling, without a consummation in seeing, is a frustration, a wish with no fulfillment; thus the singer, also a disembodied "Voice in the Air," adds that all must feel, "As I feel now, lost for ever!" While frustration heightens the desire to see the unseeable, resignation to the inevitable failure is voiced in the final line of the aubade: "they fail, as I am failing, / Dizzy, lost, yet unbewailing!" (II.v.70–71).

The paradox of representation occurs when illusion is combined with delusion. Delusion, unlike illusion, involves a loss of volitional and rational control. Delusion is the hallucination of the irrational mind. If art so excites the emotions that the reason is overwhelmed, as was argued in some eighteenth-century accounts, the effect is not illusion but delusion. If the spectator of the bourgeois drama cannot distinguish what is on the stage from reality, he may have a voyeuristic experience but not an aesthetic one. Aesthetic experience requires that we recognize the work of art as a work of art even while we enjoy the illusion of its representation. Nevertheless, we still value art for its emotional intensity and its probing beyond the normal confines of reason.

Representation becomes paradoxical when we are expected to entertain the illusion of delusion. A tale of madness may keep abnormality at metonymic distance, but the author may also invite us into the madness, into the aberrant experience of an irrational world. The tradition of the *furor poeticus* provides an immediate rationale for the irrational narrator. The inspired poet engulfs the reader in the moment of vision. Should it merely observe and describe, sustaining the distance of a clinical case study or symptomatology, a narrative about madness might not involve any paradox at all. To the extent, however, that the author endeavors to recreate the madness and its hallucinations, he entangles us in the paradox of a sane mind representing insanity. Romantic narratives provide numerous versions of the visionary excursion beyond the boundaries of reason: Novalis in *Heinrich von Ofterdingen* (1800); Hoffmann in *Der goldne Topf* (1814); Shelley in *Alastor* (1816); Eichendorff in *Das Marmorbild* (1819); De Quincey in *Confessions of an English Opium-Eater* (1821); Nodier in *Jean-François les Bas-Bleus* (1833). These narratives not only instigate the fundamental paradox of representation, they involve further variations and complications: the paradox of the unreasonable truth, the paradox of manifest nothingness, the paradox of the perfect stranger.

Metonymy has impressed modernist and postmodernist critics as a far more sophisticated trope than metaphor. Metonymy, after all, requires an awareness of semiotic differentiation, whereas metaphor seems to be little more than the tropical equivalent of "naive realism." In spite of Roman

Jakobson's learned and persuasive essay to the contrary, metaphor and metonymy are not bipolar but bimodal. Jakobson's ground for arguing their polar opposition, after all, was the pathological response to language in the polar extremes of aphasia. One type of aphasic brain disorder undermines the ability to observe the similarities, the other the contiguities of verbal signs. Jakobson compares this pathological polarity to the relative dominance of metaphor in romanticism and metonymy in realism.[19] I have no objection to his clinical evidence that certain mental afflictions cause the mind to lose its ability to perform rapid and subtle metalinguistic operations. For a deranged mind, all language might become immediately connected to material things, or aloofly detached and abstracted from reality. But such polar extremes, by Jakobson's own argument, are abnormal. A mind that is healthy and alert may easily juggle both the metaphorical and metonymical referentiality of words. The two modes of response can be appreciated at the same time. Indeed, literary response is enhanced by a bimodal appreciation of the possible identity as well as alterity of signifier and signified. Because each provides operative leverage to the other, the metaphoric and metonymic modes are complementary.

Novalis appreciates the utility of such leverage, for he emphasizes the bimodality throughout the opening chapters of *Heinrich von Ofterdingen* (1799; published 1802). To be sure, his purpose is to encourage the magical dominance of metaphor. His narrative strategy is to extend, little by little, the appreciation of metaphor's momentary illusion of immediacy. The practical reminders of metonymic differentiation gradually lose importance as Heinrich moves into the realm of poetic fulfillment. But Novalis makes us feel their insistent presence at the outset. For the dream of the blue blossom as an omen of love and good fortune, Novalis simply adapts from Thuringian folklore.[20] The dream, however, transforms it into a grand and complex symbol of desire. After penetrating the cavern and plunging naked into a shimmering pool of light, Heinrich luxuriates in erotic sensation:

> It seemed to him as if a colorful sunset cloud floated around him; a heavenly feeling flooded through his inner being; with ardent desire innumerable thoughts strove to merge within him; new, never

19. Roman Jakobson, "The Metaphoric and Metonymic Poles," in Roman Jakobson and Morris Halle, *Fundamentals of Language.*

20. Novalis 1:605. For discussion of relevant folklore and literature, see Jutta Hecker, "Das Symbol der Blauen Blume in Zusammenhang mit der Blumensymbolik der Romantik"; Friedrich Hiebel, "Zur Interpretation der Blauen Blumen des Novalis"; and A. Leslie Wilson, "The Blaue Blume."

seen images arose, and intermingled, and became visible beings
surrounding him, and every wave of the lovely element pressed
pliantly like a tender bosom against him. The inundation seemed
to be a solution of enticing maidens whose liquid form became
flesh as it flowed over him.[21]

Like Florio in *Das Marmorbild*, Heinrich experiences a baptismal ritual of
initiation; although he, too, finds himself inundated with caressing femi-
ninity, he has no fear of sinking in a sea of sirens. Intoxicated with pleasure, he swims with the current of light flowing out of the basin. He slumbers and awakens on the side of a spring where he sees the blue blossom
amid a field of flowers. Just as a face begins to form within the blossom
Heinrich is roused from his dream by his mother.

As in Coleridge's "Kubla Khan" (1797; published 1816), we have the
symbols of a fountain within a cave. Coleridge's orgasmic fountain bursts
but "momently" only to sink again in "a lifeless ocean." The fountain has
the power to animate the rocks, to make them dance as if they were vital
"grain beneath the thresher's flail," yet its "swift half-intermitted burst" is
not sustained. Novalis's fountain, however, is a continuing source of energy. In spite of separation and loss upon waking, Heinrich accepts the
dream-promise of union with that energy. The mingling of human and
plant, organic and inorganic being, may seem grotesque when viewed
from the outside; seen from within, the interpenetration—a universal
metempsychosis—is a beatific consummation. Through the dream Heinrich experiences an interpenetration that restores the divided and fragmented self to wholeness. Heinrich has no sooner awakened from his
vision of the "blaue Blume," than he hears his father's chiding. But his
father, too, has had such a dream as a young man, and a stranger promised him "das höchste irdische Los," if he would only return on the Eve of
Saint John to pluck the blue blossom. The father has now forgotten the
magic of the dream and dismisses his son's enthusiasm: "Träume sind
Schäume."

The journey the father failed to pursue now commences for the son.
The mother takes Heinrich on a trip from Eisenach to Augsburg where he
meets the poet Klingsohr and his daughter Mathilde. During the journey,
the discussion with the merchants sets up the antithetical modes of per-

21. Novalis 1:196–97: "Es dünkte ihn, als umflösse ihn eine Wolke des Abendrots; eine
himmlische Empfindung überströmte sein Inneres; mit inniger Wollust strebten unzählbare
Gedanken in ihm sich zu vermischen; neue, niegesehene Bilder entstanden, die auch inein-
anderflossen und zu sichtbaren Wesen um ihn wurden, und jede Welle des lieblichen Elements schmiegte sich wie ein zarter Busen an ihn. Die Flut schien eine Auflösung reizender
Mädchen, die an dem Jünglinge sich augenblicklich verkörperten."

ception: outer experience and inner contemplation ("der Weg der Er-
fahrung" and "der Weg der innern Betrachtung"). The merchants conde-
scendingly praise Heinrich's teacher, the court chaplain, for his religious
wisdom but emphasize his unfamiliarity with the world. Because musicians work with instruments and sounds, artists with paint, color, and
light, both seem more comprehensible to the material-minded merchants
than the poet, whom they nevertheless admire for his magical power over
language. When they recommend the accomplishments of the poet, it is
in terms of his material gains. Thus they tell the tale of a poet who recovered a treasure lost at sea, and of another who married a princess and
inherited a kingdom.

Parallel to the contrast between merchant and poet (chapters 2 and 3),
the contrast between soldier and poet (chapter 4) again poses the external at odds with the introspective way of seeing. The Knight sings of the
Crusade and the battle for the Holy Land, and Heinrich is thrilled by the
adventure but appalled by the slaughter. He imagines a Christ at the holy
grave tormented by the brutal victory. The Knight describes sexual conquest as a warrior's reward ("wenn du das Schwert gut zu führen ver-
stehst, so kann es dir an schönen Gefangenen nicht fehlen"). Afterward, in
the garden, Heinrich hears the lament of the captive Zulima, whose tale of
misfortune and suffering moves Heinrich to compassion and counters the
Knight's praise of conquest.

In the scene with the Miner and the Hermit (chapter 5), Novalis makes
the underground labyrinth the metaphorical place of introspection. In his
account of the seemingly organic and hieroglyphic manifestation of the
subterranean minerals, Novalis has, in De Quincey's words, made "the
stream of the miraculous . . . confluent with the stream of the natural"
(*DQ* 8:410). Heinrich marvels at the internal beauties revealed by the
Miner, but he still stands as an outsider before the Hermit's book. In the
Hermit's book Heinrich discovers engravings of himself. The book seems
to tell his story, but it is incomplete; worse, it is written in a language he
cannot read. Heinrich's curiosity as he covertly inspects the Hermit's
book replicates the initiation of the reader into the text. As witness to
Heinrich's estrangement from the meaning of his own life, the reader, too,
becomes involved in the inside/outside paradox.

The meaning of love and poetry are revealed to Heinrich through his
meetings with Mathilde and Klingsohr in the concluding chapters of part 1
(*Erwartung*). After meeting Mathilde, Heinrich dreams that her boat is
caught in a maelstrom. This second dream repeats and enlarges the imagery of the first. Again Heinrich swims; again he "sleeps" within his dream
and awakens to find himself by a fountain on a hillside. The trees and
flowers talk; he finds Mathilde, who points to the whirlpool in the sky's

"blaue Wellen." The blue blossom has become a huge vortex presaging her death. Klingsohr's Märchen, in which Fabel drives off the Fates who inhibit perception and Freya is galvanically revived to embrace Eros, prepares for the magic interpenetration in part 2 (*Erfüllung*) of the unfinished novel.

Although Novalis pits the material world of conquest and possession against the magical world of poetic vision, he insists that material reality is sustained by the very power revealed to the poet. Novalis intends to close part 2 with a simple family, thus inverting the structure of the Märchen. The divine mission of Heinrich's pilgrimage will be fulfilled in the family, realizing the blessing of the Holy Family. Heinrich's way to this apotheosis is through madness. By accepting a voluntary madness ("freiwilliger Wahnsinn"), he is able to escape the constraints of materiality and discover the essence of being. Heinrich allows his poetic madness to carry him through all the whole evolution of poetic consciousness: the mythic, the lyric, the epic, the dramatic. The world is transformed into the poetic ideal (Paralipomena, 1:344–48). The more completely Novalis succeeds in convincing us that the paradox has been resolved *inside* the narrative, the more powerfully we feel its lack of resolution *outside* the narrative.

In *Der goldne Topf*, by contrast, the two worlds coexist in mutual suspicion if not outright hostility. Anselmus, like Heinrich, is initiated into the magic of poetic vision. Unlike the *pícaro*, who begins his adventures in maladroit folly but gradually acquires the cunning not only to survive but to prosper in the material world, the romantic *Sonderling* remains a misfit precisely because he is preoccupied with an ideal world. Heinrich, as one who transforms the world rather than merely transforming himself, is an inverse *pícaro*. Although Novalis's apprentice at Sais blames himself for being more clumsy than the others (1:81), Heinrich is merely timid, not a *Sonderling*, when he is introduced to the festivities at the home of his grandfather. Anselmus, however, is incapable of walking across the parlor without knocking over a tea tray. Hoffmann heightens narrative tension by holding Anselmus in the madness between alternate possibilities. The two value systems—materialism and idealism—are pitted against each other in irresolvable antagonism. But they do coexist. Indeed, they reflect each other like strangely distorting mirrors. Their relationship is paradoxical, for each proclaims "truth" for itself and observes the antics of the other as "folly."

In this respect, Registrator Heerbrand is as much counterpart as rival to Anselmus. Heerbrand's wedding to Veronika in Dresden is the bourgeois reflection of the magical union of Anselmus and Serpentina in Atlantis. His pretensions to artistic sensibility accompany his philistine incapacity to recognize artistic expression. When Anselmus describes his vision of the singing serpents in the elderberry tree, Konrektor Paulmann brusquely informs him that only madmen and fools dream with their eyes wide open. Veronika tries to redeem his seeming irrationality by suggesting that perhaps he was actually asleep. Heerbrand claims a greater appreciation of waking visions:

> "Is it not possible for one to sink sometimes into a kind of dreamy state even while awake? I have myself had such an experience; for instance, one afternoon while at coffee, in the kind of mood produced by that special time of salutary physical and spiritual digestion, I suddenly remembered—as if by inspiration—where a misplaced manuscript lay—and only last night a magnificent large Latin paper came dancing before my open eyes in the very same way."[22]

Heerbrand's version of "inspiration" is to recall what happened to a misplaced paper. But even a mental flight thus reduced to a flea-hop seems all too mystical to Konrektor Paulmann, who cautions Heerbrand that such an inclination to the poetic may cause a lapse into "das Fantastische und Romanhafte." When such lapses do occur, the spirits of punch, not of poetry, are to blame. Upon first hearing Lindhorst's tale of Phosphorous, Prince of Spirits, and his love for the Fire Lily, Heerbrand calls it "orientalischer Schwulst" and tells Lindhorst to confine himself to the truth. When Anselmus repeats the tale over the punch bowl, Heerbrand comes to his defense. Paulmann accuses him of madness, but Heerbrand swears that Lindhorst is indeed a salamander and reports seeing him strike a fire by snapping his fingers. Of course, Heerbrand was drunk on that occasion, too. Drunkenness, apparently, enables Heerbrand to witness that world of Lindhorst's magic into which Anselmus enters daily as an ardent and devoted scribe.

As long as he believes in the magic and dedicates his love to Serpentina, Anselmus completes his task of transcribing the mysterious texts with ease and grace. When his thoughts of Veronika intrude, following the mad punch-party, the accursed blot of ink mars his work and he is imprisoned in the crystal bottle. There he beholds other students similarly

---

22. Hoffmann, *Selected Writings*, 1:69; *Sämtlicher Werke* (1905) 1:185: "Sollte man denn nicht auch wachend in einen gewissen träumerischen Zustand versinken können? So ist mir in der That selbst einmal nachmittags beim Kaffee in einem solchen Hinbrüten, dem eigentlichen Moment körperlicher und geistiger Verdauung, die Lage eines verlornen Aktenstücks wie durch Inspiration eingefallen, und nur noch gestern tanzte auf gleiche Weise eine herrliche große lateinische Frakturschrift vor meinen hellen offenen Augen umher."

confined, who do not realize their confinement. Worse, they laugh at him and call him mad for imagining he is in a bottle. Who is confined? The person who accepts the values of the bourgeois world? Or the one enraptured by the imaginative ideal? In positing the paradox of "liberty," Foucault reminds us that the word *delirium* (from Latin *lira*, a rut) means literally "to get out of a rut." The advantage of being in a rut is that one is joined by the masses who also follow custom and tradition.[23] Those few who deviate from the path are, *ipso facto*, deviant and delirious.

Imagination enables Anselmus to enter the magical world; intoxication gives Heerbrand his occasional glimpses; superstition prompts Veronika to indulge its illusions. In contrast to Lindhorst, who seeks neither power nor gain in the material world, Liese deals with her forbidden arts in the marketplace of desire. She dwells only in the shadows of the two worlds. In the magical world, she is the misbegotten progeny of dark forces. In the real world, she identifies herself as Veronika's old nurse, but she also peddles apples at the Black Gate as well as black magic to credulous young ladies. For knocking over her applecart, Anselmus earns her curse: she grins at him from Lindhorst's door knocker and mocks him in his bottled captivity. Catering to Veronika's ambition to become a Frau Hofrathin, Liese implicates her in magical rites performed at the crossroads in the midnight hour of the equinox. From her cauldron she casts a mirror in which Veronika may behold the captive image of Anselmus. Her curse, "ins Krystall bald dein Fall," is thus doubly fulfilled: Anselmus is kept in the mirror in Veronika's sewing box as well as in the bottle in Lindhorst's laboratory. When Anselmus expounds on the salamander's magic, the punch-inspired Heerbrand calls Liese an old witch. Anselmus grants that she has power, but denounces her low birth ("ihr Papa ist nichts als ein lumpichter Flederwisch und ihre Mama eine schnöde Runkelrübe"). Veronika defends her as a wise woman and declares that Liese's cat, an educated young man with refined manners, is her first cousin. Unable to restore rational order to this mad debate, Paulmann cries out: "But I must be in a lunatic asylum. Have I gone crazy myself? What kind of gibberish am I uttering? Yes, I am mad! I am also insane!"[24]

Hoffmann's contribution to the romantic thematization of delusion resides in his peculiar skill in sustaining uncertainty and heightening sus-

23. Foucault 99–100: "*delirium*: 'This word is derived from *lira*, a furrow; so that *deliro* actually means to move out of the furrow, away from the proper path of reason'"; quoted from Robert James, *Dictionnaire universel de médicine* (French trans., Paris, 1746–48), 3:977. On the paradox of liberty, see also Foucault 209, 212–13, 260–61.

24. Hoffmann, *Werke*, 1:228; *Selected Writings*, 1:117: "Aber bin ich in einem Tollhause? bin ich selbst toll? —was schwatze ich denn für wahnwitziges Zeug?—ja ich bin auch toll— auch toll!"

pense by keeping his characters thus teetering between reason and madness. Throughout the tale, Anselmus appears to drift in and out of delusion. If gifted with an inspired imagination, he has yet to learn how to control his own mental capacities. Anselmus spends most of his introspective moments trying to sort out his doubts and divided impulses. Hoffmann is fully aware of that assault by which the bourgeoisie preempts and stifles imaginative expression. Call it "mad" and it withers stillborn, denied the chance to become art. The momentary immediacy of inspiration and insanity cannot be neatly discriminated. Reason forfeits its authority when it wanders within this border zone; nor can any witness give reliable testimony to enable the reason to adjudicate the border skirmishes. Foucault explains why the truth of the encounter cannot be subjected to scientific scrutiny:

> In this opposition, to which Tasso and Swift bore witness after Lucretius—and which it was vain to attempt to separate into lucid intervals and crises—was disclosed a distance where the very truth of art raised a problem: was it madness or a work of art? Inspiration, or hallucination? A spontaneous babble of words, or the pure origins of language? Must its truth, even before its birth, be taken from the wretched truth of men, or discovered far beyond its origin, in the being that it presumes? The madness of the writer was, for other men, the chance to see being born, over and over again, in the discouragement of repetition and disease, the truth of the work of art. (Foucault 285–86)

The truth may be rationally irretrievable, but Hoffmann delivers his doubtful testimony of the border conflict with obvious delight in its paradoxicality. A parrot does battle with a cat; a fiery salamander struggles against a witch. When the smoke and stench subside, a nasty beet and a tuft of black hair are the only remaining signs of the vanquished fiends. The long-tormented student is liberated and embraces the salamander's serpent daughter. A victory is granted to art, for the golden pot is restored and Anselmus is redeemed. But the victory can be celebrated only in the world of art. In Dresden, where he had been a madman, bungler, and fool, he is soon forgotten (that is, by the fictitious inhabitants of a fictitious Dresden). In Atlantis, he becomes knight of his own domain, a domain that can be witnessed (thus Archivarius Lindhorst kindly reassures the author who struggles to write a credible conclusion) as a poetic possession of the inner mind.

Hoffmann's authorial intrusions, often occasion for ironic play with the "Dear reader" strategies of fiction, implicate that self-reflective engagement which distinguishes illusion from delusion. Hoffmann, of course, tries to bring illusion as close as possible to that boundary of delusion which Foucault called the "equinox between the vanity of night's hallucinations and the non-being of light's judgments" (Foucault 111). Thus, on that equinox of the witch's rite, Hoffmann wishes that the reader might be transposed into the scene as witness: "Gentle reader, I sincerely wish that you had been travelling towards Dresden on this twenty-third day of September." In narrating this impossibility, deliberately sustaining the subjunctive, he conjures the semblance of Aristotelian probability (*Poetics* 1460:26–36). The circumstances of one fiction are interwoven with those of another. Veronika is persuaded by Liese to take part in these dark equinoctial rites on the crossroads. The reader is similarly compelled by the author to abandon the comfort of an inn and risk the supernatural encounter in the darkness of the equinox. Entering into the demonic scene, likened to a painting by Rembrandt or Brueghel suddenly brought to life, the reader is assured that his courageous presence will dispel the witch's magic. Whether the reader will then find the fair Veronika, as sole survivor of this "Illusionszerstörung," Hoffmann admits is doubtful. After conditionally entertaining this impossible probability of breaking the magic spell, the "Illusionszerstörung" is itself destroyed: "Alas, gentle reader, neither you nor anyone else drove or walked this way on the twenty-third of September during that stormy night so favorable to witches."

In implicating the reader, Hoffmann moves progressively from the mundane to the magical. At the beginning of the Fourth Vigil, the reader, still supposed to be much like some citizen of Dresden, is asked if he has ever found himself annoyed and discontent with all his efforts, if everything normally held in value suddenly seemed trivial and absurd. In the Seventh Vigil, when the reader is put in a coach bound for Dresden at midnight, he is certainly asked to assume a more immediate role in the magical encounter. In the Tenth Vigil, when the narrator grants that the reader has probably never been sealed up in a glass bottle, the reader is nevertheless expected to enter imaginatively into the splendor and terror of the confinement. Although both thematization of delusion and the implication of reader illusion are already developed in Cervantes's *Don Quixote*, what Foucault calls "madness by romantic identification" involves a more elaborate paradoxicality of belief and disbelief, truth and fiction. The reader is called upon not merely to witness, but to participate in the madness. In transmitting the fictive chimeras from author to reader, "what was fantasy on one side becomes hallucination on the other." The romantic narrative thus exploits the "enormous anxiety concerning the relationships, in a work of art, between the real and the imaginary, and perhaps also concerning the confused communication between fantastic invention and the fascinations of delirium" (Foucault 29).

Claiming that the workings of imagination are misconceived in the traditional lore that equates genius with madness, Dilthey insists that "beneath these paradoxes is concealed a legitimate problem" (Dilthey 6:91). The legitimate problem, according to Dilthey, is how the imagination organizes images and impressions into the work of art. The equation of genius with madness results in a misleading paradox, because it either attributes to madness a high degree of control over organization, which it does not possess, or it denies that control to genius. Foucault, in the conclusion to *Madness and Civilization*, may seem to agree with Dilthey when he exclaims that "*where there is a work of art, there is no madness.*" Although he italicizes these words, he immediately adds that "madness is contemporary with the work of art."[25] For Foucault, the paradox cannot be shunted aside by an attention to organization. Irrationality, too, has its highly wrought structures. Art may be twin-born with madness, but it escapes madness because it participates in the discourse of the rational world.

The paradoxicality, however, is inescapable. The *furor poeticus*, as Foucault defines it, is no mere invention of social convenience to excuse artistic idiosyncrasies. To be sure, the advent of the asylum and the rise of behavioral psychology brought about a different way of perceiving the peculiarities of artistic inspiration. As a result, coinciding with the close of the Enlightenment and the advent of romanticism, the poet has had to bear a greater social burden. In spite of the effort to discriminate art and madness, the polarization of reason versus emotion in Enlightenment thought forced an either/or diagnosis, which meant, in turn, that art and madness were nevertheless united, "paradoxically, at the point where they limited one another. For there existed a region where madness challenged the work of art, reduced it ironically, made of its iconographic landscape a pathological world of hallucinations; that language which was delirium was not a work of art. And conversely, delirium was robbed of its meager truth if it was called a work of art" (Foucault 285–86). Since the end of the eighteenth century, when new criteria of mental pathology began to be used, the dilemma of the mad rhapsodist has had epidemic consequences:

From the time of Hölderlin and Nerval, the number of writers, painters, and musicians who have "succumbed" to madness has

25. Foucault 287: "Madness is precisely the *absence of the work of art*, the reiterated presence of that absence, its central void is experienced and measured in all its endless dimensions. . . . Madness is the absolute break with the work of art; it forms the constitutive moment of abolition, which dissolves in time the truth of the work of art."

increased; but let us make no mistake here; between madness and the work of art, there has been no accommodation, no more constant exchange, no communication of languages; their opposition is much more dangerous than formerly; and their competition now allows no quarter; theirs is a game of life and death. (Foucault 286–87)[26]

The paradox of the *furor poeticus* is that the source of inspiration becomes the ground for rejecting its expression. The truth of art depends on that fleeting moment in its very birth pangs in which it separates itself from the truth of madness. Born of the irrational, art must take up residence in a world of rational discourse. Madness, born of the same womb, renounces all pretenses to art in order to nourish its own truth.

In Dilthey's formulation, "the highest and most difficult task of the inner life consists in bringing an acquired sense of their relationship to bear upon the perceptions, images, and conditions immediately present in the consciousness." In madness and dreams, the mind fails to perform this regulative function. In genius, the task is performed with superior power: "A genius is no pathological manifestation, but the healthy, the perfect man" (Dilthey 6:94). For Foucault, art, no less than madness, reveals the dark secrets of its origin. The madman organizes that truth for himself alone. The artist gives it to the world. The truth of art, nevertheless, is an unreasonable truth. Art, by its very nature, opposes the rational judgment of orthodoxy.

This paradox provides Shelley the argumentative structure for his *Alastor* (1819). In the opening forty-nine lines, and again in the concluding forty-nine lines, the narrator laments the folly of the poet-hero, who ignores the reality of human love in his quest for an ideal union with Spirit of Beauty. Within the central episodes of the narrative, however, Shelley recreates the fascination and visionary obsession with such ardent intimacy that neither the skeptical disclaimer of the author's preface nor the combined force of the prologue and epilogue can adequately dissuade the reader of the truth of the poet's vision. By giving suasory support to both believing and disbelieving, he not only leaves the paradox of the *furor poeticus* fully intact, he also exploits the meontic paradox of manifest nothingness and the self-reflexive paradox of the perfect stranger.

26. Ibid. 212: "In the disparity between the awareness of unreason and the awareness of madness, we have, at the end of the eighteenth century, the point of departure for a decisive movement: that by which the experience of unreason will continue, with Hölderlin, Nerval, and Nietzsche, to proceed ever deeper toward the roots of time—unreason thus becoming, *par excellence*, the world's *contra-tempo*—and the knowledge of madness seeking on the contrary to situate it ever more precisely within the development of nature and history."

As explained in the preface, the poem "represents a youth of uncorrupted feelings and adventurous genius led forth by imagination and purified through familiarity with all that is excellent and majestic, to the contemplation of the universe." Because his genius is "insatiate," he soon ceases to be content with "the magnificence and beauty of the external world." His mind seeks, instead, "for intercourse with an intelligence similar to itself." Thus "he images to himself the Being whom he loves." At this juncture, from the vantage of the narrator, the poet loses his tranquil self-possession and falls victim to self-delusion: "The intellectual faculties, the imagination, the functions of sense, have their requisitions on the sympathy of corresponding powers in other human beings. The Poet is represented as uniting these requisitions, and attaching them to a single image. He seeks in vain for a prototype of his conception. Blasted by his disappointment, he descends to an untimely grave." In his wanderings, he is tended by an Arab maiden, but he is blind to her devotion (129–39). Rather than seek sympathy and correspondence in a human companion, the poet creates a phantom image. He dedicates himself to the Spirit of Beauty whom he has engendered in dream (149–91). She appears as narcissistic reflection in female form: "Her voice was like the voice of his own soul / . . . / Herself a poet." Awakening from his erotic vision, he begins his search for the vanished image.

The impelling force of inspiration leads him on a voyage that is, at once, a quest of love and a quest of death. The poet's devotion to the illusory image seems madness, but he is also aware of the impossibility of realizing the ideal:

> As one
> Roused by some joyous madness from the couch
> Of fever, he did move; yet, not like him,
> Forgetful of the grave, where, when the flame
> Of his frail exultation shall be spent,
> He must descend.
>
> (517–22)

The nonbeing for which he searches is always with him. This is the meontic paradox of his quest.[27] Even when he embarks on the vain search, he ponders the illusion of sleep and death as

27. Ibid. 106–7, on the paradox of manifest nothingness: "The presence of images offers no more than night-ringed hallucinations, figures inscribed at the corners of sleep, hence detached from any sensuous reality; however vivid they are, however rigorously established in the body, these images are nothingness; as for erroneous judgment, it judges only in appearance: affirming nothing true or real, it does not affirm at all; it is ensnared in the nonbeing of error. Joining vision and blindness, image and judgment, hallucination and lan-

                              a shadowy lure,
With doubtful smile mocking its own strange charms.
Startled by his own thoughts he looked around.
There was no fair fiend near him, not a sight
Or sound of awe but in his own deep mind.

                                                    (294–98)

Like Novalis in *Heinrich von Ofterdingen* and Coleridge in *Kubla Khan*,
Shelley, too, uses the evocative imagery of the river and the cave (352–
420). After plunging down the "windings of the cavern," the poet finds
himself in a dark mysterious dell. Here, "as led / By love, or dream, or
god, or mightier death," he feels the presence of his long-sought love:

                              his regard
Was raised by intense pensiveness, . . . two eyes,
Two starry eyes, hung in the gloom of thought,
And seemed with their serene and azure smiles
To beckon him.

                                                    (488–92)

Even here the presence remains absent. The verb "seemed" keeps the
illusion from lapsing into delusion. The poet, fully aware that his vision is
only a vision, is nevertheless "Obedient to the light / That shone within
his soul." In the moment of his death he is described as liberated from
"Hope and despair," free of "mortal pain and fear": "he lay breathing
there / At peace, and faintly smiling" (639–45).

In telling us that the poet searched in vain and was blasted by disappointment, the narrator contradicts the conclusion of his tale, for the
poet has obviously reconciled himself to the elusive nature of his own
illusion. By Foucault's definition, however, the poet may well be confined
to madness, for he is denied the discourse of art. But here, too, the paradox is turned back upon itself: the poet's story has indeed been rendered
forth as poem. How? The poet, after all, has lived and died in isolation. He
is called a poet, but his only poem seems to be the poem of his own life.
But who has written it? The poet has not communicated the events and
circumstances of his solitary pursuit. Yet the narrator knows his story. He
can know it only as the story of the self, a self from which the narrator
seeks to maintain distance as "the perfect stranger," the one who objec-

guage, sleep and waking, day and night, madness is ultimately nothing, for it unites in them
all that is negative. But the paradox of this *nothing* is to *manifest* itself, to explode in signs,
in words, in gestures."

tifies himself in the eyes of reason and conceals the strangeness of his own desires.[28]

Shelley's self-reflexive paradox is also evident in *Julian and Maddalo* (1819; published 1824). As in *Alastor*, Shelley relies on the opposition between the visionary and the skeptic to generate philosophical tension. That tension is more dramatic, because Shelley has brought the two characters into dialogue. Julian affirms "the power of man over his mind" and "the power over ourselves to do / And suffer." It is only pride that undermines creative potential. Maddalo considers human beings utterly dependent on Providence, incapable of directing their own destinies.[29] Although Maddalo scoffs at his utopian visions, Julian defends his confidence in the human mind:

> "... it is our will
> That thus enchains us to permitted ill—
> We might be otherwise—we might be all
> We dream of happy, high, majestical.
> Where is the love, beauty, truth we seek
> But in our mind? and if we were not weak
> Should we be less in deed than in desire?"
> "Ay, if we were not weak—and we aspire
> How vainly to be strong!" said Maddalo:
> "You talk Utopia." "It remains to know,"
> I then rejoined, "and those who try may find
> How strong the chains are which our spirit bind;
> Brittle perchance as straw . . . We are assured
> Much may be conquered, much may be endured,
> Of what degrades and crushes us."
>
> (170–84)

To demonstrate to Julian the folly of his faith in the human mind, Maddalo proposes that they visit the madhouse to observe "'one like you / Who to this city came some months ago, / With whom I argued in this sort, and he / Is now gone mad'" (196–98).

Although the dialogue between Julian and Maddalo may well echo Shel-

28. Ibid. 249–50; to feign normalcy "the madman is obliged to objectify himself in the eyes of reason as the perfect stranger, that is, as the man whose strangeness does not reveal itself."

29. On the problem of free will and destiny, which some critics have tried to align with the Platonism and Godwinian necessaritarianism in Shelley's poetry, see Peter Thorslev, *Romantic Contraries*, 31, who calls attention to "the paradox that Plato was certainly no defender of an indeterminate free will."

ley's conversations with Byron, the Byronic Maddalo is as much a spokesman of Shelley's own doubts and deliberations as is the narrator of *Alastor*. This is a dialogue of self. Shelley challenges and questions his beliefs in the debate between his skeptical and his idealistic personae. They are not two, but one. Their essential identity, their primal oneness in the dark center of consciousness, is presented in the monologue of the madman (300–510). The visit to the madman, proposed as a test to show which of two opposing philosophies is apt to lead to madness, provides instead a haunting encounter with the irrationality of the self which precedes and yet accompanies all attempts to rationalize the nature of human being. The madhouse, for Maddalo, is "the emblem and the sign" of the vanity of human aspirations. For Julian, the madhouse is rather the refuge of spirits too proud to struggle against ignominy and failure. Both recognize in the madman's lamentation the voice of poetry. Julian observes that "the wild language of his grief was high, / Such as in measure were called poetry." As Maddalo puts it, "'Most wretched men / Are cradled into poetry by wrong. / They learn in suffering what they teach in song'" (541–46). Both weep without shame; they forget their argument.

Julian's position is nevertheless compromised in this encounter. He contemplates a vigil in the madman's cell, where he might "by patience find / An entrance to the caverns of his mind" and "might reclaim him from his dark estate" (572–74). He leaves, however, without offering aid. The only comfort to the forlorn madman is provided, ironically, by the seemingly misanthropic Maddalo. The madman has suffered much. He has lost his fortune, lost his love, lost his wits. The betrayal of his love seems to be the most immediate cause of his madness. He is temporarily revived when his beloved returns. When they part once more, both perish. The secret of their love and death is concealed from Julian, whose idealism, in contrast to Maddalo's pessimism, is the more ready to stand in moral judgment. As Maddalo sees it, all are flawed. For Julian, madness is the mark of some moral weakness that should be conquered. By hiding the circumstances of the madman's love and death, Shelley forestalls judgmental closure. The origin of madness is left in mystery.

When "madness by romantic identification" is enacted in *Das Marmorbild* (1819), the moral judgment is made very clear. Florio's meontic visions are at once his temptation and his punishment.[30] The visions of love are confounded with visions of death. Drawing from the lore of St. John's Eve, Eichendorff describes the "Johanniskranz" of "neunerlei Kräuter" or

---

30. Foucault 158, on moral consequences and pyschological effect: "Every thing in madness that designated the paradoxical manifestation of non-being would become the natural punishment of a moral evil."

"neunerlei Blumen," which is presumed to influence dreams. A maiden is instructed to wear the wreath in her hair, to sleep with it under her pillow, or to burn it in her chamber fire. In Eichendorff's tale, Bianka wears a St. John's wreath only to have her dream disappointed (4:41). On the very same night that Bianka has her dream, Florio wanders into a strange garden and sees an enchanting statue of Venus. The demonic spell of Venus counters the benign charm of Bianka.

Upon arriving in Lucca with the singer Fortunato, Florio joins in the summer-eve festival. He is immediately attracted to Bianka, whom he sees wearing her floral wreath, and with his song he wins from her a kiss. The happy festival is disrupted by the intrusion of the fell Donati, who claims Florio as his kinsman. When Donati's horse rears at the city gate and refuses to carry the rider across, poor Florio is as inept as Coleridge's Christabel in reading the omens. Nor does he understand Fortunato's perception of Donati as "one of those pale, misshapen moths of night, which, as if they were fleeing a fantastic dream, whir through the dusk and, with their long cat-whiskers and large horrid eyes, pretend to have an ordinary face."[31] The markings of the death-moth seem to resemble the face of a human corpse. Donati, as Fortunato sees him, is such a creature pretending to human life. To Florio's displeasure, Fortunato persists in describing the cavalier as "a moonshine hunter, a starvling cock, a braggart in melancholy" [einen Mondscheinjäger, einen Schmachthahn, einen Renommisten in der Melancholie].

A generic constituent in the tale of demonic seduction is the mesmeric fascination that enthralls the perception of the protagonist. If there is an evil presence, it cannot be seen through the aura of seductive beauty; either the narrator must tell us directly that things are not what they seem, or introduce another character to perceive and warn against the danger. When young Anthemion abandons Calliroë, in Peacock's tale of the witch of the laurel-rose, *Rhododaphne* (1818), it is a wise old sage whose "eye severe" perceives the enchanting gleam in Rhododaphne's "dark eyes so dazzling bright" and warns of her evil powers (7:1–94). Because the discrimination of good and evil is not always a simple matter, many a poet has engulfed the contest of perception in confusion and ambiguity. The seduction of the poet in *Alastor* is so luscious, the fulfillment of his quest so poignant, that the poet's "truth" persists in paradoxical opposition to the narrator's skeptical prologue and epilogue. Nor does Keats allow us to trust the sage Apollonius in *Lamia*; nor Coleridge his

---

31. Eichendorff 4:15: "einer von den falben, ungestalten Nachtschmetterlingen, die, wie aus einem phantastischen Traume entflogen, durch die Dämmerung schwirren und mit ihrem langen Katzenbarte und gräßlich großen Augen ordentlich ein Gesicht haben wollen."

perplexed and uncertain narrator in *Christabel*. The perception of good and evil in *Das Marmorbild* is much more clearly defined. Although Eichendorff has us follow the baffled perception of Florio, he also lets us appreciate the clear-sighted Fortunato, who praises the dawn, the world of color and vitality. Florio, however, is caught in the spell of his moonlight vision.

When he seems to be sinking into a sea of Bianka-like sirens, Florio awakens from his midsummer-night's dream; still he continues to see and move as if caught by the currents in his dream. He rises from his bed, looks out into the fertile Serchio, and beholds a landscape submerged in moonlight, echoing with the siren-song of his dream. He wanders forth into the night and comes upon a marble statue of Venus. In his dream, he sails "mit schwanenweißen Segeln einsam auf einem mondbeglänzten Meer." In his nocturnal wandering, "viele weißglänzende Schlößer . . . ruhten wie eingeschlafene Schwäne unten in dem Meere von Stille." In the mysterious garden, he sees the moonlit statue of Venus, seeming to gaze upon her own image mirrored in the water among the circling swans. The permutations of the dream-imagery begin to take a nightmarish turn. With his eyes fixed upon the statue as if he suddenly found a long-sought love, he sees the Venus slowly open her eyes to return his look. Florio closes his eyes "vor Blendung, Wehmut und Entzückung." When he opens them again the enchanting illusion of life is gone; he sees only the cold, inanimate stone: "das Venusbild, so fürchterlich weiß und regungslos, sah ihn fast schreckhaft mit den steinernen Augenhöhlen aus der grenzenlosen Stille an." The perceptual shift has rendered the beautiful horrible.

The perceptual shift is repeated, more starkly and with nightmarish exaggeration, in Florio's second encounter in the Venus-garden. Costumed like Bianka at the masquerade ball, her disguised double succeeds in winning Florio's attention, leaving Bianka to lament "die trügerische Blumen" and the disappointment of her dream. Donati takes Florio to the palace of the unidentified lady. Surrounded by the splendor of a pagan temple, "Florio's gaze wandered as if dazzled among the bright images, always returning with new intoxication to the beautiful mistress of the castle." He looks on her "mit flammenden Augen," ready to succumb to her enticements, when he hears Fortunato singing from the distance. At once he seems to recognize among the mythic figures in the tapestries the mistress of the castle. He realizes that she is the embodiment of his own dream fantasy. Disturbed by the uncanny identity, he looks out the window. Lightning strikes. Fortunato's song rides the gathering storm. "Herr Gott," Florio prays, "laß mich nicht verlorengehen in der Welt!" The *Legenda Aurea* tells more than one tale of evil fornicators held back by a thunderstorm. The polished marble of the palace appears old, crumbling, weed-covered. A snake slithers across the wall. He looks back into the room. By the glare of lightning, the beautiful lady seems transformed into a pale and frightening figure. The storm rises; the song continues; the statues begin to move:

> Then he was stricken with a deadly fear. For even the high blossoms in the vases began to rear and entwine themselves like colorfully speckled snakes, and upon the tapestries all the knights suddenly mirrored his features and they all laughed at him maliciously; the two arms, which held the candles, struggled and stretched themselves ever longer, as if a monstrous man was working his way out of the wall; the hall was filling more and more; the flames of lightning threw horrid shimmers among the figures, and through their swarming throng Florio saw the marble statues break loose and press toward him with such force that his hair stood on end. The horror overwhelmed all of his senses . . .[32]

Aware that he is lapsing into delusion, Florio begins to doubt his own perception. As he flees through the garden where he first saw the Venus statue, he thinks he sees Fortunato, but, now doubting his own senses, he thinks it another nocturnal delusion ("ein verwirrendes Blendwerk der Nacht"). The "Mondscheinjäger," as Fortunato had warned, not only nurtures his own subjective fantasies, he loses his ability to distinguish reality. The cure is aptly pronounced, not by Fortunato, but by a simple farmer on his way to his field:

> Now gone is the dark of night,
> With its evil sorcery and blight.
> To work call the dawn's clear rays;
> Arise, those who God still praise![33]

32. Ibid. 4:49–50: "Da erfaßte ihn ein tödliches Grauen. Denn auch die hohen Blumen in den Gefäßen fingen an, sich wie buntgefleckte bäumende Schlangen gräßlich durcheinander zu winden, alle Ritter auf den Wandtapeten sahen auf einmal aus wie er und lachten ihn hämisch an; die beiden Arme, welche die Kerzen hielten, rangen und reckten sich immer länger, als wolle ein ungeheurer Mann aus der Wand sich hervorarbeiten, der Saal füllte sich mehr und mehr, die Flammen des Blitzes warfen gräßliche Scheine zwischen die Gestalten, durch deren Gewimmel Florio die steinernen Bilder mit solcher Gewalt auf sich losdringen sah, daß ihm die Haare zu Berge standen. Das Grausen überwältigte alle seine Sinne . . ."
33. Ibid. 4:51:
> Vergangen ist die finstre Nacht,
> Der Bösen Trug und Zaubermacht,
> Zur Arbeit weckt der lichte Tag;
> Frisch auf, wer Gott noch loben mag!

Donati and his dwelling have vanished. The marble palace is an ancient ruin. After another night "in solchem unseligen Brüten und Träumen," Florio leaves Lucca and joins with travelers on the road—and finds himself reunited with Fortunato and Bianka.

Paintings, statues, and other effigies are presumed to offer oracular and prophetic counsel in St. John's Night. But Eichendorff has drawn from other lore for his story of the seductive statue. It is a surprisingly extensive tradition, including many variations on Ovid's tale of Pygmalion. From Eberhard Werner Happel, *Größeste Denkwürdigkeiten der Welt* (1687), he had the tale of the "seltzahmer Lucenser-Gespenst." In those same pages in Burton's *Anatomy of Melancholy* where Keats found Philostratus's account of the Lamia, the story is told, from Florilegus, of a man whom a statue of Venus claims as her husband. While playing tennis on his wedding day, he left his wedding-ring upon the finger of the statue and later could not remove the ring for Venus had bent her finger. That night when the husband intended to consummate the marriage, Venus appeared between him and his bride to receive the nuptial homage. Brentano planned to include a version of this same tale in his *Romanzen vom Rosenkranz* (1810).[34] By calling attention to artistic form and denying its fixity, the animation of the work of art may contribute to the play of irony. Yet even in inviting an open conjuring, the presence of the seductive artifact is not merely an interior text, it is a countertext.

Das Marmorbild describes two modes of art, or of perceiving art, one of which Eichendorff morally opposes. It is not merely the contrasting conceptions of love and beauty, represented in Bianka and Venus, but the opposing modes of perception, represented in Fortunato and Donati, that engages Florio in his contest and struggle toward an active, vital involvement. In contrast to Goethe's claim about which was sick and which healthy, it is the classical artifact that is stultifying and lethal (Eckermann, *Gespräche mit Goethe*, 2 April 1829). Rather than repress, Eichendorff seeks to exorcise. In representing the oppositions as life and death, good and evil, divine and demonic, Eichendorff reinforces social and religious fears of the delusory "other." That "other," of course, resides within the self. Only by expressing these fears can the artist hope to exorcise them. Nor could one possibly exorcise the delusory "other" in solipsistic isolation. As Eichendorff reaffirms in his poetry and his prose, one must also discover harmony in human fellowship and learn to commune with the immanence of God in nature. "By a strange paradox," Foucault writes,

---

34. Ovid, *Metamorphosis*, 10.243–97. Robert Burton, *Anatomy of Melancholy*, 649; Florilegus (Matthew of Westminster), *Flores historiarum*; Heinrich Kornmann, *Mons Veneris*, 77; Clemens Brentano, "Paralipomena zu *Romanzen vom Rosenkranz*," in *Werke* 1:996. See P. E. Baum, "The Young Man Betrothed to a Statue," and Robert Mühler, "Der Venusring."

"what is born from the strangest delirium was already hidden, like an inaccessible truth, in the bowels of the earth. When man deploys the arbitrary nature of his madness, he confronts the dark necessity of the world; the animal that haunts his nightmares and his nights of privation is his own nature, which will lay bare hell's pitiless truth" (23). By giving form to that dark truth, the artist also defines and limits. Whether or not the explicit accounts of his hallucinations Coleridge recorded in his notebooks were therapeutic, they are further testimony of the romantic desperation in coming to terms with the irrational depths of consciousness.

So, too, we can observe De Quincey's effort, in *Confessions of an English Opium-Eater* (1821), to concretize his hallucinations in the controlled medium of language. But, once this Pandora's box is opened, can the narrator actually control the language? Just as Coleridge claimed that from his opium trance "Kubla Khan" arose complete, not only in image but also in word, De Quincey frequently surrenders his authority as narrator to "eloquent opium"(*Confessions* 71). "Not the opium-eater, but the opium, is the true hero of the tale," he announces at the close of the original narrative, as published in 1821 (100). Although he thus humbles himself to the status of passive witness, he still grasps the reins of discourse. "I triumphed," he claims, but with little jubilation, for his suffering continues. "Motives external to myself," he acknowledges, "supplied me with conscientious supports, which mere personal interests might fail to supply to a mind debilitated by opium" (101). This liberation, however, is prematurely announced. Having reduced his dosage, he thought "the victory was in effect achieved." The *Suspiria de Profundis*, the sequel to the *Confessions* published twenty-four years later, relates a far more "dreadful visitation from opium excess." During the intervening years, climaxing in his third opium crisis of 1839, he experienced utter subjugation and helpless vitiation of the will. In the *Suspiria*, the irrational seizes control of the very medium of rational discourse and usurps the role of the narrator.

Even in the *Confessions*, when he turns from "The Pleasures of Opium" to "The Pains of Opium," De Quincey admits his incapacity to give his narrative "any regular and connected shape" (84). In his "intellectual torpor" and "dormant state," he cannot write at all. He loses none of "his moral sensibilities or aspirations, . . . but his intellectual apprehension of what is possible infinitely out runs his power, not of execution only, but even of power to attempt" (89). Nevertheless, strange texts are written: "Whatsoever things capable of being visually represented I did but think of in the darkness immediately shaped themselves into phantoms of the eye; and by a process apparently no less inevitable, when thus traced in faint and visionary colors, like writings in sympathetic ink, they were drawn out by the fierce chemistry of my dreams into insufferable splendor that fretted my heart" (90). The simile of the "sympathetic ink" is apt. For De Quincey, who elsewhere describes his mind as a palimpsest, the dream texts thus inscribed need only that peculiar reagent, the mind, to spring forth. He is blessed, or cursed, with a retentive memory, and it requires but a momentary "thaw" to release "all the thoughts which had been frozen up for a decade of years by opium" (105).

Still hoarded within his mind, he says at the outset of the *Suspiria*, is "the imagery of my dreams, which translated everything into their own language" (116). Denying authorship, he insists that his visions were self-engendering. They created themselves. He compares his narrative structure to "a *caduceus* wreathed about with meandering ornaments or the shaft of a tree's stem hung round and surmounted with some vagrant parasitical plant." He is merely the rod upon which they have climbed, the host to their parasitical life; he is "the dry, withered pole, which shoots all the rings of the flowering plants and seems to do so by some dexterity of its own, whereas, in fact, the plant and its tendrils have curled round the sullen cylinder by mere luxuriance of *theirs*" (120). During his third crisis, "new and monstrous phenomena began slowly to arise" (116). These are the irrational "sighs from the depths" which he reveals to the rational world in 1845. To make known their unreasonable truth, not his own pathological condition, is his only justification for publishing this work (120).[35]

De Quincey's peculiar formulation of the separate vitality of his own dreams is but another variation on that schizophrenic split of "self" and "other" which produces the paradox of the perfect stranger. The dreamer may be sick but he is sane. Not responsible for that florid growth of insanity which feeds upon him, he is only an "ugly pole" supporting exotic flowers: "those parasitical thoughts, feelings, digressions, which climb up with bells and blossoms round about the arid stock; ramble away from it at times with perhaps too rank a luxuriance" (120). A similar effort to disown the frightening impulses from within gives rise in romantic literature to that disjuncture of "self" and "other" as the doppelgänger. Brother Medardus, in Hoffmann's *Die Elixiere des Teufels* (1815), is in danger of surrendering his own identity to the powerful presence of the mad alterity of his double: "Mein eignes Ich schwamm ohne Halt wie in einem Meer all der Ereignisse, die wie tobende Wellen auf mich hereinbrausten." Robert Wringhim, in Hogg's *Confessions of a Justified Sinner* (1824), is plagued by a friend/fiend capable of perfectly duplicating his appearance. Hogg gives

---

35. Foucault, on the paradox of the truth of illusion, 111; on the paradox of the unreasonable truth, 113: "The truth appears in this paradoxical twilight, in this matinal night where the cruelty of truth will be transformed into the fury of hallucination."

the self/other narrative an additional twist by telling the tale twice: once from outside observation, then again from inside Wringhim's own experience. In Hoffmann's tale, the "self" is ultimately redeemed from his mad delusions. In Hogg's tale, the "self" perishes under the relentless persecution of the "other." For both, the "other" torments and undermines the efforts of the "self" to become the perfect stranger and mask the tumultuous inner strangeness from the eyes of the world (Foucault 249–50).

The narrator of Charles Nodier's *Jean-François les Bas-Bleus* (1833) sets forth the relationship of "self" and "other" as reminiscence. He recreates his own schoolboy identity, forty years earlier. But if the narrator is that boy, so, too, he is the madman, whom the boy encounters in the street. The madman harbors ideological sympathies with the aristocracy, which in the midst of the Revolution, the boy must disown. In the dialogue on the fantastic with which he introduces his tale, Nodier describes its basic elements as paradoxical rather than marvelous.[36] As he observes in *Du Fantastique en littérature*, superstition is not vanquished by reason and science, it simply becomes covert, perhaps not even consciously acknowledged. Arguing that "the true and believable fantastic story in an era without beliefs could be placed with ease only in the mouth of a madman," Nodier proposes a contrast between two sorts of madmen: a fantast who is obsessed by occult intrigues, and a doubter "who consoles himself intentionally over his lost illusions with the illusions of the imaginary world" (*Oeuvres Complètes* 4:13–15).

According to Todorov, the fantastic, as the genre of uncertainty, is delicately balanced between the uncanny ("l'étrange") and the marvelous ("le merveilleux"). The uncanny restores "reality" by finding some rational explanation for the fantastic; the marvelous invents new laws of nature to account for unnatural phenomena. Todorov cites the tale of *Inès de las Sierras* as an example of Nodier's compulsion to provide a rational resolution rather than sustain the fantastic. This two-part tale, which he labels fantastic-uncanny, is a convenient choice for Todorov's structural argument. The first part elaborates the perplexity; the second part provides an "improbable" but "rational" solution. Todorov's critique, then, is that Nodier surrendered to the sway of rationalism and relied on utterly artificial coincidences to conclude his tale. If he had cited *Jean-François les Bas-Bleus*, however, he would have had to label it fantastic-marvelous. Although I consider Todorov's classifications hypersubtle, I appreciate his attention to an equipollence of rationality and irrationality in the fantastic

36. Charles Nodier, *Contes*, 362–64. In a note to this dialogue, Castex writes: "Nodier est fidèle aux idées exprimées dans la seconde préface de *Smarra* (p. 37) et au début de l' *Histoire d'Hélène Gillet*, en opposant au fantastique conventionnel un 'fantastique sérieux', qui fait état de phénomènes étranges, mais dûment constatés."

(Todorov 43, 46, 84, 90).[37] This is the operative paradox, and it matters little whether it is resolved or unresolved. Because Nodier develops this paradox with insistent dialogical opposition, his various concluding gambits, in spite of Todorov's objections, do not make it easy for the reader to return to the comfort of unquestioned convictions. Even if the paradox is resolved, the orthodox has been effectively challenged.

Although Jean-François is very much the "ingenious madman" who has steeped himself in metaphysics and occult lore, the narrator is by no means the jaded and disillusioned madman Nodier elsewhere proposed as fitting foil. The narrator is a schoolboy, and narrative credibility is enhanced with a strong sense of autobiographical presence. Nodier was born in 1780. The tale is set in 1793. The narrator, for all practical purposes, is Nodier himself, recollecting an episode from his childhood. We are given two explanations of Jean-François's madness. At first, it is simply "à force d'être savant." Later, the boy's father recounts the story "d'une passion invincible." To repress his impossible love for the daughter of his aristocratic patroness, Jean-François plunged himself into "études périlleuses pour la raison." In his flight from emotional duress, he delved too deeply into occult science and exalted spiritualism. Since then, his father says, no light has penetrated into his mental darkness ("le ténèbres des son esprit"). But, as our schoolboy narrator has already discovered, the light does indeed penetrate his mind. The peculiarity of his madness is that Jean-François only speaks in wild and disconnected words when asked about commonplace things. If he is given an intellectual or moral question of some importance, the scattered rays of his sick mind gather and focus "comme ceux du soleil dans la lentille de Archimède." The most difficult problems he quickly solved with such precision and ease that one might well have doubted whether he had ever been more clear, persuasive and scholarly when in full possession of his reason.

The schoolboy has thus discovered that Jean-François has a "double life": a madman amidst the mundane world, a savant in the higher realm of intellect. He attempts to gain access to the rational mind concealed within Jean-François's irrational mind by posing questions from his own "double study" of tropes and logarithms. In a moment of compassion, however, he one day forgets his purpose with a seemingly trivial remark: "Comme te voilà seul." He bites his lip and anticipates the usual barrage of impenetrably confused words. Instead, the concept "alone" prompts a dialogue on the interconnectedness of all things which leaps immediately

---

37. For my critique of Todorov's structural classification, see *The Haunted Eye*, 15, and my review of Tobin Siebers, *The Romantic Fantastic*.

into the paradox of rationality. Only a madman, Jean-François tells him, is alone ["Il n'y a que l'insensé qui soit seul"].

The boy at first fails to comprehend the paradoxical wisdom, and tries to redirect Jean-François's thoughts by giving cosmic dimension to the impossibility of being "alone." Perhaps, he suggests, Fontanelle was right in claiming the plurality of worlds (*Entretiens sur la pluralité des mondes*, 1686). But Jean-François is not to be manipulated; rather, he draws the boy into a dialogue on interconnectedness. What is a world? What is a planet? What is space? What holds all matter together? What fills the seeming void? As the boy grapples with makeshift answers, Jean-François leads him to consider how a divine providence might penetrate all things. Would God, who filled all physical space with occupants and who inspired his imperfect creatures with the desire for a better life, have left space unoccupied? The boy agrees that he, too, believes that space must be occupied by finer beings enveloped in a more subtle matter which connects us all. "But how can I know them?" he asks. "By learning to see them," answers Jean-François.

The "double life" of the madman has opened the schoolboy's mind to possibilities previously untouched by his "double studies." He returns home still perplexed by the possibility of an ethereal interconnectedness, wondering, indeed, whether Jean-François might have two souls, one captive in the coarse world in which we live, the other dwelling in the subtle atmosphere of pervasive mind. His father warns him against the doctrines of Swedenborg and Saint-Martin which Jean-François has appropriated into his "double speech." These visionary beliefs must be brought back into their "true expression" in reason. Jean-François's memory is intact, the father explains, but his understanding is gone. He no longer can distinguish the speculative from the practical. The boy accepts his father's advice, confessing to himself the seductive attraction of the imaginary— the tales of *A Thousand and One Nights* are incomparably more congenial than Bezout's mathematics.

Nodier has already introduced several dimensions of doubleness in defining the paradox of reason and madness: the sciences versus the arts, the practical versus the speculative, the reason versus the passion, the mundane versus the intellectual. The crucial opposition he has saved for the crisis of his narrative: the political versus the visionary. The year, we should recollect, is 1793; the place, Besançon, is 350 kilometers southeast of Paris. Just before noon on October 16 (the schoolboy remembers the exact time and date because he was on his way home from the first day of school following the six-week vacation), the narrator encounters the madman in his usual place in the Rue d'Anvers. Jean-François is staring into the seemingly empty sky. "Tell us, Jean-François," the schoolboy asks, "what you observe again today in that subtle matter of space in which all worlds move?" "Don't you know as I well as I?" the madman replies, "Follow with your eyes the traces of blood, and you will see Marie Antoinette, Queen of France, on her way to heaven."

At home, the schoolboy finds his father with several cronies. They are discussing the outcome of the trial in Paris. The most recent newspapers, dated October 13, contain no mention of the event and no letters of more recent date have arrived. The schoolboy announces the news he has just heard. When his father learns his source, the report is dismissed as mere chance ravings. Two days pass before the madman's report is confirmed. Still the vision is dismissed as coincidence. Not until the end of the following spring (the schoolboy now uses the revolutionary calendar) does he learn of the madman's death. Jean-François died on the 29th of Predial. He had been standing all day in the Rue d'Anvers, staring into the heavens. A few minutes after 4:00, he cried out the names of his former patroness and her beautiful daughter, then fell dead. As reported in the newspaper three days later, the aristocratic lady and her family had been brought to the guillotine on 29 Predial, a few minutes after 4:00. "Promise me," the father tells the boy, "that if you should ever tell this story when you are a grown man, you will never claim that it is true, for it would expose you to ridicule." "Are there reasons," the boy responds, "that could possibly dissuade a person from loudly proclaiming what he knows to be true." "One reason that outweighs all others," the father replies, "the truth is useless."

Nodier's madman, of course, is the spokesman of two different sorts of truth. As conventional "fool," he may safely express the mad truth of love and loyalty to the old regime. As prophet and seer, he is the voice of the paradoxical truth of unreason. In the rational world, either truth must remain "useless." The one must be resigned to the fate of that paradox which counters but, no matter how trenchant, cannot convert the entrenched orthodox. The other draws from that vast and volatile region of primordial energy which the rational world seeks to suppress. When it erupts, now as art, now as madness, its power is far too manifold and extensive to be comprehended in terms of meager value judgments, whether moral or aesthetic.

As mediators of the provocative illusion of delusion, the mad personae of romantic literature expose that inner ferment of mind which is somehow always a part of artistic expression. Novalis, Hoffmann, Eichendorff, Shelley, De Quincey, Nodier have elaborated the modes of inspiration, each in their own peculiar way, and have exposed the paradoxical tensions of irrationality and manifest nothingness. Just as literary reference is enriched by a bimodal appreciation of the possible identity as well as alterity of signifier and signified which enables us to witness the interchange of metaphor and metonymy, the mimetic and meontic, so, too, the literary representation of madness, the illusion of delusion, is enhanced by an awareness of the inherent and operative paradoxicality. Whether that primordial irrationality which precedes and participates in the creative act is to be feared or pursued, condemned or embraced, must be decided by some rational scheme of moral judgment which *follows* the artistic expression. In the moment itself, as these romantic writers demonstrate, the paradoxical encounter with the unreasonable truth is ineluctable.

6

BLAKE AND THE
BLIGHTED CORN

Although an entire community in Manchester fell victim to the nervous tremors and hallucinations of ergotism in 1927 (Barger 64–65; Ainsworth 126), as did 300 residents of Pont Saint Esprit as late as 1951,[1] such outbreaks of ergot poisoning have been virtually eliminated in modern Europe. Throughout earlier centuries, however, epidemics were frequent. In Blake's time, widespread cases commonly followed when rainstorms felled the rye before harvest. While the lysergic acid in ergot fungus contributed to mental derangement, other ergot alkaloids caused muscular spasms and violent constriction of blood vessels (Barger 125–210). Among the symptoms, then, were delusions and convulsions. Severe cases might even result in respiratory failure, permanent mental impairment, or, as happened in France and Germany, gangrenous loss of limbs (Barger 59–78; Brackman 305–6). Blake's concern with the blight that "cuts the tender corn," evident as early as his sketches of the "The Good

---

1. Fuller recounts a case of rye-bread poisoning in August 1951, affecting 300 persons in Pont Saint Esprit near Avignon in southern France. Most of the victims experienced hallucinations; twenty were temporarily insane; four died. Although medical doctors identified ergotism as the cause and found traces of ergot alkaloids in the bread, their testimony in the court hearings was opposed by toxicologists who found traces of mercury salts apparently from the pesticides and fungicides used to spray the grain. No similar poisonings were caused elsewhere by agricultural spraying. The doctors pointed out that mercury affects the liver and kidneys, which were not damaged in the victims at Pont Saint Esprit. Fuller cites the medical reports prepared by Dr. Giraud and Dr. Latour for the French Academy of Medicine to argue that LSD-25, not mercuric poisoning, had caused the bizarre hallucinations experienced by victims. Bové, 166, summarizes the case and cites Gabbai, Lisbonne, and Pourquier, "Ergot Poisoning at Pont St. Esprit."

Farmer" (c. 1780–5), becomes an important motif in the prophetic works, where the hallucinatory blight provides an apt metaphor for Urizenic oppression and exploitation.

In the seven extant sketches of "The Good Farmer" (Butlin, cat. 120r, 120Ar, 121, 122r and v, 123r, 124), Blake progressively intensified the drama of the impending blight. In the last version (Fig. 1), Christ offers the good grain to the people while a storm rages in the background. In the distance beyond Christ's head, Blake depicts the demon of the storm felling the grain. The communion of Christ, as "the living bread" (John 6:35, 48–51), is contrasted with the contagion and blight being spread by the storm demon.

Only the poor suffered the curse of the blighted grain, for the ergot fungus (*claviceps purpurea*) grows principally on rye. And rye bread was a staple for the lower classes. Wheat, which provided white bread for the tables of the wealthy, was, if infected, seldom marketed (Ashley). But it might well be milled by the laborers. The outbreak in 1762 near Bury St. Edmunds, where there were no fields of rye, was traced to ergot in the bread prepared from "clog-wheat, or revets, or bearded wheat" (Wollaston 99; Barger 63). The ergot fungus (Fig. 2) grows quickly in the wet,

Fig. 1. Blake, *The Good Farmer* (ca. 1780–85), Humanities Research Center, University of Texas, Austin.

Fig. 2.   Friedrich Severa, *claviceps purpurea*: 2.1, blighted rye; 2.2, sclerotia; 2.3, germinating sclerotium.

ripening grain. As the fungus grows within the kernel it swells into a peculiar and distinctive shape, which gives the ergot-infected grain its name: *secale cornutum*, or horned rye. The swollen sclerotia, or corn-mother, splits and sends forth its spiraling purple tendrils (see Fig. 2.3).

Now deliberately cultivated in Europe, in former Czechoslovakia, for extracting ergot alkaloids (D-lysergic acid amide, D-isolysergic acid amide), the rye sclerotia may provide a valuable pharmaceutical source for psychiatric medicine (Starý and Jirásek 140). But the corn-mother also contains alkaloids that can cause severe cramps and spasms.

Hippocrates recommended the use of the corn-mother in childbirth to restrict bleeding and promote uterine contractions (Bové 138–41), and potions of ergot were administered in the midwifery of Blake's time (Akerly; Bordot; Desgranges; Neale; Paulizky; Prescott; Stearns). The sacred seeds used by Mexican Indians two to three thousand years ago in their religious ceremonies have been analyzed as especially potent in the hallucinogenic ergot alkaloids (Bové 137). During the Middle Ages, peasants stricken by the epidemic had no notion of the cause of their plight. The effects were painfully obvious. The delusions and the burning sensations in the arms and legs, often medically diagnosed as *erysipelas* in the nineteenth century, were known popularly as St. Anthony's fire, or *ignis sacer* (Brackman 295–312). The symptoms of ergot poisoning prompted association with the sufferings of St. Anthony, who was visited by demons in his desert hermitage. The Order of St. Anthony was founded in 1093 to care for the sufferers (Bové 151–52). Well into the eighteenth century ergot hallucinations were interpreted as demonic possession or divine revelation (Hutchinson). Even after the black swollen kernels had been identified as causing the epidemics, the disease continued to be attributed to admixtures of other impurities (Barger 65–72). The distinguished Linnaeus, in 1763, claimed the poison derived from raphanus or turnip radish (Barger 29, 79). In spite of the growing consensus that blighted wheat or rye was to blame, little was done to stop the milling of bad grain.

Why make bread from bad grain? The answers are as complicated as Blake's account of what precipitated the "awful division" of the Four Zoas. One answer is that there was often nothing else to eat. Knowing that the grain was bad, the farmer would nevertheless sift away some of the swollen sclerotia, sometimes mixing the remaining rye with other grain, or with peas or mullet, hoping to stave off starvation and risk no worse than temporary intoxication. Since his livelihood depended upon the harvest, he might also take his bad grain to the mill. And the miller, who might indeed see evidence of ergot, would buy cheap and hope to sell at a profit. And who was to blame? The farmer, the miller, or the economic conditions that prompted them to act in desperation and deceit?

Mild poisonings, typically marked by fevers, chills, cramps, dizziness, and hallucinations, went unreported. England was spared the severe epidemics that ravaged whole communities in France and Germany with crippling convulsions or gangrene (Barger 59–78). The nervous disorders were familiar to the lower classes. An early account of the disease, *Of Agues and Fevers* (1658), described it as "grievous, dangerous and hard to be cured" and noted that the infection would invade "the brain and all the nerves," causing fits and delirium. Mistakenly classifying it as a scurvy, Thomas Beddoes in 1793 was nevertheless right in identifying ergot as the cause of nervous disorder and calling for inspection of the rye (Beddoes 209). Erasmus Darwin, in his *Botanic Garden* (1791), also sounds a warning against the devastating blight:

> Shield the young Harvest from devouring blight,
> The Smut's dark poison, and the mildew white;
> Deep-rooted Mould, and Ergot's horn uncouth,
> And break the Canker's desolating tooth.
>   (Part I, canto 4, 511–14)

Darwin might as well have asked the rainstorms to turn away. The fields were blighted and, just as inexorably, reaped by peasants who needed the harvest to survive. As is evident from a case reported in 1847, doctors were unaware of the widespread occurrences of ergotism. In treating a young man at Dublin hospital, the examining physicians thought his symptoms rare and unusual (hair and fingernails had fallen out, a gangrenous toe had dropped off). He explained that he had lost his nails three years before, and that his relatives and neighbors were similarly afflicted (Nuttall; Colles). The disease and its delusions were all too familiar to the poor villagers, who seldom turned to the hospitals in their desperation.

Bread, "the staff of life," also threatened death. Perhaps it was a merciful death, for its onset was accompanied by intoxicated delusions that left the victim oblivious to pain and enraptured by visions. Although the mental derangement had been noted (Sennert; Hoffmeyer), doctors treated only the physical symptoms. Not until the very end of the nineteenth century did they begin to concern themselves with ergot psychosis (Siemens; see also Gurewitsch, von Bechterew, Kolossow). One man, thinking he could fly, leapt from a second story, breaking both legs; he then rose up on his shattered legs and ran fifty meters before he could be stopped. According to the testimony of many victims, common objects were mystically transformed, radiating intense and beautiful colors, and seeming to reveal divine presence (Fuller 95–97).

The strange gift of the ergot rye is a moment of vision. It comes to its victim with a rapture as sudden and irresistible as a young William Blake is reported to have experienced when, standing in the field at Peckham Rye, he saw a tree full of angels. Blake's initiation into vision began early, and as a visionary poet he tells of the mildew blight and the poisoned bread many times in his prophetic works. The bread of torment and delusion is contrasted with the bread of love and communion. When Los in indignation strikes his beloved emanation, in Night the First of *The Four Zoas*, Urizen smiles on the violence and discord and calls upon Los to punish Luvah and follow Urizen's law. Los recognizes in Urizen, however, "one of those who when most complacent / Mean mischief most" (*FZ* 1 12:18–19). Urizen scorns Los as "a visionary of Jesus the soft delusion of Eternity" and declares himself "God the terrible destroyer." Los regrets his jealous anger and seeks Enitharmon's forgiveness.

> Los now repented that he had smitten Enitharmon he felt
>   love
> Arise in all his Veins he threw his arms around her loins
> To heal the wound of his smiting
>
>   (*FZ* 1 12:41–44)

The embrace is not merely a gesture of love and reconciliation, it becomes a communion in which they together "eat the fleshly bread" and "drink the nervous wine" (*FZ* 1 12:45). The communion provides a moment of harmony, but fails to resolve rivalry and strife.

Even as their nuptial bonds are celebrated, the singers at "The Feast of Los & Enitharmon" announce the threat of bad bread being prepared in the land.

> Let us refuse Plow & Spade, the heavy Roller & spiked
> Harrow, burn all these Corn fields, throw down all these
>   fences
> Fattend on Human blood & drunk with wine of life is bet-
>   ter far
>
> Than all these labours of the harvest & vintage. See the
>   river
> Red with the blood of Men. swells lustful round my rocky
>   knees
> My clouds are not the clouds of verdant fields & groves
>   of fruit
> But Clouds of Human Souls, my nostrils drink the lives of
>   Men

> The Villages Lament. they faint outstretchd upon the
>   plain
> Wailing runs round the Valleys from the Mill & from the
>   Barn
>
> (*FZ* 1 14:8–16)

Because of the visionary manner of Blake's prophetic poetry, his indictment of social evils may often seem surreal, a mere mental conjuration. But his description of the lamenting villages, inhabitants "outstretchd upon the plain," and wailing "from the Mill & from the Barn," has documentary accuracy in reporting the events that recurred seasonally in the rye-producing regions of Ireland, Scotland, and northern England.

The division of the Four Zoas is at work in the individual brain as well as in the collective mind of Albion's England. As Los tells Enitharmon, "in the Brain of Man we live, & in his circling Nerves" (*FZ* 1 11:15). Because the outside world of villages, mills, and barns is perceptually mirrored in the mythic consciousness, which is Blake's poetic terrain, whatever factors influence the social or political conditions also alter individual perception. And conversely, whatever affects the individual mind has an impact on England as a whole. Because the Urizenic specter fosters jealousy and greed throughout the land, his reasonings are the source of irrationality: "the Spectre is in every man insane" (*FZ* 1 5:38; *FZ* 7 84:36). The very struggle with that insanity, however, gives rise to vision. The "blighted corn" represents both the poison spread by exploitation and the senses expanded by vision.

Harvesting and bread making, dominant symbols in the apocalyptic conclusion to Night the Ninth, are well anticipated earlier in the narrative. If, to avoid the blight that leaves the villagers "outstretchd upon the plain," the threat in Night the First to "burn all these Corn fields" were actually carried out, the villagers would have been left penniless and starving. At the close of Night the Second, Enion laments the seemingly inescapable plight:

> Wisdom is sold in the desolate market where none come
>   to buy
> And in the witherd field where the farmer plows for bread
>   in vain
> It is an easy thing to triumph in the summer sun
> And in the vintage & to sing on the waggon loaded with
>   corn
>
> .   .   .   .
>
> It is an easy thing to laugh at the wrathful elements

> To hear the dog howl at the wintry door, the ox in the
> slaughter house moan
> To see a god on every wind & a blessing in every blast
> To hear sounds of love in the thunder storm that de-
> stroys our enemies house
> To rejoice in the blight that covers his field, & the sick-
> ness that cuts off his children
>
> . . . .
>
> It is an easy thing to rejoice in the tents of prosperity
> Thus could I sing & thus rejoice, but it is not so with me!
> (*FZ* 2 35:14–17; 36:3–8, 12–13)

Experience, she laments, is purchased at the price "Of all that a man hath his house his wife his children" (*FZ* 2 35:13). The cost is high. Enion has already learned enough to reject the hypocrisy of rejoicing "in the tents of prosperity," but she does not pursue the possibility that the experience she has purchased may have value.

Urizen denies that there can be any other than purely material value. Under his reign in alliance with Vala, thoughts are linked to things with chains of iron. His books of law define only the conditions of have and have not. His sons teach war. His daughters knead the "bread of Sorrow." But the bread of sorrow is also the bread of incipient rebellion, the bread of Orc.

> Urizen answerd Read my books explore my Constella-
> tions
> Enquire of my Sons & they shall teach thee how to War
> Enquire of my Daughters who accursd in the dark depths
> Knead bread of Sorrow by my stern command for I am
> God
> Of all this dreadful ruin Rise O daughters at my Stern
> command
>
> Rending the Rocks Eleth & Uveth rose & Ona rose
> Terrific with their iron vessels driving them across
> In the dim air they took the book of iron & placd above
> On clouds of death & sang their songs Kneading the
> bread of Orc
> Orc listend to the song compelld hungring on the cold
> wind
> That swaggd heavy with the accursed dough. the hoar
> frost ragd

> Thro Onas sieve the torrent rain pourd from the iron pail
> Of Eleth & the icy hands of Uveth kneaded the bread
> The heavens bow with terror underneath their iron hands
> Singing at their dire work the words of Urizens book of
>   iron
> While the enormous scrolls rolld dreadful in the heavens
>   above
> And still the burden of their song in tears was pourd
>   forth
> The bread is Kneaded let us rest O cruel father of chil-
>   dren
>
> But Urizen remitted not their labours upon his rock
>   (*FZ* 7 79:20–38)

Nor need he remit, so long as the forces of authority can "Compell the poor to live upon a Crust of bread by soft mild arts" (*FZ* 7 80:9). Urizen, who dictates the sowing, reaping, threshing, does not anticipate that the "Crust of bread" might have conjuring powers of its own.

The Christian paradox of suffering and rebirth informs Blake's celebration of the harvest and vintage in Night the Ninth. In their thorough commentary, Brian Wilkie and Mary Lynn Johnson identify the grapes with the passions, the grain with intellect. The distinction is useful in interpreting the redemptive value of the bread and the wine. Treading the grapes in the winepress, they propose, is necessary for liberating the passions, while "the suffering symbolized in bread making is intellectual" (233). But if there is to be a communion, a restoration of harmony, the division of reason and passion must be overcome. It is the Eternal Man, not the fallen Albion, who announces the harvest and vintage. "Luvah prince of Love" is cheered as the ripe seed is brought into the barns, and the Bulls of Luvah lick the children in rites of initiation.

> I hear the flail of Urizen his barns are full no room
> Remains & in the Vineyards stand the abounding sheaves
>   beneath
> The falling Grapes that odorous burst upon the winds.
>   Arise
> My flocks & herds trample the Corn my cattle browze
>   upon
> The ripe Clusters The shepherds shout for Luvah prince
>   of Love

Let the Bulls of Luvah tread the Corn & draw the loaded
   waggon
Into the Barn while children glean the Ears round the
   door
Then shall they lift their innocent hands & stroke his fu-
   rious nose
And he shall lick the little girls white neck & on her head
Scatter the perfume of his breath while from his moun-
   tains high
The lion of terror shall come down & bending his bright
   mane
And couching at their side shall eat from the curld boys
   white lap
His golden food and in the evening sleep before the Door
                                                   (*FZ* 9 135:8–20)

The harvesting of the grain is no assurance that suffering and sorrow are at an end. The blight has already been scattered among the fields. The task is to tame "the lion of terror" when it descends.

Although they contrast the bread of knowledge in Night the Ninth with the bread of sorrow in Night the Seventh, Wilkie and Johnson also argue that "it is possible for sorrow to become knowledge" (233). If the Preacher of Ecclesiastes was right, it is a possibility with vexing consequences, for "he that increaseth knowledge increaseth sorrow" (Eccles. 1:17–18). Indeed, making bread from "the Corn out of the Stores of Urizen" might merely perpetuate the cycles of sorrow, for the men "are bound to sullen contemplations" and "knead the bread of knowledge with tears & groans":

Then Dark Urthona took the Corn out of the Stores of
   Urizen
He ground it in his rumbling Mills Terrible the distress
Of all the Nations of Earth ground in the Mills of Urthona
In his hand Tharmas takes the Storms. he turns the whirl-
   wind Loose
Upon the wheels the stormy seas howl at his dread com-
   mand
And Eddying fierce rejoice in the fierce agitation of the
   wheels
Of Dark Urthona Thunders Earthquakes Fires Water
   floods
Rejoice to one another loud their voices shake the Abyss

> Their dread forms tending the dire mills The grey hoar
>   frost was there
> And his pale wife the aged Snow they watch over the fires
> They build the Ovens of Urthona Nature in darkness
>   groans
> And men are bound to sullen contemplations in the night
> Restless they turn on beds of sorrow. in their inmost
>   brain
> Feeling the crushing Wheels they rise they write bitter
>   words
> Of Stern Philosophy & knead the bread of knowledge
>   with tears & groans
>
> (*FZ* 9 138:1–15)

To liberate knowing from the repetitions of suffering and sorrow, Blake insists upon vision. Urizen reaps the blighted corn and grinds it "in his rumbling Mills." "Dark Urthona" then bakes the bread, which, paradoxically, enables those who eat it to step forth from the evils and strife and "behold the Angelic spheres."

> Such are the works of Dark Urthona Tharmas sifted the
>   corn
> Urthona made the Bread of Ages & he placed it
> In golden & silver baskets of precious stone
> And then took his repose in Winter in the night of Time
>
> The Sun has left his blackness & has found a fresher
>   morning
> And the mild moon rejoices in the clear & cloudless
>   night
> And Man walks forth from midst of the fires the evil is all
>   consumd
> His eyes behold the Angelic spheres arising night & day
> The stars consumd like a lamp blown out & in their stead
>   behold
> The Expanding Eyes of Man behold the depths of
>   wondrous worlds
>
> (*FZ* 9 138:16–25)

Because the bread of "blighted corn" may expand vision and reveal "wondrous worlds," the communion at the close of *The Four Zoas* affirms freedom from the bondage of Urizen.

Fig. 3.   Blake, *Milton*, plate 49. Rare Book Division, New York Public Library.

Blake again evokes harvest and vintage in the conclusion of *Milton* (Fig. 3), when the clouds of Los and Enitharmon "roll over London," and "soft Oothoon / Pants in Vales of Lambeth weeping oer the Human Harvest" (42 [49]:31–33). As in *The Four Zoas*, "the Ovens are prepar'd." The final plate (Fig. 4) depicts the human grain, male seeds still sheathed in unwin-

Fig. 4.   Blake, *Milton*, plate 50. Rare Book Division, New York Public Library.

nowed ears, and the liberating Harvest, a female lifting away the con-
straining veil, ready "To go forth to the Great Harvest & Vintage of the
Nations" (43 [50]:1). The harvest and vintage are visually anticipated in
the opening plate of Book the First (Fig. 5), which depicts the star of

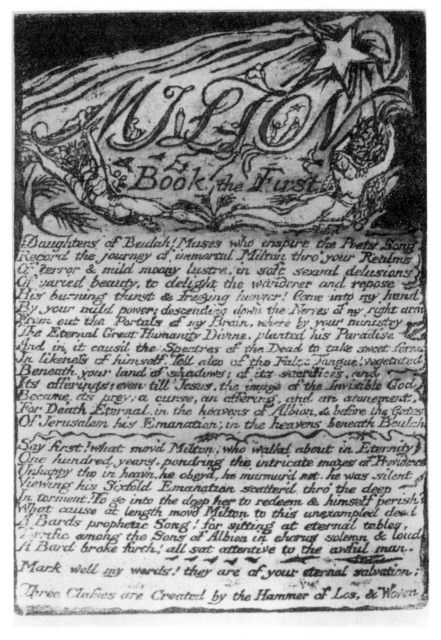

Fig. 5.   Blake, *Milton*, plate 2. Rare Book Division, New York Public Library.

Milton's return shining down on Adam outstretched among the fallen grain and Eve reclining on a cluster of grapes. In *Jerusalem*, too, Urizen's reign is a mildew blight. The world is engulfed in clouds of sexual conflict and "the Spectre like a hoar frost & a Mildew rose over Albion" (*J* 54:15). Although the paradox of the "blighted corn" and expanded vision is not developed until the *Four Zoas*, Blake makes use of its essential constituents, vision aroused by maddening blight, in *America* and *Europe*.

Blight and pestilence are the weapons that Albion's Angel seeks to send against the rebellious American colonies:

> His plagues obedient to his voice flew forth out of their
> clouds
> Falling upon America, as a Storm to cut them off
> As a blight cuts the tender corn when it begins to appear.
> *(America* 14:4–6)

He succeeds in sweeping the land with a wind of "Fury! rage! madness!" America would have been "o'erwhelmed," and Earth would have "lost another portion of the infinite," had not that very wind rallied the American spirit and united the colonies. They turn their "Fury! rage! madness!" back upon Albion's Guardians who drop their weapons and flee. The American Revolution sets loose the demon Orc, who hides in the mists, "Till Angels & weak men twelve years should govern o'er the strong: / And their end should come, when France receiv'd the Demons light." The final plate of *America* foretells the expansion of the five senses and the liberation of Europe:

> France Spain & Italy,
> In terror view'd the bands of Albion, and the ancient
> Guardians
> Fainting upon the elements, smitten with their own pla-
> gues
> They slow advance to shut the five gates of their law-
> built heaven
> Filled with blasting fancies and with mildews of despair
> With fierce disease and lust, unable to stem the fires of
> Orc
> *(America* 16:16–20)

Although "the ancient Guardians" seek to close the senses with "blasting fancies" and "mildews of despair," the "fierce disease and lust" kindles rather than extinguishes "the fires of Orc."

Plate 9 of *America* apparently depicts an abandoned babe beneath the blighted corn. The immediately preceding plates have already taught the reader to be alert to the ironic disjuncture between text and illustration. Plate 7 is inscribed with the burning wrath of Albion's Angel:

> Art thou not Orc; who serpent-form'd
> Stands at the gate of Enitharmon to devour her children;
> Blasphemous Demon, Antichrist, hater of Dignities;
> Lover of wild rebellion, and transgressor of Gods Law;
> Why dost thou come to Angels eyes in this terrific form?
>
> (*America* 7:3–7)

The accompanying illumination, however, is a scene of tranquillity, with two naked children and a ram slumbering together under a birch tree. Plate 8 gives the Terror's answer, depicting not Orc but his auditor, Albion's Angel, supporting himself in the clouds as he listens to Orc's reply. When we behold in plate 9 the smitten grain arching over an infant lying alone and naked in the field (Fig. 6), we must not leap to conclusions. Whose field is this, America's or Albion's? And whose babe? Is the babe abandoned and dead, or sheltered and protected. Perhaps the ambiguity is deliberate. Albion's Angel is speaking, calling for his "loud war-trumpets" to sound alarm among the colonies. By his own account, however, his effort to blight the land has failed:

> America is darkned; and my punishing Demons terrified
> Crouch howling before their caverns deep like skins dry'd
>   in the wind.
> They cannot smite the wheat, nor quench the fatness of
>   the earth.
>
> (*America* 9:3–5)

He sees "Children take shelter from the lightnings," not alone in the fields but in the robes of the patriots—"Washington / And Paine and Warren." His ability to perceive the events taking place in America is obscured by clouds and usurped by "a vision from afar." The vision reveals his own fears of what Urizenic oppression has fostered: the harlot mother gives birth to the rebellious serpent.

> Writhing in pangs of abhorred birth; red flames the crest
>   rebellious
> And eyes of death; the harlot womb oft opened in vain
> Heaves in enormous circles, now the times are return'd
>   upon thee,

Devourer of thy parent, now thy unutterable torment renews.
.   .   .   .
terrible birth! a young one bursting! where is the weeping
    mouth?
And where the mothers milk? instead those ever-hissing
    jaws
And parched lips drop with fresh gore; now roll thou in
    clouds
Thy mother lays her length outstretch'd upon the shore
    beneath.

(America 9:17–25)

The babe that lies beneath the smitten grain may well be another victim
of oppression, or it may be the newborn child of revolution.

In contrast to plate 9 of *America*, plate 9 of *Europe* represents "the
blighted corn" as a source of visionary power (Fig. 7). In his commentary
on this plate, Erdman is probably correct in suggesting that these naked
dancers "are trumpeting the apocalypse." But there is more to support
that argument than a biblical allusion to the seven plagues of the Book of
Revelation. The blight is spread by naked male and female spirits who
dance through the toppled stalks of rye blowing the ergot rusts as silent
music from their curved horns. Blake's literal rendering of the *secale cornutum*, the horned rye, imitates the spiraling tendrils of the sclerotia.
That Albion's Angel is to be "smitten with his own plagues," helps to
explain why the harbingers of blight are beautiful. They are beautiful not
just for the political liberation they prophesy, they are intrinsically beautiful in their capacity to expand vision and reveal "wondrous worlds."

Blake has not hesitated in *Europe* to provide scenes of violence and
horror. He depicts malevolence (plate 1), the strangler and his victims
(plate 2), the dying infant before the hearth (plate 6), those stricken with
pestilence (plate 7), imprisoned in chains (plate 13), fleeing the confla-
gration (plate 15). The dancers of the blighted corn possess a dreamy
detachment from the dreary scenes of human suffering. Throughout the
grim torments of *Europe* Blake sustains a visionary transcendence that
enables him and the reader to bear the oppression, to escape the spider's
web of decay (plate 12), and to anticipate the new day of "enormous
revelry" (plate 14).

The narrative begins with the playfulness of Blake's catching a fairy
who then dictates the prophecy. Akin to this fairy, the naked dancers
appear as effects in the very dream they cause. They are delusions in the
blight they propagate. They are also dancers in Enitharmon's dream. Enitharmon has slept and "Man was a Dream!" For "eighteen hundred years"
she has dreamt her "female dream!" It is a dream of Europe's history

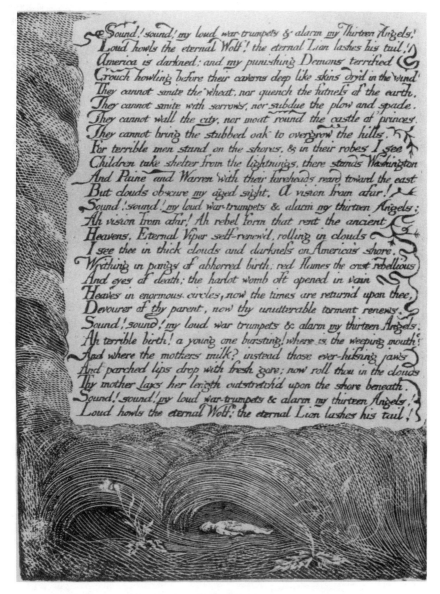

Fig. 6. Blake, *America*, plate 9. Auckland Public Library.

since the time of Christ, a dream of division and war, a dream that now reveals "Albions Angel smitten with his own plagues" and a looming cloud "Fill'd with immortal demons of futurity" (*Europe* 9:1–10). In her dream, she feels none of the paroxysms of the blight. As that futurity unfolds,

Enitharmon slept,
Eighteen hundred years; Man was a Dream!
The night of Nature and their harps unstrung:
She slept in middle of her nights song.
Eighteen hundred years a female dream!

Shadows of men in fleeting bands upon the winds:
Divide the heavens of Europe;
Till Albions Angel smitten with his own plagues fled with his bands
The cloud bears hard on Albions shore:
Fill'd with immortal demons of futurity:
In council gather the smitten Angels of Albion
The cloud bears hard upon the council house; down rushing
On the heads of Albions Angels.

One hour they lay buried beneath the ruins of that hall:
But as the stars rise from the salt lake they arise in pain,
In troubled mists oercloulded by the terrors of struggling times.

Fig. 7.   Blake, *Europe*, plate 9. Auckland Public Library.

however, she is awakened from her delusions. Orc descends from "the heights of Enitharmon" to blaze in fury amidst "the vineyards of red France." The revolution rages and "Enitharmon groans & cries in anguish and dismay" (*Europe* 15:8).

Beginning with his sketches of "The Good Farmer" early in the 1780s, Blake appropriated the recurrent threat of ergot blight into his artistic vision of redemption. With its hallucinatory effects, ergot poisoning expressed precisely those conditions which Blake sought to describe in the mental storms and fires of *The Four Zoas* and the political strife of *America* and *Europe*. Like the victim of "the blighted corn," the Blakean redeemer—Orc, Los, Christ, Milton, Blake himself—knows both bliss and agony, "behold[s] the Angelic spheres arising night & day," and "walks forth from midst of the fires."

This chapter on Blake brings us to the very threshold of the problem to be addressed in the next three chapters. Although I have chosen to include my discussion of the Blakean redeemer in this section devoted to the literary representations of madness, other critics, more in accord with Paul Youngquist's argument in *Madness and Blake's Myth*, might be inclined to place Blake together with those poets discussed in the final three chapters. Blake, no less than Hölderlin, Clare, or Nerval, it might be argued, exhibits the duality of the sane and insane hero as well as the dependency on intertextuality that, according to Evelyne Keitel, are characteristic of psychopathic writing. Such characteristics, to be sure, may be seen in the grand struggle between Los and Urizen and the frequent reliance on the prophets of the Old Testament. Blake himself, however, never falters in that struggle, never loses the hermeneutic center in his biblical appropriations. Most important, he remains clearly conscious of the distinction between the redemptive rage of the mad prophet and the debilitating infection of madness that is propagated among the poor by forces of greed and power.

PART III
MAD POETS

7

ARNIM'S "WALKS WITH HÖLDERLIN"

It may well seem a paradox that Arnim, in his pursuit of a practical aesthetics capable of reconciling the arts with political conditions of turmoil and unrest, should find his model in the works of Hölderlin. Hölderlin's mental breakdown, after all, had been attributed to his inability to reconcile poetic sensibility with real life. Impressed by the wisdom and practicality of the earlier writings, especially *Hyperion*, Arnim believed that Hölderlin, much in the manner of his own Empedocles, had commenced a journey of exploration. Empedocles justified his leap into the volcano as a search for the quintessence of mind. Hölderlin, similarly, fell into madness in order to chart that subjective *terra incognita* beyond the reach of rationality. Still writing poetry, even while totally dependent on the Zimmer family, Hölderlin kept sending his messages from the realm of madness. Some day he might return, Arnim wrote, to tell us what he had seen in the "lonely abyss."[1] In the meantime, these poetic messages required an interpreter. Grounding his hermeneutic on Hölderlin's earlier works, Arnim defined the conditions for rendering Hölderlin's later poetry accessible to the rational mind.

In 1818 Arnim commented on the neglect of Hölderlin's poetry and called for a critical edition. *Hyperion* was long out of print and individual poems were scattered in periodicals. From the close of *Hyperion*, he quoted the passage that laments "empty words" and praises the inspired soul as "the beauty of the world."[2] The passage prompts a wish that "the

1. "Ausflüge mit Hölderlin."
2. Friedrich Hölderlin, *Hyperion*, in *Sämtliche Werke* 2:124, 123: "O Seele! Seele! Schönheit der Welt! Du unzerstörbare, du entzückende [Arnim: *entzündende*] mit deiner ewigen

works of Hölderlin, of Germany's greatest elegiac poet," might be "gathered into a complete collection by a careful hand." The edition must be complete, "for he never wrote an empty word." As brilliant as they were, a strange fate had befallen his words, "like stars, with which he experienced a like destiny: that their terrestrial eye could not adjust to the magnitude of the light which they beheld, their loving disposition could not overcome the afflictions of life; so their spirit was withdrawn from humanity, while their body still lives among them."[3] Hölderlin might not return to dwell again among men, but his words can be restored.

When Gustav Schwab, Ludwig Uhland, and Justinus Kerner brought out their edition of Hölderlin's *Gedichte* (1826), Arnim welcomed the contribution but lamented its limited compass. Many of the poems that he had admired were missing. In "Ausflüge mit Hölderlin" (1828) he expressed his frustration that his own collection of transcriptions had been scattered so that he could no longer supplement the edition. He had once had copies of the nine poems published as "Nachtgesänge" in 1805.[4] And in 1808, he had published in his *Zeitung für Einsiedler* excerpts from "Der Rhein" (from strophe 14) and "Patmos" (the first and last strophes), poems that had appeared in Seckendorf's *Musenalmanach für das Jahr 1808*.[5] "Patmos" is the poem which for Arnim best illustrates Hölderlin's bold exploration into the realm beyond rationality. Shame, Arnim declares, inhibited most poets from tracing the origin of their being ("die Wurzelkeime ihres Daseins").[6] They feared the risks, he explains, in trying to rediscover the primal ground in the unconscious. Hölderlin was too

---

Jugend! Du bist; was ist denn der Tod und alles Wehe der Menschen? Ach, viel der leeren Worte haben die Wunderlichen gemacht! Geschiehet doch Alles aus Lust und endet doch alles mit Frieden." And "Frei sind wir, gleichen uns nicht ängstig [Arnim: *ängstlich*] von außen; wie sollte nicht wechseln die Weise des Lebens? Wir lieben den Aether doch alle und innigst im Innersten gleichen wir uns!"

3. "Literatur-Notizen": "Gleich Sterne, mit welchem ihn ein gleiches Geschick traf: daß ihr irdisches Auge die Fülle des angeschauten Lichtes nicht ordnen, ihr liebevolles Gemüth die Kränkungen des Lebens nicht überwinden konnte; so ward den Menschen ihr Geist entzogen, während ihr Leib noch unter ihnen fort lebte."

4. Of the nine "Nachtgesänge" ("Chiron," "Thränen," "An die Hoffnung," "Vulkan," "Blödigkeit," "Ganymed," "Hälfte des Lebens," "Lebensalter," and "Der Winkel von Hart"), which had appeared in Wilman's *Taschenbuch* (1805), copies of the first seven are in the Arnim-Nachlaß (no. 452), Goethe- und Schiller-Archiv, Weimar; this manuscript file also contains Arnim's copies of Hölderlin's poems from Vermehren's *Musenalmanach* (1803) and Seckendorf's *Musenalmanach* (1807 and 1808).

5. Achim von Arnim and Clemens Brentano, *Zeitung für Einsiedler*, 20 April, 4 and 11 May; see also Arnim's letter to Bettina, 27 February 1808, in *Achim von Arnim und die ihm nahe standen*, ed. Reinhold Steig and Herman Grimm, 2:99. Bettina von Arnim also writes of Hölderlin in *Die Günderode*, 134–39, and records her visits with Hölderlin (in Homburg, 1804–1806), 249–51 (August 1805), 403–4.

6. FDH ms 7212; in the published version of "Ausflüge," the phrase is altered to "Wurzelkeime ihres Wirkens."

earnest in his art to be confused by such an investigation. But even he, at the beginning of his "Patmos," asks for aid "to cross over and return" [Hinüberzugehn und wiederzukehren]. It was to be regretted, then, that Hölderlin had not charted the way. The only recourse was to follow him on his journey.

Tracing that journey, Arnim quotes from "Herbstfeier" ("Stutgard"), "Die Nacht" ("Brod und Wein"), "Die Wanderung," as well as passages from *Empedokles*. His key text, however, is "Patmos," which he possessed only in faulty transcription. Part of his effort, therefore, was editorial. He wanted an accessible rather than an "accurate" version. As he had asserted in his dispute with the Brothers Grimm, the truth of art is not best served by scholarly pretension to the authority of some mechanical replication on the printed page.[7] For Arnim, the active rather than the mechanical reception is crucial. When Andreas Thomasberger examined the variants in Arnim's version of the poem, he emphasized, contrary to Arnim's intention, a split between poem and reception. Having created his own image of the poet, "der gedichtete Dichter," Arnim constructed a new text to suit his fictive poet.[8] Because Thomasberger builds his case on deviations from an "accurate" text, he has rendered himself vulnerable to a similar charge of having invented his own Arnim, for his transcription of Arnim's manuscripts contains over thirty errors in text and punctuation.[9]

If it is valid to look at Arnim's text of "Patmos" as a part of the historical reception of Hölderlin, then it is also necessary to reconsider the dismissal of his text as a copy thrice removed from the "ideal" (apparently based on Schlosser's copy of Sinclair's copy of the draft in the author's own hand). Rather than holding to some static and objective rendition as an "accurate" text, Arnim maintained that art, as a "bildende, fortschaffende Trieb," persists exclusively in its historicity.[10] If we take Arnim at his word, as Roswitha Burwick has proposed, his adaptation of Hölderlin's text should be seen as informing, rather than departing from, his role as mediator between Hölderlin and the reader.[11] His purpose was to document Hölderlin's endeavor to represent the "other half."

Indeed, Arnim had argued that a practical aesthetic might well be based on Hölderlin's *Hyperion*. What he had in mind, as he explained in a letter to Savigny (13 August 1814), would perform the usual hermeneutic function of elucidating a specific text, but would proceed historically as well as in accord with his own peculiar practice. That practice, evident in

---

7. Steig and Grimm 3:242, 248–49; R. Burwick, *Dichtung und Malerei bei Achim von Arnim*, 56–60.

8. Andreas Thomasberger, "Der gedichtete Dichter," 283–300.

9. Arnim, *Werke*, vol. 6, "Kommentar."

10. Steig and Grimm 3:248–49.

11. R. Burwick, *Dichtung und Malerei*, 82–84.

any number of Arnim's essays, would involve a narrative re-creation of how the work was produced. In his "Taschenbuch" (ms B44) he gives a seven-point outline describing how his lectures on aesthetics might be organized.[12] As elsewhere, he insisted that the approach be positive: an author should be praised for what he has done, not condemned for what he has failed to do. Arnim compares the aesthetic endeavor to the descriptive and analytic method of a geologist or chemist. A practical aesthetic works with immediate evidence, but also with the mediated affect—it is a "Wirkungsästhetik."[13] While historical and biographical circumstances are important, an explication must also reconstruct the feeling of a work. In his "Taschenbuch" he specifically proposes Hölderlin's *Hyperion* as the text upon which he intends to construct his aesthetics; and in his letter to Savigny he refers to it as a comprehensive source: "My compendium would be Hölderlin's *Hyperion*. From this wonderfully deep and lucid book I have derived many notions. It was the only book which still completely comforted me during the most uncertain time in the previous year. Much can be connected with it, especially political science."[14] The connection between aesthetics and political science was not remote for Arnim. In his defense of the Danish government in 1815, for example, Arnim quoted from *Hyperion* Hölderlin's charge that violence, greed, and deceit are promulgated by suppressing the aesthetic sensibility of the people:

> Where a people love the beautiful, where they honor the genius of their artists, there stirs, like the breath of life, a pervasive spirit, and the shy sense unfolds; the dark shadows of the self vanish, and all hearts become pious and great, and enthusiasm gives birth to heroes. But where divine nature and its artists are wronged, there

12. "Vorlesungen über praktische Ästhetik nach Hölderlins Hyperion," in Arnim's "Taschenbuch" (ms B44), 185, in the Freies Deutsches Hochstift in Frankfurt. A transcription of the "Taschenbücher" (mss B44 and B69) is currently being prepared for publication by Jürgen Knaack and Ulfert Ricklefs.

13. R. Burwick, *Dichtung und Malerei*, 62–84 ("Positive Kritik und die offene Form der Theorie"), 85–129 ("Wirkungsästhetik").

14. *Arnims Briefe an Savigny* 96: "Mein Compendium würde Hölderlins Hyperion, von diesem wunderbar tiefen und klaren Buche sind mir viele Betrachtungen ausgegangen, es war das Einzige das mir in dem vorigen Jahre in der zweifelhaftesten Zeit noch immer ganz behagte, vieles läst sich daran anschliessen, insbesondre Staatswissenschaft." Cf. Arnim's letter to Brentano, 3 August 1813, in which he says that following the "Landsturm" of 1813, "Außer dem Hyperion sind mir in dieser Zeit keine andern [Bücher] als meine eignen treu geblieben" (Steig and Grimm 1:316–17); and to the Brothers Grimm, 21 September 1817: "Schon vor ein paar Jahren machte ich mir einen Plan, eine Aesthetik nach Hölderlins Hyperion auszuarbeiten, denn elegisch wird sie ihrer Natur nach, und diese herrlichsten aller Elegieen giebt dazu den mannigfaltigsten Anlaß" (Steig and Grimm 3:402).

the best joys of life are driven away, and every other star is better than the earth. Ever more bleak and barren men become, although all are nobly born. The sense of servitude increases, and with it a coarser mood; a delirium grows with cares, and with haughtiness hunger and a fear of finding sustenance; the blessings of the seasons become a curse, and all gods flee.[15]

Hölderlin himself was victimized by the very political brutality he decried in his "profound" ("tiefsinnig") *Hyperion*. Arnim finds in Hölderlin's words the power to arouse resistance to the continuing plight of oppression.[16]

As Arnim saw it, Hölderlin's distress over the Napoleonic intervention, combined with his "most unfortunate attraction" to Susette Gontard, precipitated his mental breakdown. In "Ausflüge mit Hölderlin" Arnim builds upon a series of quotations to document the historical and biographical circumstances. The story he tells is intended to anticipate and elucidate the narrative in "Patmos." He begins with "Herbstfeier" ("Stutgard," 1–10) addressed to his friend Siegfried Schmidt on his return from the war. These lines show that the poet, "der so vieles Leid der Menschheit darstellte, ihren Freuden innig zu gewendet war." That joy is soon blighted by the military turmoil. The lines he quotes from "Die Nacht" ("Brod und Wein," 1–18) reveal the poet's anguish. The public suffering, resulting from the French assault on Frankfurt, compounded his personal misery. It is from this period, too, that Arnim dates "die Scheltrede an die Deutschen" with which Hölderlin concluded volume 2 of *Hyperion* (the first volume was published in April 1797, the second in October 1799). Arnim describes an increasing tension between Hölderlin's love for his country and his disgust with the corruption of German politics: "His anger at the demise of Germany's splendor is a reflection of his burning love for his unfortunate Fatherland, which he had beautifully expressed in the festive song he addressed to Schmidt."[17] Here Arnim quotes again from "Herbst-

15. *Hyperion*, in *Sämtliche Werke* 2:118: "wo ein Volk das Schöne liebt, wo es den Genius in seinen Künstlern ehrt, da weht, wie Lebensluft ein allgemeiner Geist, da öffnet sich der scheue Sinn; der Eigendünkel schmilzt, und fromm und groß sind alle Herzen, und Helden gebiert die Begeisterung. Wo aber so beleidigt werden die göttlich Natur und ihre Künstler, da ist des Lebens beßte Lust hinweg, und jeder andere Stern ist besser denn die Erde. Wüster immer, öder werden da die Menschen, die doch alle schöngeboren sind. Der Knechtsinn steigt, mit ihm der grobe Muth, der Rausch wächst mit den Sorgen und mit der Üppigkeit der Hunger und die Nahrungsangst, zum Fluche wird der Segen des Jahres, und alle Götter fliehen."

16. [Die Verteidigung der dänischen Regierung].

17. "Ausflüge mit Hölderlin": "Dieser Zorn über den Untergang aller Herrlichkeit Deutschlands, er ist eben ein heller Widerschein seiner glühenden Liebe für dieses unglückliche Vaterland, die er eben in jenen Festgesänge an Schmidt so schön ausspricht."

feier" (29–36), as well as from Hölderlin's praise of his native Swabia in "Die Wanderung" (1–28). In Hyperion's polemic—"ich kann kein Volk mir denken, das zerrißener wäre, wie die Deutschen"—Arnim sees a growing discontent which prompted Hölderlin to leave Stuttgart two years later (December 1801); "Hölderlin actually made an attempt to flee Germany. As a teacher for young boys, he traveled to Bordeaux, but the trip itself brought on a feeling of boundless misery and undermined his health."[18] On 22 June 1802, his beloved Susette Gontard died. He returned to Stuttgart in an obvious state of mental distraction. Although he found support in Homburg upon his return, circumstances, both personal and political, were deteriorating. His friends—Emerich, Sinclair, and Schmidt—were to suffer with Hölderlin under Napoleon's reconstruction of German rule. Emerich was confined in the insane asylum at Würzburg (17 November 1802); Sinclair was arrested (26 February 1805); and Schmidt was sent to the insane asylum at Haina (16 April 1806). In fear of his life, Hölderlin renounced Jacobin politics.

Until the court at Homburg was dissolved (11 September 1806), Hölderlin was able to persist with the composition of his hymns and odes. The first two volumes of his translation of Sophocles appeared in 1804.[19] Arnim assumes that "traces of confusion prevented their continuation" [Spuren der Verwirrung hinderten die Fortsetzung]; nevertheless, he affirms the value of the critical commentaries to *Oedipus* and *Antigone*. Although "one feels the full power even here already broken in theorizing" [man fühlt die volle Kraft auch hier schon gebrochen im Theoretisiren], Hölderlin's remarks are relevant to his late poetry. In describing the dilemma of Sophoclean tragedy, Hölderlin turns his own personal crisis into a vigorous new aesthetic. To establish hermeneutic access to "Patmos," Arnim excerpts Hölderlin's account of the disruption of harmony between mind and nature.

The concept of harmony cannot be made intelligible by philosophy, Hölderlin argues, for philosophy can address only one faculty of the soul ("Vermögen der Seele"), treating that one as a whole and calling the unity of its parts logic. Poetry, on the other hand, deals with the manifold powers, so that its representation of connections among the parts creates a coherent whole that is truly harmonic: "rhythm in its higher sense" ("Rhythmus in höhern Sinne"). Whereas philosophy relies on logic, poetry

---

18. Ibid.: "Wirklich machte Hölderlin einen Versuch Deutschland zu entfliehen, er reiste als Jugendlehrer nach Bordeaux, doch soll gerade diese Reise ihn ein grenzenloses äußerres Elend geführt und sein Gesundheit untergraben haben."

19. A copy of *Sophocles Trauerspiele. Übersetzt von Hölderlin* (Frankfurt: Friedrich Wilmans, 1804), vol. 1, stamped "Ludwig Achim von Arnim," is listed in the catalogue (9 May 1929) prepared by Freimund von Arnim of the collection at Wiepersdorf.

engages rhythm, "the calculable law" ("das kalkulable Gesetz") of coherence. Even in its most fundamental elements rhythm operates through
contrast or opposition. A strong stress can only be heard or felt when
accompanied by an alternating weak stress. According to Hölderlin's metrical analysis of ideas, a "rapidity of enthusiasm" ("Rapidität der Begeisterung") is an *ictus* that compels some relief or release.

Hölderlin's sense of the tragic rhythm is not just the active and passive,
such as the alternations of rage and remorse in Reynolds's portrait of *Mrs.
Siddons as the Tragic Muse*. For him that rhythm is defined by the *arsis*
and *thesis* of mind and nature, spiritual and physical being. Although the
mortal mind is physically confined, Hölderlin argued, the moment of inspiration enables it to experience the "other half": "The keenest moment
of daily life or of a work of art is where the spirit of time and nature, the
divine which seizes the human, and the object in which he is interested,
are juxtaposed in their wildest extreme, for the sensual object reaches
only half way, but the mind is most powerfully awakened where the second half commences."[20] As Arnim recognizes, Hölderlin does not conceive
of this confrontation with the "other half" in terms of a religious ecstasy,
an *unio mystica*. Achieved through wild excess and rage, it is monstrous
rather than beatific. Antigone's claim of divine union and her sublime
scorn at the mocking response from the chorus (852–61) together form
such a "monstrous" moment: "Her sublime scorn, so far as holy madness
is the highest human manifestation and is here more soul than spoken
word, surpasses all of her other speeches" [Der erhabene Spott, sofern
heiliger Wahnsinn höchste menschlicher Erscheinung und hier mehr
Seele als Sprache ist, übertrifft alle ihre übrige Äußerungen]. Fulfillment
occurs, paradoxically, only in its loss: "Tragic representation rests principally therein, that the monstrous, as God and man couple and nature is
made boundless and in anger becomes one with man's innermost being,
thereby leads to the awareness that the boundless union is purified
through boundless division."[21] Only in "boundless division" does the
"boundless union" gain its meaning. An *arsis* must complement the *thesis*.
In Arnim's interpretation, Hölderlin's poetry became progressively preoc-

20. Hölderlin, *Sämtliche Werke*, 5:266: "Der kühnste Moment eines Taglaufs oder Kunst-
werks ist, wo der Geist der Zeit und Natur, das Himmlische, was den Menschen ergreift und
der Gegenstand, für welchen er sich interessirt, am wildesten gegen einander stehen, weil
der sinnliche Gegenstand nur eine Hälfte weit reicht, der Geist aber am mächtigsten erwacht, da wo die zweite Hälfte angeht."

21. Ibid. 195: "Die Darstellung des Tragischen beruht vorzüglich darauf, daß das Un-
geheure, wie der Gott und Mensch sich paart und grenzenlos die Natur macht und des
Menschen Innerstes im Zorn Eins wird, dadurch sich begreift, daß das grenzenlose Eins
werden durch grenzenloses Scheiden sich reinigt."

cupied with this rhythm. Rather than seeking the liberation announced at the close of *Hyperion*, "Poor suffering Hölderlin had in the meantime derived another consolation" [Der arme Dulder Hölderlin, er hatte inzwischen schon einen andren Trost gewonnen]. As Arnim saw it, Hölderlin had turned his poetic effort inward, seeking in the "calculable law" of rhythm a control over harmonic complementation.

Arnim apparently assumed that Hölderlin had endeavored to write his tragedy on Empedocles at the time he was translating the tragedies of Sophocles. The fragments included in *Gedichte* (1826) certainly seemed to exhibit the theory of tragic rhythm. Arnim did not know, nor did the editors, that the fragments were from act 1, scene 1, of the second version (summer 1799) and act 1, scene 3, of the third version (winter 1799–1800). Arnim thought these were scenes from the first and final acts. He was perfectly correct, however, in relating Hölderlin's conception of Empedocles to his study of Sophocles. As we now know from his theoretical deliberations on the "Form des Trauerspiels" and "Grund zum Empedokles,"[22] Hölderlin had already formulated in 1799 his concept of the tragic hero as martyr to the destiny of his time ("das Schicksal seiner Zeit").

On the basis of the fragments published in 1826, Arnim endeavors to construct a plot summary.[23] As Arnim observes in his "Vorrede zum Stoff des Empedokles," Empedocles is torn between "göttlich" and "gottlos":

> [Empedocles is] a divine nature corrupted by power precisely because he appears godless to a humanity who cannot recognize his divine nature. He is blissfully reminded of the desire which begot him, otherwise he is beyond mere appearances which no longer bind him. He becomes firm through the friendship of Pausanias. . . . He betrayed the favors of the gods to the common people.
>
> His brother curses him, and it can be concluded that Empedocles alone is a son of a god and that his brother feels that the honor of his house is thereby wronged. Because a lover is nowhere mentioned, one could well think that Empedocles also despises this

22. "Form des Trauerspiels" (from letter to Neuffer, 3 July 1799) 6:338–41; and "Grund zum Empedokles" 4:149–62.

23. As Heinz Röllecke himself admits, there is no internal evidence to support the assumption that Arnim made use of additional manuscripts. The commentary in "Ausflüge mit Hölderlin" as well as in the "Vorrede zum Stoff des Empedokles" contains no reference to text from "Empedokles" not printed in *Gedichte* (1827). See Rölleke, "Achim von Arnim und Friedrich Hölderlin," 149–58.

earthly tie and yearns to be with the gods. He was worshiped in a base manner, which means material gifts were expected of him, and that seems to be the point which determines his doom. If we may dare to speculate, an apotheosis should close the play. The favors of the gods lift him out of the crowd, and the timorous people, returning from the old abyss, search for him.[24]

Although he speculates on a possible conclusion in this earlier draft, Arnim omits the notion of an apotheosis from his published essay. Such a conclusion is no longer consonant with the argument that he has extracted from Hölderlin's commentaries to Sophocles. Nor does he further elaborate the suggestion that Empedocles seeks death because he cannot fulfill the expectations of the people. Instead, he emphasizes those conditions of the "monstrous" union of man and God described in the commentaries to Sophocles. As Hölderlin's raging alter ego, Empedocles is caught in the threshold of "boundless union" and "boundless division": "Empedocles, designated as a descendent of the gods because of his heavenly intellect, is made the enemy of Mecades and Hermocrates precisely because of this monstrous power within him, the way in which he appears to be both man and god. They do not envy him; rather, they believe that such a condition, such a power over the people, cannot be endured. He appears to them in titanic stature; he enkindles their passions like dry grass."[25] To reveal how Empedocles' divine power aroused fear and jealousy among those incapable of understanding it, Arnim quotes the dia-

---

24. "Vorrede zum Stoff des Empedokles": "Eine göttliche Natur von Herrschaft verdorben eben weil sie gottlos ist, weil die Menschen sie nicht erkennen können. Dieser wird selig an ein Lusten gemahnt, von dem er abstammt, sonst über das Äussere hinaus, das ihn nicht mehr fesselt, wird fest durch die Freundschaft Pausanias. . . .
Er hat die Gunst der Götter den Gemeinen verrathen.
Sein Bruder flucht ihm es läßt sich das annehmen, daß eben nur er ein Göttersohn ist und jener die Ehre seines Hauses dadurch gekränkt fühlt. Da nirgend eine Geliebte erwähnt könnte man wohl denken, das er auch dieses irdische Band verachtet und zu den Göttern sich sehnt. Sie haben ihn in gemeiner Art vergöttert, das heißt sie erwarten alles Irdische von ihm und das scheint der Punkt wo er untergehen muß. Sollten wir eine Vermuthung wagen, so müßte eine Apotheose das Stück schließen, die Gunst der Götter ihn aus der Menge erheben und das zaudernde Volk vom alten Abgrund zurückkehrend ihn suchen <unleserlich>."

25. "Ausflüge mit Hölderlin": "Empedokles als ein Abkömmling der Götter wegen seines himmlischen Geistes bezeichnet, wird von Mekades und Hermokrates eben wegen dieses Ungeheuren in ihm, wie er zugleich Gott und Mensch zu sein scheint, angefeindet, sie beneiden ihn nicht, sie glauben nur, daß solch ein Zustand, solch ein Gewalt über das Volk nicht bestehen könne, er erscheint ihnen in Titangröße; er entzündet die Menschen wie dürres Gras."

logue between Mecades and Hermocrates. Mecades declares that the people worship Empedocles as a king or god. Hermocrates answers that Empedocles does not understand the use of power and has erred in attending to the common people: "His very soul he cast before the people, / Good-naturedly betrayed to vulgar men / The grace of gods" [Die Seele warf er vor das Volk, verriet / Die Götter Gunst gutmütig den Gemeinen]. Although he had quoted these same lines in his earlier draft, Arnim now sees in Empedocles a Promethean hero who has inspired the people. When he turns to the next scene, he anticipates a conclusion on Mount Etna that will confront the dilemma of the divided self:

> Nowhere is it indicated how it has come about, but at the close we find Empedocles driven into exile at the top of Aetna, cursed by his brothers, his appearance desecrated, accompanied by no one but his follower Pausanias, from whom he endeavors to separate before he throws himself into Etna. Then there comes to him an aged man from Egypt, who in earlier times revealed many things to him, and who now once more relates to him his entire life by asking him: And who am I?[26]

Again Arnim gives a quotation in which he finds autobiographical resonance. Hölderlin observed that in both *Oedipus* and *Antigone* the blind prophet Tiresias provided the caesura, the reflective pause to balance the dramatic stress. Such a role Hölderlin has given to Manes, the old Egyptian, who challenges Empedocles to confront his own identity. Empedocles, however, defines self only in terms of other—the other half, which has infused his merely mortal being:

> And now the ruler comes within his beam,
> And thereupon, to prove ourselves his kin,
> We follow him down amid the holy flames.[27]

26. Ibid.: "Nirgends ist angedeutet, wie es gekommen, aber wir finden Empedokles am Schlusse ausgestossen am Aetna, verflucht von seinem Bruder, sein Angesicht geschändet, von niemand begleitet als von einem Jünglinge Pausanias, den er von sich zu entfernen trachtet, ehe er sich in den Aetna stürzt. Da tritt zu ihm ein Greis aus Aegypten der ihm früher viel verkündet, ihm erschließt er noch einmal sein ganzes Leben, indem er ihn fragt: Und wer bin ich?"

27. Hölderlin, "Empedokles," 3d version, scene 3.478–80, in *Poems and Fragments* 360:
> Und itz der Herrscher kömmt in seinem Strahl,
> Dann folgen wir, zum Zeichen, daß wir ihm
> Verwandt sind, hinab in heil'ge Flamme.

The holy flame consumes the flame of mortal being. Hölderlin resolves the contraries, as Arnim recognizes, not in an apotheosis of the living self but the self in the moment of death.[28]

Confident in a progressive history, Arnim had little patience with the classic-modern dialectics that captivated many of his contemporaries—Friedrich Schlegel and Schelling as well as Hölderlin. In a draft version of his "Ausflüge," Arnim excused as a kind of escapism Hölderlin's preoccupation with the Greek past: "No wonder that in his thoughts he transported himself completely into antiquity, fleeing to happier times, especially Greece; no one felt more vital sympathy when the Greeks, at the time of the Russian Campaign, made their first attempt at liberation and forsaken perished."[29] For Hölderlin, Greek culture provided a model for understanding modern culture. All art seeks to complement the prevailing weakness. The Greeks found strength in a concept of destiny to complement their own inability to comprehend the human condition. With the advent of Christianity, the belief in the individual soul replaced the belief in fate or destiny. As a result, the tragic sense has become all the more intense. Greek tragedy is circumstantially mediated, because it concerns only the physical body. Modern tragedy is immediate, because it involves the spiritual body. For the Greeks, the word had causal reality. For the moderns, the word dissolves in idea.

> For us, since we are under a more true Zeus, who not only pauses between this earth and the wild world of the dead, but also more decisively forces to the ground the natural process, eternally hostile to man, on its way to the other world, and since this greatly changes the essential and national conceptions, and our poetry must be national, so that its themes are selected according to our worldview and its conceptions are national, the Greek conceptions are changed insofar as their main tendency is to be able to compose themselves, because that was their weakness, while by con-

28. "Anmerkungen zur Antigone" 5:195–202: "Die tragische Darstellung beruhet, wie in den 'Anmerkungen zum Oedipus' angedeutet ist, darauf, daß der unmittelbare Gott ganz eines mit dem Menschen (denn der Gott eines Apostels ist mittelbarer, ist höchster Verstand in höchstem Geiste), daß die *unendliche* Begeisterung *unendlich*, das heißt in Gegensätzen, im Bewußtsein, welches das Bewußtsein aufhebt, heilig sich scheidend, sich faßt, und der Gott in der Gestalt des Todes gegenwärtig ist."

29. Because of the errors in Thomasberger's transcriptions in "Der gedichtete Dichter," 292–300, I have relied on Roswitha Burwick's transcriptions of FDH mss. 20128 and 7212. "Ausflüge mit Hölderlin": "Kein Wunder daß der sich in Gedanken völlig in die Vorzeit versetzte, nach glücklicheren Zeiten sich flüchtete, vor allem nach Griechenland, daß keiner lebendiger mitfühlte, als die Griechen zur Zeit des Russischen Krieges den ersten Versuch der Befreiung wagten und verlassen untergingen."

trast the main tendency in the conceptions of our time is to be able to effect something, for the lack of destiny is our weakness.[30]

In this argument from Hölderlin's commentary to Sophocles, Arnim thinks he has discovered an apt link to "Patmos." The poet is not escaping into the past, he is resurrecting from the past a vision of apocalypse and salvation for the present.

Although he confesses that he has only an "unclear transcription" ("undeutliche Abschrift"), his emendation addresses not a faulty text but obscure meaning. The poet, "with beating pulse and echoing words has ascended the mountain peak" and has peered beyond mortal bounds. "Is it different," Arnim asks, "in that mental realm?" [Ist es im Geistigen anders?]. The answer must be yes, for Hölderlin's language became strange and perplexing.

Many a word was uncertain, some fully veiled in highest contemplation, some had to be omitted or a couple of explanatory words added. No effort was spared. What need is there to excuse how I made clear to him who is far remote as well as to myself, we who scarcely perceived a whisper in the air, this wonderful mirage, which revealed for a moment all wisdom and glory of the world to the prophet in the desert, to the others, however, who threw themselves down, seemed only a suffocating desert wind.[31]

Arnim thus defines himself as mediator as well as interpreter. His task is to render the vision clear and accessible. Even though the poet may have left the realm of rationality in order to experience it, the vision itself may bear meaning for the rational world.

30. Hölderlin, *Sämtliche Werke*, 5:269–70: "Für uns, da wir unter dem eigentlicheren Zeus stehen, der nicht nur zwischen dieser Erde und der wilden Welt der Todten inne hält, sondern den ewig menschenfeindlichen Naturgang auf seinem Wege in die andre Welt, entschiedener zur Erde zwinget, und da dies die wesentlichen und vaterländischen Vorstellungen groß ändert und unsre Dichtkunst vaterländisch sein muß, so daß ihre Stoffe nach unsrer Weltansicht gewählt sind und ihre Vorstellungen vaterländisch, verändern sich die griechischen Vorstellungen in so fern, als ihre Haupttendenz ist sich fassen zu können, weil darin ihre Schwäche lag, da hingegen die Haupttendenz in den Vorstellungen unsrer Zeit ist, etwas treffen zu können, da das Schicksallose unsre Schwäche ist."

31. Arnim, "Ausflüge mit Hölderlin": "Manches Wort war ungewiß, einiges verhüllte sich völlig in höchster Anschauung, einiges mußte weglassen, ein Paar Worte erklärend zugefügt werden. Mühe ist nicht gespart, was bedarfs der Entschuldigung, wie ich diese wunderbare Luftspiegelung, die dem Seher in der Wüste alle Weisheit und Herrlichkeit der Welt für einige Augenblicke nahte, den andern aber, die sich nieder warfen, wie der erstickende Wind der Wüste erscheinen mochte, hier den Weitentfernten und mir verdeutliche, die wir kaum ein Sausen in der Luft vernahmen."

Arnim titled one of his drafts "Aesthetische Ausflüge mit Hölderlin," and another, with his reading of "Patmos," has the heading "Erster Ausflug." Recollecting his earlier plan for a "Vorlesungen über praktische Ästhetik nach Hölderlins Hyperion," Arnim seems ready to write a series of "Aesthetische Ausflüge" in which he will travel to the very brink with the poet and endeavor to interpret the strange language from beyond: "Once I had a plan very dear to me to construct a so-called Aesthetic upon a poet such as Hölderlin, who plunged so magnificently into a crater in order to experience something that not even he could communicate."[32] What might lie beyond the threshold of his Hyperionic farewell or his Empedoclesian *salto mortale* the poet left concealed in silence. In his "Patmos," however, he continued to sing even as he entered into the prophetic vision of St. John. If Arnim is to satisfy the hermeneutic task of his practical aesthetic, he will have to follow the poet even "zur Höhe des Geistigen."

This is the stuff which penetrates him in Hyperion. Then he sings praises to the sun and earth in their magnificence. Thus the spirit leads him through loneliness to salvation. Already in departing from mankind, dazzled by magnificence, he beholds Patmos; expression becomes infinitely difficult for him, and his thoughts are confused even retrospectively. Breathless, with pounding pulse, with fading words the mortal approaches the peak of the mountain. How shall he reach the lofty heights of mind without similar danger? Painful destiny, the most unfortunate love had broken his strength. The poem excites in every moment, but it wraps itself in obscurity as it approaches the highest intuitions.[33]

32. Again I rely on Roswitha Burwick's transcriptions of FDH mss 20128 and 7212; the brackets indicate her conjectural reading; the word "ebenfalls" in Thomasberger's transcription is incorrect. FDH ms 20128: "Es war einmal ein Plan, der mir scheint <ausgestrichen: sei es> <darüber: ? ordentlich> lieb wurde, die sogenannte Aesthetik an einem Dichter wie Hölderlin abzuhandeln, der sich so großartig in den Krater stürzt um etwas zu erfahren, was er doch nicht mittheilen kann."

33. Roswitha Burwick corrects Thomasberger's reading "Ziel" and "verhallenden" to "Heil <?>" and "verschallenden." FDH ms 7212: "Dieser Stoff ist es der ihm im Hyperion durchdringt. Dann besingt er Sonne und Erde in ihrer Herrlichkeit. So führt ihn der Geist durch Einsamkeit zum Heil <?> und schon im Abscheiden von den Menschen, geblendet von Herrlichkeit, erblickt er Pathmos, der Ausdruck wird ihm unendlich schwer, er verwirrt sogar seine Gedanken rückwirkend, athemlos, mit schlagenden Pulsen, mit verschallenden Worten naht sich der Sterbliche den Gipfel der Berge, wie soll er zur Höhe des Geistigen ohne ähnliche Gefahr gelangen? Schmerzliche Schicksale, die unglücklichste Liebe hatten seine Kraft gebrochen. Das Gedicht regt an in jeden Momente, aber es verhüllt sich nahe den höchsten Anschauungen."

Arnim admits his limited access to this dangerous realm and confesses "that much had to be omitted as unintelligible" [daß manches als unverständlich ganz weggelassen werden muß]. Conscious of the constraints on his own hermeneutic endeavor, he recognizes that Hölderlin, too, had assumed a very similar hermeneutic mission.

"Patmos" begins with the poet feeling "the nearness of the divine in its incomprehensiblity" [die Nähe der Gottheit in ihrer Unbegreiflichkeit]. Arnim provides a seven-point outline that reconstructs the steps in Hölderlin's visionary hermeneutic of the Revelation: (1) To penetrate and elucidate that incomprehensiblity; (2) the poet undertakes his mental journey to Patmos; (3) when he enters into the mental range of St. John, the stories of the New Testament surround him, especially the institution of the Lord's Supper; (4) the mystery of the Crucifixion and the confusion of the Apostles is resolved through the diffusion of the Holy Ghost; (5) with heightened awareness the poet is able to perceive from the vantage of the biblical past the course of corruption in the present; he interprets this as the chaff to be purged by the Sower who casts the grain (Matt. 3:12); (6) he understands the paradox of death and resurrection ("das Geistige aufersteht wie er sich wiedergeliebt fühlt, wie er die Welt begreift"); (7) commending his divine revelation, "er bringt seinen Gesang als Opfer dar."

As Hölderlin's poem is a visionary hermeneutic of Johannine vision,[34] Arnim's essay is a hermeneutic of that hermeneutic. The love of God requires, Hölderlin declares at the end of his poem, that the biblical text should be cherished and its enduring truth rightly interpreted,

> that we keep the letter
> Fast in our care and well interpret
> What endures. Which German song obeys.[35]

Although Arnim seeks to interpret Hölderlin's interpretation, to make "clear to him who is far remote as well as to myself," he fails to elucidate

34. Jochen Schmidt, *Hölderlins geschichts-philosophische Hymnen*, 185–97, documents Hölderlin's hermeneutic task in "Patmos" as a response to the request of the landgrave of Homburg, who wanted a poem that would effectively refute the biblical exegesis of deism and the higher criticism.

35. With one exception, the English rendering of "Patmos" is from Hölderlin, *Hymns and Fragments*, translated by Richard Sieburth. The exception (lines 212–13) is quoted from Hölderlin, *Poems and Fragments*, translated by Michael Hamburger. The latter is more literal and endeavors to retain the often convoluted syntax. The German text is quoted from Hölderlin, *"Bevestiger Gesang,"* 224–26:

> daß gepfleget werde
> Der feste Buchstab, und Bestehendes gut
> Gedeutet. Dem folgt deutscher Gesang.

several passages of the poem: "Many a word was uncertain, some fully veiled in highest contemplation, some had to be omitted." Among the forty-nine "veiled" lines Arnim omits, the major lacunae are lines 106–15, 130–40, 142–46, and 162–82 (briefer omissions are 70–71 and 190). It is not Hölderlin's "holy madness," but his biblical exegesis that baffles Arnim. His difficulties occur at the fifth point in his outline of the poem. He does not understand how "die Ausgießung des Geistes" has given the poet "erhöhte Einsicht." He has presumed a "Luftspiegelung," an airy vision of splendid images. Hölderlin's poetic argument, however, is that the divine truth is imageless.

The passages that Arnim omits are precisely the passages in which Hölderlin insists upon the invisible manifestation of spirit. Although he might well have informed his interpretation with Hölderlin's account of the "boundless division" as the necessary complement to the "boundless union," he does not seem to comprehend Hölderlin's affirmation of that division. The "boundless union" with Christ is followed by the "boundless division" of the Holy Ghost. In strophe 8, Arnim omits the passage that tells us of division and darkness:

> Now that he appeared to them
> Once again in farewell.
> And now the kingly sun's
> Light went out and broke
> His sceptered beams
> In godly pain, due
> To return when times
> Were right. Far worse, had it
> Happened later, brutally tearing men
> From their work.[36]

In the presence of Christ, John could directly behold the face of God. Now that the divine light is eclipsed, its beams, as a divine scepter, no longer touch mortal eyes. It will be restored with the Resurrection. In the mean-

---

36. Hölderlin, "Patmos," 106–15:
> Itzt, da er scheidend
> Noch einmal ihnen erschien.
> Denn erlosch der Sonne Tag,
> Der Königliche, und zerbrach
> Den geradestrahlenden,
> Den Zepter, göttlichleidend, von selbst,
> Denn wiederkommen sollt es,
> Zu rechter Zeit. Nicht wär es gut
> Gewesen, später, und schroffabbrechend, untreu,
> Der Menschen Werk.

time human effort is vain and "untreu." Arnim does quote the lines which immediately follow:

> so from now on
> It was a joy
> To live in loving night, to keep
> Abysses of wisdom
> Fixed in clear eyes. And living images
> Grow green in depths of mountains.[37]

These lines affirm the joy of dwelling "in liebender Nacht." Even for "einfältige Augen" there is wisdom in the dark abyss. With the death of Christ, the realm of spirit becomes an imageless darkness. The sensory images of the material world cannot supplant the imageless abyss of the spirit. That Arnim failed to comprehend Hölderlin's distinction between the spiritual and material is evident in his altering "lebendige Bilder" to "lebendige Wälder."

The poetry of vision, Arnim no doubt thought, would be characterized by strong visual imagery. The symptoms of madness, should they be present, would most likely be exhibited in hallucinations and visual delusions. His reading of "Patmos" goes awry when the inspired "Seher" denies vision. The passages he omitted were not unintelligible, but given his set of expectations it is not surprising that he found them obscured "in höchster Anschauung." The longest passage he deleted is the one in which the poet most vigorously refuted the temptation of images. The poet describes that temptation at the close of strophe 11:

> Just as mines yield ore
> And Etna glows with resins,
> I would have enough in my possession
> To shape an image of him and
> Contemplate Christ as he was.[38]

---

37. Ibid. 115–20:

> und Freude war es
> Von nun an,
> Zu wohnen in liebender Nacht, und bewahren
> In einfältigen Augen, unverwandt
> Abgründe der Weisheit. Und es grünen
> Tief an den Bergen auch lebendige Bilder.

38. Ibid. 162–66:

> Zwar Eisen träget der Schacht,
> Und glühende Harze der Ätna,
> So hätt ich Reichtum,

Building materials abound for the artist to create an image of Christ. The material image, "wie er gewesen," would necessarily be bound in time, a static icon rather than a dynamic truth. In strophe 12 the poet goes on to reject the error of worshiping the material image instead of remaining open to spiritual revelation.

> as if a slave
> Could imitate the image of God—
> I once saw the lords of heaven
> Visibly furious that I wanted to *be* something
> Rather than learn.[39]

Hölderlin's lyrical language, of course, is never without an image. The unmined "Eisen" and the volcanic "Harz" from which he might sculpt an image are images against image-making. The rich appeal to material imagery celebrates God's creation. The "himmlischer Triumphgang" may be "der Sonne gleich," but no physical similitude can suffice as an adequate image of God. The poet thus offers a paradoxical "Losungszeichen"—the signless sign of poetic song (179–82).

Although Arnim could not follow the poet's appropriation of the biblical warning against worshiping images,[40] he certainly understood the argument that the song is a hymn of praise. His sixth and seventh points appropriately interpret the concluding section of the poem, and his transcription omits only the reference to "der goldene Zaum" as image of imageless of faith:

> Yet many timid
> Eyes await a glimpse
> Of the light, reluctant
> To flower in the glare,
> Their courage bridled by the gold.[41]

Ein Bild zu bilden, und ähnlich
Zu schaun, wie er gewesen, den Christ.

39. Ibid. 169–73.

und von dem Gotte
Das Bild nachahmen möcht ein Knecht—
Im Zorne sichtbar sah ich einmal
Das Himmels Herrn, nicht, das ich sein sollt etwas, sondern
Zu lernen.

40. Exod. 20:4–5; Lev. 26:1; Deut. 4:16–18, 5:8–9, 27:15; Isa. 40:18–20; in the New Testament, see especially Acts 17:22–25.

41. Hölderlin, "Patmos," 185–90.

Es warten aber
Der scheuen Augen viele,

Because Arnim has read "Patmos" as visionary hermeneutic, he has emphasized how the poet has assimilated the Johannine vision. Strophe 15 he interprets as the poet's offering for divine revelation: "Er preiset das Himmlische, was sich ihm offenbart hat, er bringt seinen Gesang als Opfer dar, indem er die Quelle des deutschen Gesanges entdeckt."[42] The final strophe commences with the lament,

> Too long, too long now
> The honour of the Heavenly has been invisible.[43]

Arnim has apparently understood that this imageless condition has already been alleviated by the poetic vision. He is right, of course, yet not because the poet has retrieved the invisible into visionary perception, rather because the poet has relied on faith and the Bible without turning away from the visible and palpable glories of God's material creation.

The landgrave of Homburg expected a poem that would answer the higher criticism and overthrow the "exegetischen Träume" of rationalist Bible interpretation.[44] To fulfill that expectation in his "Patmos," Hölderlin adhered to Pietist readings of the Johannine texts.[45] If the landgrave truly thought that a mighty poem would achieve victory once and for all in the Pietist battle against the rationalists, he certainly wanted far more than Hölderlin could achieve. The battle was still raging twenty-five years later when Arnim wrote his "Ausflüge." Even orthodox Lutherans had grown more hostile to the Pietist movement. Rather than urge tolerance, Wilhelm III of Prussia sought to establish a *Kirchenordnung* that would unite the Protestant sects under one ecclesiastical governance. The response, of course, was an increase of factional tensions as the various religious groups rallied for due representation. Arnim's novella, *Die Kirchenordnung* (1817; published 1822), vividly narrates events following the Reformation as analogous to the current strife. He, too, hoped for a resolution, but not one purchased by repression.

Zu schauen das Licht. Nicht wollen
Am scharfen Strahle sie blühn,
Wiewohl den Mut der goldene Zaum hält.

42. FDH ms 7212; in the published version of "Ausflüge," Arnim states only: "Er bringt seinen Gesang als Opfer dar."

43. Hölderlin, "Patmos," 211–12. "Zu lang, zu lang schon ist / Die Ehre der Himmlischen unsichtbar."

44. Schmidt 185–86.

45. Ibid. 194, refers to Hölderlin's sources: Johann Albrecht Bengel, *Erklärte Offenbarung Johannis und vielmehr Jesu Christi* (1740); Bengel, *Sechsig erbauliche Reden über die Offenbarung Johannis* (1747); and Jung-Stilling, *Gemeinnützigen Erklärung der Offenbarung Johannes* (1799).

Among the advocates of the *Kirchenordnung*, Friedrich Schleiermacher was instrumental in reorganizing the Prussian church. In spite of many years devoted to the effort, he failed to bring about a reconciliation of the Lutheran and Reformed churches. When his book of hymns intended for a unified congregation stirred further quarrels, Schleiermacher wrote a defense of his efforts. His persistent error, Arnim declared, was in neglecting to consult the very community he sought to bring together. He could have solicited their advice, encouraged their participation.[46] Apparently he had forgotten too much of his own Pietist background. Arnim, for his part, recognized that the great appeal of Pietism lay in liberating the individual from the dictates of dogma by nurturing intellectual inquiry and faith.

In "Sonntags-Erzählung des Landpredigers" (from *Landhausleben*, 1826), Arnim (*Werke*, vol. 4) satirizes that religious pretension which sacrifices essential faith to mode or fashion. Even though he criticizes one character as a most extreme man of fashion transformed into the worst sort of Pietist, his objections are leveled against overzealous polemics, not against personal conviction.[47] His review of Varnhagen von Ense's *Leben des Graf von Zinzendorf* (1830) begins by urging religious tolerance: "Certainly it is a fine testimony of higher learning when even a follower of the Catholic faith can laud our Zinzendorf at the close of his book, with a blessing as may be allotted to very few men; yes, we can therefore promise that a book will have many more satisfied readers, the more the author shows himself ready to eschew the passion for dividing, segregating, and damning, such as flames up from time to time as it does even now."[48] Arnim appreciates Zinzendorf primarily as a teacher, one

46. Arnim, "Ueber das berliner Gesangbuch. Ein Schreiben an Herrn Bischof Ritschl in Stettin, von Friedrich Schleiermacher. Berlin, Reimer, 1830," *Blätter für literarische Unterhaltung*, 8 November 1830, 1248; in *Werke* 6:1026–29. Granting that Berlin is a large city, Arnim suggests that Schleiermacher could have turned to the press, "um Fragen ausgehen zu lassen, um Erklärungen, Berichtigungen zu empfangen." Although he neglected a supporting constituency, he was effective in responding to his adversaries: "Da also die Verständigen sich von der Besserung des Werkes ausgeschlossen sahen und übrigens dankbar das Gute erkannten, was die Arbeit auszeichnete, so ließen sich nur die leidenschaftlichen Stimmen vernehmen, mit deren Uebereilungen der Verf. leicht fertig wird."

47. Thomas Sternberg, "'Und auch wenn wir entschiedne Protestanten sind.' Achim von Arnim zu Religion und Konfession," in *Neue Tendenzen der Arnim forschung*, ed. Roswitha Burwick and Berndt Fischer, 25–59.

48. "Leben des Grafen von Zinzenforf. Von Varnhagen von Ense. Berlin, Reimer. 1830," *Blätter für literarische Unterhaltung*, 1 August 1830, 849–51, in *Werke* 6:980–82: "Gewiß ist es ein schönes Zeugniß höherer Bildung, wenn auch ein Bekenner der katholischen Glaubensansicht unsern Zinzendorf am Schlusse des Buches . . . selig preisen kann, und zwar selig, wie es nur wenig Menschen bescheiden; ja, wir können dem Buche eben deswegen um so mehr befriedigte Leser versprechen, je weniger der Verfasser auf die Liebhaberei am Son-

who gave the Pietist community a practical as well as spiritual system of education. Zinzendorf urged a disciplined introspection with attention to feeling. In feeling one discovers a deep personal sense of holy love, which inspires the quest for knowledge. Thus feeling is the wellspring of all learning. The schools he established for the Moravian Brethren, Arnim observes, fulfilled two goals: education and missionary expansion.[49]

A similar praise for Pietist pedagogy informs Arnim's essay on Jung-Stilling. The way in which God directs human action is for Jung-Stilling the important message of Revelation. His *Gemeinnützigen Erklärung der Offenbarung Johannes* (1799) calls for an individual receptivity to divine presence. His autobiography, Arnim observes, reveals the author's belief that he could observe "eine höhere milde Hand in den Ereignissen seines Lebens." His *Geisterkunde* attempts to establish a reliable ground for distinguishing true supernatural manifestations from superstitious delusions. Originally drafted in 1808 as a review of *Geisterkunde*, Arnim's essay was transformed into a fitting memorial on the occasion of Jung-Stilling's death in 1817. Although Arnim acknowledged that extremes of religious enthusiasm merged rather easily with madness, his defense of *Geisterkunde* validates enthusiasm as an alert sensitivity to the possibilities of spiritual being.

"My favorite study was always the physics of spirits," declares the protagonist of Arnim's "Die Majoratsherren."[50] With ideas similar to those Friedrich Schelling promulgated in his *Zeitschrift für spekulative Physik* (1800), Jung-Stilling elaborates a spiritual physics based on the current fascination with electrical energy and "animal magnetism." Arnim, who had spent his university years actively engaged in experiments with electricity and magnetism,[51] was intimately familiar with the sort of speculations that Jung-Stilling had appropriated as a theory of spiritual being. In Gilbert's *Annalen der Physik*, Arnim had published meticulous accounts of his research. He notes that Jung-Stilling is innocent of any such laboratory investigation: "Along with those wonderful magnetic exercises, which the author observes so well, we miss the analysis of the experiments, especially since the author so often warns against deliberately relying on

---

dern, Scheiden, Verdammen, die immer von Zeit zu Zeit wie eben jetzt aufflammt, einzugehen Lust bezeigt."

49. Ibid.: "Erziehung der Jugend zum geistlichen Stande, sowie die Vorbildung zu Missionen, worin die Brüdergemeinde so erfolgreich vor allen andern Bemühungen der Art such auszeichnet."

50. Migge 3:31ff, esp. 41, and 33: "Die Physik der Geister war von je mein Lieblingsstudium."

51. Frederick Burwick, "Elektrizität und Optik"; Roswitha Burwick, "Achim von Arnims Ästhetik."

intuition."[52] In spite of its scientific trappings, as Arnim recognizes, Jung-Stilling's book is about divine providence and spiritual identity. Since science has yet to discredit spirit with convincing proofs, the scientist should remain open-minded. Nor should the theologian panic in fear that mechanical physics will effectively demolish belief in God, the Bible, and the spirit (Jung-Stilling 16; Arnim, *Werke* 6:539–50).

Responding to discoveries in contemporary physics, Schelling had argued that energy was the constitutive force in all physical phenomena. Manifestations of energy as heat, light, electricity, and magnetism were explained in terms of variations in wavelength and differences in the conducting media. All matter, and therefore all life, was shaped by the informing energy. Jung-Stilling applies the physics of *Naturphilosophie* to St. John's account of the divine Logos propagated as light. It becomes the life and light of humanity, the light that shines in darkness (John 1:4–5). The divine energy is attracted to matter, says Jung-Stilling, where it manifests itself as spirit. When it enters into a human body a reciprocal change occurs: the body temporarily transforms the energy into the inner light of spiritual consciousness, while the energy permanently absorbs the identity of its host. Even after the physical death of the host, the spiritual energy retains that identity. As long as it remains in the earth's atmosphere, it is capable of manifesting itself as a figure of light.[53]

In contrast to Hölderlin's faith in invisible divinity, Jung-Stilling's sense of the divine is physically immanent. Because his understanding of Pietist faith was influenced by Jung-Stilling, Arnim had reason to anticipate visible apparitions in Hölderlin's visionary union with St. John on Patmos. Although Jung-Stilling intended to distinguish the true from the spurious cases of supernatural manifestation, Arnim regretted that he had devoted so much attention to those intuitions which come in sickness that he neglected healthy enthusiasm: "The author finds the most common development of intuition occurs in a condition of *sickness* and intends in future editions of his writing to explain in greater detail his thoughts on the healthy attributes of inspiration and on the correct external signs of their difference."[54] The distinction between a sick and a healthy vision might

---

52. Arnim, "Über Jungs Geisterkunde": "Neben jenen wunderbaren magnetischen Erfahrungen, die der Verfasser so wohl betrachtet, vermissen wir aber doch die Untersuchung über das Experimentieren damit, da der Verfasser so oft gegen die absichtliche Erweckung des Ahnungsvermögens ermahnt."

53. "Über Jungs Geisterkunde," 543.

54. Arnim, "Über Jungs Geisterkunde," 542: "Der Verfasser findet nämlich die gewöhnlichste Entwicklung des Ahnungsvermögens in einem *krankhaften* Zustande, und wollte sich in künftigen Auflagen der Schrift noch ausführlicher über den hochgesunden Zustand der Begeisterung erklären und über sichere äußere Zeichen des Unterschiedes."

well be related to the discrimination between true and false apparitions. A false apparition, if not perpetrated as a hoax, could result from a fallibility of perception or from an aberration of the mind. While Arnim wanted to affirm the good health of poetic inspiration, the case of Hölderlin was a sad reminder that it could also lapse into sickness. But it was only a crude form of rationalism that condemned "all and every faith as a sickness" (541).

As Arnim was quick to point out, Kant had radically changed the course of German philosophy. Eighteenth-century rationalism no longer held sway. Once Kant had defined time and space as a priori conditions of all representation in the mind, he successfully liberated perceptual phenomena from the inexorable determinism of physical causality. If Jung-Stilling had conceived of space and time as mental, Arnim suggests, he would not have felt compelled to annihilate space and time in order to affirm spiritual apparitions, which, after all, are always manifest in space and time. Jung-Stilling need not have seen the philosophers as the enemies to the "theokratische Freiheit" he wished to substantiate. Although Kant and his followers "did not want to rely too much on intuition, and not more than they were compelled to" [nicht zu viel ahnen wollen, und nicht mehr als sie notgedrungen sind], they still turned to intuition as crucial to the transcendental dialectic: "We are of the opinion, however, that not one of the newer philosophers taught in Germany would have any objection against intuition and prediction, which they find necessary to complementation."[55] In Kant the "Ahnungsvermögen" is especially developed but inadequately explained ("er gab etwas und wußte daß es viel sei, und wußte eigentlich doch selbst nicht, was es sei oder bedeuten werde," 544). A supernatural intuition that senses "was noch nicht gegenwärtig ist" Kant dismisses as nothing more than a "Hirngespinst." He does grant, however, prescience as a judgment about yet unformulated or undefined concepts. One kind of intuition is a mystical *salto mortale* in thinking the unthinkable; the other has the hermeneutic function of organizing obscure concepts ("dunkle Begriffe") so that they may be subjected to more precise scrutiny. The one relies on supernatural revelation, which is the death of philosophy; the other anticipates possible connections and stimulates an *as-if* mode of observation, which is the highest achievement of transcendental philosophy.[56]

---

55. Ibid. 545: "Wir meinen aber, daß überhaupt wohl keine der neueren in Deutschland gelehrten Philosophen gegen Ahnung und Vorhersagungen etwas einzuwenden habe, sie sind ihnen notwendig zur Ergänzung."

56. Kant, *Anthropologie in pragmatischer Hinsicht*, part 1, sec. 35, in *Werke* 6:491–92; *Von einem neuerdings erhobenen vornehmen Ton in der Philosophie*, in *Werke* 3:378, 384–90; *Kritik der reinen Vernunft*, in *Werke*, A669–704, in *Werke* 2:582–605; and *Träume eines Geistersehers, erläutert durch Träume der Metaphysik*, in *Werke* 1:923–89.

To the extent that intuition is directed by what Kant called "ein höheres Gefühl," it may facilitate a heuristic or hermeneutic process. Arnim objects that Jung-Stilling validates "Ahnung" principally in cases of sickness. While Arnim does not deny that spiritual grace may accompany feverish hallucinations and forebodings of imminent death, he claims that inspiration would offer a more rewarding field of investigation than intuition. Inspiration occurs when prescience, which is a passive reception, becomes an active presence and animates the mind. Inspiration, too, has its negative side: the visionary moment may end in frenzy or madness. The play with illusion ("Spiel mit Schein"), Kant warned, may become compulsive. If conscious and volitional control are lost, illusion turns to delusion.[57]

In its positive mode, Arnim asserts, inspiration is the source of all art. When the composer Johann Friedrich Richardt called Arnim mad, he meant it as the highest accolade: "He considers it genial to honor madness; he means it to characterize me as poetic." Accepting the tribute, Arnim declares that there is "no more holy madness than in art" [kein heiliger Wahnsinn als in der Kunst].[58] Because the divine moment of inspiration is consummated in the creative act of art, the *furor poeticus* encompasses and elaborates the *furor divinus*. The artist confronts two tremendous tasks: to express the inspired vision in art and to propagate the inspiration. Unless the vision is released in creative expression, the artist may remain trapped in madness. Unless the work of art communicates its inspiration, the artist will be misunderstood and isolated. Such was the entrapment of the spirit that Schiller lamented in his distich on language:

> Why cannot the living spirit appear to the spirit of another?
> Once the soul *speaks*, so speaks, alas! the *soul* no more.[59]

The frustration for Arnim is not simply that words lose their meaning, but that they fail to communicate the wonder they possessed when they were conjured "fresh und flaming" in the poet's mind.

> I speak their language, yet they do not understand me; words, for me, live fresh and flaming, yet for them die away; for me, no sylla-

57. Kant, *Kritik der Urteilskraft*, secs. 29, 54, in *Werke* 5:362, 366, 435–41.

58. R. Burwick, "Exzerpte Achim von Arnim zu unveröffentlichten Briefen," 321; cf. letter to Clemens Brentano, 25 January 1808, in Steig and Grimm 1:230.

59. Friedrich Schiller, *Taubulae Votivae*, 84: "Sprache," in *Sämtliche Werke* 1:313: "Warum kann der lebendige Geist dem Geist nicht erscheinen? / *Spricht* die Seele, so spricht ach! schon die *Seele* nicht mehr."

ble becomes a mere mechanism: each one builds and forms within me, and figures gush forth; over this marvel I could contrive many a rhyme a whole year long, and how it happened that such words came together. I would like to say that each word becomes a deed for me, and few therefore have accomplished as many deeds as I have without doing anything. Accordingly, however, I seldom act in earnest because my words would not be acceptable as such to people. Once I would often express my innermost opinions, but people always understood my words to mean something else, or, more likely, to mean nothing at all, and thus they would persist in their own opinions.[60]

Part of the problem, as he expresses it in his argument with the Brothers Grimm on the transmission of *Volkspoesie*, derives from a preoccupation with external form: "Where inspiration produces something external out of its inner pleasures, there it becomes an object for observation and no longer fulfills itself completely."[61] If the informing inspiration is to persist in the formal text, the reader must be made a participant in the process. As St. Paul wrote, God "hath made us able ministers . . . not of the letter, but of the spirit: for the letter killeth, but the spirit giveth life" (2 Cor. 3:6).

For poetry to escape the entrapment of language, the poet must make the creative moment a part of his message. A poem must be *about* the very inspiration that brought it into being. If the reader is to share the poetic inspiration, the poet must draw from a common ground of belief. This is what Hölderlin attempted by entering into the vision of St. John. Because Schleiermacher, in his hermeneutics, had emphasized participation and intersubjectivity, it is an irony that Arnim should advise him on the need to involve his congregation in collecting hymns. The Pietist hymns of Paul Gerhardt echo, with a fidelity that Arnim could appreciate, the motifs of folk song. The desires and fears that inspire a whole people

60. "Autobiographische Auszeichnungen," in Streller 110–11: "Ich spreche ihre Sprache wie sie sind und sie verstehen mich nicht, die Worte leben mir frisch und flammend, die jenen abstarben, keine Silbe ist mir zum leeren Mechanismus geworden, jede baut und bildet in mir und es quellen Gestalten hervor, ich könnte über das Wunderbare mancher Reime jahrelang nachsinnen und wie es kam, daß solche Worte zusammenkommen. Ich möchte sagen daß jedes Wort mir zur That wird und wenige haben daher so viel Thaten erkämpft als ich ohne daß ich etwas that. Aber ich handle eben darum selten ernsthaft weil meine Worte den Leuten dazu nicht passen würden, ich sprach sonst oft meine innerste Meinung aus, aber die Leute verstanden immer etwas andres dabey oder eigentlich gar nichts und blieben bey dem Ihren stehen."

61. Letter to Jacob Grimm, 18 August 1811, in Steig and Grimm 3:142: "Wo aber Begeisterung außer ihrem innern Genusse ein Aeußeres schafft, da wird sie selbst schon wieder ein Gegenstand der Beobachtung und erfüllt sich nicht mehr ganz."

take form in their legends and myths. Once the poet has experienced prescience and inspiration, he need only to reanimate the latent images of folk tradition to kindle the inspiration and imagination of readers. Without prescience, the poet could not make "der kleinste wahre Vers" ("Über Jungs Geisterkunde," 544). Intuitions of the supernatural infuse all true poetry: "There never was an inspired person who did not believe in spirits" [Es ist wohl nie ein begeisterter Mensch ohne Geisterglauben gewesen, 542].

Hölderlin's madness presented for Arnim an example of the tragic consequences of the inspired mind finding no language adequate to communicate the purity of the inspiration. Granting, with Jung-Stilling, that there is a crucial difference between supernatural vision and superstitious delusion, Arnim was confident that Hölderlin was inspired by true vision. With Jung-Stilling, Arnim affirms an inspiration that is totally healthy ("der hochgesunde Zustand der Begeisterung," 542), an intuition that is "pure, healthy, and holy" ("rein, gesund und heilig," 544). The problem for Hölderlin was that he found it increasingly difficult to communicate his ideas within the formal constraints of language. He was not one who had fallen prey to that pathological condition of the mind which confounds its own delusory phantoms with divine revelation; rather, his poetic intuition had led him far beyond the physical world and language could no longer serve as an Ariadne's thread to guide him back.

The resulting mental isolation, which held Hölderlin captive from 1806 until his death in 1843, is very different from that pathological condition in which the victim of delusion sees every shadow of the mind projected into external reality. While the poetic imagination may play with these fancies, an excessive indulgence is unhealthy, and the mind may lapse into madness when the images of fancy jostle aside those of perception.[62] The healthy imagination seeks to communicate its visions to, rather than to impose them upon, the world. If the capacity to communicate is baffled, however, the resulting alienation will also affect the mind. The starveling children of the imagination, in the metaphor with which Arnim commences his "Taschenbuch," will be treated only as orphans even if they are lucky enough to be set upon the doorstep of the understanding: "The imagination is a fruitful mother, but she does not nourish her children, and the understanding has only a little space and nursing them causes him trouble and worry."[63]

---

62. "Über Jungs Geisterkunde," 543: "Was die Einbildungskraft in allen übrigen Erscheinungen in sich verschließt und sich zueignet, diese Kraft liegt in diesen krankhaften Zuständen außer ihr in einem realen Zusammenwirken mit der übrigen Welt."

63. Arnim, "Taschenbuch," ms B44, 1, quoted in Ricklefs, Magie und Grenze, 44: "Die Einbildungskraft ist eine fruchtbare Mutter, aber sie nährt ihre Kinder nicht, und der Verstand hat nur wenige Raum und ihre Wartung macht ihm Mühe und Sorge."

Although many still look upon madness as "touched by God," the world has grown less generous toward the hallucinating seer or prophet. "Why are the mad often deemed to be divine," Arnim asks, "even though in every respect they are more wretched than the . . . rational?" He answers himself, "Because they are set beyond all the accustomed conditions of life, they commence an original life which they have derived from no one. Their life is in this sense divine, as is every original thought. As a result of their vanity, however, that which is divine only in relation to themselves becomes acknowledged by the world to which they have no connection."[64] It may be the vanity of madness which commands attention among those who are sane, but it is also the vanity of rationality to presume that it can comprehend the divine revelation in the originality that arises out of the irrational.

As the years passed by in his tower in Tübingen, Hölderlin grew progressively more estranged from the world. He found comfort playing the piano and walking along the Neckar. Arnim was not the only poet of the period to remember his great accomplishments. As they prepared the edition of his works in 1826, Kerner, Uhland, and Schwab paid him visits. He was said to be eager to please, yet he would sometimes lapse into a silent reverie. He frequently presented his guests with extemporaneous compositions. The verse of these latter years, however, seems to have sought security in the confines of form. Rather than rebel against the limits of poetic structure, he rendered his hexameter couplets all the more rigidly patterned and formulaic. These late poems often bore the signature "Scardanelli," and were dated variously 1648, 1748, 1758, 1849, and 1940. Many were dedicated to one of the seasons. He deliberately eschewed meditation and observation for the sake of convention, but the convention seems sometimes twisted awry, as if the mind of a poet was still struggling to make itself heard.

64. Ibid. 5, quoted in Ricklefs, *Magie und Grenze*, 44–45: "Warum sich Wahnsinnige so oft für göttlich halten, während sie in aller Hinsicht dürftiger als die . . . Vernünftigen sind? Die Antwort liegt nahe. Indem sie durch ihre Krankheit gerade über alles Angewöhnte des Lebens hinweggesetzt werden, so fangen sie ein uranfängliches Leben an, das ihnen von niemand überliefert worden, es ist also in diesem Sinne göttlich wie jeder eigenthümliche Gedanke, ihre Eitelkeit macht aber, daß sie das was in Beziehung auf sie nur göttlich ist in der Welt, zu der es keine Beziehung hat, also anerkannt werden soll."

8

NERVAL'S *CHIMÈRAS*

Arnim recognized in Hölderlin's "Patmos" a visionary hermeneutic of the vision of St. John. In his "Walks with Hölderlin" we have thus been reading Arnim reading Hölderlin reading John. The constellation is no less complex when we turn to Gérard de Nerval's reading of Christ on the Mount of Olives. He adapts his biblical narrative from the gospels (Matt. 24–26; Mark 13–14; Luke 19, 21; John 8, 13). In the first three of the five sonnets of "Le Christ aux Oliviers," however, Nerval is reading Madame de Staël reading Jean Paul reading the gospels. Nerval, perhaps with less constraint than most writers, immersed himself personally into his texts. His friend, Théophile Gautier, and his physician, Dr. Esprit Blanche, both recognized in his writing a rewriting of the self, a repetition and a displacement of the very agonies of his own identity. Dr. Blanche, persuading him to write an account of his illness, saw Nerval's writing as therapeutic.[1] Gautier, however, feared the consequences of his friend's autobiographical self-projection. Should his fictive self become inextricably entangled in the web of narrative displacement, the fragile hold on his own identity might well be jeopardized (a fear also expressed by other friends at the time of Nerval's first bout of madness).[2]

1. Norma Rinsler, *Gérard de Nerval*, 110. Paul Youngquist makes a similar case in *Madness and Blake's Myth*; see also Dr. Martin Orne's records on Anne Sexton, in Diane Middlebrook's, *Anne Sexton: A Biography*. The problem is most thoroughly deliberated by Michel Jeanneret in *La Lettre Perdue. Écriture et Folie dans l'oeuvre de Nerval*. Eschewing biographical and medical approaches, Jeanneret is concerned instead with the theoretical relationship between madness and literary activity. With Nerval as his case study, he examines whether writing is therapeutic, or actually stimulates madness; whether Nerval merely writes about his madness, or the madness "writes" Nerval. I thank Dr. Jeanneret for sending me a typescript of "Écriture et folie dans le XIXe siècle français," the original version of the introduction to *La Scrittura Romantica della follia. Il caso Nerval*.

2. Jean Richer, in *Nerval par les témoins de sa vie*, provides an excellent collection of

With a structural effect not unlike that achieved by Shelley in "Ode to the West Wind" (1819), Nerval developed the symbolic action of "Le Christ aux Oliviers" (1844) in a five-sonnet sequence. His motto is from Jean Paul: "God is dead! The heavens are empty . . . / Weep, children, you no longer have a father!" [Dieu est mort! le ciel est vide . . . / Pleurez! enfants, vous n'avez plus de père!].[3] The "Speech of the Dead Christ" from Jean Paul's *Siebenkäs* (1796–97) had been introduced to French readers in Madame de Staël's *De l'Allemagne* (1810). From his nightmare of the immortal soul abandoned in a godless universe, Jean Paul turns to a reaffirmation of divine immanence. His English imitators—Coleridge in "Limbo" and "Ne Plus Ultra" (1811), Carlyle in "The Everlasting No" and "The Everlasting Yea" of *Sartor Resartus* (1833), De Quincey in the vision of the eyeless face in the Orion nebula and the "Dream upon the Universe" from "System of the Heavens" (1846)—all followed Jean Paul in reaffirming divine presence after conjuring the possibility of an utterly moribund deity. Nerval's "Le Christ aux Oliviers," much like Vigny's "Le Mont de Oliviers" (also

---

contemporary documents. Nos. 1 and 2 are accounts of Nerval by Gautier and George Bell. In no. 9, sections 2 and 3, Alphonse Karr recollects a hashish party with Nerval and a conversation during Nerval's first bout of madness in 1841. No. 13, sec. 4, is Alexander Weil's record of his visit with Nerval in the sanitorium in Montmartre. No. 30 is an essay by Charles Asselineau from the *Revue fantaisiste* (September 1861), recording a conversation with Nerval during his confinement at Passy, and speculating on the relation between the poet's insanity and his interests in mythology and mysticism. No. 40 is Alexander Dumas's well-known account of Nerval's chronic melancholy, which accompanied the publication of "El desdichado" (subsequently first in the sequence of *Les Chimères*) in *Le Mosquetaire* (10 December 1853). For additional contemporary accounts of Nerval's madness, see Jules Janin, *Critique portraits et caractères contemporains*, 305–7, who avoids the usual variations on the *furor poeticus* and tells instead of the hardships that come with living a literary life; Eugène de Mirecourt who insists in his biography, which Nerval regarded as his obituary, that Nerval's madness was no more than the consequence of inspiration and imagination which the poet could only control and overcome through writing; and du Camp's *Souvenirs Littéraires*, 2:159–78, who recalls conversations with Nerval during his madness, emphasizing the intermittent periods of lucidity, describing the hallucinations about Jenny Colon, and noting how Nerval's interest in hermeticism emerged amid his deranged thoughts.

3. Nerval does not quote his epigram from de Staël's translation. De Staël: "Jésus, n'avons-nous pas de père? —et il résponit, avec un torrent de larmes: —Nou sommed tous orphelins, moi et vous nous n'avons point de père. —A ces mots, le temple et les enfants s'abîmèrent, et tout l'édiice du monde s'écroula devant moi dans son immensité." Jean Paul, *Werke*, 2:269: "Da kamen, schrecklich für das Herz, die gestorbenen Kinder, die im Gottesacker erwacht waren, in den Tempel und warfen sich vor die hohe Gestalt am Altare und sagten: 'Jesus! haben wir keinen Vater?' —Und er antwortet mit strömenden Tränen: 'Wir sind alle Waisen, ich und ihr, wir sind ohne Vater.' Da krieschten die Mißtöne heftiger—die zitternden Tempelmauern rückten auseinander—und der Tempel und die Kinder sanken unter—und die ganze Erde und die Sonne sanken nach—und das ganze Weltgebäude sank mit seiner Unermeßlichkeit vor uns vorbei."

inspired by the "Speech of the Dead Christ" and published three months after Nerval's poem), offers no such happy resolution.

Abandonment and isolation are the motifs that dominate the "Speech of the Dead Christ." Jean Paul makes no mention of betrayal, the motif that defines and directs the agonies of Nerval's "Le Christ aux Oliviers." Christ's torment, in Nerval's poem, results from the betrayal of his closest friends: "Long lost in speechless agonies, and knew / Himself betrayed by thankless friends."[4] Elaborating the motif of betrayal, Nerval adapts from the gospels Christ's prophecy that brother shall betray brother (Mark 13:12), that his followers will betray him (Matt. 26:21, Mark 14:18, John 13:21) and will in turn be betrayed by their friends and relatives (Luke 21:16) and by one another (Matt. 24:10). In Nerval's reading of the gospels, there are subtler and more insidious modes of betrayal than the overt greed and deceit in Judas's kiss. Betrayal is also in Peter's self-protective denial that he is a friend of Christ. And, specifically pertinent to that night Christ spent on the Mount of Olives, betrayal is in the failure of his friends to see his need. They slumber while he holds his lonely vigil (Matt. 26:40).

Jean Paul's text, then, informs and is informed by Nerval's reading of the biblical text. As mediator of the poet's torment, Nerval's Christ raises his arms to the skies as poets do ("comme font les poètes"), feels keenly the hurt of isolation and betrayal, and cries out in desperation to the sleeping apostles. God, he shouts, has ceased to exist ("Dieu n'est plus!"):

> They slept. *"The change*, friends—can you see it now?
> I've touched the eternal firmament with my brow;
> I've suffered many days, bleeding, broken!
>
> Brothers, I cheated you: Abyss, abyss!
> God's missing from my altar of sacrifice . . .
> There is no God! No God now!" They slept on.[5]

---

4. For the English text I cite Peter Jay's translation, *The Chimeras*; for notes and commentaries I consult Norma Rinsler's edition of *Les Chimères*; and for original text and variants I use Jean Guillaume's critical edition. Citations to "Le Christ aux Oliviers" are by stanza and line. Nerval, "Le Christ aux Oliviers," 1:3–4: "Se fut longtemps perdu dans ses douleurs muettes, / Et se jugea trahi par des amis ingrats."

5. Nerval, "Le Christ aux Oliviers," 1.9–14:

> Ils dormaient. "Mes mais, savez-vous *les nouvelle*?
> J'ai touché de mon front à la voûte éternelle;
> Je suis sanglant, brisé, souffrant pour bien des jours!
>
> Frères, je vous trompais: Abîme! abîme! abîme!
> Le dieu manque à l'autel, où je suis la victime . . .
> Dieu n'est pas! Dieu n'est plus!" Mais ils dormaient toujours!

When Christ calls out from the cross, "Eloi, Eloi, lama sabachthani," the fear of abandonment and betrayal is brought to a sublime climax: "My God, my God, why hast thou forsaken me?" Since this is the only instance in the Greek Testament in which Christ's words are recorded in Aramaic (Mark 15:34) or in Hebrew (Matt. 27:46), the act of quotation is boldly proclaimed. In repeating the words of Psalm 22, Christ speaks not of mere personal fear, but of the human agony he shares in putting on flesh and surrendering his miraculous powers. Precisely this human agony is crucial to Nerval. It is not the threat of a godless universe ("Dieu n'est pas! Dieu n'est plus!") that produces the empty pain and sad desolation of being betrayed by thankless friends. Rather, the causality works the other way around. It is the betrayal of friends that leaves the world godless, the self a martyr.

In the second sonnet, Nerval's Christ-persona, ignored by his friends, discovers that not just God, but the world, the entire universe is dead: "'Tout est mort! J'ai parcouru les mondes; / Et j'ai perdu mon vol dans leurs chemins lactés'" (2.1–2). The spheres move, "'Mais nul esprit n'existe en ces immensités'" (7–8). Nerval's Christ journeys through the same bleak desolation and beholds the same bottomless socket described by Jean Paul's Christ.[6]

> "I looked for God's eye, only saw a black
> Bottomless socket pouring out its dark
> Night on the world in ever thickening rays."[7]

In the third sonnet, again echoing Jean Paul,[8] the familiar oppositions of mechanist and vitalist thought are reevoked. Is the world governed by

6. Nerval's second sonnet appropriates but visually enhances the imagery of Jean Paul: "Christus fuhr fort: 'Ich ging durch die Welten, ich stieg in die Sonnen und flog mit den Milchstraßen durch die Wüsten des Himmels; aber es ist kein Gott. Ich stieg herab soweit das Sein seine Schatten wirft, und schauete in den Abgrund und rief: 'Vater, wo bist du?' aber ich hörte nur den ewigen Sturm, den niemand regiert, und der schimmernde Regenbogen aus Wesen stand ohne eine Sonne, die ihn schuf, über dem Abgrunde und tropfte hinunter. Und als ich aufblickte zur unermeßlichen Welt nach dem göttlichen *Auge*, starrte sie mich mit einer leeren bodenlosen *Augenhöhle* an; und die Ewigkeit lag auf dem Chaos und zernagte es und wiederkäute sich'" (*Werke* 2:269).

7. Nerval, "Le Christ aux Oliviers," 2.9–11:
> "En cherchant l'oeil de Dieu, je n'ai vu qu'un orbite
> Vaste, noir et sans fond; d'où la nuit qui l'habite
> Rayonne sur le monde et s'épaissit toujours."

8. Jean Paul, *Werke*, 2:270: "'Starres, stummes Nichts! Kalte, ewige Notwendigkeit! Wahnsinniger Zufall! Kennt ihr das unter euch? Wann zerschlagt ihr das Gebäude und mich?— Zufall, weißt du selber, wenn du mit Orkanen durch das Sternen-Schneegestöber schreitest und eine Sonne um die andere auswehest, und wenn der funkelnde Tau der Gestirne ausblinkt, indem du vorübergehest? —Wie ist jeder so allein in der weiten Leichengruft des

destiny, by cold necessity, or by chance? Or is there a mindless "puissance originelle" capable of animating, perhaps even reanimating the cycle of things and beings? Or is there some kindred creative mind truly deserving to be called "mon père"? Nerval's Christ no sooner calls forth the human image of a divine Father than he reasserts the motif of betrayal. Impossible in a universe of mechanical necessity or haphazard chance, betrayal, as Nerval knows, asserts itself in the Judeo-Christian doctrine of the Fall. While Jean Paul himself avoids any reference to Satan or a Manichean power of darkness, his image of the "Angel of Death," the "Würgengel," may have inspired Nerval's "ange des nuits" in the sestet. Nerval's own troubled relationship with his father may be heard in the appeal of his Christ, who reasserts the crisis of betrayal by evoking the primal strife. The fallen angel, in jealous rivalry, has commenced the rebellion against the Father. Perhaps the outcast renegade has won. What then?

> "Father! Within me, is it you I feel?
> Have you the strength to live and conquer death?
> Or will the outcast angel of the night
>
> Have overturned you with his final thrust?
> I am alone in suffering and grief,
> And if I die, it's death to everything!"[9]

Bereft even of the Father who has betrayed him, Christ is the sole survivor, the last vestige of life.

Stanzas 2 and 3 are given over completely to the monologue of the Nerval-Christ. In stanza 4, Nerval returns to the opening scene with the sleeping apostles so preoccupied with their selfish dreams of power (as kings, or sages, or prophets) that they cannot be roused even by Christ's urgent cries. Christ now perceives that one apostle remains awake—the traitor Judas. Nerval's collation of Jean Paul's vision and the biblical ac-

---

Alles! Ich bin nur neben mir—O Vater! o Vater! wo ist deine unendliche Brust, daß ich an ihr ruhe? —Ach wenn jedes Ich sein eigner Vater und Schöpfer ist, warum kann es nicht auch sein eigner Würgengel sein?'"

9. Nerval, "Le Christ aux Oliviers," 3.9–14:

> "O mon père! est-ce toi que je sens en moi-même?
> As-tu pouvoir de vivre et de vaincre la mort?
> Aurais-tu succombé sous un dernier effort
>
> De cet ange de nuits que frappa l'anathème . . .
> Car je me sens tout seul à pleurer et souffrir,
> Hélas! et si je meurs, c'est que tout va mourir!"

count of Christ's lonely vigil results in his emendation of both texts: the one because it has omitted the power of evil and betrayal, the other because it represents the deceit of Judas as the worst of the multiple acts of betrayal. For Nerval, the overt double-cross is far less an evil than the hidden duplicity. Nerval's Christ thus welcomes the forthright crime of Judas:

> "Judas!" he shouted, "Sell me, don't waste time
> Getting the deal done; you know what I'm worth:
> I suffer here, friend, lying on the earth,
> Come! For at least you have the strength of crime."[10]

Stanza 3 merely guesses whether the dark angel has the power to succeed in his rebellion. In stanza 4, the power is acted upon. The act, however, leaves Judas guilt-ridden. Chance, the prevailing element in the mechanistic universe at the opening of stanza 3 is joined by pity at the close of stanza 4 in Pilate's summons to seek out the madman Christ: "'Go, find this lunatic!'" ["Allez chercher ce fou!"].

In Nerval's concluding stanza, Christ is exalted as the sublime madman, "ce fou, cet insensé sublime." If not dead or overthrown, the Father has been absorbed into the Son, who has now crossed over to the world of spirit. Nerval lingers no longer as an exegete interpreting and glossing the texts of Jean Paul or Matthew or Mark. He turns instead to classical myth, where the forgotten Icarus again dons his wings, Phaeton again rides Apollo's chariot, and Cybele again resurrects the slain Attis (5.1–4). The biblical text has been relinquished, but its narrative of the Fall and Resurrection continue to resonate in Icarus, Phaeton, and Attis, whose mythic fates makes them fitting fellows of the sublime madman Christ.

Unlike Hölderlin, Nerval has penetrated into his texts to find at the core no meaning at all. His Christianity is set alongside mythology, and the whole cast of characters are reduced to reading the entrails of the sacrificial victim to interpret the meaning of life and death. Caesar himself demands to know whether a god or a devil now rules the world. The answer, if there is an answer, is not forthcoming: the oracle is silent, and the possible creator, "He who gave a soul to the sons of clay" [Celui que donna l'âme aux enfants du limon, 5.14], remains shrouded in mystery.

The notion that Christianity was spiritually bankrupt did not lead Ner-

---

10. Ibid., 4.5–8:
> "Judas! lui cria-t-il, tu sais ce qu'on m'estime,
> Hâte-toi de mi vendre, et finis ce marché:
> Je suis souffrant, ami! sur la terre couché . . .
> Viens! ô toi qui, du moins, as la force du crime!"

val to an enlightened atheism. Rather, it drove him in a relentless quest for meaning in the ruins of religion. Although the dialogue with the world of spirit had been disrupted by the new dominion of materialism, somewhere in the old beliefs there might still be a way to embrace the lost Mother and reconcile with the lost Father. Even when he was overwhelmed with hallucinations, Nerval continued writing letters to reassure and placate the father who had rejected him. Similarly, he did not cease his effort to reestablish a bond with the divine Father who had abandoned him. If Christianity could serve as mediator no longer, its essential elements, as confirmed in other religions, might nevertheless enable him to communicate with the supernatural realm.

Although he drew his knowledge of ancient religions from many sources, he was particularly influenced by Friedrich Creuzer.[11] Intrigued by popular versions of syncretism, Nerval plunged into Gnosticism, Orphism, Pythagoreanism, Zoroastrianism, and more recent cults inspired by Adam Weishaupt, Emanuel Swedenborg, and others. Syncretism, as it first emerged in the Hellenistic Age, sought to recognize and preserve individual characteristics of divine revelation, augmenting rather than synthesizing religious beliefs. Thus it is possible to recognize in Jehovah, Zeus, Jupiter, Allah, Mithra, Attis, and Osiris fully differentiated cultural manifestations of the originary Father. So, too, Isis, Ceres, Demeter, Ops, and the Virgin Mary are various forms of the Great Mother. No particular manifestation is truer than any other; rather, each has revealed its validity and power at specific intersections of history and culture. The plurality is important to Nerval, for he recognizes that what has been proclaimed as deity is merely a symbol, a fragmentary glimpse of deity. "My role," he wrote, "seemed to me to be to reestablish universal harmony by cabalistic art and seek a solution by evoking the occult forces of different religions."[12] Nerval evokes a wide array of deities (symbolic fragments, in Creuzer's sense) as syncretic lightning rods to draw down whatever powers may loom within the storm clouds that perpetually darken his mythic landscape.

He found a universal harmony, but only to recognize that he had been excluded from it. His mythic vision became increasingly self-referential.

11. Georg Friedrich Creuzer, *Symbolik und Mythologie der alten Völker* (1810–12), argued that the mythology of Homer and Hesiod were the symbolic remnants of earlier revelations transmitted by the Pelagians from Eastern religions. For the reception of Creuzer's syncretism, see Ernst Howald *Der Kampf um Creuzers Symbolik*.

12. "Mon rôle me semblait être de rétablir l'harmonie universelle par art cabalistique et de chercher une solution en évoquant les forces occulte de diverses religions." *Oeuvres de Gérard de Nerval* 1:406. Translations of *Aurélia* are from Geoffrey Wagner's translation, *Selected Writings of Gérard de Nerval*, 115–78.

Isis, the Queen of Sheeba, and the Virgin Mary were transformations of Jenny Colon, the actress whom he loved and lost. She had played in his *Piquillo* in 1837. But she married another in April 1838. When she appeared again in *Piquillo* at Brussels in 1840, he met with her briefly on December 15. Two months later, Nerval suffered his first bout of madness. Too spellbound by his mythic world to communicate with those around him, Nerval was taken to the clinic of Dr. Esprit Blanche in Montmartre.

As he tells the story of his madness in *Aurélia*, subtitled *La Rêve et La Vie*, his consciousness seems to vacillate between two modes of perception, which seem, in turn, to shift from one center of consciousness to another. Once the waking perception gives way to the perception of dream, another "I" asserts itself in the spirit realm of sleep. This "sosie" or doppelgänger commands sufficient power to enable it, on occasion, to usurp the place of the dreamer when he reawakens. The reawakened "self" is thus the "other" who escapes the invisible world of the sleep, while the original "self" is trapped within the dream: "Our dreams are a second life. I have never been able to penetrate without a shudder those ivory or horned gates which separate us from the invisible world. The first moments of sleep are an image of death; a hazy torpor grips our thought and it becomes impossible for us to determine the exact instance when the 'I,' under another form, continues the task of existence."[13]

Once the "I" has taken on another form, as the ensuing narrative of madness gradually reveals, dangerous transformations begin to follow. Far from acknowledging a lurking danger, he goes on to insist in these opening lines from *Aurélia* that the seeming illness arising "within the mysteries of my soul" [dans les mystères de mon esprit] was, in fact, no "malady" but rather the liberation of his imagination. Nevertheless, the defense of the "joys" and "infinite delight" is tinged, much in the manner of De Quincey's account of the "pleasures of opium," with a desperation and fear that he may not succeed, after all, "in recovering what men call reason."

The narrator confesses that he cannot explain "how in my own mind earthly events could coincide with those of the supernatural world" [que, dans mes idées, les événements terrestres pouvaient coïncider avec ceux du monde surnaturel, 1:384]. Nevertheless, he does maintain a recognizable chronology of exterior and interior events. The first eight chapters

---

13. "Le Rêve est une seconde vie. Je n'ai pu percer sans frémir ces portes d'ivoire ou de corne que qui nous séparent du monde invisible. Les premier instants du sommeil sont l'image de la morte; un engourdissement nébuleux saisit notre pensée, et nous ne pouvons déterminer l'instant précis où le *moi*, sous une autre forme, continue l'oeuvre de l'existence." *Oeuvres* 1:363.

record the visionary adventures during his eight months (21 March to 21 November 1841) under the care of Dr. Esprit Blanche at Montmartre. In the opening paragraph of chapter 9, Nerval leaps over the intervening ten years: "Such were the visions which filed, one by one, before my eyes. Gradually calm came back to me and I left the house which had been a paradise for me. A long while later fateful circumstances brought about a relapse which renewed this interrupted series of strange dreams."[14] He picks up the narrative at the time of his admission to the clinic of Dr. Émile Blanche at Passy (September 1851). The relapse had already begun many months before he stumbled from the terrace steps in Montmartre. His knee was sprained, his body bruised, and his chest had received a sharp blow. He recognizes familiar symptoms as he succumbs once more to fever and delirium. It is not a matter of choice: the story of *Aurélia* has recommenced.

The terrors, however, are more pronounced, for he must now grapple mentally with the double let loose from his inner world. This other self has an equal claim to existence in the physical world. Indeed, since their relationship is defined by the polarities of light and shadow, action and passion, good and evil, it may be that the "other" has a stronger claim to remain in the waking world, and he must trade places and resign himself to remain in exile among the spirits of the dream.

> I had a terrible idea. Every man has a double, I said to myself. "I feel two men in myself," a Father of the Church once wrote. The concurrence of the two souls has infused this double seed in man's body, which shows similar halves in every organ of its structure. In everyone is a spectator and an actor, one who speaks and one who answers. The Orientals have seen two enemies in that, the good and evil genius of a man.
> Am I the good or the evil? I asked myself. In any case my *other* is hostile to me . . .[15]

14. "Telles furent les images qui se montrèrent tour à tour devant mes yeux. Peu à peu le calme était rentré dans mon esprit, et je quittai cette demeure qui était pour moi un paradis. Des circonstances fatales préparèrent, longtemps après, une rechute qui renoua la série interrompue de ces étranges rêveries." *Oeuvres* 1:383.

15. "Une idée terrible me vint: «L'homme est double», me dis-je. —«Je sens deux hommes en mois», a écrit un Père de l'Église. —Le concours de deux âmes a déposé ce germe mixte dans un corps qui lui-même offre à la vue deux portions similaires reproduites dans tous les organes de sa structure. Il y a en tout homme un spectateur et un acteur, celui qui parle et celui qui répond. Les Orientaux ont vu là deux ennemis: le bon et le mauvais génie. «Suis-je le bon? suis-je le mauvais?» me disais- je. En tout cas, *l'autre* m'est hostile . . ." *Oeuvres* 1:385. From the *Confessions* of St. Augustine, Nerval quotes «Je sens deux hommes en mois»; the phrase, however, is also echoed by Faust: "Zwei Seelen wohnen, ach!

As the rival "other" gains control, the dreaming "self" is overcome with despair. All his efforts as a poet, all the struggles of the imagination, will come to nought. His place will be usurped by his double, who will reap the rewards: "Aurélia would take him for me, and the wretched spirit that animated my body, weakened, disdained, and unrecognized by her, saw itself eternally destined to despair or annihilation."[16]

Part 1 ends with the realization that he had disturbed "the harmony of the magic universe" [l'harmonie de l'univers magique, 1:389]. For himself, the experience had confirmed the immortality of the soul, but at the same time he had, like Faust, gained his knowledge only by trespassing "divine law." Part 2 confronts the consequences of the curse: apostasy and the torments of godless exile. In the exterior world, Nerval does not remain confined in the asylum. Periods of intense writing alternate with periods of agony and hallucination. During the first months of 1852, he was treated at the Maison Dubois, the municipal hospital in the Rue du Faubourg Saint-Denis, for "fièvre chaude." He saw his *Loreley* through the press in August, and he managed to complete *Les Nuits d'Octobre* and *Les Illumines*. Yet all this while he suffered in mind and body.

Whatever the nature of Nerval's madness, its first manifestations mark his transformation as a writer and his emergence as the great romantic explorer of dream consciousness. While still under the care of Dr. Esprit Blanche in 1841, he commenced the autobiography of his madness. Gérard Labrunie became Gérard de Nerval. The year following his release, he undertook his *Voyage en Orient*, a compelling travelogue through interior and exterior geography on which he wrote throughout the decade of his "recovery." Severe spells of delirium began to recur in 1849. He was a patient of Dr. Amedée Aussandon at his clinic during April 1849; of Dr. Charles Ley at the Maison de Santé in May 1849; again with Dr. Aussandon in June 1850; with Dr. Emile Blanche at Passy during September and November 1851; at the municipal clinic, Maison Dubois, in January and February 1852, again in February and March 1853; disoriented by persistent hallucinations, with Dr. Blanche at Passy from August 1853, until the end of May 1854. His relapse is accompanied a flurry of creativity during which his most memorable works are published: *Sylvie* (1853), *Les Filles du Feu* and *Les Chimères* (1854); Part 1 of *Aurélia* was published on 1 January 1855; the corrected proofs of part 2 were in his pocket when his body was found on January 26.

---

in meiner Brust" (in Nerval's translation of *Faust*: "Deux âmes, hélas! se paretagent mon sein . . . ," also used as epigraph to *La Pandora*).

16. "—pour Aurélia, c'était moi-même, et l'esprit désolé qui vivifiait mon corps, affaibli, dédaigné, méconnu, d'elle, se voyait à jamais destiné aud désespoir ou au néant." *Oeuvres* 1:386.

Among his critics and biographers there has been a continuing effort to diagnose his madness and explain its causes. The possible causes, as Richard Holmes has lamented, are too many rather than too few: the loss of his mother in childhood, the rejection and hostility that troubled his relation with his father, the loss of his inheritance and the ensuing financial worries, his disappointment in love, the frustration of his major efforts as playwright (*Léo Burckart* was stopped by the censor in 1839; *Les Monténégrins* had an unsuccessful run in 1849; *L'Imagier de Harlem* failed in 1851). Any of these difficulties could have weighed heavily on a sensitive poetic temperament. Their cumulative and collective weight may well have been what broke him. Even if we accept the diagnosis of schizophrenia or severe manic-depressive syndrome, much of the evidence is left unexplained. Was his "fièvre chaude" a physical symptom produced by his mental derangement? Or could the mental derangement itself have been precipitated by some physical cause?

The evidence is not ambiguous. During his six weeks at the Maison Dubois (6 January to 15 February 1852), Nerval was treated for ergot poisoning. The hospital recorded the diagnosis: *erysipelas* (Sowerby 120). As I explained in Chapter 6, epidemics of ergotism continued to be rampant throughout the nineteenth century. Infected rye bread caused mass outbreaks in Dauphine (1814), in Saone et Loire (1814, 1820), at Lyons (1855), and sporadic cases were common among the lower classes in all the rye-producing regions of France (Barger 45, 61–62). Severe cases of convulsive and gangrenous ergotism resulted in death. Milder cases, diagnosed as *erysipelas* or *feu Saint Antoine*, caused fever and inflammation of the skin,[17] and, as Charles Darwin noted in *Expression of the Emotions* (1872), the infection also "commonly induces delirium" (xiii, 325). During the fifty years after Nerval's death, clinical studies of ergot psychosis began to appear.[18] Once such toxins as lysergic acid diethylamide had been isolated from the ergot, scientists were able to identify its powerful hallucinogenic properties.

At least one of Nerval's friends was familiar with the symptoms of ergot poisoning and did his best to treat it. Eugène Stadler, a fellow playwright, cared for Nerval during 1852 and would rub his entire body with ointment

17. In the OED, *erysipelas* is defined as "A local febrile disease accompanied by diffuse inflammation of the skin, producing red colour; often called St. Anthony's fire." The term is used by Hippocrates (Greek: ἐρυσίπελας; cf. ἐρυσίβη, red blight on corn).

18. Eugène Bacquias, *Recherches historiques et nosologiques sur les maladies désignées sous les noms feu sacré, feu Saint Antoine, mal des ardents*; F. Siemens, "Psychosen beim Ergotismus"; W. von Bechterew, "Über neuro-psychische Störungen bei chronischem Ergotismus"; M. J. Gurewitsch, "Über die Ergotinpsychose"; and G. A. Kolossow, "Geistesstörungen bei Ergotismus."

to reduce the relentless burning and itching of the *feu Saint Antoine*. Nadar (Félix Tournachon), the photographer, describes such a scene: "I can still recall that small, high bedroom in a fourth-storey flat in the place Pigalle, the full summer sun flowing in with asphyxiating heat, and Stadler's only bed; I shall always see before me the good Samaritan rubbing [Nerval] all over with a greyish ointment, his body like a living corpse, in a bath of sweat."[19] Nadar's photograph of Nerval, taken some months before he hanged himself in the Rue de la Veille-Laterne, shows him with puffy face and blackened fingers. "Dark with nicotine," presumes Richard Holmes, whose instincts as a biographical detective prompt him to add, "Funny: in all those dozens of memoirs and articles by his friends nobody had remarked on the fact that Gérard smoked heavily" (Holmes 269). The swollen features, the darkened fingers, might actually be signs of the ravages of ergotism.

While there can be no doubt that Nerval was a victim of *le bled cornu*, it is impossible to determine on how many occasions he had imbibed or ingested *seigle ergoté*. Certainly he had experienced serious mental and emotional difficulties before the onset of the tormenting symptoms of *erysipelas*. Once the fevers and rashes, dizziness and delirium had commenced, however, they would leave him no peace. Nor is it likely that Nerval fell prey to ergot psychosis through deliberate experimentation with extracts of ergotine. Such preparations, to be sure, were available for medical use; yet it is also true that traces of ergotine in rye bread were all too common. The fevers and hallucinations of *feu Saint Antoine* had brought many victims into the hospitals and asylums. The epidemic of a severe gangrenous ergotism treated at the Hôtel-Dieu in Lyons in 1854 and 1855 revealed not only the severity of toxic infection (many victims had to have fingers, toes, even arms and legs, amputated), but also the long-lasting consequences (as Barger notes of an earlier epidemic at Orleans, "mania and other forms of insanity" were "not uncommon").[20]

The hallucinogenic alkaloids are not the only toxins found in ergot. Other toxins in ergot cause nervous convulsions, constricted breathing, as well as the characteristic burning and itching. Experiments with er-

19. Richard Holmes, *Footsteps*, 254. I quote Holmes's translation of the entry from Nadar's notebook in the Bibliothèque Nationale. Although he has assembled the crucial evidence on Nerval's *erysipelas*, Holmes does not discuss the ergot poisoning as a cause of psychotic delirium.

20. George Barger, *Ergot and Ergotism*, 61–62. Barger cites F. Barrier, "De l'épidemie d'ergotisme gangréneux observée à l'Hôtel-Dieu de Lyon en 1854 et 1855," *Gazette médicale de Lyon* 7 (1855): 181–84, and, on mental impairment and insanity, François Salerne, "Sur les Maladies que cause le Seigle ergoté," *Mémoires de mathématique et de physique, présentés à l'Academie Royale de Sciences* 2 (1755): 155–63.

gotine would be even more dangerous than those trials with opium and hashish that Charles Baudelaire began to make as student at the Sorbonne when he was living in the Hôtel-Lazun in 1840 (Hayter 151–61). *Le Club des Haschishins*, according to Gautier's autobiographical account in 1846, celebrated the drug-assisted exploration of the mind's interiors. Thomas De Quincey and Edgar Allan Poe were praised and emulated as models and guides for a new literature of travel through the inner world beneath the familiar planes of rationality. Baudelaire translated the tales of Poe (*Histoires extraordinaires*, 1856 and 1857), and he included translations from *Confessions of an English Opium Eater* in his *Paradis artificiels* (1860), in which he also went on to describe his own passage into the unearthly landscape and vast architecture of the imagination as inspired by hashish and opium.

Perhaps Nerval himself had turned to hashish during his bohemian days. Gautier gave a splendid account of their parties of "oriental" indulgence held during those brief years (1834–36) before Nerval had exhausted his inheritance. But Nerval, in recollecting those events in *Petits Châteaux de Bohème* (1852), leaves few clues that their festivities may have been perfumed by *les fleurs du mal*. The opening chapter of the "Histoire du Calife Hakem" (1847), however, is devoted to a hashish-inspired discussion of divine revelation (*Oeuvres* 2:362–69). "Le hachich rend pareil à Dieu," the guest and his host agree, but soon their gentle visions give way to shouting disagreement about the nature of the divine. Following the first attack of madness in 1841, which had totally altered his life, Nerval had no need of hashish to take him into delirium. Night after night, he could witness how his small island of rationality seemed, with each visitation of dream, to be further eroded by the rising tides from a supernatural ocean.

He looked upon that ocean with fascination and fear. *Les Chimères* are the poetic expression of the effort, described in *Aurélia*, "to reestablish universal harmony by cabalistic art and seek a solution by evoking the occult forces of different religions" (*Oeuvres* 1:406; see note 12). He comes to realize, however, that in tampering with the supernatural he has actually disrupted "universal harmony." He has ventured into a realm beyond rationality and has set loose the irrational "other." Indeed, he has been compelled to trade places with his double. Returning from his travels through Germany in 1854, he found a book about himself in a Strasbourg library. It was Eugène de Miracourt's "biographie nécrologique" with an engraved portrait by E. Gervais. Nerval "signed" the portrait with a caged raven, his own sign of the captive self, and the pentacle of Solomon, the talisman to control a conjured demon (Givry 107–14). The artist may be "un homme de talent," Nerval complained, but "*il fait*

trop vrai!" Because Gervais had portrayed the wrong Nerval, "que Mer-
cure avait pris les traits de Sosie et posé à ma place," the Nerval who had
been usurped corrected the portrait by writing under it, *"Je suis l'autre"*
(*Oeuvres* 1:1079, 1399).

To evoke the occult forces in *Les Chimères*, Nerval conjures through
his belief in syncretic complementation. The face of the divine or demonic power, when it peers into the real world is captured, as in a photo-
graphic image, in whatever configuration the immediate cultural circumstances might impose, such as a Horus, an Anteros, or a Christ. Too,
when from the real world a bold explorer dares enter, like Orpheus, the
other world, he makes it possible for a spirit to assume the place that he
had left behind. This is why the poet or the mystic required the aid of
"cabalistic art," the symbols, signs, and formulae of which were not considered means of conjuration, but means of control. As we have seen in
"Le Christ aux Oliviers," Nerval anchors his own text in other texts (the
Gospels and "The Speech of the Dead Christ") in order to grasp a narrative thread to guide his way through the labyrinth. By holding on to a
given symbol or text, Nerval is less at risk of losing the "self" he projects
onto another identity or into another realm. His Nerval-Christ can confront the betrayal of friends and of father, yet find his way home again on
the thread of narrative. The tales of myth or religion give him not only the
images of the many faces that have peered forth from the other side, they
provide him a necessary tie to this world. Crossing over is a dangerous
enterprise.

A year after "Le Christ aux Oliviers" had appeared in *L'Artiste* (31 March
1844), the same journal carried Nerval's "Vers Dorés" (first published as
"Pensée antique," 16 March 1845). To make the ancient thought explicit,
Nerval prefixed a Pythagorean motto to the poem: "Eh quoi! tout est sensible!" As Georges Le Breton has shown, the text in which Nerval has
anchored his thought is a chapter from Delisle de Sale's *De la philosophie
de la nature* (1777), which includes among its dozen Pythagorean sur-
prises a refutation of the notion that a human being is "le seul être sensible." De Sale also proffers a fragment which he purports to be the "vers
dorés de Pythagore," the doctrine of "l'âme universelle."[21]

The Nerval-Christ envisions God as dead. The Nerval-Pythagoras
teaches that everything is alive and animated by a universal soul. The last
stanza of the former poem, however, anticipates the challenge of the latter. "Les Christ aux Oliviers" closed with the resurrected Christ as "ce
fou, ce insensé sublime." Christ is "insensé" because he now wanders on
the other side. Having crossed over to the world of spirit, Christ becomes

---

21. Georges Le Breton, "Le pythagorisme de Nerval et la source des «Vers dorés»."

an Icarus again in flight, a Phaëthon again amid the thunderbolts, an Attis revivified by Cybele. Caesar called up Jupiter, demanding to know what new god or devil had been imposed upon the world. But the ancient oracle was silent, and only the mad knew. Should an answer be forthcoming, it will be communicated through the soul and only by Him who gave a soul to humanity. Indeed, an answer has already been communicated through the soul, the answer to the questions of the central stanza. The soul lives only because the spirit of Christ endures ("si je meurs, c'est que tout va mourir," *Oeuvre* 3:14). And Christ endures only because the Father persists in the Son (O mon père! est-ce toi que je sens en moi-même?" 3:9).

In "Vers Dorés," Nerval carries the argument of animating spirit much further than earlier formulations prevalent in German romanticism. Friedrich Schelling, who posited a "Weltseele," was careful to insist on an essential self-reflexivity that distinguishes sentient from nonsentient manifestations of the vital energy. Nor did he want to grant to the all-pervasive force a divine consciousness or identity. Because the very celebration of animate nature threatened to dissolve theism into pantheism, Samuel Taylor Coleridge dedicated his *Opus Maximum* to the "cherished hope," as Thomas McFarland described it, "of achieving a systematic reconciliation of the 'I am' and the 'it is'" (190). Joseph von Eichendorff, converting the sense of a diffused immanence into a moment of individual revelation, declared that it was possible to call forth the song slumbering in all things if one could observe nature with the magic of sensitivity and imagination:

> There slumbers a song in all things,
> Ever dreaming forth unheard,
> And the world wakes up and sings,
> If only you find the magic word.[22]

In terms of Nerval's Pythagoreanism, however, all things not only share the vital impulse, they also think and feel. They are awake and watching ("Crains dans le mur aveugle, un regard qui t'épie"), whether or not the human mind is sufficiently alert to behold them. For Nerval, it is not a question of finding the "magic word." Confident as he is in the power of signs, Nerval affirms an Adamic naming of things as a holy act: "Tied to the heart of all matter is a word . . . / Make matter serve no use that's

---

22. Eichendorff, "Wünschelrute," in *Werke* 1:127:

> Schläft ein Lied in allen Dingen
> Die da träumen fort und fort,
> Und die Welt hebt an zu singen,
> Triffts du nur das Zauberwort.

impious!"[23] The word, like the divine Logos, belongs equally to mind and to matter. Spoken or written, it is the material manifestation of idea, mediating between thoughts and things. All words resonate with spirit, like echoes of the Orphic song of one who has crossed over to that other realm. Pride in our own powers has led us to ignore the powers of nature. Once we perceive that animals possess "un esprit agissant," that "Un mystère d'amour dans le métal repose," we should become less arrogant and learn to attend to the God who may dwell hidden in "l'être obscur."

Nerval's "Delfica" (with the title "Vers Dorés," which he later gave to "Pensée antique") was the third of the "Chimèras" to appear in L'Artiste (28 December 1845). Again he sings of "un mystère d'amour" haunting all things, a "chanson d'amour" ever recommencing. Ovid had told of Apollo's love for Daphne, how she fled from his passion and was turned into a laurel tree (Metamorphoses 1.448–611). Nerval asks Daphne, now enrooted amidst other daphne laurels, whether she recognizes "cette ancienne romance," whether she remembers the Temple of Apollo and the Delphic cave. Once the virgin Pythia in frenzied ecstasy drew her oracular secrets from its depths.[24] In this cave, "fatal aux hôtes imprudents," still slumbers the ancient seed of the vanquished dragon. With this sexual image of generative seed within the cave, Nerval enhances the myth of Apollo's slaying the Python of the cave with the myth of the Theban warriors sprung from the teeth of the dragon sown by Cadmus (Metamorphoses 3.1–187).[25] The lemon marked with the teeth of Daphne ("les citrons amers où s'imprimaient tes dents"), echoed again in his tale of Octavie ("elle imprimait ses dents d'ivoire dans l'écorce d'un citron," Oeuvres 1:310), is an image of erotic attraction and, in both instances, unfulfilled desire, a night of love on Posilipo turned to disappointment and despair. The teeth of Daphne thus leave their mark as a symbolic challenge to the seed of the dragon. The serpent, the cave, both await revival:

> They will come back, those gods you always mourn!
> Time will return the order of old days;
> The land has shivered with prophetic breath . . .[26]

23. Nerval, "Vers Dorés," 9–12: "A la matière même un verbe est attaché . . . / Ne la fais pas servir à quelque usage impie!"

24. For the erotic nature of the chthonian cult of the Delphic Pythia, see J. E. Fontenrose, Python: A Study of the Delphic Myth and its Origins (1959).

25. In her commentaries to Les Chimères, 77, Norma Rinsler points out that the Apollo and Cadmus myths are also combined in Nerval's reference to the dragon's teeth in "Antéros" and in his play Léo Burckart.

26. Nerval, "Delfica," 9–12.

> Ils reviendront ces dieux que tu pleures toujours!
> Le temps va remener l'ordre des anciens jours;
> La terre a tresailli d'un souffle prophétique . . .

Although the prophecy promises a revival of mythic vitality, Nerval's final tercet suggests that it may well be long before the gods return, for the ancient world lies in ruin, and nothing disturbs the Sibyl asleep beneath the Arch of Constantine.[27]

In the sonnet "Myrtho" Nerval sings his praise to the "divine enchanteresse." Branches of the myrtle, as Nerval described "La messe de Vénus" (1844), are used to feed the fires on her altar (*Oeuvre* 2:70). As mythic personification of the myrtle sacred to Venus, Myrtho bears an arboreal kinship to Daphne. Many are the maidens who, in mythic lore, were transformed into trees. Phaeton's sisters, who gathered to mourn him, were turned to trees at his tomb; Bacchus avenged the murder of Orpheus by turning the Thracian women into trees (*Metamorphoses* 2.380–443, 11.104–30). An "ancienne romance" of the maiden changed into a myrtle never found its way into the *Metamorphoses*. Nevertheless, when Plautus writes of the myrtle as a symbol of sexual desire ("haec myrtus Veneris est," *Vidularia* 17), he relies on the same old tradition that enabled Lucianus to refer to a debauchee as μύρτων (*Lexiphanes* 12). The divine enchantress of Nerval's poem is a debauchee now greeting the dawn after a night of Bacchic revels:

> Your forehead in a flood of Eastern rays,
> Your braids of gold entangled with black grapes.
>
> In your cup too I tasted drunkenness,
> And in the furtive lightning of your smile
> Seeing me at the feet of Bacchus kneel,
> For the Muse elected me a son of Greece.[28]

27. Curtis Bennett, *God is Dead*, interprets Nerval's turn to pagan myth as an attempt to escape the restrictive doctrines of the church. While there is some truth in Bennett's thesis, overstating it leads him to distort the meaning of Nerval's poetry in his translation of *Les Chimères*. The final tercet of "Delfica":

> Cependant la sibylle au visage latin
> Est endormie encor sous l'arc de Constantin:
> —Et rien n'a dérange le sévère portique.

becomes in Bennett's translation:

> But the prophetic sibyl in her Western home
> Lies sleeping under the arch of St. Peter's dome,
> And nothing has shattered yet that repressive bow.

28. Nerval, "Myrtho," 3–8:

> A ton front inondé des clartés d'Orient,
> Aux raisin noirs mêlés avec l'or de ta tresse.
>
> C'est dans ta coupe aussi que j'avais bu l'ivresse,
> Et dans l'éclair furtif de ton oeil souriant,
> Quand aux pieds d'Iacchus on me voyait priant,
> Car la Muse m'a fait l'un des fils de la Grèce.

As in "Delfica," Nerval tells once more of a night on Posilipo where desire is unconsummated. Amid the Bacchic revels, the poet drinks too deeply from Myrtho's cup. Bent to the feet of Bacchus, he looks up to behold the furtive lighting flash in her smiling eye. Her cup, her eye, have compounded his drunkenness, and the very touch of her foot, he says in the sestet, has aroused the fires within the volcano. They have burst forth, and now, the morning after, the sky is still darkened with ashes. Also as in "Delfica," Nerval reminds us in the concluding tercet of that ancient world of myth left lying in ruin. The Norman conquerors have shattered the statues of the gods. Myrtho, the bacchante, has now become the tree. At Virgil's tomb, she entwines her green branches with the pale blossoms of Hortensia, whose name identifies the cultivated garden, not the hidden altar and wild revels of yore.

The mood of "Delfica" and "Myrtho" is the peculiarly Nervalian *tristesse*: once-ardent longings have undergone a sad metamorphosis, desire has turned to melancholy and regret. The opening line of "Antéros" announces a very different mood. Anger, not disappointment, swells in the voice of Nerval-Anteros, who proceeds to tell why he has "so much rage at heart." This was the mood of the Nerval-Christ: anger and defiance.

Abandoned by the Father, he challenged God: "Have you the strength to live and conquer death?" Betrayed by his friends, he shouted out to Judas, "Sell me, don't waste time!" The Nerval-Anteros is moved with the same defiance: "I throw the spears back at the conquering god" [Je retourne le dards contre le dieu vainqueu].

When Byron's Manfred recounted his history to the Witch of the Alps, he described his "lone wanderings, to the cave of death," where he endeavored to call forth the spirits:

> I made
> Mine eyes familiar with Eternity,
> Such as, before me, did the Magi, and
> He who from out their fountain dwellings raised
> Eros and Anteros, at Gadaras
>
> (II.ii.89–93)

The story of how Eros and Anteros were conjured by Jamblichus, Byron explained, he had read in Eunapius's *Lives of the Sophists* (A.D. 396). In narrating the Life of Jamblichus, Eunapius, a vigorous opponent of Christianity, emphasized the ability of the sophist to tap powers inaccessible to the adherents of the new religion. Charles Lamb, in his well-known description of the "inspired charity-boy," described how the youthful Coleridge would "unfold, in . . . deep and sweet intonations, the mysteries of Jamblichus or Plotinus" (7:24–25). A sophist and Neoplatonist of a very different stamp from Plotinus, Jamblichus was more given to magic than to mysticism. It was precisely his indulgence of superstitious ritual and Pythagorean lore that made him attractive to the youthful Coleridge, to Byron, and to Nerval.

At Gadara, Jamblichus summoned Eros, god of love, and Anteros, god of unrequited love, to explain how their two springs could flow from the same fountain. Nerval dons the identity of Anteros to give Jamblichus his answer: "You ask why I have so much rage at heart" [Tu demandes pourqoui j'ai tant de rage au coeur]. Because Eros is silent here, the sonnet has none of the erotic reference of "Myrtho" and "Delfica." Instead, it tells of torment in metaphors that aptly describe his physical as well as his mental agonies:

> Yes, I am one of those the Avenger fires,
> He marked my forehead with his angry mouth,
> At times I've Cain's relentless flush beneath
> The pallor of poor Abel's bloodstained face.

By taking these lines as referring in a very literal sense to the burning rash of *erysipelas*, I do not mean to deny the equally pertinent depiction of himself as, at once, both Cain and Abel, murderer and victim. Conscious of his own trespasses and failings, Nerval believed that in his guilt he had deserved the Avenger's wrath. He felt morally responsible for the erratic behavior he confesses in *Aurélia*. As Charles Darwin observed, in the passage cited above from *Expression of Emotion*, "erysipelas of the head" was likely to be accompanied by delirium. In the account he gives as Anteros, it was indeed his head that had been especially marked by the Avenger's fire, the *feu Saint Antoine*.

In the sestet, Anteros turns to denounce the Judeo-Christian God. The Satan, whom Jehovah had cast into hell, Anteros identifies as Baal or Dagon ("mon aïeul Bélus ou mon père Dagon"). Throughout the sonnet, Nerval's Anteros asserts his ancestry: he is of the race of Antaeus (3); a descendent of Baal, Dagon was his father (11); and his mother was an Amalekite (13). As descendent of Antaeus, he draws his energy from the earth. As heir of "Baal le Dieu Soleil " (*Oeuvre* 2:717), whom Nerval associates with Apollo, he is quite at home amid the fires of hell into which his progenitor has been cast by the usurping Jehovah. Nerval left no record acknowledging that his illness derived from the ergot of rye. Nevertheless, in his role as Anteros he identifies himself as a son of Dagon, a Canaanite god of grain. His mother, he said, was an Amalekite, the clan of desert warriors who sought to block the Israelites from entering Canaan

(Gen. 36:12, 16; 1 Chron. 1:36). As her sole protector ("protégeant"), he now sows at her feet "the teeth of the old dragon" ["les dents du vieux dragon"]. These are the same dragon seed which, as we were told in "Delfica," were left in the fatal cave. He has entered that cave, and, in the trial of penetrating its darkness, "They plunged me in the Cocytus three times" [Ils m'ont plongé trois fois dans les eaux du Cocyte].

In *Aurélia*, Nerval refers often to his asylum experience as a trial ("épreuve"). The water therapy to which he was subjected becomes in his delirium a mythic trial by water.[29] One recollection of that water therapy is strangely combined with the very sort of mythic vision that forms the substance of *Les Chimères*: "I felt myself thrust into cold water, and a colder water trickled down my forehead. I turned my thoughts to the eternal Isis, sacred mother and spouse; all my aspirations, all my prayers were mingled in that magic name, and I seemed to live again in her; sometimes she appeared to me in the guise of Venus of the ancients, sometimes as the Christian Virgin."[30] Nerval's syncretism is not merely a theoretical or historical exercise; it is an informing attribute of his experience. The goddess of his hallucinatory dreams promises to fulfill all empty, hopeless longings: "During my sleep I had a marvelous vision. It seemed to me that the goddess appeared to me saying, 'I am the same as Mary, the same as your mother, the same being as you have always loved under every form. At each of your ordeals I have dropped one of the masks with which I hide my features and soon you shall see me as I really am.'"[31] Schiller ("Das verschleierte Bild zu Sais") and Novalis (*Die Lehrlinge zu Sais*) wrote on the enchantments of the image of Isis and how the priests of her temple always felt the dangerous temptation to lift the veils concealing her true features. For Nerval, the veils or masks themselves are part of her power. She is his lost mother, his bride, his salvation.

That he recognizes the danger, as well, is evident in "Horus," a sonnet that reveals the power of her passion. Nerval sets the scene for the birth

29. On baths or showers of cold water as therapy for patients suffering hallucinatory derangement, see Jan Goldstein, *Console and Classify*, 102, and Roy Porter, *Mind-Forg'd Manacles*, 29, 30, 106, 221.

30. Nerval, *Aurélia*, in *Oeuvres* 1:408: "Je me sentais plongé dans une eau froide, et une eau plus froide encore ruisselait sur mon front. Je reportai ma pensée à l'éternelle Isis, la mère et l'épouse sacrée; toutes mes aspirations, toutes mes prières se confondaient dans ce nom magique, je me sentais revivre en elle, et parfois elle m'apparaissait sous la figure de la Vénus antique, parfois aussi sous les traits de la Vierge des chrétiens."

31. Ibid. 403: "Pendant mon sommeil, j'eus une vision merveilleuse. Il me semblait que la déesse, m'apparaissait, me disant: «Je suis la même que Marie, la même que ta mère, la même aussi que sous toutes les formes tu as toujours aimée. A chacune de tes épreuves, j'ai quitté l'un des masques dont je voile mes traits, et bientôt tu me verras telle que je suis.»"

of Horus, the son she has conceived in her union with Osiris, her brother-lover. It is also the scene, therefore, in which she repudiates her old father-husband, Kneph. Her successive roles—daughter, bride, mother—may replicate a natural sequence, but at each stage she acquires new powers that enable her finally to emerge as a redeeming goddess.

Kneph is the earth-god, who took Nuth, the sky-mother, as his bride. Isis and Osiris are their offspring, but old Kneph grew enamored of his daughter's beauty and sought to keep her in his bed. Tiring of his lust, Isis brings Osiris back from the dead and takes him as her lover. Nerval's sonnet suggests the parallels to the story of Venus, wed to old Vulcan, embracing Mars in his absence. The octave of the sonnet dramatizes her scorn for her aged spouse:

> Trembling, the god Kneph shook the universe:
> Then mother Isis rose up on her bed,
> Gestured at her savage spouse in hatred,
> And the old passion blazed in her green eyes.
>
> "See him?" she said. "He's dying now, that brute,
> The frosts of all the world are in his gut;
> Put out his squint eye, tie his twisted foot—
> He's king of winters, the volcanoes' god!"[32]

What may seem ruthless and brutal, here, is actually a necessary step in spiritual growth. The old father is bound to the material world. Isis and Osiris, guided by Thoth (Hermes), seek to lead humanity out of its primitive savagery. In giving birth to Horus, the sun-god, Isis prepares to drive off the hostile darkness that still has a hold on Osiris and her realm.

"The eagle has flown," Isis declares, announcing the ascent of Horus (his sign is the bird of prey, and it is said that he ascended the skies in the form of a falcon). Isis, as mother, has put on the robe of Cybele. Then, reversing the course of Venus (as in Botticelli's well-known painting), she rides upon a shell back into the sea. In the final line her veil is lifted. It is

---

32. Nerval, "Horus," 1–8:

> Le dieu Kneph en tremblant ébranlait l'univers:
> Isis, la mère, alors se leva sur sa couche,
> Fit un geste de haine à son époux farouche,
> Et l'ardeur d'autrefois brilla dans ses yeux verts.
>
> «Le voyez-vous, dit-elle, il muert, ce vieux pervers,
> Tous les frimas du monde ont passé par sa bouche,
> Attachez son pied tors, éteignez son oeil louche,
> C'est l'enfant bien-aimé d'Hermès et d'Osiris!»

the veil of Iris, the rainbow, exulting in the light of the newborn god ("Et les cieux rayonnaient sous l'écharpe d'Iris").

Although often regarded a precursor of the Symbolists, Nerval, as I have argued, elaborated his system of mythic reference and cabalistic signs not as an aesthetic end in itself, in spite of his belief in "l'art pour l'art," but as a means of controlling the fierce spirits his visionary conjurations had set loose. The poet who ventures into a world of spirits has need of "cabalistic art." Nerval's reliance on symbols and signs in *Les Chimères* is especially prominent in "Artémis" and "El Desdichado."

Often in these sonnets Nerval borrowed his operative metaphor, as Georges Le Breton has shown, from the Tarot cards. "Artémis" and "El Desdichado" become more accessible when one glances at the Tarot cards, which inform his imagery. In "Artémis," four cards are played in the opening quatrain—XIII, the Grim Reaper; III, the Queen; VI, the Lover; IV, the King:

> The Thirteenth comes back . . . is again the first,
> And always the only one—or the only time:
> Are you then queen, O you! the first or last?
> You, the one or last lover, are you king?[33]

Even in laying out the cards, the poet struggles to comprehend their meaning. What do these symbols tell of his fate? The Reaper takes the Queen, so that the Lover, who follows her, is denied his love; and the King, bereft of his bride, stands alone.

The second quatrain laments the fatal message. The mother and bride, "who loved you from the cradle to the hearse" [qui vous aima du berceau dans la bièr], is dead; she bears to her tomb not the red rose of passion, but the mallow rose. A lady with a mallow rose had appeared to him once while he was in the garden of the asylum at Montmartre, where, even as he watched her, she seemed to blend into the flowerbeds and vanish: "'Don't leave me!' I cried, 'For with you Nature itself dies'" [«Oh! ne fuis pas! m'écriai-je . . . car la nature meurt avec toi!» *Oeuvres* 1:379]. The Queen of the Tarot deck conjures her image once again, carrying the mallow rose: she is Artemis, with powers of death, yet also of birth.

Born as female twin of Apollo, Artemis has no dominion over music, philosophy, or the arts. Quietly, from her golden throne in Ortygia, Artemis influences the very causes of life and death. As a birth-goddess, she

---

33. Nerval, "Artémis":

> La Treizième revient . . . C'est encor la première;
> Et c'est toujours la seule, —ou c'est le seul moment:
> Car es-tu reine, ô toi! la première ou dernière?
> Es-tu roi, toi le seul ou le dernier amant? . . .

grants sexual potency to man and beast. As a death-goddess, she causes sudden, inexplicable death. The poet expresses this paradox of her identity with his exclamation "O délice! ô tourment!" Her mythic character has, perhaps, been influenced by the coincidence of her name (Ἄρτεμις) with the word for slaughterer or butcher (ἄρταμος). Because the hunter Actaeon had surprised her while bathing and gazed upon her nakedness, she punished him with the cruel death of being chased and killed by his own hounds. Yet she could also administer a gentle death, as when she killed the mighty hunter Orion "with a visitation of painless arrows" (*Odyssey* 5.124).

The sestet makes a radical leap, turning its attention to Naples and a very different figure—a virgin saint. As a reader familiar with Nerval might well suspect, he has merely shifted syncretic parameters. The Tarot cards revealed the Queen of Love and Death, in whom he recognized the Greek goddess Artemis and the lady of the mallow rose. She, in turn, prompts him to think of two other ladies of the flowers, one of whom he beheld in Naples, the other in Brussels.

The identification of the "Neapolitan saint" as St. Rosalia rests, in part, upon his own marginal glosses to the poem. Opposite the reference to the return of the "La Treizième," Nerval noted that the thirteenth hour is "pivotale." The exclamation "O délice! ô tourment!" is glossed with a reference to "Philomène," the medieval French version of Ovid's tale of Philomela, whom Tereus, her sister's husband, ravished then cut out her tongue so that she could not betray him. Transformed into a nightingale, she continues to sing her sorrow (*Metamorphoses* 6.424–888). And the passage describing the saint "with her hands full of fire" [aux mains pleines de feux], is glossed as "Rosalie" (see Guillaume's critical edition, «*Les Chimères*», 114).

Another reference occurs in *Octavie*, where Nerval describes her room in Naples as heaped with mystical, mythic, antique, and religious ornaments, including "une figure de sainte Rosalie, couronée de roses violettes" (*Oeuvres* 1:312). Rosalia, her legend records, shielded her virginity by fleeing to the mountains when she was only fourteen. Taking only her crucifix and her books, she found refuge first in a cave atop Mount Quisquita, then on Mount Pellegrino, where angels nourished her with the Host and protected her from the freezing snows by bringing her handfuls of fire. Rosalia thus has a kinship with the goddess of chastity and with the sibyl of the cave. Her "Rose a coeur violet" also associates her, in a leap that would have been spontaneous and irresistible in Nerval's mind, with St. Gudula. He saw her statue, far from Naples, at the Place Sainte Gudule in Brussels—Brussels, where he bid his final farewell to Jenny Colon. A complex set of images, laden with personal memories, prompt the curse of the concluding tercet. He damns the white rose of purity, the white phantoms of the sky, and blesses the saint of the abyss, who still dwells within the cave of the dark underworld.

"El Desdichado" is a sonnet of self-definition in which the poet endeavors to reconcile his conflicting impulses, the split into *self* and *other*. The first definition of self is proposed in the title, in which he identifies himself with the unfortunate Don Blaz Desdichado in Le Sage's *Le Diable boteux*, who went mad after his wife died and he lost all claim to her fortune. "El Desdichado" is also the device which the Disinherited Knight bore on his shield when he rode into the tournament to challenge Brian de Bois-Guilbert to mortal combat in *Ivanhoe*. Whether from Scott or Le Sage, Nerval has identified himself as one who had lost his fortune and had fallen into misery and madness. Having dubbed himself Gérard *de Nerval*, he must also claim for himself an estate, a noble lineage. Thus he becomes, not only "the shadowed, —the bereaved, —the unconsoled," but also the dispossessed "Aquitanian Prince of the stricken tower" [Je suis le ténébreux, —le veuf, —l'inconsolé, / Le prince d'Aquitaine à la tour abolie]. Upon a troubadour's lute rather than a knight's shield, he bears his heraldic emblem borrowed from Dürer's well-known engraving: "the *Black Sun* of *Melancholia*" [le *Soleil noir* de la *Mélancholie*].

As in "Artémis," he uses the opening quatrain to tell his fortune, or misfortune, with a series of Tarot images: XV, the Devil ("le Prince de Ténèbres"); XVI the Lightning-Struck Tower ("La Maison Dieu"); XVII, the Star ("Ma seule étoile est morte") (Le Breton 31–38). In the second quatrain he returns to the Neapolitan landscape of "Myrtho," "Delfica," and "Artémis," sonnets which invoke symbolic landmarks: the cave of the Cumaean sibyl, the tomb of Virgil, the temples once buried in ashes at the foot of Vesuvius. Again, he recollects the nocturnal tryst at the grotto of Posilipo:

> You who consoled me, in the tombstone night,
> Bring back my Posilipo, the Italian sea,
> The *flower* that so pleased my wasted heart,
> And the arbour where vine and rose agree.[34]

Here the "unconsoled" is momentarily "consoled." The vine and the rose are in harmonious balance. As he confessed in "Myrtho," the flower and the grape have also been in opposition.

34. Nerval, "El Desdichado," 5–8:
>   Dans le nuit tombeau, toi qui m'as consolé,
>   Rends-moi le Pausilippe et la mer d'Italie,
>   La *fleur* qui plaisait tant à mon coeur désolé,
>   Et la treille où le pampre à la rose s'allie.

In the sestet he reflects upon his inability to resolve the opposition: "Suis-je Amour ou Phébus? . . . Lusignan ou Biron?" Love pulls him in one direction, poetry in another. As lover, he is a Lusignan who loses his beloved Melusina; as poet, he is a Byron who wanders in lonely exile. The dilemma is further complicated by fits of madness and torments of *erysipelas*: "My brow is red still from the kiss of the queen; / I've dreamed in the cavern where the siren swims . . ."[35] The image contrasts with that in "Antéros," where it was the Avenger who "marked my forehead with his angry mouth." The agony of the burning rash is sweetened by splendid visions, such as those recounted in *Aurélia*. Like the bacchante Myrtho greeting the dawn, he bears his inflamed brow as a mark of the wild revelry of the dream.

It is not only the dream of the siren that enables the poet to appraise his fate more positively. Even if he cannot overcome the affliction that assails his mind and body, he has learned to turn his delirium into poetry. In the concluding tercet of "Antéros," he wrote that he had thrice been plunged into the Cocytus. The parallel passage in "El Desdichado" states that he has twice crossed the Acheron as a conqueror. What enables him to vanquish the spell of the underworld is the gift of the Orphic lyre. Armed with that instrument, or the troubadour's lute of the first quatrain, he sings his songs of ecstasy and agony: "The sighs of the saint, and the fairy's screams" [Les soupirs de la sainte et les cris de la fée].

35. Ibid. 10–11: "Mon front est rouge encor du baiser de la reine; / J'ai rêvé dans la grotte où nage la syrène . . ."

9

CLARE'S "CHILD HAROLD"

When Thomas De Quincey wrote on John Clare for the *Edinburgh Review*, he assumed the role of apologist. The fits of severe depression that Clare had suffered in 1824 De Quincey readily diagnosed as an "affection of the liver," a morbid reaction to the tumultuous and licentious habits of London, a mode of life for which the "Peasant Poet" was ill-prepared. As De Quincey saw it, Clare was a Wordsworthian poet of nature, who thrived upon "his own humble opportunities of enjoyment in the country."[1] The artificial excitements of London were detrimental to his mental health.

De Quincey, of course, had strong preconceptions about the susceptibility of the creative mind to bouts of madness. His long-time friend, Charles Lloyd, best known for his fictionalized account of Coleridge in *Edmund Oliver*, had been in and out of institutions before he was permanently consigned to the asylum in Chaillot where he had died just the year before. De Quincey had not only cared for Lloyd in his delirium, he had also struggled with his own frightening hallucinations wrought by his opium addiction. With Coleridge he had discussed the problems of medical treatment of mental disturbances, and in his periodical essays, he not only deliberated on the affinities of genius and madness, he also wrote psychological portraits of such idiosyncratic characters as Walking Stewart. It is not surprising, then, that De Quincey should turn his attention to John Clare who, since 1837, had been sequestered in the asylum at Epping Forest as a patient of Dr. Matthew Allen.

Although fits of melancholy had troubled Clare when they first met in London, De Quincey recollects that the "Peasant Poet" had found a thera-

1. Thomas De Quincey, "Sketches of Life and Manners," Tait's *Edinburgh Magazine*, December 1840, 771–72; in *DQ* 3:144–45.

peutic relief in the poetry of Wordsworth. "Even in this season of dejection," wrote De Quincey, Clare "would uniformly become animated when anybody spoke to him of Wordsworth—animated with the most hearty and almost rapturous spirit of admiration" (*DQ* 3:145). From *Poems Descriptive of Rural Life and Scenery* (1820) and *The Village Minstrel* (1821) through *The Shepherd's Calendar* (1827) and *The Rural Muse* (1835), Clare continued to inform his lyric with precise botanical descriptions of nature. Whatever Wordsworthian attributes Clare might seem to display in his early poetry, he resisted the mold into which he felt he was being cast by his publishers. Edward Drury warned his cousin, the publisher John Taylor, in a letter of 2 January 1820, that they must be patient with Clare: "It is to be feared that the man will be afflicted with insanity if his talent continues to be forced as it has been these 4 months past; he has no other mode of easing the fever that oppresses him after a tremendous fit of rhyming except by getting tipsy." Requesting books of Chaucer and the "old poets," Clare asserted that he "must have Poetry to read otherwise I cannot rhyme; & these Wordsworth's, Bowles &c that Mr Gilchrist lends do me no good" (Storey, *Critical Heritage*, 34). Taylor was, for a time, a patient publisher, and Clare promptly had his copy of Chaucer.

Twenty years later, after long "fits of rhyming" and many more bouts of "getting tipsy," Clare was indeed "afflicted with insanity." When Cyrus Redding visited him in Dr. Allen's asylum, he still wanted books: not Chaucer now, but Byron. In much of the poetry Clare produced in the asylum he adopted a deliberate and self-conscious Byronic pose. De Quincey, of course, had no notion of this belated, perhaps benighted, turn to Byron. No less than Edward Drury, however, he observed the symptoms of mental duress threatening Clare's sanity. Drury hinted that alcohol was Clare's bane. De Quincey, too, noted that Clare suffered "from an affection of the liver." As one who had recorded his own chaste cohabitation with "Ann of Oxford Street," De Quincey saw Clare's downfall abetted by an ardent attraction to London prostitutes.

Once the "brilliant parties" and "glittering theatres" had "made his rural life but too insupportable to his mind," Clare went in quest of stimulation. "It is singular that what most fascinated his rustic English eye was not the gorgeous display of English beauty," De Quincey recalls, "but the French style of beauty, as he saw it amongst the French actresses of Tottenham Court Road" (*DQ* 3:145). Clare's Wordsworthian sensibility was finely tuned to nature, according to De Quincey's diagnosis, but too easily distracted and debauched by the wanton enticements of the city. De Quincey's appraisal is confirmed by Clare himself in brooding over his sins in "Child Harold" and in jesting about the whorehouses of London in "Don Juan." Such matters, to be sure, are well suited to his Byronic identity in these poems. But there is no sense that the poet has simply invented remorse and self-recrimination for the sake of the pose.

When they first met, Clare may well have recognized in De Quincey a kindred spirit, one who seemed just as overwhelmed and ill at ease amidst the social whirl as himself. At the gala dinners hosted by Taylor and Hessey, Clare met the London literati and contributors to the *London Magazine*: Reynolds, Lamb, Coleridge, and Hazlitt. The author of the "Confessions of an English Opium-Eater," which had appeared in the issues of September and October 1821, was also among the company. Clare describes him as friendly yet not unlike a little boy lost: "A little artless simple-seeming body something of a child overgrown in a blue coat & black neckerchief for his dress is singular with his hat in his hand steals gently among the company with a smile turning timidly around the room It is De Quincey the Opium Eater & that abstruse thinker in logic & metaphysic X.Y.Z." (*Prose*, 91). Clare read the "Confessions" and followed the articles by "X.Y.Z." in the *London Magazine*. When a second printing of *The Village Minstrel* was called for in 1823, Clare wrote to Hessey asking that copies be given to the other contributors to *London Magazine*. He also requested "a copy of the Opium Eater he is a great favorite of mine" (April 1823). De Quincey's review of Goethe's *Wilhelm Meister* (August 1824) he considered "excellent" and, along with an essay by Elia in the same issue, "sufficient to make a bad no. interesting" (Journal, 11 September 1824; also letter to C. A. Elton, 18 December 1824). Readily granting that De Quincey had "contended right enough that women had an inferior genius to men," Clare observed that De Quincey's essay "False Distinctions" (June 1824) stirred a debate in subsequent numbers of the *Surrey* and the *Lion's Head* (Journal, 6 October 1824). Clare followed, too, the controversy over *Walladmor*, the German forgery of a Scott novel that De Quincey not only reviewed (October 1824) but also translated in a two-volume edition published by Taylor and Hessey. Conceding that "some parts of the novel" were "alive with action," Clare added the wish that "De Quincey had better subjects for his genius" (Journal, 13 October 1824).

By this time, after submitting several pieces on natural history, Clare had abandoned his effort to write for the *London Magazine*. Hessey began to sound more patronizing than supportive, and Taylor did not hesitate to ridicule both his poetry and his prose (Clare, *Natural History* [= *NH*], xxxvi–xxxviii). Both were well aware of Clare's precarious mental health. When he wrote Taylor to report that Dr. Arnold (of Stamford) had helped quiet his fits, Clare complained that he still felt "a numbness all over just as I should suppose a person to feel when bitten by a serpent" (August 1824). Worried about this reaction to Dr. Arnold's treatment, he wrote to Hessey asking him to secure the advice of Dr. G. Darling, the physician who had subjected Keats to "copious bleedings."

I have gave up doctoring save the taking of opening pills occasionally I am as stupid as ever & blood comes from me often my insides feels sinking & dead & my memory is worse & worse nearly lost the sensation as if cold water was creeping all about my head . . . I feel desirous Hessey of having Dr. Darlings advice & would feign get to London if I could. (20 August 1824)

As Clare recorded in his autobiography, Dr. Darling was successful in allaying temporarily "the complaint . . . in my head & chest." But his visit to London in 1824 was also an occasion of willed and unwilled fantasies, illusions that slipped into delusions. "I amused my illness by catching the most beautiful women faces in the crowd as I passed on in it," he wrote, "till I was satiated as it were with the variety & the multitude & my mind lost its memory in the eternity of beautys successions & was glad to glide on in vacancy with the living stream." But the beauties of daytime perception were replaced by the terrors of night. Although he declared himself "a stubborn disbeliever" of the supernatural, he confessed an utter failure in resisting his fears:

At night their terrors came upon me tenfold & my head was as full of the terrible as a gossip's thin death-like shadows & goblins with saucer eyes were continually shaping on the darkness from my haunted imagination & when I saw anyone of a spare figure in the dark passing or going on by my side my blood curdled cold at the foolish apprehension of his being a supernatural agent whose errand might be to carry me at the first dark alley we came to. (*Prose* 94)

Because he was painfully conscious of his own mental debilities, it may be a deliberate omission that he made no mention of De Quincey's "Madness" (June 1824), which, like "False Distinctions," appeared in the "Notes from the Pocket-Book of a late Opium-Eater." Whatever the cause of Clare's "affection of the liver," De Quincey presumed that it was directly to blame for Clare's mental condition. In his account for the *London Magazine*, he confidently postulated that "all madness, or nearly all, takes its rise in some part of the apparatus connected with the digestive organs, most probably the liver." The brain is merely the organ that through a sympathetic response to disruptions in the stomach or liver, produces those symptoms of irrationality. The fact that the brain of a lunatic might, upon dissection, reveal "some lesion or disorganization" does not mean the disease originated in the brain itself. A lesion in the brain may merely mark the ravages that commenced, most probably, in a diseased liver. Because opium had played havoc with his own digestive tract, De Quincey was particularly sensitive to the powerful influence the inner organs could work upon the mind. He therefore takes as the primary ground of his argument on the cause of madness the evidence of his own experience:

> For some years opium had simply affected the tone of my stomach; but, as this went off, and the stomach, by medicine and exercise, &c., began to recover its strength, I observed that the liver began to suffer. Under the affection of this organ, I was sensible that the genial spirits decayed far more rapidly and deeply, and that with this decay the intellectual faculties had a much closer sympathy. Upon this I tried some scores of experiments, raising or lowering alternately for periods of 48, 60, 72, or 84 hours, the quantity of opium. The result I may perhaps describe more particularly elsewhere; in substance, it amounted to this, —that, as the opium began to take effect, the whole living principle of the intellectual motions began to lose its elasticity, and, as it were, to petrify; I began to comprehend the tendency of madness to eddy about one idea; and the loss of power to abstract—to hold abstractions steadily before me—or to exercise many other intellectual acts, was in due proportion to the degree in which the biliary system seemed to suffer. (*DQ* 10:446–47)

Through his opium addiction, De Quincey had come to experience the conditions of madness. He fought its awful hold on his mind, yet endeavored to document all the symptoms, physical and mental, that the addiction had imposed upon him.

If there is some truth in De Quincey's insistence on the salubrious effects of Wordsworth, it may well be possible that in his turn to Byron, notorious as prodigy turned prodigal of Regency London, Clare indulged a hazardous mode of homeopathic therapy. In writing his "new cantos" for "Child Harold" and "Don Juan," he developed his own version of the Byronic identity. The poems of Clare's madness use this Byronic identity to explore the dark interiors of desire and guilt. These interiors, however, also resemble the haunted realms of De Quincey's nightmare visions. As Mark Storey has noticed, Clare had begun to imitate De Quincey in "The Dream" and "The Nightmare," and he returned to the De Quinceyan bifurcation of self in the recurring apocalyptic visions of "Child Harold" (*Critical Introduction* 167, 216). The sense of Clare reading Byron is subordinate to Clare adopting and transforming Childe Harold as his own *alter ego*. Clare, to be sure, was fully aware that Byron's poetic strategy involved a subtle in-and-out relationship of narrator and character. If this is parody, it is desperately earnest and far more complex than a mere appropriation of a Byronic "self." The tormented dreams of the Opium-Eater also inform the intertextuality. Nor has Clare abandoned his former habits as the "Peasant Poet" who could lose himself in act of observing the "minute particulars," as Blake would say, of a wayside weed.

As in Hölderlin's "Patmos" and Nerval's "Le Christ aux Oliviers," Clare writes his text by reading himself into another text. An outcast from the society of the London *beau monde* where he had been feted for a season, Clare no doubt felt a certain sympathy with the poet who left England amid scandal. He recognized too, and appropriated, the ironic displacement of self that Byron accomplished in engendering his poetic persona. Most critical commentary on Clare's "Don Juan" and "Child Harold" has been preoccupied with the mimicking of Byron. In line with the preceding investigation of Hölderlin and Nerval, I stress instead Clare's hermeneutic penetration into Byron's text where he recovers the "wandering outlaw of his own dark mind" and engenders his own "being more intense" (canto 3, stanzas 3 and 6). This is Clare's poem, not Byron's. Clare's Spenserian stanza is more roughshod (often ignoring the convention of a final Alexandrine),[2] and his Child Harold is the form of his own fancy, the image of his own life, as its opening stanza tells us.

> Many are the poets—though they use no pen
> To show their labours to the shuffling age
> Real poets must be truly honest men
> Tied to no mongrel laws on flatterys page
> No zeal have they for wrong or party rage
> —The life of labor is a rural song
> That hurts no cause—nor warfare tries to wage
> Toil like the brook in music wears along—
> Great little minds claim right to act the wrong.

Clare stubbornly insists on his right to be a poet. Reared among the hovels of farm laborers, he is an "honest" man who has heard a song amid the sweat and toil. During the 1820s he won acclaim, but soon discovered that he had been received as little more than a curiosity and a freak, a minstrel plowboy. His early poems are notable for their keen observation of nature; his asylum poems are introspective and tinged with irony and defiance. With this shift from a Wordsworthian to a Byronic mode, Clare denies the ideological contests of the established par-

---

2. Clare had used the Spenserian stanza in "The Village Minstrel" (the title poem of the 1821 collection) as well as in many of the poems of *The Shepherd's Calendar* (which owes more to Spenser than stanza and title).

ties. He champions the voice of the marginalized working class: "Great little minds claim right to act the wrong."

Undercutting the posturing of his poetic self-projection, Clare's "honest" persona does not conceal the squalor of his existence and the sad confrontation with the futility of his ideals and ambitions:

> My life hath been one of love—no blot it out
> My life hath been one chain of contradictions
> Madhouses Prisons wh-reshops—never doubt
> But that my life hath had some strong convictions
> That such was wrong—religion makes restrictions
> I would have followed—but life turned a bubble
> (145–50)

Clare's Child Harold does not range across the nations of Europe; he travels the lonely backroads, a man abandoned and betrayed.

> Life is to me a dream that never wakes
> Night finds me on this lengthening road alone
> Love is to me a thought that never aches
> A frost bound thought that freezes life to stone
> (255–58)

His Child-Harold self, in the stanzas just quoted, seems to confess some sexual disorder. The cause of Clare's debility has been variously attributed to epilepsy or alcoholism. Although medical records at the Northampton General Lunatic Asylum typically made note of such evidence, the certification of his insanity, signed by Dr. William Page and Dr. Fenwick Skimshire, mentions neither epilepsy nor venereal infection. When Patty's "temper or injudicious conduct" drove him away from home in 1826, he had a brief affair with another woman. His guilt in the aftermath of this episode grew into the conviction that he had contracted a disease (letter from Eliza Emmerson, 1826; letter from James Hessey, 18 June 1828; in Tibble and Tibble 305). Although his symptoms were not manifest in lesions of the flesh, they were real enough to provide a recurrent motif of "Child Harold," in which the retribution for his sins is manifest as the freezing blight that "fell in youths mayday" (32–33).

Because the cottage in Helpston was overcrowded after their seventh child was born, Lord Milton arranged for Clare and his family to move into a house with some five acres in Northborough in 1832. Unsettled by the move, Clare complained to Dr. Darling that he could no longer concentrate: "I cannot sleep for I am asleep as it were with my eyes open & I feel chills come over me & a sort of nightmare awake. . . . I cannot keep my mind right as it were for I wish to read & cannot—there is a sort of numbing through my private parts which I cannot describe" (Autumn 1835; *Letters* 183). He told Thomas Inskip that an "appoplectic fit" had left "a numbing pain" in his head and "an acking void at the pit of my stomach" (10 August 1824). Such "fits," Clare thought, had commenced when, as a child, he witnessed a man break his neck in a fall from a wagon (*Sketches* 70). He also suffered, by his own account, periods of severe melancholy. His letters contain detailed descriptions of a numbness penetrating his head and a lethargy overwhelming his body. "A tottering trembling state of nerves & . . . sickly sensibility" were the symptoms he described to Taylor (March–April 1821). During the next ten years Clare's recurrent agonies became more severe. He told Eliza Emmerson that "my very brains seemed to boil up almost into madness & my arms & legs burnt as it were with a listless feebleness" (13 November 1832).[3]

Eliza Emmerson had advised him to avoid "anything that may affect your *Head*" (December 1825). As the torment of mind and body increased, Clare curtailed his drinking. Answering Taylor's suspicion that he might be lapsing into former habits and probably had too much to drink as a guest of the mayor of Boston (in Lincolnshire), Clare explained that he had merely indulged an incautious enthusiasm when "a lady of the table talked so ladily of the Poets that I drank off my glass very often without knowing." He felt the influence of the wine, precisely because "I was not used to the drink." He then adds: "I dont think I have drank a pint of ale together these two years in fact I can drink nothing strong now in any quantity & as to spirits I never touch them & yet without them I feel hearty & hale & have quite recovered from my last ailments & hope to prolong the lease of life for a good season" (3 January 1829).

Clare was never long free of his ailments. The "fits" of melancholy were also accompanied by hallucinations. Clare's letter to Dr. Darling (Autumn 1835) is filled with fear that he is losing his mind; he declares desperately that he "can scarcely bear up against my fancys or feelings." When Taylor, accompanied by a doctor, visited him in December 1836, they found Clare enfeebled by delusion and able to speak only in repetitive babbling (Grigson 6). At Taylor's recommendation, Clare was sent to Dr. Allen's asylum in Epping Forest (near Enfield, Essex).

De Quincey, we recall, was certain that madness arose from an "affection of the liver." Dr. Allen argued that there was a link between kidney function and certain forms of insanity. He consequently advocated regular observation of the color and clarity of the urine (*Classification of the Insane* 36). Clare's portrait of "Doctor Bottle imp" confirms that Dr. Allen put his theory into practice at his High Beech asylum:

3. John Clare, *Letters*, 73, 85, 135, 136, 147, 175, 110, 147, 157–58, 165, 208.

> There is Doctor Bottle imp who deals in urine
> A keeper of state prisons for the queen
> As great a man as is the Doge of Turin
> And save in London is but seldom seen
> Yclep'd old A–ll–n—mad brained ladies curing
> Some p–x–d like Flora and but seldom clean
> The new road oer the forest is the right one
> To see red hell and further on the white one
> ("Don Juan," 223–30)

By calling attention only to the female patients under Dr. Allen's care, Clare seems to detach himself from confinement, to stand some distance from Epping Forest, and merely to point the way to the "red hell and . . . the white one" (the lodge and clinic at High Beech).[4] The reference to the "mad brained ladies" might echo some persisting gossip among the attendants about the court case over Dr. Allen's treatment of one of the women patients four years before Clare's arrival at the asylum.[5]

In spite of Dr. Allen's advocacy of proper medical and moral treatment (*Cases of Insanity*, part 1, vol. 1), the attendants did not always act with the prescribed benevolence. Indeed, records at other asylums during this period reveal that brutality to the patients was all too common (Digby 140–70). After his escape, Clare wrote to Dr. Allen that the "servants & stupid keepers" had made life in the asylum unbearable:

> I can be miserably happy in any situation & in any place & could have staid in yours in the Forest if any of my friends had noticed me or come to see me but the greatest annoyance in such places as yours are those servants & stupid keepers who often assumed as much authority over me as if I had been their prisoner & not liking to quarrel I put up with it till I was weary of the place altogether so I heard the voice of freedom & started (August 1841; *Letters* 294)

The only belongings abandoned in his escape which he wished to have forwarded were his volumes of Byron's poetry. His journey home from Epping Forest to Northborough, a distance of 100 miles, would have been

4. Referring to the three separate buildings at High Beech, Geoffrey Grigson, *Poems of John Clare's Madness*, 363, reports that "Leppit's Hill Lodge housed the incipients, the convalescents, and the partially deranged."

5. *Allen versus Dutton* documents the suit brought by Dr. Matthew Allen to vindicate himself against Richard Dutton who had alleged malpractice in the treatment of Mrs. Frances Louise Dutton during her stay as a patient in his asylum.

less arduous if Clare had a proper pair of shoes and some food. As it was, he arrived on the road north from Petersborough limping and hungry. Two nights he slept in fields, one night he took shelter on the porch of a cottage, and he chewed grass and tobacco to allay the hunger pangs. Just a few miles from his home, he was met by a woman in a cart. "When nearing me the woman got out & caught fast hold of my hands & wished me to get into the cart but I refused & thought her either drunk or mad" (*Prose* 247). It was his wife Patty.

His failure to recognize his wife may have been the consequence of having long dwelt upon his fantasy of Mary Joyce, his first love. "Young as my heart was," he recollected in his autobiography, "it would turn chill when I touched her & tremble & I fancyd her feelings were the same for as I gazd earnestly in her face a tear would hang in her eye & she would turn to wipe it away." Even in its inception, the relationship was "romantic or Platonic" and nourished in Clare's own fancy. "I fancyd her eyes told me her affections," he wrote of those days when "we walked together as school-companions." Whatever her eyes may have told him, they soon ceased to look upon him. "When she grew to womanhood she felt her station above mine at least I felt that she thought so for her parents were farmers, & farmers had great pretensions to something then" (*Prose* 44).

In later years, he began to elaborate this "fancyd" love into an almost mystical ideal. From Epping Forest, he addressed letters to "My dear Wife Patty" and "My dear Wife Mary." After his escape from the asylum, he was informed that Mary Joyce had died in 1838, one year after his confinement. "Mary has been dead eight years," he wrote to Dr. Allen. The lapse of time is garbled—three years became six or eight—and the very fact of her death is challenged. In the account of his escape, "The Journey from Essex," he scoffs at "the old story of her being dead six years ago." Such a tale "might be taken from a bran new old newspaper printed a dozen years ago but I took no notice of the blarney having seen her myself about a twelvemonth ago alive & well & as young as ever" (*Prose* 250). Indeed, she came to him in a dream and lay at his side on that very journey homeward.

The love affair with Mary blossomed in the poet's imagination at High Beech. It is her image, not Patty's, that becomes his muse and mental companion:

> Here where Mary loved to be
> And here are flowers she planted
> Here are books she loved to see
> And here the kiss she granted
> (125–28)

In the very next quatrain of this song from "Child Harold" Clare recognizes that Mary's haunting presence is expelled and eradicated by the physical evidence of absence. Not even her picture remains, "Both walls and rooms are naked now / No Marys nigh to hear me."

In the asylum version of their childhood love, Mary had been his bride and, only after she was taken from him amid "maledictions," had he "made the error double" by wedding a second wife. His imprisonment in the madhouse enforces his separation from both:

> Yet absence claims them both and keeps them too
> And locks me in a shop in spite of law
> Among a low lived set and dirty crew
> Here let the Muse oblivions curtains draw
> And let man think—for God hath often saw
> Things here too dirty for the light of day
> For in a madhouse there exists no law—
> Now stagnant grows my too refined clay
> I envy birds their wings to flye away
>
> (154–62)

Byron's "Prisoner of Chillon," after the death of his two brothers, falls into madness, a dark despair of "no thought" and "stagnant idleness." When the song of a bird "broke in upon my brain," rather than envy its freedom to fly, he is glad that it is not caged like him. Byron's prisoner, his mind and will broken, made friends with spiders and mice and "my very chains."

Clare, too, may have gradually resigned himself to captivity during his twenty-two years as an inmate at the Northampton General Lunatic Asylum. But at Epping Forest he continued to protest: "No one knows how sick I am of this confinement"; "If I was in prison for felony I could not be served worse"; "Having been cooped up in this Hell of a Madhouse till I seem to be disowned & even forgot by my enemies. . . . I am almost mad in waiting for a better place & better company"; "It Would Seem By Keeping Me Here One Year After Another That I Was Destined For The Same Fate Agen & I Would Sooner Be Packed On A Slave Ship For Africa Than Belong To The Destiny of Mock Friends & Real Enemies" (*Letters* 290–92). Some of the letters that he drafted in his High Beech notebook may well have been intended for the eyes of his keepers, who no doubt also had occasion to peruse the satirical diatribe against the Madhouse in Clare's "Don Juan" as well as the spiritual meditations of his "Child Harold." Although he had been meeting "with some gipseys one of whom offered to assist in my escape from the madhouse," Clare was careful not to reveal the plan in his notebook. But he did leave a broad hint in the small High Beech notebook, when he drafted a letter to "My Dearest Mary": "This Will Be My Last Letter To You Or Any One Else—Let My Stay In Prison Be As Long Or As Short As It May" (*Letters* 293). Five nights before his escape, he inserted into his "Child Harold" the lines "Written in a Thunder storm July 15th 1841":

> My soul is apathy—a ruin vast
> Time cannot clear the ruined mass away
> My life is hell—the hopeless die is cast
> And manhoods prime is premature decay
>
> Roll on ye wrath of thunders—peal on peal
> Till worlds are ruins and myself alone
> Melt heart and soul cased in obdurate steel
> Till I can feel that nature is my throne
>
> . . . .
> Smile on ye elements of earth and sky
> Or frown in thunders as ye frown on me
> Bid earth and its delusions pass away
> But leave the mind as its creator free
>   (221–28; 233–36)

It would be clutching at straws to relate Clare's language to specific passages from Byron; nevertheless, his rhetoric and rhythms are not without Byronic resonance. While Grigson had more ample warrant to see in "Maid of Walkherd" Clare's indigenous version of Byron's "Maid of Athens" (Grigson 9), the opening line of "Written in a Thunder storm" echoes the agony of the mad Saul in "My Soul is Dark," and the apostrophe to the "wrath of thunders" celebrates the power of the elements much in the manner of Byron's Childe Harold when looking down upon the sea from Alban Mount: "Roll on, thou deep and dark blue Ocean— roll!" (stanza 4, line 174). And the final quatrain anticipates the ultimate liberty of mind in terms similar to Childe Harold's when he imagines that moment "when, at length the mind shall be all free / From what it hates in this degraded form" (stanza 3, line 74).

In his asylum poetry, Clare sings of an anguish which has long fermented in his bouts of dark depression: "My Mind Is Dark and Fathomless And Wears / The Hues Of Hopeless Agony" (1011–12). Byron's heroic personae—the exile, the outlaw, the madman—have been seen as projections of the poet's own troubled mind. Byron may have empathically identified with the madman in his cell in "Prisoner of Chillon" or "Lament of Tasso," but the experience was never his own. Clare's "Child Harold" speaks of real confinement, not imaginary, when he cries out, "I'm not an outlaw in this midnight deep" (266), and laments that in his imprisonment, "Day seems my night and night seems blackest hell" (272).

Clare did not think that he was Byron in residence at Epping Forrest, but he may well have enjoyed the ruse to baffle his madhouse attendants.[6] In "Don Juan" he dons and doffs his Byronic identity with the alacrity of Charles Mathews in one of his "polymonologues." "Now this day is the eleventh of July / And being sunday I will seek no flaw / In man or woman," he declares a the beginning of stanza 29. Satire is unsuited for the sabbath, and all modes of irony and humor are unsuited for the madhouse. Because his keepers have no sense of humor, he declares that "In a madhouse I can find no mirth pay." The odd phrasing of "mirth pay" serves to call forth the rhyming line: "—Next Tuesday used to be Lord Byron's birthday." The rhyme is forced, the date is wrong. Wrong, at least, from one mode of reckoning. "Next Tuesday," July 13, was Clare's birthday.

So there is one Byron, a historical figure who happened to be born on January 22, and whose funeral procession Clare had witnessed in London. And there is another Byron, who persists in dispelling lies through his poetry. And yet another Byron, among the fools "still in Allens madhouse caged and living":

> Lord Byron poh—the man wot rites the werses
> And is just what he is and nothing more
> Who with his pen lies like the mist disperses
> And makes all nothing as it was before
> Who wed two wives and oft the truth rehearses
> And might have had some twenty thousand more
> Who has been dead so fools their lies are giving
> And still in Allens madhouse caged and living
> ("Don Juan," 263–70)

In the notoriety of Byron, Clare saw justification of his own troubled lot. Byron, like Clare, had been pampered then rejected by the fickle society

6. When Cyril Redding visited Clare in May 1841, he found him lucid and "communicative." The only sign of "mental eccentricity," Redding reported, was his mention of an engagement as a prize-fighter, which was "brought in abruptly, and abandoned with equal suddenness" (Storey, *Critical Heritage*, 248) Later, at Northampton, February 1847, Clare told his visitors that Byron had written a lengthy review of *Poems Descriptive of Rural Life* (it had been reviewed by Octavius Gilchrist). By 1850, according to the account of G. J. de Wilde, Clare was quoting from *Childe Harold* and Shakespeare passages which he declared to be his own (Grigson 35, 42–43; Storey, *Critical Heritage*, 266).

of London. Eliza Emmerson and Lord Radstock had sought to squelch Clare's satirical voice. Byron defied the disapproval of the Regency and wielded his pen as weapon against hypocrisy and corruption. Byron, too, had "wed two wives . . . / And might have had some twenty thousand more." Embalmed in spirits the body of Byron had been brought back from Greece. As the coffin was carried from the London Docks through Oxford Street, Clare had watched in awe. Not the death of the poet, but the adulation of the onlookers is what most impressed Clare: "A young girl that stood beside me gave a deep sigh & uttered 'Poor Lord Byron' I looked up at the young girl's face it was dark & beautiful & I could almost feel in love with her for the sigh she had uttered" (Autobiography, July 1824, in *Prose* 99).

Clare respected Byron's reputation and poetic accomplishment, yet he knew he was no Byron. He could, however, adapt a Byronic pose to his own homely manner. The rhetorical flourishes of the exiled aristocrat, the noble outlaw, were too bold to be absorbed with ease into Clare's native idiom. Rather than abandoning or suppressing the Wordsworthian strain that had come into his poetry in the 1820s, Clare returned in his asylum poetry to the Wordsworthian strategies of recollecting the exuberant self of the past and mocking the myopic self of the present. In his Journal, Clare described a conversation with "a sensible & well informed man" who "talkd much of the poets but did not like Wordsworth": "When I told him I did he instantly asked me wether I did not like Byron better I don't like these comparisons to knock your opinions on the head when I told him I read Wordsworth oftener than I did Byron & he seemd to express his surprise at it by observing that he could not read Wordsworth at all" (Journal, 3 April 1825, in *Prose* 142). He was fascinated by the grand manner of Byron, but Wordsworth was a poet whom he could read and re-read. Clare confessed that he had originally resisted the efforts of Drury and Hessey to push him into a Wordsworthian mode. To his surprise, once he began to explore Wordsworth's poetry he found himself enthralled:

> Read some poems of Wordsworth his 'Lucy Gray' or Solitude 'The Pet Lamb' 'We Are Seven' the Oak & Broom 'the Eglantine & the Fountain' Two April Mornings are some of my favorites When I first began to read poetry I dislikd Wordsworth because I heard he was dislikd & I was astonishd when I lookd into him to find my mistaken pleasure in being delighted & finding him so natural & beautiful in his 'White Doe of Rylstone' there is some of the sweetest poetry I ever met with tho full of his mysteries. (Journal, 29 October 1824, in *Prose*, 118)

A Wordsworthian communion with nature was never as important to Clare as the simpler modes of observation and description. In the asylum, however, Wordsworthian evocations of childhood memories become increasingly important. His "Child Harold" often pauses to reaffirm the mind's capacity to revisit scenes from the otherwise inaccessible landscape of the past:

> Dull must that being live who sees unmoved
> The scenes and objects that his childhood knew
> The school yard and the maid he early loved
> The sunny wall where long the old Elms grew
> The grass that e'en till noon retains the dew
> Beneath the wallnut shade I see them still
> Though not such fancy's do I now pursue
> Yet still the picture turns my bosom chill
> And leaves a void—nor love nor hope may fill
>   (603–11)

When Byron calls upon memories of the past, his purpose is show how past joys have been blighted. The pattern, as in *Hours of Idleness* or the first two cantos of *Childe Harold*, is to conjure a memory even in the declared act of abjuring it. Recollections of the past, for Byron, are strangely imageless, dominated by feelings rather than perceptions. The painful opposition of joy and loss prompts the Byronic hero to call for oblivion and forgetfulness. Clare, tempering the Byronic tensions with Wordsworthian tranquillity, continues to cherish images of the past even if they ultimately leave him all the more forlorn in a bleak and hopeless present.

> After long abscence how the mind recalls
> Pleasing associations of the past
> Haunts of his youth—thorn hedges and old walls
> And hollow trees that sheltered from the blast
> And all that map of boyhood overcast
> With glooms and wrongs and sorrows not his own
> That oer his brow like the scathed lightning past
> That turned his spring to winter and alone
> Wrecked name and fame and all—to solitude unknown
>   (612–20)

While such "associations of the past" in "Child Harold" turn from the Byronic to the Wordsworthian, Clare's rapt attention to nature remains as selflessly unWordsworthian as it had been in *Poems Descriptive of Rural Life and Scenery* (1820) and *The Village Minstrel* (1821).

> The blackbird startles from the homestead hedge
> Raindrops and leaves fall yellow as he springs
> Such images are natures sweetest pledge
> To me there's music in his rustling wings
> 'Prink prink' he cries and loud the robin sings
> The small hawk like a shot drops from the sky
> Close to my feet for mice and creeping things
> Then swift as thought again he suthers bye
> And hides among the clouds from the pursuing eye
> (770–78)

In his solitary walks around the asylum grounds, he is still alert to the sights and sounds of nature. If this lonely stance, as observer rather than as participant, is Wordsworthian, it is a Wordsworth in anguish over his own sense of isolation and numbness: "The things which I have seen I now can see no more" ("Intimations of Immortality," 9). As Clare put it, "nature to me seems dead & her very pulse seems frozen to an icicle in the summer sun" (letter to "My Dear Wife Mary," 1841).

Isolation and estrangement were conditions that Clare, from the time he wrote his first poems, found inescapable. "I always felt anxiety to control my scribbling," Clare said of the necessary stealth, "& woud as leave have confessed to be a robber as a rhymer." A would-be poet could expect no sympathy or encouragement, only envy and hostility. His illiterate fellow laborers hated him for his learning, and his employers condemned him as a lazy shirker or as a pretentious upstart (*Prose* 30–33, 48, 60, 62, 66–67). Even Drury, who claimed to have "discovered" Clare's talent, did not hesitate in his letter to Taylor to mention his lethargy and his affectations (Storey, *Critical Introduction*, 3). It was Clare's folly, according to many of his contemporaries, to struggle against his place in society, to oppose the labors proper to his class. Much the same judgment was recorded on the medical papers consigning Clare, five months after his escape from Epping Forest, to the General Lunatic Hospital in Northampton. His employment, the doctors recorded, was gardening, and his present mental condition was attributed to "years of Poetical prosing" (Grigson 22).

Robert Southey, in *Our Uneducated Poets* (1831), sought to put a kinder light on the poetic efforts of those among the lower classes. But his kindness is condescending, a smug and patronizing *noblesse oblige*:

> When we are told that the thresher [Stephen Duck], the milkwo-
> man [Ann Yearsley], and the tobacco-pipe-maker [John Frederick
> Bryant] did not deserve the patronage they found, —when it is laid
> down as a maxim of philosophical criticism that poetry ought
> never to be encouraged unless it is excellent in its kind, —that it is
> an art in which inferior execution is not to be tolerated, —a lux-
> ury, and must therefore be rejected unless it is of the very best, —
> such reasoning may be addressed with success to cockered and
> sickly intellect, but it will never impose upon a healthy under-
> standing, a generous spirit, or a good heart. (164)

What Southey expects of "a generous spirit" is a tolerance for "bad poetry," which "can do no harm, unless it passes for good, becomes fashion-
able, and so tends to deprave still further a vitiated public taste, and still
further to debase a corrupted language." He grants that "mediocres have
long been a numerous and increasing race," but he insists that it can be
no "offence against the public, to publish verses no one is obliged either
to purchase or to read." The benevolent motives of "a healthy understanding" in forwarding the cause of one of "our uneducated poets," is not
"the hope of rearing a great poet, but for the sake of placing a worthy
man in a station more suited to his intellectual endowment, than that in
which he was born" (165–66). The class system remains intact. The aspir-
ing poet, thus co-opted by the benevolent establishment, is allowed to
ascend a rung or two up the ladder of privilege.

Arrogance disguised as patronage was not new to Clare. In a letter to
Taylor, he expressed his anger: "Mr Southey seems to hold uneducated
poets in very little estimation & talks about the march of mind in a sneer-
ing way—as to education it aids very little in bringing forth that which is
called poetry—& if it means [a] humble station in life is to be the tolera-
tion for people to praise him I should say much admiration is worth but
little" (7 March 1831). Those who enjoyed the advantages of education
and who deigned to admire his works, Clare learned early in his career,
were seldom to be trusted. His letters and journal record many false
promises. Worse, a patron could assume the right to dictate and to censor what the poet should write. Lord Radstock felt particularly incensed
that Clare should rail against the poor conditions of field laborers. Why,
the world might think that there was such exploitation on his own estates! Eliza Emmerson is called upon to bring Clare to his senses. He must
"expunge certain highly objectionable passages":

> Passages, wherein, his then depressed state hurried him not only
> into error, but into the most flagrant acts of injustice; by accusing

those of pride, cruelty, vices, and ill-directed passions—who, are
the very persons, by whose truly generous and noble exertions he
had been raised from misery and despondency. . . . It has been my
anxious desire of late, to establish our poets character, as that, of
an honest and upright man—as a man feeling the strongest sense
of gratitude for the encouragement he has received—but how is it
possible I can continue to do this if he suffers another Edition of
his poems to appear with those vile, unjust, and now would be
ungrateful passages in them? —no, he must cut them out . . . he
must give me unquestionable *proofs*, of being that man I would
have him to be—he *must expunge*! (11 May 1820, in Storey, *Critical
Heritage*, 61)

Eliza Emmerson thus reports the benefactors command, and she adds her
own request that he remove the "*Radical* and *ungrateful* sentiments" from
his poetry (she has marked the passages for him). Lord Radstock had his
way. Grudgingly, Clare informed Taylor that he must "leave out the 8
lines in 'Helpstone' beginning 'Accursed wealth' and two under 'when
ease and plenty'—and one in 'Dawning of Genius' 'That necessary tool'
leave it out and put ***** to fill up the blank this will let em see I do it as
negligent as possible D—n that canting way of being for to please I say—I
cant abide it and one day or other I will show my Independence more
strongly than ever" (16 May 1820). When the new edition was brought
out, Clare was angry to find that Taylor had taken even further liberties in
rendering the poetry acceptable. He wrote to Hessey, in whom he thought
he had an ally:

I have seen the third Edition I am cursed mad about it the Judgement of T. is a button hole lower in my opinion—it is good—but
too subject to be tainted by medlars *false delicasy* damn it I hate it
beyond everything those frumpt up misses brought up in those
seminaries of mysterious wickedness (Boarding Schools) what will
please em? why we well know—but while their heart and soul
loves to extravagance (what we dare not mention) false delicasy's
seriousness muscles up the mouth and condemns it. (July 1820)

Hessey wrote back to placate their "vexed" poet. The changes were made,
he insists, in the "firm conviction that your own Interest would be most
essentially served" (11 July 1820, in Storey, *Critical Heritage*, 63). Editors
were worse than patrons: the latter demanded "gratitude," the former enforced propriety. "Editors are troubled with nice amendings," Clare asserted, "& if Doctors were as fond of amputation as they are of altering &

correcting the world woud have nothing but cripples" (Journal, 30 April 1825, in *Prose* 146).

After his literary career had been effectively frustrated and stifled, Clare grew increasingly despondent. The editors and the doctors had indeed left him a cripple. His Byronic stance at the asylum in Epping Forest allowed him the only "Independence" and the only "honest" poetic voice that he could muster: the irony of an honest confession that he had capitulated to a world of deception.

> This life is made of lying and grimace
> This world is filled with whoring and decieving
> Hypocrisy ne'er masks an honest face
> Story's are told—but seeing is believing
> And I've seen much from which there's no retrieving
> I've seen deception take the place of truth
> I've seen knaves flourish—and the country grieving
> Lies was the current gospel in my youth
> And now a man—I'm further off from truth
>
> (526–34)

The truth that he had dared to tell was only a momentary light. It passed and the poet was left to a world of darkness and blighted hope.

> Fame blazed upon me like a comets glare
> Fame waned and left me like a fallen star
> Because I told the evil of what they are
>
> (426–28)

More than either Hölderlin or Nerval, Clare turns within the precincts of his hermit-crab text to shake his fist at the society that rejected and incarcerated him.

In spite of the profound and disturbing insights that emerge from the poetry of Hölderlin, Nerval, and Clare, their debilitating sickness progressively destroyed their creativity. Nerval's condition was brought about by ergotism; Hölderlin most probably suffered from schizophrenia; Clare, too, may have been a victim of schizophrenia, but the diagnosis of his case is less certain. Schizophrenia may be a more precise term than madness, but its symptoms and manifestations are various, as are its causes. Even after the rise of psychology as a science, the boundaries between idiosyncracy and insanity, neurosis and psychosis, have often been shifted and redefined. Although the relation between various mental aberrations and artistic creativity still seems uncertain, substantial progress has been made in the treatment of manic-depressive illness. Thomas Caramagno, in *The Flight of the Mind: Virginia Woolf's Art and Manic-Depressive Illness* (1992), argues that a Freudian diagnosis of Woolf's disorder as a neurosis subjected her to an onus of blame, as if the biological imbalance had been caused by some deliberate quirk in her personal character. The drug therapy currently available could have prevented the periods of dark suffering that plagued her career. The advent of psychiatric medicine, to be sure, has been accompanied by many false promises. What restores psychological equilibrium to one patient, may produce dangerous side effects in another and lead to chemical abuse in a third.

Nevertheless, the clinical research of Nancy Andreasen, Kay Redfield Jamison, and others has provided a much better understanding of the relationship between bipolar affective disorders and artistic creativity. In responding to the problems I have been addressing in this book, Dr. Nancy Andreasen emphasized the importance in recognizing the difference between schizophrenia and manic-depressive illness. "In general," she wrote, "schizophrenia is not very compatible with creativity, since people with this illness for some reason tend to deteriorate rather badly and in particular to lose volition, drive, and richness of thought. People with mania, on the other hand, tend to be very intact between episodes, and they are often very clever and interesting while in the midst of an episode" (letter to author, 23 November 1992).

The epigrams from Plato, Aristotle, and Seneca with which I opened my introduction come from an age that could not appeal to Freudian psychology and psychiatric medicine in formulating its concepts about the creative process. This does not mean that Seneca's declaration, "There is no genius without some touch of madness" (*De tranquillitate*), is without truth. It does mean, however, that we must be careful how we interpret references to "madness." It has often become a term leveled by authority against a voice of insurgency. Any assertion of the imaginary, as Luiz Costa Lima has argued, may be deemed a threat to the established order. Dryden hoists the banner of "Reason" on behalf of Charles II when he condemns the Earl of Shaftesbury in the well-known couplet from *Absalom and Achitophel*: "Great wits are sure to madness near allied, / And thin partitions do their bounds divide" (163–64). Franciscus Junius also writes on the side of "Reason" when he denounces Sir William Draper for the "vipers" that "dance through your letters in all the mazes of metaphorical confusion." These "vipers," Junius declares, "are the gloomy companions of a disturbed imagination; the melancholy madness of poetry, without the inspiration" (3 March 1769). Emily Dickinson, although she is ready to acknowledge her place on the wrong side of the partition, refers to "madness" in much the same in sense:

Much madness is divinest sense
To a discerning eye;
Much sense the starkest madness.
'Tis the majority
In this, as all, prevails.
Assent, and you are sane;
Demur, —you're straightway dangerous,
And handled with a chain.

(No. 435, *Poems*, 209)

The mad rhapsodist, at various moments in history, has been revered as a prophet, tolerated as harmless lunatic, condemned as dangerous conspirator. The age of Junius and Sir William Draper was also the age of William Cowper and Christopher Smart, poets whose madness was not merely conjured by antagonists but arose within their own being, an internal source of persecution and agony. The "viper thoughts" that Coleridge felt "coil around my mind" (*Dejection: An Ode*, 94), stifling the last efforts of creativity, are very different from those metaphorical "vipers" condemned by Junius. When Wordsworth fears that the poet will lose the "gladness" of youth and end his days in "despondency and madness" (*Resolution and Independence*, 48–49), he, too, refers to a real loss of vitality brought about by progressively enervating and enfeebling depression.

The dilemma of the mad rhapsodist results, in part, from the irrational wellings that accompany the creative process, whether or not the artist endeavors to reassert rational order. The very endeavor rationally to contain the irrational, as we observed in Chapter 5, results in an paradox of representation. The literary representation of madness is further confounded by the multiple meanings of madness. Shelley, who meant one thing by "madness" in *Julian and Maddalo*, clearly meant something very different when he asked, in *To a Skylark*, for the bird's gladness so that he, too, might sing forth in "harmonious madness" (stanza 21). "Madness" may mean liberation, yet it may also mean persecution. Whether Shelley is talking about the "madness" of Torquato Tasso's resistance to his exploitation and torment, the hallucinations of Laon or Cythna, or his own lyrical flight, the word "madness" retains in its manifold connotations Shelley's sense of opposition to the oppression of reason, an opposition that may end in agony or in freedom.

For Hölderlin, Nerval, and Clare, "madness" was by no means merely metaphorical or imaginary. It was an insidious invader of the mind and body that relentlessly destroyed the being that it conquered. Yet it also aroused its victim to a valiant struggle, and to a creative endeavor that, because of its intertextuality, unwinds a thread of reason as it wanders through the dark labyrinth of irrationality. It maintains its literary integrity as poetry of the interior realm of experience. While the poetry of irrationality may baffle literary critic and psychologist alike, it nevertheless exercises a powerful appeal precisely because the "unknown" is hauntingly familiar. The mad rhapsodist exposes a dark side of the mind that is as intimate as the shadows of our own repressed consciousness.

BIBLIOGRAPHY

Anonymous. Review: John Hanson, *Observations of Madness and Melancholy*, 2d ed. (London, 1809); J. Davis, *Pinel's Treatise on Insanity* (Sheffield, 1806); J. M. Cox, *Practical Observations on Insanity*, 2d ed. (London, 1806); Thomas Arnold, *On the Management of the Insane* (London, 1809); *Quarterly Review* 2, no. 3 (August 1809): 155–80.

Anonymous. Review: *Selections, Grave and Gay, from the Writings, published and unpublished by Thomas De Quincey*, 14 vols. (1854–60). *Quarterly Review* 110 (July 1861): 1–35.

Anonymous. "Rezension: Trauerspiele von C. F. Weiße." *Allgemeine deutsche Bibliothek* (1782): 136–37.

Abercrombie, John. *Inquiries concerning the Intellectual Powers, and the Investigation of Truth*. Edinburgh, 1830.

———. *Pathological and Practical Researches on Diseases of the Brain and Spinal Cord*. Edinburgh, 1830.

———. "Spectral Illusions." *Edinburgh Journal of Science*, n.s., 4, no. 4 (1831): 218–19; no. 6 (1831): 244; no. 7 (1831): 261.

Adams, Franklin Pierce, ed. *Innocent Merriment: An Anthology of Light Verse*. New York: McGraw-Hill, 1942.

Addison, Joseph. *The Works of the Right Honorable Joseph Addison, with notes by Richard Hurd, D.D.* 6 vols. London, 1856.

Ainsworth, G. C. *Introduction to the History of Medical and Veterinary Mycology*. Cambridge: Cambridge University Press, 1986.

Akerly, Samuel. "Account of the Ergot or Spurred Rye as employed in Certain Cases of difficult Parturition." *Medical Repository*, 2d hexad (New York, 1809), 6:341–47.

Allen, Matthew. *Cases of Insanity, with medical, moral, and philosophical observations*. London, 1831. .

———. *Essay on the Classification of the Insane*. London, 1837.

Allen versus Dutton. Published at the request of the friends of Dr Allen. London, 1833.

Andreasen, Nancy, J.C. "Creativity and Mental Illness: Prevalence Rates in Writers and Their First-Degree Relatives." *American Journal of Psychiatry* 144 (October 1987): 1288–92.

———. "Creativity and Psychiatric Illness." *Psychiatric Annals* 8 (March 1978): 113–19.

———. "Mood Disorders and Creativity." *Creative Psychiatry* 13 (1977): 1–27.

Andreasen, Nancy, J.C., and Arthur Center. "The Creative Writer: Psychiatric Symptoms and Family History." *Comprehensive Psychiatry* 15 (March/April 1974): 123–31.

Andreasen, Nancy, J.C., and Ira D. Glick. "Bipolar Affective Disorder and Creativity: Implications and Clinical Management." *Comprehensive Psychiatry* 29 (1988): 207–17.

Andreasen, Nancy, J.C., and Pauline S. Powers. "Creativity and Psychosis. An Examination of Conceptual Style." *Archive of General Psychiatry* 32 (January 1975): 70–73.

Aristotle. *The Basic Works of Aristotle*. Ed. Richard McKeon. New York: Random House, 1941.

———. *Problemata Physica*. Trans. and ed. Hellmut Flashar. Berlin, 1983.

———. *The Rhetoric of Aristotle*. Ed. Lane Cooper. New York: Appleton, Century, Crofts, 1932.

Arnim, Achim von. *Achim von Arnim und die ihm nahe standen*, 3 vols. Ed. Reinhold Steig and Herman Grimm. Stuttgart and Berlin: Cotta, 1894–1913; rpt. Bern: Herbert Lang, 1970.

———. "Aesthetische Ausflüge mit Hölderlin." Freies Deutsches Hochstift mss 7212, 20128.

———. *Arnims Briefe an Savigny, 1803–1831, mit weiteren Quellen als Anhang*. Ed. Heinz Härtl. Weimar: Herman Böhlaus Nachfolger, 1982.

———. "Ausflüge mit Hölderlin." *Berliner Conversationsblatt* 2, nos. 31–35 (1828). In Arnim, *Werke*, 6:862–68.

———. "Autobiographische Auszeichnungen." Goethe- und Schiller-Archiv Weimar. Arnim-Nachlaß 226, U8 and U11. In Streller, "Achim von Arnim und das Drama," 110–12.

———. "David der Prediger und Spinner." *Die Wünschelruthe*, 22–25 June 1818, 197–98, 201–2. In Arnim, *Werke*, 6:622–25.

———. "Hölderlins Gedichte." Goethe- und Schiller-Archiv Weimar. Arnim-Nachlaß 452.

———. "Literatur-Notizen." *Der Gesellschafter oder Blätter für Geist und Herz* 2, no. 199 (1818). In Arnim, *Werke*, 6:636–40.

———. *Sämtliche Romane und Erzählungen*. 3 vols. Ed. Walther Migge. Munich: Carl Hanser, 1963–65.

———. "Taschenbuch." Freies Deutsches Hochstift, Frankfurt. Manuscript B44.

———. "Theoretische Untersuchung." In *Achim von Arnim und die ihm nahe-standen*, 3:242–44.

———. "Über Jungs Geisterkunde." *Der Gesellschafter, oder Blätter für Geist und Herz*, ed. F. W. Gubitz, 13–16 June 1817, 385–86, 389–91, 394–95. In Arnim, *Werke*, 6:535–46.

———. [Die Verteidigung der dänischen Regierung.] *Rheinischer Merkur*, 23 March 1815. In Arnim, *Werke*, 6:490–92.

———. "Vorrede zum Stoff des Empedokles." Manuscript 1826? Goethe- und Schiller Archivs Weimar. Arnim-Nachlaß 92, U12.

———. *Werke*. 6 vols. Ed. Roswitha Burwick, Jürgen Knaack, Paul Michael Lützeler, Renate Moering, Ulfert Ricklefs, and Hermann Weiss. Munich: Deutsche Klassiker Verlag, 1989–92.

Arnim, Achim von, and Clemens Brentano, eds. *Zeitung für Ensiedler*. Heidelberg: Mohr & Zimmer, 1808. Facsimile reprint, ed. Hans Jessen. Darmstadt: Wissenschaftliche Buchgesellschaft, 1962.

Arnim, Bettina von. *Die Günderode*, Leipzig: Insel Verlag, 1980.

Ashley, William James. *The Bread of our Forefathers. An Enquiry in Economic History*. Oxford: Clarendon Press, 1928.

Backman, E. Louis. *Religious Dances in the Church and Popular Medicine*. London: Allen & Unwin, 1952.

Bacquias, Eugène. *Recherches historiques et nosologiques sur les maladies désignées sous les noms feu sacré, feu Saint Antoine, mal des ardents*. Troyes, 1865.

Baeumler, Alfred. *Das Irrationalitätsproblem in der Ästhetik des 18. Jahrhunderts bis zur Kritik der Urteilskraft*. Darmstadt: Wissenschaftliche Buchgesellschaft, 1967.

———. *Das Irrationalitätsproblem in der Ästhetik und Logik des 18. Jahrhunderts bis zur Kritik der Urteilskraft*. Halle, 1923. 2d ed. Darmstadt: Wissenschaftliche Buchgesellschaft, 1967.

Baillie, Joanna. *A Series of Plays: in which it is attempted to delineate the stronger passions of the mind, each passion being the subject of a tragedy and a comedy*. 3 vols. London, 1802–12.

Baillie, Matthew. *The Morbid Anatomy of some of the most important Parts of the Human Body*. London, 1793. 2d ed. 1797.

Barger, George. *Ergot and Ergotism*. London: Gurney & Jackson, 1931.

Barrell, John. *The Idea of Landscape and the Sense of Place, 1730–1840. An Approach to the Poetry of John Clare*. Cambridge: Cambridge University Press, 1972.

Barth, J. Robert, S.J. *Coleridge and Christian Doctrine*. Cambridge: Harvard University Press, 1969. Revised ed. New York: Fordham University Press, 1987.

———. *The Symbolic Imagination. Coleridge and the Romantic Tradition*. Princeton: Princeton University Press, 1977.

Baudelaire, Charles. *Oeuvres complètes*. 2 vols. Ed. Claude Pichois. Bibliothèque de la Pléiade. Paris: Gallimard, 1975–76.

Bauer, F. "On the Ergot of Rye." *Transactions of the Linnean Society* 18 (1841): 475–82.

Baum, P. E. "The Young Man Betrothed to a Statue." *PMLA* 34 (1919): 523–29.

Baumgarten, Alexander Gottlieb. *Aesthetica*. Frankfurt, 1750. Reprint, Hildesheim: Georg Olms Verlag, 1961.

Beattie, James. *An Essay on the Nature and Immutability of Truth* (1770). 2d ed., corrected and enlarged. Edinburgh, 1771.

Bechterew, W. von. "Über neuro-psychische Störungen bei chronischem Ergotismus." *Neurologisches Centralblatt. Originalmittheilungen* 11 (1892): 769–75.

Beddoes, Thomas. *Observations on the Nature of Demonstrative Evidence . . . together with . . . other Subjects of Physiology and Pathology*. London, 1793.

Behler, Ernst. "Schellings Ästhetik in der Überlieferung von Henry Crabb Robinson." *Philosophisches Jahrbuch* 83 (1976): 133–83.

Belavel, Yvon. *L'Esthétique sans Paradoxe de Diderot*. Paris: Gallimard, 1950.

Bennett, Curtis. *God Is Dead! The Gods Return. An English Version of "Les Chimères" of Gérard de Nerval*. Special Studies, no. 44. Buffalo: Council on International Studies, State University of New York at Buffalo, 1973.

Berkeley, George. *Works*. 4 vols. Ed. Alexander Campbell Fraser. Oxford: Clarendon Press, 1871.

Bertaux, Pierre. *Friedrich Hölderlin*. Frankfurt: Suhrkamp, 1978.

Beys, Charles. *Les Illustres Fous*. Ed. Merle I. Protzman. The Johns Hopkins Studies in Romance Literatures and Languages, 42. Baltimore: Johns Hopkins University Press, 1942.

Blake, William. *The Complete Poetry and Prose of William Blake*. Ed. David Erdman, commentary by Harold Bloom. Revised ed. Berkeley and Los Angeles: University of California Press, 1982.

———. *The Illuminated Blake*. Ed. David Erdman. Garden City, N.Y.: Anchor Books, 1974.

Bollacher, Martin. *Der junge Goethe und Spinoza. Studien zur Geschichte des Spinozismus in der Epoche des Sturms und Drangs*. Tübingen, 1969.

Bones, J. "Extract of letter from the Rev. J. Bones, M.A., minister of Wattisham, near Stowmarket in Suffolk, to George Baker, M.D., F.R.S, relating to the case of mortification of limbs in a family there," and "Extract of a second letter from the Rev. Mr. Bones to Dr. Baker," *Philosophical Transactions of the Royal Society* 52 (1762): 526–29, 529–33.

Bordot, Louis. *Nouvelles recherches sur l'emploi du seigle ergoté comme propre à faciliter et accélérer l'accouchement, suivies de quelques observations*. Paris, 1826.

Borges, Jorge Luis. *Inquisiciones*. Buenos Aires: Editoral Proa, 1925.

Böschenstein, Bernhard. "Hölderlins späteste Gedichte." *Hölderlin-Jahrbuch* 14 (1965–66): 35–56.

Böttger, Fritz. *Bettina von Arnim. Ein Leben zwischen Tag und Traum*. Berlin: Verlag der Nation, 1986.

Bové, F. J. *The Story of Ergot*. Basel: S. Karger, 1970.

Brackman, E. Louis. *Religious Dances in the Christian Church and Popular Medicine*. London: Allen & Unwin, 1952.

Brand, C. P. *Torquato Tasso: A Study of the Poet and His Contribution to English Literature*. London: Cambridge University Press, 1965.

Bremner, Geoffrey. *Order and Change. The Pattern of Diderot's Thought*. Cambridge: Cambridge University Press, 1983.

Brentano, Clemens. *Werke*. 4 vols. Ed. Wolfgang Frühwald, Bernhard Gajek, and Friedhelm Kemp. Munich: Hanser, 1968.

Brewster, Sir. David. *Letters on Natural Magic, Addressed to Sir Walter Scott*. London: John Murray, 1832.

Brose, Karl. "Jean Pauls Verhältnis zu Fichte. Ein Beitrag zur Geistesgeschichte." *Deutsche Vierteljahres Schrift* 49 (1975): 66–93.

Büchner, Georg. *Sämtliche Werke und Briefe*. 4 vols. Ed. Werner Lehmann. Hamburg: Christian Wegner, 1967–75.

Buck, August. "Über einige Deutungen des Prometheus-Mythos in der Literatur der Renaissance." In *Romanica. Festschrift für Gerhard Rohlfs*, ed. H. Lausberg and H. Weinrich. Halle, Gesellschafts- und Sprachwissenschaftliche Reihe, Martin-Luther Universität, 1958.

Buckley, Michael J., S.J. *At the Origins of Modern Atheism*. New Haven: Yale University Press, 1987.

Burnet, Thomas. *Archaeologiae philosophicae, sive Doctrina antiqua de rerum originibus*. 2 vols. London, 1692.

Burton, Robert. *Anatomy of Melancholy*. Ed. Floyd Dell and Paul Jordan-Smith. New York: Tudor, 1938.

Burwick, Frederick. *Damnation of Newton: Goethe's Color Theory and Romantic Perception*. Berlin and New York: De Gruyter, 1986.

———. "The Dream-Visions of Jean Paul and Thomas De Quincey." *Comparative Literature* 20 (Winter 1968): 1–26.

———. "Elektrizität und Optik: Zu den Beziehungen zwischen wissenschaftlichen und literarischen Schriften Achim von Arnims." *Aurora* 46 (1986): 19–47.

———. *The Haunted Eye: Perception and the Grotesque in English and German Romanticism*. Heidelberg: Carl Winter, 1987.

———. "Kant and Hegel: Organicism and Language Theory." In *Approaches to Organic Form*. Boston Studies in the Philosophy of Science. Dordrecht: D. Reidel, 1987.

———. "The Language of Causality in *Prometheus Unbound*." *Keats-Shelley Journal* 31 (1982): 136–58.

———. Review: "Tobin Siebers, *The Romantic Fantastic*." *Romanticism Past and Present* 10 (Summer 1986): 71–76.

Burwick, Roswitha. "Achim von Arnims Ästhetik. Die Wechselwirkung von Kunst und Wissenschaft, Poesie und Leben, Dichtung und Malerie." In *Neue Tendenzen der Arnimforschung*, ed. Roswitha Burwick and Berndt Fischer. Bern: Peter Lang, 1990.

———. *Dichtung und Malerie bei Achim von Arnim*. Berlin: De Gruyter, 1989.

———. "Exzerpte Achim von Arnim zu unveröffentlichten Briefen." *Jahrbuch des Freien Deutschen Hochstifts* (1978): 298–395.

Butler, Marilyn. *Peacock Displayed. A Satirist in his Context*. London: Routledge & Kegan Paul, 1979.

Butlin, Martin. *The Paintings and Drawings of William Blake*. 2 vols. New Haven: Yale University Press, 1981.

Bynum, W. F., Roy Porter, and Michael Shepherd, eds. *The Anatomy of Madness*. 2 vols. London: Tavistock, 1985.

Byron, George Gordon, Lord. *Byron's Letters and Journals*. 12 vols. Ed. Leslie A. Marchand. Cambridge: Belknap Press of the Harvard University Press, 1973–82. Supplementary Volume. Newark: University of Delaware Press, 1994.

———. *Poetical Works*. London: Oxford University Press, 1904.

Campbell, George. *Dissertation on Miracles* (1762). Reprinted in *Lectures on Ecclesiastical History*. Philadelphia, 1807.

Caramagno, Thomas. *The Flight of the Mind: Virginia Woolf's Art and Manic-Depressive Illness*. With an afterword by Kay Redfield Jamison. Berkeley and Los Angeles: University of California Press, 1992.

Cassirer, Ernst. *Individuum und Kosmos in der Philosophie der Renaissance*. Berlin, 1927. Reprint, Darmstadt: Wissenschaftliches Buchgesellschaft, 1977.

Castel, Robert. *The Regulation of Madness: The Origins of Incarceration in France*. Trans. W. D. Halls. Berkeley and Los Angeles: University of California Press, 1988.

Cicero. *De senectute, De amicitia, De divinatione*. Loeb Classical Library, 1923. Reprint, 1971.

Clairon, Claire-Joseph. *Mémoires d'Hippolyte Clairon*. Paris, 1799.

Clare, John. *John Clare*. Ed. Eric Robinson and David Powell. Oxford: Oxford University Press, 1984.

———. *The Letters of John Clare*. Ed. J. W. Tibble and Anne Tibble. London: Routledge & Kegan Paul, 1951.

———. *The Natural History Prose Writings of John Clare* (= *NH*). Ed. Margaret Grainger. Oxford: Clarendon Press, 1983.

———. *The Poems of John Clare*. 2 vols. Ed. J. W. Tibble and Anne Tibble. London: Routledge & Kegan Paul, 1935.

———. *The Prose of John Clare*. Ed. J. W. Tibble and Anne Tibble. London: Routledge & Kegan Paul, 1951.

———. *Sketches in the Life of John Clare, Written by Himself*. Ed. Edmund Blunden. London: Cobden-Sanderson, 1931.

Coleridge, Samuel Taylor. *Aids to Reflection* (= *AR*). Ed. Derwent Coleridge. 7th ed. London, 1854.

———. *Biographia Literaria* (= *BL*). 2 vols. Ed. James Engell and Walter Jackson Bate. In *The Collected Works of Samuel Taylor Coleridge*, vol. 7, ed. Kathleen Coburn and Bart Winer. Bollingen Series 75. Princeton: Princeton University Press; London: Routledge & Kegan Paul, 1983.

———. *Biographia Literaria*. 2 vols. Ed. J. Shawcross. London: Oxford University Press, 1907.

———. *Coleridge on the Seventeenth Century*. Ed. Roberta Brinkley. Durham: Duke University Press, 1953.

———. *Collected Letters of Samuel Taylor Coleridge* (= *CL*). 6 vols. Ed. Earl Leslie Griggs. Oxford: Clarendon Press, 1956–71.

———. *The Complete Poetical Works of Samuel Taylor Coleridge*. 2 vols. Ed. Ernest Hartley Coleridge. Oxford: Clarendon Press, 1912.

———. *Complete Works*. 7 vols. Ed. W.G.T. Shedd. New York: Harper & Brothers, 1853–58.

———. *Confessions of an Inquiring Spirit*. Ed. H. St. J. Hart. Stanford: Stanford University Press, 1957.

———. *The Friend*. 2 vols. Ed. Barbara Rooke. In *The Collected Works of Samuel Taylor Coleridge*, vol. 4. Princeton: Princeton University Press; London: Routledge & Kegan Paul, 1969.

———. *Lay Sermons* (= *LS*). Ed. R. J. White. In *The Collected Works of Samuel Taylor Coleridge*, vol. 6. Princeton: Princeton University Press; London: Routledge & Kegan Paul, 1972.

———. *Lectures 1808–1819: On Literature* (= *LL*). 2 vols. Ed. Reginald A. Foakes. In *The Collected Works of Samuel Taylor Coleridge*, vol. 5. Princeton: Princeton University Press; London: Routledge & Kegan Paul, 1987.

———. *Lectures 1795: On Politics and Religion*. Ed. Lewis Patton and Peter Mann. In *The Collected Works of Samuel Taylor Coleridge*, vol. 1. Princeton: Princeton University Press; London: Routledge & Kegan Paul, 1971.

———. *Letters, Conversations and Recollections of S. T. Coleridge*. 2 vols. Ed. Thomas Allsop. London: Edward Moxon, 1836.

———. *Logic*. Ed. J. R. de J. Jackson. In *The Collected Works of Samuel Taylor Coleridge*, vol. 13. Princeton: Princeton University Press; London: Routledge & Kegan Paul, 1981.

———. *Marginalia* (= *M*). 2 vols. Ed. George Whalley. In *The Collected Works of Samuel Taylor Coleridge*, vol. 12. Princeton: Princeton University Press; London: Routledge & Kegan Paul, 1980–81.

———. "Memorandum on Miracles" (August 1807). British Museum Add Ms 34, 225 ff75–75DvU.

———. *The Notebooks of Samuel Taylor Coleridge* (= *CN*). 4 vols. of text and 4 vols. of notes. Ed. Kathleen Coburn. New York: Pantheon, 1957, 1961; Princeton: Princeton University Press, 1973, 1990.

———. *Philosophical Lectures of Samuel Taylor Coleridge, Hitherto Unpublished*. Ed. Kathleen Coburn. London: Pilot Press, 1949.

———. *Poems. Second Edition to Which are Now Added Poems by Charles Lamb and Charles Lloyd*. London, 1797.

———. *Table Talk*. Ed. Hartley N. Coleridge. London, 1894.

Coleridge, Samuel Taylor, and Robert Southey. *Omniana, or Horae Otiosiores*. 2 vols. London, 1812.

Colles, W. "Cases of Injurious Effects following the Use of Rye as Food." *Dublin Quarterly Journal of Medical Science* 4 (1847): 243.

Colley, Ann C. *Tennyson and Madness*. Athens: University of Georgia Press, 1983.

Costa Lima, Luiz. *O Fingidor e o Censor*. Rio de Janiero: Forense-Universitaria, 1988.

———. *Sociedade e Discurso Ficcional*. Rio de Janiero: Editora Guanabara, 1986.

Creuzer, Georg Friedrich. *Symbolik und Mythologie der alten Völker*. 4 vols. Heidelberg, 1810–12.

Curtius, Ernst Robert. *European Literature and the Latin Middle Ages*. Trans. Willard Trask. New York: Harper & Row, 1953.

Dante. *Divine Comedy*. Trans. with commentary by Charles S. Singleton. 2d ed. Princeton: Princeton University Press, 1977.

Darwin, Charles. *Expression of the Emotions*. London: John Murray, 1872.

Darwin, Erasmus. *The Botanic Garden: A Poem in Two Parts*. London, 1790.

———. *The Botanic Garden*, Part Two: "The Loves of the Plants." London: J. Johnson, 1789. Reprint, Oxford: Woodstock Books, 1991.

Davies, H. "On the Secale cornutum, Clavus or Ergot of Rye." *The London Medical and Physical Journal* 54 (1825): 1, 100.

Delatte, Armand. *Les conceptions de l'enthousiasme chez les philosophes présocratiques*. Paris: Société d'édition "Les Belles Lettres," 1934.

DePorte, Michael V. *Nightmares and Hobbyhorses. Swift, Sterne, and Augustan Ideas of Madness*. San Marino, Ca.: The Huntington Library, 1974.

De Quincey, Thomas. *The Collected Writings of Thomas De Quincey* (= *DQ*). 14 vols. Ed. David Masson. Edinburgh, 1889–90.

———. *Confessions of an English Opium-Eater and Other Writings*. Ed. Aileen Ward. New York: New American Library, 1966.

———. "'Let Him Come Down from the Cross,'" Wordsworth Library. Grasmere, England.

———. "On Miracles." Author's collection. Claremont, Calif.

———. *The Posthumous Works of Thomas De Quincey* (= *PW*). 2 vols. Ed. Alexander H. Japp. London, 1891.

Desgranges. "Sur la propriété qu'a le Seigle ergoté d'accélérer la marche de l'accouchement. et de hâter sa terminaison (extrait)." *Nouveau Journal de Médecine, Chirurgie, Pharmacie* 1 (1818): 54–61.

Dhaenens, Jacques. *Le destin d'Orphée, étude sur «El Desdichado» de Nerval*. Paris: Minard, 1973.

Dickinson, Emily. *The Poems of Emily Dickenson*. Ed. Thomas H. Johnsom. Cambridge: The Belknap Press of Harvard University Press, 1979.

Diderot, Denis. *Oeuvres Complètes* (= *OC*). 20 vols. Ed. J. Assézat and M. Tourneaux. Paris, 1875–77.

———. *Oeuvres esthétiques* (= *OE*). Ed. P. Vernièe. Paris: Garnier, 1959.

———. *Paradoxe sur le Comédien, avec recueilles et présentées sur l'art du Comédien*. Ed. Marc Blanquet. Paris: Librairie Théâtrale, 1958.

———. *The Paradox of Acting*, trans. Walter Herries Pollock (1883), and William Archer, *Masks or Faces? A Study in the Psychology of Acting* (1888). Introductory essay by Lee Strasberg, ed. Eric Bentley. New York, 1957.

————. *Salons*. 4 vols. Ed. Jean Seznec and Jean Adhémar. Oxford: Clarendon Press, 1957–67.

Dieckmann, Herbert. Review: Yvon Belaval, *L'Esthétique sans Paradoxe de Diderot*. *Romanic Review* 42 (1951): 63.

Digby, Anne. *Madness, Morality and Medicine. A Study of the York Retreat, 1796–1914*. Cambridge: Cambridge University Press, 1985.

Dilthey, Wilhelm. "Dichterische Einbildungskraft und Wahnsinn" (1886). In *Gesammelte Schriften*, vol. 6. Ed. Georg Misch. Leipzig and Berlin: B. G. Teubner, 1924.

Dobat, Klaus-Dieter. *Musik als romantische Illusion*. Tübingen: Niemeyer, 1984.

Dodd, C. H. *The Interpretation of the Fourth Gospel*. Cambridge: Cambridge University Press, 1953.

Dodds, E. R. *The Greeks and the Irrational*. Berkeley and Los Angeles: University of California Press, 1951.

Doerner, Klaus. *Madmen and the Bourgeoisie: A Social History of Insanity and Psychiatry*. Trans. Joachim Neugroschel and Jean Steinberg. Oxford: Basil Blackwell, 1981.

Donaldson, John William. *A Vindication of Protestant Principles*. London, 1847.

Du Camp, Maxime. *Souvenirs Littéraires*. 2 vols. Paris: Hachette, 1882–83.

Duff, William. *Critical Observations on the Writings of the Most Celebrated Geniuses in Poetry*. London, 1770.

————. *Essay on Original Genius; and its Various Modes of Exertion in Philosophy and the Fine Arts, particularly in Poetry*. London, 1767.

Dussinger, John A. "Madness and Lust in the Age of Sensibility." In *Sensibility in Transformation: Creative Resistance to Sentiment from the Augustans to the Romantics*, ed. Syndy McMillen Conger. Rutherford, NJ: Farleigh Dickinson University Press.

Eaton, Horace Ainsworth. *Thomas De Quincey, A Biography*. London: Oxford University Press, 1936.

Eckermann, Johann Peter. *Gespräche mit Goethe*. Ed. Fritz Bergemann. Wiesbaden: Insel Verlag, 1951.

Eichendorff, Josef von. *Werke*. 6 vols. Ed. Heinz Amelung. 2d edition. Berlin: Propyläen, 1920.

Erasmus, Desiderius. *Opera omnia*. 11 vols. Ed. Joannis Clericus. Leyden, 1703–6.

Eunapius. *Vitae Sophistarum* (A.D. 396). *The Lives, opinions, and remarkable sayings of the most ancient philosophers. Written in Greek by Diogenes Laertius, to which are added, the lives of several other philosophers, written by Eunapius of Sardis. Made English by several hands*. London, 1696.

Faurisson, Robert. *La Clé des "Chimères" et "Autres Chimères" de Nerval*. Paris: J.-J. Pauvert, 1977.

Fénelon, François de Salignac de la Mothe-. *Oeuvres complètes*. 10 vols. in 11. Paris: J. Leroux et Jouby, 1848–52.

Fichte, Johann Gottlieb. *Versuch einer Kritik aller Offenbarung*. 2d ed. Königsberg, 1793.

Ficino, Marsilio. *De vita triplici* (1482, 1489). Trans. and ed. Dieter Benesch. 2 vols. Frankfurt, 1977.

————. *Opera*. 2 vols. Basel, 1576.

————. *Theologia Platonica de immortalitate animorum duo de viginti libris, Marsilio Ficino Florentino, Philosopho sacerdote ac Medico, Graecè Latinesque doctissimo, authore comprehensa.* Paris, 1559. Facsimile reprint, Hildesheim: Georg Olms, 1975.

Field, M. "On the Origin of Ergot." *Annals of Philosophy* 29 (1826): 14–17.

Flew, Antony. *Hume's Philosophy of Belief.* London: Routledge & Kegan Paul, 1961.

Florilegus (Matthew of Westminster). *Flores historiarum* (1307). London, 1567. Trans. C. D. Yonge under the title *The Flowers of History.* London, 1847.

Fontenrose, Joseph Eddy. *Python: A Study of the Delphic Myth and Its Origins.* Berkeley and Los Angeles: University of California Press, 1959.

Foucault, Michel. *Madness and Civilization. A History of Insanity in the Age of Reason.* Trans. Richard Howard. New York: Vintage Books, 1988.

Friedrich, Otto. *Going Crazy: An Inquiry into Madness in Our Time.* New York: Simon & Schuster, 1976.

Fuller, John G. *The Day of St. Anthony's Fire.* New York: Macmillan, 1968.

Furst, Lilian R. *Fictions of Romantic Irony.* Cambridge: Harvard University Press, 1984.

Fuseli, Henry. *Lectures on Painting* (1801). London, 1833.

Gabbai, A., J. Lisbonne, and R. Pourquier. "Ergot Poisoning at Pont St. Esprit." *British Medical Journal* 2 (1951): 650–51.

Garrick, David. *Private Correspondence.* 2 vols. Ed. James Boaden. London, 1832.

Garrison, Fielding Hudson, ed. *An Introduction to the History of Medicine.* 4th ed. London and Philadelphia: W. B. Saunders, 1929.

Geninasca, Jacques. *Analyse structurale de "Chimères" de Nerval.* Neuchatel: La Baconnière, 1971.

Gerard, Alexander. *An Essay on Genius.* London and Edinburgh, 1774.

———. *An Essay on Taste. With Three Dissertations on the Same Subject, by Voltaire, D'Alembert, and Montesquieu.* 3d ed. London, 1780. Facsimile reprint, Gainesville, Fla.: Walter J. Hipple Jr., 1963.

Gilman, Sander L. *Disease and Representation: Images of Illness from Madness to Aids.* Ithaca: Cornell University Press, 1988.

Givry, Grillot de. *Witchcraft, Magic, and Alchemy.* Trans. J. Courtney Locke. New York: Dover, 1971.

Goethe, Johann Wolfgang von. *Collected Works.* 12 vols. New York: Suhrkamp Publishers, 1983–89.

———. *Werke.* 14 vols. Ed. Erich Trunz. Hamburg: Christian Wegner, 1948–78.

Goldstein, Jan. *Console and Classify. The French Psychiatric Profession in the Nineteenth Century.* Cambridge: Cambridge University Press, 1987.

Goodwin, Frederick, and Kay Redfield Jamison. *Manic-Depressive Illness.* London: Oxford University Press, 1990.

Gräf, Hans Gerhard. *Goethe über seine Dichtungen. Versuch einer Sammlung aller Äusserungen des Dichters über seine poetischen Werke.* 6 vols. Frankfurt: Rutten & Loening, 1908.

Grierson, Herbert, J.C. "Classical and Romantic." In *The Background of English Literature.* London: Chatto & Windus, 1925.

Grigson, Geoffrey, ed. *Poems of John Clare's Madness.* London: Routledge & Kegan Paul, 1949.

Guiguené, Pierre Louis. *Rapport sur les travaux de la classe d'histoire et de littérature Ancienne.* Paris, 1807.

Gurewitsch, M. J. "Über die Ergotinpsychose." *Zeitschrift für die gesammte Neurologie und Psychiatrie, Originalien* 5 (1911): 269–92.

Haeger, J. H. "Samuel Taylor Coleridge and the Romantic Background to Bergson."

In *Crisis in Modernism: Bergson and the Vitalist Controversy*, ed. Frederick Burwick and Paul Douglass. Cambridge: Cambridge University Press, 1992.

Haile, H. G. *Artist in Chrysalis: A Biographical Study of Goethe in Italy*. Urbana: University of Illinois Press, 1973.

Hamann, Johann Georg. *Briefwechsel*. 6 vols. Ed. W. Ziesemer and A. Henkel. Wiesbaden, 1955–75.

———. *Sämmtliche Werke*. 6 vols. Ed. Josef Nadler. Vienna: Verlag Herder, 1949–53.

Hamlin, Cyrus. "'Stimmen des Geschiks': The Hermeneutics of Unreadibility (Thoughts on Hölderlin's 'Griechenland')." In *Jenseits des Idealismus. Hölderlins letzte Homburger Jahre (1804–1806)*, ed. Christoph Jamme and Otto Pöggeler. Bonn: Bouvier Verlag, 1988.

Happel, Stephen. *Coleridge's Religious Imagination*. Salzburg: Salzburg Studies in English Literature, 1983.

Harding, Anthony. *Coleridge and the Inspired Word*. Kingston and Montreal: McGill-Queen's University Press, 1985.

Hartley, David. *Observations on Man, his Fame, his Duty, and his Expectations* (1749). 3 vols., with notes and additions by Herman Andrew Pistorius, trans. from the German edition (Rostock and Leipzig, 1772). London, 1801.

Hayter, Alethea. *Opium and the Romantic Imagination*. Berkeley and Los Angeles: University of California Press, 1968.

Hazlitt, William. *The Complete Works of William Hazlitt*. 24 vols. Ed. P. P. Howe. London: J. M. Dent & Sons, 1933. Reprint, London: Frank Cass, 1967.

Hecker, Jutta. "Das Symbol der Blauen Blume in Zusammenhang mit der Blumensymbolik der Romantik." *Jenaer Germanistische Forschungen* 17 (1931).

Heidegger, Martin. *Sein und Zeit*. Tübingen: Max Niemeyer, 1979.

Henslow, Rev. J. S. "Report on the Diseases of Wheat." *Journal of the Royal Agricultural Society* 2 (1841): 14–19.

Herder, Johann Gottfried. *Werke*. 33 vols. Ed. Bernard Suphan. Berlin: Wiedmann, 1877–1913. Reprint, Hildesheim: Georg Olms, 1967.

Hershman, D. Jablow, and Julien Lieb. *The Key to Genius: Manic-Depression and the Creative Life*. Buffalo, NY: Prometheus Press, 1988.

Hewitt, Regina. "Torquato Tasso—A Byronic Hero?" *Neophilologus* 7 (1987): 431–46.

Hibbert, Samuel. *Sketches of the Philosophy of Apparitions: or, An Attempt to trace such Illusions to their physical Causes*. Edinburgh, 1824.

Hiebel, Friedrich. "Zur Interpretation der Blauen Blumen des Novalis." *Monatshefte für den deutschen Unterricht* 43 (1951): 327–34.

Hobson, Marian. *The Object of Art. The Theory of Illusion in Eighteenth-Century France*. Cambridge: Cambridge University Press, 1982.

———. "Le 'Paradox sur le comédien' est un paradoxe." *Poétique* 15 (1973): 320–39.

Hodgson, John A. "Transcendental Tropes: Coleridge's Rhetoric of Allegory and Symbol." In *Allegory, Myth, and Symbol*, ed. Morton W. Bloomfield. Cambridge: Harvard University Press, 1981.

Hoffer, A., and H. Osmond. *The Hallucinogens*. New York: Academic Press, 1967.

Hoffmann, E.T.A. *Sämtliche Werke*. 15 vols. Ed. Eduard Grisebach. Leipzig: Max Hesses Verlag, 1905.

———. *Sämtliche Werke*. 5 vols. Ed. Walter Müller-Seidel, with notes by Wolfgang Kron and Wulf Segebrecht. Munich: Winkler, 1960–63.

———. *Selected Writings*. 2 vols. Ed. and trans. Leonard J. Kent and Elizabeth C. Knight. Chicago: University of Chicago Press, 1969.

Hoffmeyer, Johann Jacob. *D. Joh. Jacob Hoffmeyer's königl. Landphysici zu Oranienburg Send-Schreiben an einen vornehmen Geistlichen, von der bisher an viel Personen in seiner Gegend gefundenen Grübel- oder Krummen- und Schwere-Noths-Kranckheit, deren Ursach und Heilungs-Mitteln*. Berlin, 1742.

Hogg, James. *The Private Memoirs and Confessions of a Justified Sinner*. New York: W. W. Norton, 1970.

Hölderlin, Friedrich. *"Bevestigter Gesang." Die neu zu entdeckende hymnische Spätdichtung bis 1806*. Ed. Dietrich Uffhausen. Stuttgart: J. B. Metzler, 1989.

———. *Gedichte*. Ed. Gustav Schwab, Ludwig Uhland, and Justinus Kerner. Stuttgart and Tübingen: Cotta, 1826.

———. *Hymns and Fragments*. Trans. Richard Sieburth. Princeton: Princeton University Press, 1984.

———. *Poems and Fragments*. Trans. Michael Hamburger. Cambridge: Cambridge University Press, 1980.

———. *Sämtliche Werke*. 7 vols. Ed. Friedrich Beißner and Adolf Beck. Stuttgart: Kohlhammer, Cotta, 1943–77.

Holmes, Richard. *Footsteps: Adventures of a Romantic Biographer*. London: Hodder & Stoughton, 1985.

———. *Shelley, The Pursuit*. New York: Dutton, 1975.

Horace. *The Complete Works of Horace*. Ed. and trans. Charles E. Passage. New York: Frederick Ungar, 1983.

Howald, Ernst, ed. *Der Kampf um Creuzers Symbolik. Eine Auswahl von Dokumenten*. Tübingen: Mohr, 1926.

Hughes, Patrick, and George Brecht, eds. *Vicious Circles and Infinity. An Anthology of Paradoxes*. Harmondsworth, Middlesex: Penguin Books, 1978.

Hume, David. *An Enquiry Concerning Human Understanding* (1748). Ed. L. A. Selby-Bigge. Oxford: Clarendon Press, 1902.

———. *The Natural History of Religion* (1757). Ed. H. E. Root. Stanford: Stanford University Press, 1957.

———. *A Treatise of Human Nature* (1739). Ed. L. A. Selby-Bigge. 2d ed., revised by P. H. Nidditch. Oxford: Clarendon Press, 1978.

Hutchinson, Francis. *An Historical Essay concerning Witchcraft* (1718). Enlarged 2d ed. London, 1720.

———. *Historischer Versuch von der Hexerey*. Trans. Theodoro Arnold. Leipzig, 1726.

Inchbald, Elizabeth. *The British Theatre; or, A Collection of Plays, which are acted at the Theatres Royal, Drury Lane, Covent Garden, and Haymarket. Printed under the authority of the Managers from the Prompt Books. With Biographical and Critical Remarks*. 25 vols. London, 1808.

Jacobi, Friedrich Heinrich. *Über die Lehre des Spinoza*. 2d ed. Breslau, 1789.

Jakobson, Roman, and Morris Halle. *Fundamentals of Language*. The Hague: Mouton, 1956.

Jamison, Kay Redfield. "Mood Disorders and Patterns of Creativity in British Writers and Artists." *Psychiatry* 52 (1989): 125–34.

Jamme, Christoph. "'ein kranker oder gesunder Geist'? Berichte über Hölderlins Krankheit in den Jahren 1804–1806." In *Jenseits des Idealismus. Hölderlins letzte Homburger Jahre (1804–1806)*, ed. Christoph Jamme and Otto Pöggeler. Bonn: Bouvier Verlag, 1988.

Janin, Jules. *Critique portraits et caractéres contemporains.* Paris, 1841.

Jauß, Hans Robert. "Der dialogische und der dialektische *Neveu de Rameau* oder: Wie Diderot Sokrates und Hegel Diderot rezipierte." In *Das Gespräch. Poetik und Hermeneutik*, 11. Munich: Fink, 1984.

———. "Diderots Paradox über das Schauspiel (Entretiens sur le Fils Naturel)." *Germanisch-Romanische Monatsschrift* 24 (1961): 380–413.

———. "Nachahmungsprinzip und Wirklichkeitsbegriff in der Theorie des Romans von Diderot bis Stendhal." In *Nachahmung und Illusion. Poetik und Hermeneutik*, 1. Munich: Fink, 1964.

Jean Paul [Richter]. *Werke.* 6 vols. Ed. Walter Höllerer, Gustav Lohmann, and Norbert Miller. *Werke, Abteilung II.* 4 vols. Ed. Norbert Miller and Wilhelm Schmidt-Biggemann. Munich: Hanser Verlag, 1959–63, 1974–85.

Jeanneret, Michel. *La Lettre Perdue. Écriture et Folie dans l'oeuvre de Nerval.* Paris: Flammarion, 1978.

———. *La Scrittura Romantica della follia. Il caso Nerval.* Naples: Ligouri, 1984.

Johnson, Samuel. *The Works of Samuel Johnson.* 16 vols. Cambridge: Harvard Cooperative Society, 1912.

Jung-Stilling, Johann Heinrich. *Theorie der Geister-Kunde, in einer Natur- Vernunft- und Bibelmäßigen Beantwortung der Frage: Was von Ahnung, Gesichten und Geistererscheinungen geglaubt und nicht geglaubt werden müsse.* Nuremberg, 1808.

Junius, Franciscus. *The Letters of Junius.* 2 vols. Ed. John Wade. London, 1850.

Kant, Immanuel. *Werke.* 6 vols. Ed. Wilhelm Weischedel. Darmstadt: Wissenschaftliche Buchgesellschaft, 1966.

Keats, John. *The Letters of John Keats.* 2 vols. Ed. Hyder Edward Rollins. Cambridge: Harvard University Press, 1958.

———. *The Poems of John Keats.* Ed. Jack Stillinger. Cambridge: Belknap, Harvard University Press, 1978.

Keitel, Evelyne. *Reading Psychosis. Readers, Texts and Psychoanalysis.* Trans. Anthea Bell. Oxford: Basil Blackwell, 1989.

Klinckowstroem, Carl Graf von. "Beitrag zur Geschichte der Wünschelrute und verwandte Erscheinungen, namentlich der Ritterschen Pendelversuche." *Physische Studien* 25 (1908): 523–31.

———. "Johann Wilhelm Ritter und die Wünschelrute." *Die Wünschelrute*, supplemental issue, "Das Wasser," no. 32–34 (1913): 1–3.

———. "Die Stellungnahme der Münchner Königlichen Akademie der Wissenschaften zu den Experimenten Ritters mit Campetti." *Physische Studien* 26 (1909): 33–40, 148–53, 351–59.

Kolossow, G. A. "Geistesstörungen bei Ergotismus." *Archiv für Psychiatrie und Nervenkrankheiten* 53 (1914): 1118–29.

Konner, Melvin. "Art of Darkness." *The Sciences* 29, no. 6 (1989): 2–5.

Kornmann, Heinrich. *Mons Veneris.* Frankfurt, 1614.

Kraepelin, Emil. *Manic-depressive Insanity and Paranoia.* London: Churchill Livingston, 1921.

Krieger, Murray. *Ekphrasis: The Illusion of the Natural Sign.* Baltimore: Johns Hopkins University Press, 1992.

———. *Poetic Presence and Illusion.* Baltimore: Johns Hopkins University Press, 1979.

Lamb, Charles. *The Works of Charles and Mary Lamb.* 7 vols. Ed. E. V. Lucas. London: Methuen, 1903–5.

Lancaster, H. C. *French Tragedy in the Time of Louis XV and Voltaire, 1715–1774.* Baltimore, 1950.

Lavater, Johann Caspar. *Aphorisms on Man.* Trans. Henry Fuseli. London, 1788.

———. *Physiognomische Fragmente zur Beförderung der Menschenkenntnis und Menschenliebe.* 4 vols. Leipzig and Winterthur, 1775–78. Facsimile reprint, Leipzig, 1968.

Le Breton, Georges. *Nerval, poète alchimique.* La Bégude-de-Mazenc: Curandera, 1982.

———. "Le Pythagorisme de Nerval et la source des «Vers dorés»." *La Tour Saint-Jacques* 13–14 (January–April 1958): 79–87.

Lefebure, Molly. *Samuel Taylor Coleridge: A Bondage of Opium.* New York: Stein & Day, 1974.

Lenz, Jakob Michael Reinhold. *Gesammelte Schriften.* 3 vols. Ed. Ludwig Tieck. Berlin, 1828.

Le Sage, Alain-René. *The Adventures of Gil Blas, of Santillane* (1715). Trans. Tobias Smollett. London, 1748; Lyons, 1815.

———. *Le Diable boiteux* (1707). 2 vols. Paris, 1886.

Lessing, Gotthold Ephraim. *Werke.* 8 vols. Ed. Herber G. Göpfert. Munich: Hanser Verlag, 1974.

Levin, Samuel R. *Metaphoric Worlds: Conceptions of a Romantic Nature.* New Haven: Yale University Press, 1988.

Levinson, Marjorie. *The Romantic Fragment Poem: A Critique of a Form.* Chapel Hill: University of North Carolina Press, 1986.

Lichtenberg, Georg Christoph. *Schriften und Briefe.* 5 vols. Ed. Wolfgang Promies. Munich: Hanser, 1967–71.

Liebrucks, Bruno. *Irrationaler Logos und rationaler Mythos.* Würzburg: Königshausen und Neumann, 1982.

Lloyd, Charles. *Edmund Oliver.* 2 vols. Bristol, 1798. Reprint, Oxford: Woodstock Books, 1990.

———. *The Tragedies of Vittorio Alfieri translated from the Italian.* London, 1815.

Loewenthal, Erich, ed. *Sturm und Drang. Kritische Schriften.* 3 vols. Heidelberg: Lambert Schneider, 1949.

Lokke, Kari. *Gerard de Nerval: The Poet as Social Visionary.* Lexington, Ky.: French Forum, 1987.

———. "Weimar Classicism and Romantic Madness: Tasso in Goethe, Byron and Shelley." *European Romantic Review* 2 (January 1992): 195–214.

Lombroso, Cesare. *The Man of Genius.* London: Walter Scott; New York: C. Scribner's Sons, 1891.

Lowth, Robert. *De sacra poesi Hebraeorum.* Oxford: Clarendon Press, 1753. 3d ed. 1775.

Lucian. *Luciani Opera.* 4 vols. Ed M. D. Macleod. Oxford: Clarendon Press, 1972–87.

Lützeler, Paul Michael. "Der Briefwechsel zwischen Bettina und Achim von Arnim. Sozialgeschichte und Roman." In *Horizonte. Festschrift für Herbert Lehnert zum 65. Geburtstag,* ed. Hannelore Mundt, Egon Schwarz, and William J. Lillyman. Tübingen: Max Niemeyer, 1990.

Marin, Louis. *Études Semiologiques.* Paris: Klincksieck, 1971.

Marlowe, Christopher. *Marlowe's "Doctor Faustus." 1604–1616.* Ed. W. W. Greg. Oxford: Clarendon Press, 1950.

Marmontel, Jean François. "Illusion." In vol. 8 of the *Encyclopédie, ou Dictionnaire Raisonné des Sciences, des Arts et des Métiers.* 3d ed. Geneva, 1777–79.

————. *Poétique Française*. 2 vols. Paris, 1763.

Martin, Robert L. *The Paradox of the Liar*. Reseda, Calif.: Ridgeview Publishing, 1978.

Marx, Karl. *Critique of the Hegelian Philosophy of Right*. In *Karl Marx, Frederick Engels, Collected Works*, vol. 3. New York: International Publishers, 1975.

McFarland, Thomas. *Coleridge and the Pantheist Tradition*. Oxford: Clarendon Press, 1969.

————. "The Origin and Significance of Coleridge's Theory of the Secondary Imagination." In *New Perspectives on Coleridge and Wordsworth*, ed. Geoffrey Hartman. New York, London: 1972.

————. *Originality and Imagination*. Baltimore: Johns Hopkins University Press, 1985.

————. *Romanticism and the Forms of Ruin: Wordsworth, Coleridge, and Modalities of Fragmentation*. Princeton: Princeton University Press, 1981.

Mercier, Louis Sébasten. "De Défauts à éviter dans le Drame." In *Du Théâtre, ou nouvel essai sur l'art dramatique*. Amsterdam, 1773.

Merivale, Patricia. "The Raven and the Bust of Pallas: Classic Artifact in the Gothic Tale." *PMLA* 89 (October 1974): 960–66.

Michell, William. *On Difficult Cases of Parturition and the Use of Ergot of Rye*. London, 1828.

Michelsen, Peter. *Laurence Sterne und der deutsche Roman des 18. Jahrhunderts*. Göttingen: Vandenhoeck & Rupprecht, 1962.

Middlebrook, Diane. *Anne Sexton: A Biography*. Boston: Houghton Mifflin, 1991.

Mirecourt, Eugène de. *Gérard de Nerval*. Paris, 1854.

Mühler, Robert. "Der Venusring. Zur Geschichte eines romantischen Motivs." *Aurora* 17 (1957): 50–62.

Müller, Adam. *Die Lehre vom Gegensatze*. Berlin, 1804.

————. *Vorlesungen über die deutsche Wissenschaft und Literatur*. 2d ed. Dresden, 1807.

Müller-Seidel, Walter. "Hölderlin in Homburg. Sein Spätwerk im Kontext seiner Krankheit." In *Homburg vor der Höhe in der deutschen Geistesgeschichte. Studien zum Freundeskreis um Hegel und Hölderlin*, ed. Christoph Jamme and Otto Pöggeler. Stuttgart: Klett-Cotta, 1981.

Nägele, Rainer. *Literatur und Utopie. Versuche zu Hölderlin*. Heidelberg: Lothar Stiehm Verlag, 1978.

Neale, Adam. *Researches respecting the Natural History, Chemical Analysis and Medical Virtures of the Spur, or Ergot of Rye*. London, 1828.

Nerval, Gérard de. *Chimeras*. Trans. Peter Jay, with essays by Richard Holmes and Peter Jay. Redding Ridge, Conn.: Black Swan Books, 1984.

————. *Les Chimères*. Ed. Norma Rinsler. London: Athlone Press, 1973.

————. *«Les Chimères» de Nerval. Édition critique*. Ed. Jean Guillaume. Namur: Bibliothèque de Faculté de Philosophie et Lettres, 1966.

————. *Oeuvres de Gérard de Nerval*. 2 vols. Ed. Albert Béguin and Jean Richer. Paris: Gallimard, 1952–56.

————. *Selected Writings of Gérard de Nerval*. Trans. Geoffrey Wagner. New York: Grove Press, 1957.

Newman, John Henry. *An Essay on the Development of Christian Doctrine*. London, 1845.

Nivelle, Armand. *Kunst- und Dichtungstheorien zwischen Aufklärung und Klassik*. Berlin: De Gruyter, 1960.

Nodier, Charles. *Contes*. Ed. Pierre-George Castex. Paris: Garnier, 1961.
――――. *Oeuvres complètes*. 12 vols. 1832–37. Reprint, Geneva: Slatkine, 1968.
Novalis. *Schriften*. 5 vols. Ed. Paul Kluckhohn and Richard Samuel. 2d ed. Vols. 1–3, Stuttgart: Kohlhammer Verlag, 1960. Vols. 4 and 5, Darmstadt: Wissenschaftliche Buchgesellschaft, 1975 and 1988.
Nuttall, R. R. "Case of Injurious Effects resulting from the Use of Ergot of Rye." *The Medical Times* 16 (London, 1847): 390–91.
Ovid. *Metamorphosis*. Translated into English Verse under the direction of Sir Samuel Garth by John Dryden, Alexander Pope, Joseph Addison, William Congreve, and other Eminent Hands. London, 1717. Reprint, Verona: Officina Bodoni, 1958.
Packer, Barbara. "Mania and Depression from the Writer's Point of View: The Case of William Cowper." In *Literature and Psychology*. Lisbon: Instituto Superior de Psicologia Applicada, 1991.
Page, H. A. [Alexander H. Japp]. *Thomas De Quincey. His Life and Writings. With Unpublished Correspondence*. 2 vols. New York, 1877.
Paley, William. *Evidences of Christianity* (1794). Ed. Thomas Rawson Birks. London, 1872.
Parker, John. "Some Reflections on Georg Büchner's *Lenz* and Its Principal Source, the Oberlin Record." *German Life and Letters* 21 (1968): 103–11.
Patten, Janice. "Dark Imagination: Poetic Painting in Romantic Drama." Ph.D. diss., University of California, Santa Cruz, 1992.
Paulizky, F. "Pulvis ad partum aus dem Mutterkorn." *Baldinger's Neues Magazin für Ärzte* 9 (1787): 44.
Peacock, Thomas Love. *Works*. 10 vols. Ed. H.F.B. Brett-Smith and C. E. Jones. London: Constable, 1924–34. Reprint, AMS, 1967.
Plato. *The Collected Dialogues of Plato*. Ed. Edith Hamilton and Huntington Cairns. Princeton: Princeton University Press, 1961.
Plautus, Titus Maccius. *Comoediae*. 4 vols. Ed. Friedrich Ritshcel. Leipzig: Teubner, 1884–93.
Plinius Secundus. *Natural History*. 10 vols. Loeb Classical Library. 1938–63.
Plotinus. *Enneads*. 7 vols. Loeb Classical Library. 1978–88.
Plutarch. *Plutarch's Morals: Theosophical Essays*. Ed. C. W. King. London: George Bell & Son, 1898.
Pope, Alexander. *The Works of Alexander Pope*. 12 vols. London, 1764.
Porter, Roy. *Mind-Forg'd Manacles. A History of Madness in England from the Restoration to the Regency*. Cambridge: Harvard University Press, 1987.
Poundstone, William. *Labyrinths of Reason: Paradox, Puzzles, and the Frailty of Knowledge*. New York: Doubleday, 1988.
Prescott, Oliver. *A Dissertation on the Natural History and Medicinal Effects of Secale cornutum, or Ergot*. Boston, 1813.
Prickett, Stephen. *Romanticism and Religion*. Cambridge: Cambridge University Press, 1976.
Priestley, Joseph. *Discourses Relating to the Evidences of Revealed Religion*. 3 vols. London: J. Johnson, 1794–97.
――――. *An History of the Corruptions of Christianity*. 2 vols. Birmingham, 1782.
――――. *Institutes of Natural and Revealed Religion*. 3 vols. London, 1772–74.
Rasch, Wolfdietrich. *Goethes "Torquato Tasso." Die Tragödie des Dichters*. Stuttgart: J. B. Metzler, 1954.
Read, C. Stanford, ed. S.v. "Insanity," *Encyclopaedia Britannica*.

Reiman, Donald, ed. *Shelley and His Circle, 1773–1822: Manuscripts*. Cambridge: Harvard University Press, 1973.

Richards, I. A. *Philosophy of Rhetoric*. New York: Oxord University Press, 1936.

Richards, Ruth, Dennis Kinney, Inge Lunder, Maria Benet, and Ann Merzel. "Creativity in Manic-Depressives, Cyclothemes, Their Normal Relatives, and Control Subjects." *Journal of Abnormal Psychology* 97 (1988): 281–88.

Richer, Jean. *Nerval par les témoins de sa vie*. Paris: Menard, 1970.

Ricklefs, Ulfert. "Arnims poetologische Theorie." In *Magie und Grenze. Arnims 'Päpstin Johanna'-Dichtung*. Göttingen: Vandenhoeck & Ruprecht, 1990.

Rinsler, Norma. *Gérard de Nerval*. London: Athlone, 1973.

Rölleke, Heinz. "Achim von Arnim und Friedrich Hölderlin. Ein neuentdecktes Fragment Arnims über 'Empedokles.'" *Hölderlin-Jahrbuch* 18 (1973/74): 149–58.

Roston, Murray. *Prophet and Poet: The Bible and the Growth of Romanticism*. London: Faber & Faber, 1965.

Rothenberg, Albert. *Creativity and Madness: New Findings and Old Stereotypes*. Baltimore: Johns Hopkins University Press, 1980.

Rüfener, V. "Homo secundus deus. Eine geistesgeschichtliche Studie zum menschlichen Schöpfertum." *Philosophisches Jahrbuch* 63 (1955): 249–91.

Ryan, Thomas E. *Hölderlin's Silence*. Frankfurt: Peter Lang Verlag, 1988.

Sackville-West, Edward. *Thomas De Quincey, His Life and Work*. New Haven: Yale University Press, 1936.

Salerne, François. "Sur les Maladies que cause le Seigle ergoté." *Mémoires de mathématique et de physique, présentés à l'Académie Royale de Sciences*, 1755. 2:155–63.

Schelling, Friedrich, W.J. *Sämtliche Werke*. 14 vols. Ed. K.F.A. Schelling. Stuttgart and Augsburg: Cotta, 1856–61.

———. *Sämtliche Werke*. 13 vols. Ed. Manfred Schröter. Munich, 1927–59. Reprint, C. H. Beck, 1962–71.

Schiller, Friedrich. *Sämtliche Werke*. 5 vols. Ed. Gerhard Fricke and Herbert G. Göpfert. 3d ed. Munich: Carl Hanser, 1962.

Schink, Johann Friedrich. *Dramaturgische Fragmente*. 4 vols., continuous pagination. Graz, 1781–82.

Schlegel, August Wilhelm. *Kritische Schriften*. 2 vols. Berlin: Georg Reimer, 1828.

———. *Kritische Schriften und Briefe*. 7 vols. Ed. Edgar Lohner. Stuttgart: Kohlhammer Verlag, 1965–74.

———. *Sämtliche Werke*. 12 vols. Ed. Eduard Böcking. Leipzig, 1846–47. Reprint. 126 vols. Hildesheim: Georg Olms, 1971–72.

Schlegel, Friedrich. *Kritische Friedrich Schlegel Ausgabe*. 35 vols. Ed. Ernst Behler, Jean-Jacques Anstett, and Hans Eichner. Paderborn: Schöningh, 1958– .

———. *Lectures on the History of Literature, Ancient and Modern*. Trans. Edinburgh, 1818; New York, 1841.

Schmidt, Jochen. *Die Geschichte des Genie-Gedankens in der deutschen Literatur, Philosophie und Politik, 1750–1945*. 2 vols. Darmstadt: Wissenschaftliche Buchgesellschaft, 1985.

———. *Hölderlins geschichts-philosophische Hymnen "Friedensfeier," "Der Einzige," "Patmos."* Darmstadt: Wissenschaftliche Buchgesellschaft, 1990.

———. *Hölderlins später Widerruf in den Oden "Chiron," "Blödigkeit," und "Ganymed."* Tübingen: Max Niemeyer Verlag, 1978.

———, ed. *Dichter über Hölderlin*. Frankfurt: Insel Verlag, 1969.

Schmidt-Dengler, W. *Genius. Zur Wirkungsgeschichte antiker Mythologeme in der Goethezeit.* Munich: Fink, 1978.

Schmitt, Albert R. "Christian Felix Weißes *Jean Calas*—Dokumentarisches Theater im 18. Jahrhundert." In *Aufnahme—Weitergabe: Literarische Impulse um Lessing und Goethe,* ed. John A. McCarthy and Albert A. Kipa. Hamburg: Buske, 1982.

Schneider, Elizabeth. *The Aesthetics of William Hazlitt.* Philadelphia: University of Pennsylvania Press, 1933.

Schulz, Max F. *The Poetic Voices of Coleridge.* Detroit: Wayne State University Press, 1963.

Schweikert, Uwe. *Jean Pauls "Komet." Selbstparodie der Kunst.* Stuttgart: Metzler, 1971.

Scott, Sir Walter. *Letters on Natural Magic, Addressed to J. G. Lockhart, Esq.* 2d ed. London, 1830.

———. *Waverley Novels.* 25 vols. London: Oxford University Press, 1912.

Seneca. *Moral Essays.* Loeb Classical Library. 1928.

Seneca, the Elder. *Ortatorum sententiae divisiones colores.* 3 vols. Ed. A. Kiessling. Leipzig: Teubner, 1872.

Sennert, Daniel. *Of Agues and Fevers: their differences, signes, and cures.* Trans. N.D.B.M., late of Trinity College in Cambridge. London, 1658.

Shaftesbury, Anthony Ashley Cooper, 3d earl of. *Characteristics of Men, Manners, Opinions, Times.* 3 vols. 5th ed. Birmingham, 1773.

Shakespeare, William. *The Complete Works of Shakespeare.* Ed. Hardin Craig. Chicago: Scott, Foresman, 1951.

Sharp, Francis Michael. "Büchner's *Lenz.* A Futile Madness." In *Psycho-analytische und psychopathologische Literaturinterpretationen,* ed. Bernd Urban and Winfried Kudszus. Darmstadt: Wissenschaftliche Buchgesellschaft, 1981.

Shelley, Percy Bysshe. *The Letters of Percy Bysshe Shelley.* 2 vols. Ed. Frederick L. Jones. Oxford: Clarendon Press, 1964.

———. *Shelley's Poetry and Prose.* Ed. Donald H. Reiman and Sharon B. Powers. New York: W. W. Norton, 1977.

Shumaker, Wayne. *Literature and the Irrational: A Study in Anthropological Backgrounds.* Englewood Cliffs, N.J.: Prentice-Hall, 1960.

Siebers, Tobin. *The Romantic Fantastic.* Ithaca: Cornell University Press, 1984.

Siemens, F. "Psychosen beim Ergotismus." *Archiv für Psychiatrie und Nervenkrankheiten* 11 (1881):108–16, 336–90.

Skilton, Vieda. *English Madness. Ideas on Insanity, 1580–1890.* London: Routledge & Kegan Paul, 1979.

Southcott, Joanna. *Life and Sacred Writings.* London, 1814.

Southey, Robert, ed. *Attempts in Verse, by John Jones, and old servant: with some account of the writer, written by himself: and an Introductory Essay on the Lives and Works of our Uneducated Poets.* London, 1831.

Sowerby, Benn. *The Disinherited: The Life of Gérard de Nerval, 1808–1855.* New York: New York University Press, 1974.

Spinoza, Benedictus de. *Werke.* 2 vols. Ed. Günter Gawlick and Friedrich Niewöhner. Darmstadt: Wissenschaftliche Buchgesellschaft, 1979.

Staël, Germaine de. *De l'Allemagne.* 5 vols. Ed. Jean de Pange and Simone Balayé. Paris: Hachette, 1958–60.

Starý, Friedrich, and V. Jirásek. *Heilpflanzen.* Munich: Bertelsmann; Prague: Artia, 1972.

Stearns, John. "Account of the Pulvis Parturiens, a Remedy for Quickening Child-birth." *Medical Repository of New York* 5 (1808): 308–9.

Stendhal [Henri Beyle]. *Racine et Shakespeare* (1823). Ed. Roger Fayole. Paris: Garnier-Flammarion, 1970.

Sternberg, Thomas. " 'Und auch wenn wir entschiedene Protestanten sind.' Achim von Arnim zu Religion und Konfession." In *Neue Tendenzen der Arnim-forschung*, ed. Roswitha Burwick and Bernd Fischer. Bern: Peter Lang, 1990.

Storey, Mark. *The Poetry of John Clare. A Critical Introduction.* New York: St. Martin's Press, 1974.

———, ed. *Clare: The Critical Heritage.* London: Routledge & Kegan Paul, 1973.

Streller, Dorothea. "Achim von Arnim und das Drama." Diss., Göttingen 1956.

Sulzer, Johann Georg. *Allgemeine Theorie der schönen Künste.* 4 vols. Leipzig, 1792–94.

———. *Allgemeine Theorie der schönen Künste, Zweyter Theil.* 2d ed. Leipzig, 1792. Facsimile reprint, Hildesheim: Georg Olms, 1967.

Talford, Thomas Noon. *Final Memorials of Charles Lamb.* 2 vols. London, 1848.

Tasso, Torquato. *Discourses on the Heroic Poem.* Trans. with notes by Mariella Cavalchini and Irene Samuel. Oxford: Clarendon Press, 1973.

———. *Jerusalem Delivered.* Trans. with an introduction by Joseph Tusiani. Rutherford: Farleigh Dickinson University Press, 1970.

Taylor, Shelley E. *Positive Illusions. Creative Self-Deception and the Healthy Mind.* New York: Basic Books, 1989.

Thomasberger, Andreas. "Der gedichtete Dichter. Zum metaphorischen Charakter der 'Ausflüge mit Hölderlin' von Ludwig Achim von Arnim." *Aurora* 45 (1985): 283–300.

Thorslev, Peter. *Romantic Contraries: Freedom versus Destiny.* New Haven: Yale University Press, 1984.

Tibble, J. W., and Anne Tibble. *John Clare: A Life* (1932). Revised edition. London: Routledge & Kegan Paul, 1972.

Todorov, Tzvetan. *The Fantastic: A Structural Approach.* Trans. Richard Howard. Cleveland: Case Western University Press, 1973.

Trousson, Raymond. *Le thème de Promethée dans la littérature euopéenne.* 2 vols. Geneva: Librairie Droz, 1964.

Ul-Haque, Intisar. *A Critical Study of Logical Paradoxes.* Peshawar: University of Peshawar, 1970.

Villiers, André. "A propos du *Paradoxe* de Diderot." *Revue d'Histoire du Théâtre* 4 (1952): 379–81.

Walzel, Oskar. *Das Prometheussymbol von Shaftesbury zu Goethe.* 2d ed. Munich: M. Hueber, 1932.

Weiße, Christian Felix. *Das Fanatismus, oder Jean Calas. Ein Historisches Schauspiel in fünf Aufzügen, Samt einer kurzen Geschichte von seinem Tode.* Frankfurt and Leipzig, 1780.

Welsford, Enid. *The Fool. His Social and Literary History.* London: Faber and Faber, 1935.

Wilkie, Brian, and Mary Lynn Johnson. *Blake's Four Zoas: The Design of a Dream.* Cambridge: Harvard University Press, 1978.

Willis, Thomas. *Pathologiae cerebri, et nervosi generis specimen. In quo agitur de morbis convulsivis, et de scorbuto.* Oxford, 1667; Amsterdam, 1668.

Wilson, A. Leslie. "The Blaue Blume: A New Dimension." *Germanic Review* 34 (1959): 50–58.

Wolfart, Karl Christian. *Mesmerismus. Oder System der Wechselwirkungen.* Vol. 1, *Theorie und Anwendung des thierischen Magnetismus als die allgemeine Heilkunde zur Erhaltung des Menschen.* Vol. 2, *Erläuterung zum Mesmerismus . . . als zweiter Theil des Mesmerismus.* Berlin, 1814–15.

Wölfel, Kurt. "'Ein Echo, das sich selber in Unendliche nachhallt.' Eine Betrachtung von Jean Pauls Poetik und Poesie." In *Jean Paul,* ed. Uwe Schweikert. Darmstadt: Wissenschaftliche Buchgesellschaft, 1974.

Wollaston, Charlton. "Extract of a letter from Charlton Wollaston, M.D., F.R.S., to William Heberden, M.D., F.R.S., dated Bury St. Edmunds, April 13, 1762, relating to the case of mortification of limbs in a family at Wattison in Suffolk." *Philosophical Transactions of the Royal Society* 52 (1762): 523–26.

Wordsworth, William. *Poetical Works.* Ed. Thomas Hutchinson, rev. Ernest De Selincourt. London: Oxford University Press, 1969.

———. *The Prose Works of William Wordsworth.* 3 vols. Ed. W.J.B. Owen and Jane Smyser. Oxford: Clarendon Press, 1974.

Young, Edward. *Conjectures on Original Composition,* in a letter to the Author of *Sir Charles Grandison.* London, 1759.

Youngquist, Paul. *Madness and Blake's Myth.* University Park: Pennsylvania State University Press, 1989.

Zimmerman, J. G. von. *A Treatise on Physic.* London, 1782.

INDEX